Royal and Ancient Peebles

A New History of one of the original
Royal Burghs of Scotland
its story from its beginnings
and its place in Scotland's history

RONALD IRELAND

By the same Author
The Bloody Covenant Crown and Kirk in Conflict
Published by The History Press, 2010

First published 2021

The Loaningwood Press
Loaningwood
Edderston Road
Peebles, Scottish Borders EH45 9DT

 A CIP catalogue record for this book is available from the British Library

ISBN 978-1-3999-0493-3

Printing by Elmbank Print, 8 Elcho Street, Peebles EH45 8HU

Contents

Illustrations

1. The Edston Hoard of 290 Roman coins from about AD 222 found near a hill fort at Edston Farm, Peebles *(Tweeddale Museum and Gallery Collection)*
2. Roman copper alloy statuette of Jupiter, found on banks of the River Tweed and believed to have been brought by a Roman soldier visiting Eshiels, Lyne or Happrew *(Tweeddale Museum and Gallery Collection)*
3. St.Gordian's Cross, Manor Valley *(photograph by the author)*
4. Acca's Cross. *(photograph by Chris Britton, copyright Hexham Abbey)*
5. Statuette of Alexander III *(photograph by the author with permission of the Kirk Session of Peebles Old Parish Church of Scotland)*
6. Conjectural Image of Peebles *Castle circa 1250 (Water colour by Gareth Hughes Design and Illustration, reproduced with permission of Peebles Civic Society)*
7. Conjectural image of Peebles High Street, circa 1500, showing Chapel of St Mary (W*ater colour by Gareth Hughes Design and Illustration, reproduced with permission of Peebles Civic Society)*
8. The Cross Church before Reformation of 1560. *From drawing by Alex Blackwood*
9. Cross Church and Monastery on north side *From drawing by Alex Blackwood*
10. Cross Church Cloister and Garth and tomb of Earl of March 1560 *From drawing by Alex Blackwood*
11. Plan of Cross Kirk *(© Crown Copyright: HES)*
12. Portrait of John Stuart, 1st Earl of Traquair – School of George Jamieson *(by kind permission of the Traquair Charitable Trust, Photograph by Alasdair MacFarlane)*
13. Siege of Neidpath: Watercolour by Jack Roney. *(by kind permission of Lady Elizabeth Benson, Photograph by Alasdair MacFarlane)*
14. Portrait of Sir James Hay, 1st Baronet of Smithsfield and Haystoun, 1586-1654 School of Sir Anthony van Dyck *(by kind permission of the Hon. Mrs Mary Coltman, Photograph by Alasdair MacFarlane)*
15. Rev.William Veitch. First Church of Scotland Minister of Peebles, 1690 – 1694 *(With permission of the Kirk Session of Peebles Old Parish Church of Scotland)*

16. Falconry lure and hawk hood associated with James Naesmyth of Posso in Manor (1575–1658) who was appointed Royal falconer to King James VI. *(Tweeddale Museum and Gallery Collection)*
17. Whisky toddy ladles carved from rowan wood by shepherd at Gameshope, Tweedsmuir, 1763. *(Tweeddale Museum and Gallery Collection))*
18. 16th century wooden ball carved by a Flemish monk, showing the Shrine of the Nativity. Donated by Mrs Fergusson of Spittalhaugh in 1854 *(Tweeddale Museum and Gallery Collection)*
19. Detail of Nativity scene
20. Plan of Castle hill 1779 from *The Book of the Parish Church of Peebles AD 1784-1885* by Dr Gunn (1917)
21. Print of St Andrews Church reproduced from *Antiquities of Scotland by Francis Grose 1797*
22. Print of Cross Kirk reproduced from *Antiquities of Scotland by Francis Grose 1797*
23. Hilt of Jacobite sword owned by Naesmyths of Dawyck and Posso 1745 *(Tweeddale Museum and Gallery Collection)*
24. Engraving on scabbard
25. Municipal measures for liquid and dried goods, circa 1800 *(Tweeddale Museum and Gallery Collection)*
26. Portrait of Mungo Park by Atkinson Horsburgh *(Tweeddale Museum and Gallery Collection)*
27. Mungo Park's surgery circa 1870 *(Tweeddale Museum and Gallery Collection)*
28. Example of model ship of war made of bone, made by French prisoners of the Napoleonic Wars 1810-14 *(Tweeddale Museum and Gallery Collection)*
29. Burgess ticket 1804 *(Tweeddale Museum and Gallery Collection)*
30. Provost's chain first presented to James Kerr in1823 *(Tweeddale Museum and Gallery Collection)*
31. Portrait of William Chambers by John A Horsburgh *(Tweeddale Museum and Gallery Collection)*
32. Contemporary Wemyss Ware plate with image of house, BiggieskOwe, birthplace of Chambers brothers.
33. Frontispiece of *Memoir of Robert Chambers with Autobiographical Reminiscences of William Chambers*
34. Portrait of Robert Chambers by John Horsburgh

(Tweeddale Museum and Gallery Collection)
35. Miss Vere's visit to the Black Dwarf from *The Black Dwarf and a Legend of Montrose* by Sir Walter Scott (*Portrait edition Vol V – 1913)*
36. Statue of the Black Dwarf, Hallyards House, Manor
    (Photograph by the author with kind permission of Mr & Mrs Michael Gush)
37. Print of Church from south of River Tweed circa 1800 *From lithograph by A & J Macpherson, Edinburgh*
38. Tweed Green by Charles Blyth 1836
    (Tweeddale Museum and Gallery Collection)

Illustration Numbers 1,2,16,17,18,19,23,24,25,26,27,28,29,30,31,34, and 38 are from the collection of Scottish Borders Council administered by Live Borders (Tweeddale Museum & Gallery) and included with its permission.

Chronology of Life and Times

79	Roman invasion of Southern Scotland.
118	Construction of Hadrian's Wall.
143	Construction of the Antonine Wall.
400(circa)	Roman withdrawal from Britain
1116	Inquest of David – first detailed description of Peebles.
1124	David I becomes King of Scots.
1130(circa)	Castle established and Peebles becomes a Royal Burgh.
1195	Church (later St Andrews Parish Church) established in Peebles.
1249	Alexander III becomes King of Scots
1261	'a stately and venerable cross' found at Peebles. A church, the Cross Kirk, built on the site. Peebles becomes place of pilgrimage.
1286	Death of Alexander III. Margaret, the Maid of Norway becomes Queen of Scots.
1290	Death of Margaret on her way from Norway to Scotland. Edward I becomes arbiter in the "Great Cause".
1292	Edward I claims to be Overlord of Scotland. Start of the Wars of Independence.
1296	Scottish landowners, churchmen and burgesses, including 71 representatives of the burgh and county of Peebles called to swear allegiance to Edward I by signing the "Ragman Roll"
1298	William Wallace appointed Guardian of Scotland. Robert Bruce, Earl of Carrick (later Robert Bruce King of Scots) and John, the "Red" Comyn fight at Peebles.
1301	Edward I in Peebles on 4th August.
1302	William de Durhame appointed by Edward I as Governor of the castle of Peebles.
1304	Edward I again in Peebles.
1305	Wallace captured and executed in London on 23 August.
1306	Robert Bruce crowned King of Scots on 25thMarch.
1314	Battle of Bannockburn 23 June.
1328	Earliest exchequer record of fixed rent paid by the Royal Burgh to the King. Treaty of Edinburgh, recognising Bruce as King of an independent Scotland.

1329   Death of Robert Bruce, Succeeded by David II aged 5 years.

1346   Robert II captured by English at the battle of Neville's Cross.

1357   Robert II freed on payment of a ransom and returns to Scotland.

1362   David II issues letters assigning an area at the west end of the High Street as site for erection of a Chapel dedicated to St Mary.

1371   Death of David II. Succeeded by Robert the Steward as Robert II. Stewart dynasty founded.

1388 (circa) Peebles burned by forces of Richard II of England led by Sir Robert Umphraville.

1390   Death of Robert II. Succeeded by his son, John Earl of Carrick as Robert III.

1395   Hospice of St Leonard established at modern day Eshiels.

1406   James, son of Robert III captured by English. Death of Robert III. Succeeded by his son as James I.

1424   James I released and returns to Scotland. First reference to "Play of Peebles" about this time.

1437   Murder of James I at Perth. Succeeded by his son as James II.

1452   Charter granted by James II to Peebles on 5th February.

1456   First record of a meeting of the town Council held on 4th October.

1458   Earliest reference to the tolbooth located at the foot of the Briggait.

1460   James II killed by exploding canon at siege of Roxburgh. Succeeded by his son as James III.

1465   First mention in the records of bridge across the Tweed.

1473   Establishment of Conventual Monastery of Trinity Friars under patronage of James III and Queen Margaret. Peebles now a major religious centre and place of pilgrimage.

1488   Rebellion against James III who is fatally injured at Battle of Sauchieburn. Succeeded by his son as James IV. James comes to Cross Kirk as an act of penitence for his part he rebellion against his father.

1497   James IV in Peebles again.

1506   James IV grants Charter of Confirmation and Novodamus to the town.

1507   James IV commissions a gold cross for Cross Kirk.

1509   Henry VIII becomes King of England.

1513   Battle of Flodden on 9th September. James IV killed together with many of the nobility and representatives of Peebles. James, the fourteen month old son of James IV succeeds as James V.

1517   Declaration against the Sale of Indulgences by Martin Luther. The start of the Protestant Reformation.

1525   First recorded visit to Peebles by James V.

1529   James V starts expeditions to quell unrest in the Borders from Peebles.

1542   Last visit by James V to Peebles in November. Birth of Mary Queen of Scots. Death of James V.

1543   Start of the "Rough Wooing". Border raids by forces of Henry VIII. Church of St Andrew made a collegiate church.

1545   After further raids on the Borders by the English. The Earl of Angus musters an army at Peebles and defeats an English army at the Battle of Ancrum Moor.

1547   Army assembled at Peebles by Privy Council of Scotland. Scotland invaded by English forces, defeating the Scottish army at Pinkie Heuch in East Lothian.

1548   Mary Queen of Scots sent to France for her safety.

1549   Peebles severely damaged by an English force. Church of St Andrew largely destroyed and never rebuilt.

1552   First mention of the name "provost" in burgh records.

1554   New charter granted to the town on behalf of her daughter, Mary Queen of Scots, by Mary of Guise, Regent of Scotland.

1555   First recorded election of town council on 30th September.

1560   The Scottish Estates meet in Edinburgh on 1st August and endorse the Protestant Confession of Faith drawn up by John Knox and abolish the authority of the Pope and outlaw the Mass in Scotland. First meeting of General Assembly.

1559   John Knox returns to Scotland from Geneva. A number of Scottish nobles supporting Protestantism come together as the "Lords of the Congregation".

1561   First Kirk Session of the parish of Peebles established. John Allan (or Allane) elected as first minister of the Reformed Kirk. Nineteen year old Mary Queen of Scots returns from France.

1563   First recorded visit to Peebles by Mary Queen of Scots. Weavers Guild officially recognised.

1565   Mary Queen of Scots marries Henry Stuart, Lord Darnley. Darnley in Peebles at Christmas.

1566   Birth of a son James on 15th June. Mary and Darnley at Traquair in August.

1567   Darnley killed by an explosion at Kirk O'Fields, Edinburgh. Mary marries the Earl of Bothwell. Civil war follows. Mary and Bothwell defeated at Battle of Carberry Hill. Mary captured and imprisoned in Loch Leven Castle. Signs Deed of Abdication. The infant James, crowned James VI at Stirling Castle. The Earl of Moray appointed Regent.

1568   Mary escapes from Loch Leven Castle; defeated at Battle of Langside, flees to England; remains there in captivity for the rest of her life.

1569   Moray urges the provost and bailies of Peebles to build a proper defensive wall to oppose the earls of Northumberland and Westmorland.

1570   Thomas Cranstoun appointed as first Reformed minister of Peebles in February. Moray killed at Linlithgow. Succeeded as Regent by Earl of Lennox.

1571   Town ordered to raise reinforcements for the army. Construction of town wall starts.

1574   Regent Morton issues an order to men aged between 16 and 60, in the Sheriffdoms of Lanark, Peebles and Selkirk to assemble at Peebles.

1583   Raid on Peebles by four Border clans, inflicting considerable damage. A new "Synod" created, linking Peebles, Melrose, Chirnside and Dunbar.

1585   First record of visit to Peebles by James VI.

1587   Mary Queen of Scots executed at Fotheringay Castle.

1597   Presbytery of Peebles established.

1602   Last recorded visit to Peebles by James VI.

1603   Death of Elizabeth I of England on 24th March. James VI proclaimed as James I of England, Wales and Ireland.

1604   "Ane grayte fyir" in Peebles. Outbreak of bubonic plague in Peebles.

1605   Further spread of plague. An undertaking given to build a tolbooth and prison.

1609	Act of Parliament requires that all future holders of the offices of provost and magistrates be restricted to those who live and work in the burgh. John Dickisoun elected first commoner to hold the office of provost.
1610	Commissiary Court set up in Peebles.
1621	James VI & I grants a Charter of Confirmation and Novodamus to Peebles.
1623	Execution by drowning in Peebles, in the Eddleston Water of Thomas Paterson for theft of sheep.
1624	Plague again spreading. Parade of townsfolk with their weapons held, the first for many years.
1625	Death of James VI & I. Succeeded by his son Charles I
1628	Three "witches" burned on the Calf Knowe.
1629	Weavers Guild officially incorporated.
1633	Charles I comes to Edinburgh to be crowned King of Scots. Attempts to introduce Episcopacy to Scotland
1636	Visit to Peebles in May by Patrick Lindsay, Archbishop of Glasgow.
1637	Service held in St Giles Cathedral, Edinburgh to introduce Episcopal Liturgy. Riot follows. Representatives of the nobility, lairds, the burghs and Kirk establish "The Tables". Text of the "National Covenant" approved.
1638	National Covenant signed in Greyfriars Kirkyard, Edinburgh. Copies distributed round Scotland. General Assembly meets and demands an Assembly and Parliament free from the control of the King.
1639	Warships of the King's navy sail up the Forth to Leith. The Burgh of Peebles is called upon to raise a defence force. Charles gathers an army at Berwick. Covenanter army led by Alexander Leslie including contingent from Peebles encamps at Duns Law. John Stuart, 1st Earl of Traquair appointed Lord High Commissioner to General Assembly.
1640	Town Council of Peebles raises troops and finance for a contingent to join the Scottish army. Covenanting Army led by General Leslie crosses the Tweed and captures Newcastle. Charles meets with Scots Commissioners at Ripon. Scots halt their advance after agreeing a substantial payment.
1641	English parliament agrees terms and Scottish army returns to Scotland. Charles comes north to Edinburgh in

an unsuccessful attempt to gain support from the
Scottish Parliament. The Earl of Traquair impeached.

1642 Charles raises his standard at Nottingham on 22nd August.
Start of the Civil War.

1643 The Estates (the Scottish Parliament) ratify the Solemn
League and Covenant. Scottish Commissioners meet with
representatives of the English Parliament and sign
Westminster Confession of Faith. Whole of Scotland put
on war footing. War Committees set up in every county.

1644 Scottish army heads south, reaches York and joins up
with army of Oliver Cromwell. Joint force defeat Royalist
force at Marston Moor. Scots march as far south as
Hereford and on return besiege Newark. Charles joins
Scots and siege lifted. Joins Scots on return north to
Newcastle. English Parliament demands withdrawal of
Scots army from England. English Parliamentary army
arrest Charles. The Solemn League and Covenant at an
end.

1645 James Graham, Marquis of Montrose starts campaign in
support of Charles. Defeats Covenanter army at
Inverlochy, but is heavily defeated at Philiphaugh. Plague
returns to Peebles.

1647 Scottish force including a contingent from Tweeddale led
by Earl of Traquair, heavily defeated at Battle of Preston.
Traquair captured and imprisoned in Warwick Castle. First
election of Dean of Guild to town council.

1649 Charles I executed. His son, proclaimed King Charles II.

1650 Scottish Covenanter army, including a small force from
Peebles, defeated by Cromwell at Dunbar. Cromwell
Takes control of Lothians and Borders. Large contingent
of Cromwell's New Model Army arrives in Peebles.
Neidpath Castle besieged.

1651 Peebles occupied by troops of New Model Army for next 9
Years.

1652 Commonwealth of England, Wales and Scotland
established by Cromwell. Cromwell becomes Lord
Protector.

1654 "Ordinance of Union" issued by Cromwell setting up a
united parliament.

1659 Death of Oliver Cromwell. Protectorate abolished.

1660 Restoration of the Monarchy. Charles Stuart proclaimed in Edinburgh as Charles II, King of Scots.

1661 Restoration of the Beltane Fair and its horse race, suspended during The Commonwealth. Episcopalianism re-established. All magistrates and councillors required to take an oath of allegiance to the Crown.

1669 The Cordiners and Shoemakers guild formally recognised by the town council.

1662 All ministers admitted to the Kirk since 1649 suspended and only reinstated as Episcopalians.

1666 Rebellion by those opposed to Episcopacy (known as Covenanters) breaks out in south west. Scotland. Covenanter Army heavily defeated at Rullion Green. Start of a period of repression known as "The Killing Times".

1668 Militia formed in Peebles in October.

1679 James Graham of Claverhouse appointed commander of Government Forces; defeated by Covenanters at Drumclog. Large force of Covenanters defeated at Bothwell Bridge by government army led by Duke of Monmouth. Contingent from Peebles present in support of government. James Nicol, a merchant burgess of Peebles also present in support of the Covenanters.

1680 Presbytery of Peebles seriously concerned about Covenanting activity. The Tailors Guild formally approved by the town council.

1681 The Test Act introduced in Scotland. Members of the town council take "The Test".

1682 Major riot in the town on March 1st in protest at a proposal by the town council to let a small area of the town's common grazings.

1684 Royal proclamation in May names those charged with rebellion, among them, James Nicol. Four communion cups dedicated in Peebles Parish Church. James Nicol apprehended in Edinburgh and hanged in the Grassmarket.

1685 Charles II dies on 5th February. His brother James, Duke of York, proclaimed James VII & II.

!686 Election of town councils suspended. It is the first time that the Crown attempted to interfere with the workings of local government.

1688 A group of Presbyterian ministers meet at Stobo in March and form a Presbyterian congregation in Peebles. A new Indulgence, granting freedoms to Catholics issued by James. A son born to him in June. James, his wife, Mary of Modena and his son flee to France, in December never to return.

1689   Estates meeting as a Convention in March, issue a "Claim of Right". William III (of Orange) and Mary II proclaimed joint sovereigns.

1690   "Call" issued by Presbyterian group in Peebles to William Veitch to become minister of Peebles.

1692   Peebles called upon by a letter issued by King William to elect a Commissioner to attend a Convention of Estates. Powers of town councils restored. First General Assembly of restored Kirk of Scotland which expels all Episcopalians. Appointment of William Veitch supported by the General Assembly, the first minister to be appointed as a minister of Peebles of the Church of Scotland as it remains constituted to the present day.

1693   Town council issue strict rules for public order. Darien Scheme launched with disastrous financial consequences for Scotland.

1699   Start of a period of severe economic decline and austerity in Peebles.

1702   The town's mills and cauld in poor state of repair and taken back into the council's own hands pending repairs. Death of King William. Succeeded by his sister in-law Queen Anne, the last Stuart monarch.

1706   A meeting of the Convention of Royal Burghs, held to discuss a possible Treaty of Union with England.

1707   Treaty of Union agreed and parliaments of Scotland and England united. Peebles, Selkirk, Lanark and Linlithgow entitled jointly, to send one representative to the House of Commons.

1708   First election to the new parliament of representative of combined burghs.

1713   The Guild of Masons, Wrights, Glaziers and Smiths is recognised and Incorporated.

1714   Death of Queen Anne on 1st August. She is succeeded by the Elector of Hanover, as George I.

1715   Jacobite Rebellion starts when Earl of Mar raises the standard of James, Stuart, son of James VII & II at Braemar.

1729   A water supply brought from St Mungo's Well to a well in the High Street. The first public supply in Peebles.

1732   General Assembly of the Church of Scotland passes an Act prohibiting election of ministers by congregations, prompting a split in the church.

1744   "First Secession" from Church of Scotland.

1745   Jacobite rebellion led by Charles Edward Stuart starts at Glenfinnan. He captures Edinburgh. A large detachment the Jacobite army, mainly of Highlanders marches south reaching Peebles, where it encamps for several days.

1746   The council attempts to raise a volunteer force to defend The town. The services of this "Association of Volunteers" never required as retreating Jacobite army does not return by way of Peebles.

1749   Decision taken to build a new "Town House" to replace the steeple and tolbooth.

1755   Secession congregation established in Peebles.

1756   First meeting of council within the Town House.

1758   Decision taken to demolish remains of West Port and reduce the street level.

1760   Death of Rev John Hay on 1st June, after 43 years as minister of Peebles and Manor. Succeeded by the Rev William Dalgleish D.D.

1766   Action taken to improve Water supply by building a reservoir in the Eastgate.

1770   Building of new manse on east side of Hay Lodge. Cross Kirk in poor state of repair. Proposal to construct new road to Edinburgh. Agreement reached to promote Turnpike Act for that purpose.

1771   Street lighting first introduced.

1776   Remains of tolbooth, the steeple and the Chapel of St Mary demolished. Dr Dalgleish presents proposal to the town council for the building of a new church.

1778   Agreement reached to build the new church on Castle Hill on condition that it includes a steeple, with the town's clock and bells.

1779   Council rules revised to limit length of service of provost to five years. Act of Parliament requires all burghs to provide adequate jail facilities.

1780   A well sunk at the Ludgate (Young Street) to supply the Old Town.

1782   Building of the steeple completed.

1784   First services held in new church.

1789   Council decide to build new jail at foot of Castle Hill. Storming of the Bastille in Paris on 14th July. Start of French Revolution.

1793   Additional well sunk at foot of the Old Town. Council decide to compile a register of people in poverty and distress.

1797   Publication of *The First Statistical Account of Scotland*. Gytes Meetinghouse built by Secession congregation

1799   Three arches added to Tweed bridge at south end. First regular transport to Edinburgh started.

1803   Britain and France at war. Peebles chosen as location for prisoners of war. Dutch and Walloon prisoners come to the town.

1806   Start of transport to Edinburgh by "the Fly". Leading members of community meet in October and agree to build a new Hotel financed on the "Tontine" principal.

1808   Construction of The Tontine Hotel completed.

1810   Large group of French prisoners of war arrive. First printing press set up in Peebles.

1814   French prisoners of war repatriated.

1817   Poverty among lower classes a particular problem following the Napoleonic Wars

1820   Death of King George III after the longest reign of any monarch up to that time. Succeeded by his son, the Prince Regent as George IV.

1822   Visit of George IV to Edinburgh from 12th to 29th August, the first visit by a reigning monarch to Scotland since 1633.

1823   Town council decide that a gold medal and chain should be provided for the Provost.

1825   Introduction of stage coach services to Edinburgh. Branch of British Linen Bank opened, the first bank in Peebles.

1828   Gas company established. Gas works established on Old Town Green. Gas lighting introduced.

1829   Decision made to build new cauld across the Tweed.

1830   Reform Bill presented to Parliament. Death of George IV.

Succeeded by his brother, as William IV.

1832   The Scottish Bill for Parliamentary Reform passed. *Chambers Edinburgh Journal* first published. Outbreak of cholera in England raises fear s of an epidemic.

1833   Burgh reform Act introduced. First council election under new rules held in November.

1837   Death of William IV on 20th June. Succeeded by his niece, Alexandra Victoria as Queen Victoria. First parliamentary election after passing of Reform Act.

1836   Scottish Episcopal church built in Peebles

1839   Attempt to establish textile factories with modern machinery fails.

1840   Marriage of Queen Victoria to Prince Albert of Saxe-Coburg and Gotha.

1841   Decision to build a new court house adjacent to town jail. *New Statistical Account of Scotland* published.

1844   Courthouse opened. Branch of the Free Church of Scotland opened.

1845   The first local newspaper, the *Peeblesshire Monthly Advertiser and Tweeddale Journal* set up.

1846   Company set up to supply water to the town from springs on Venlaw.

1850   Roman Catholic Mass held in a flat in the High Street in July, the first held in the Royal Burgh since the Reformation.

Postscript – Principal Events

1851   Peebles Railway Company set up to join the Edinburgh to Hawick line at Eskbank, Midlothian. Line opened on 2nd April,1855.

1858   Symington, Biggar and Broughton railway line, joining the Caledonian Railway, established. Opened on 1st February 1864.

1859   The Chambers Institution, gifted to the town and county by William Chambers, opened.

1860   Tweedside Mill opened.

1866   New station and extension to link Peebles to Innerleithen and Galashiels completed in October.

1869   Damdale Mill opened.

1880   Peebles Hydropathic Establishment (Peebles Hotel Hydro) opened.
1883   March Street Mill opened.
1884   Parish church on Castlehill closed and demolished.
1887   New parish church on Castle hill opened.
1889   Court House and Jail converted and become the "County Building".
1905   Peebles Hydro destroyed by fire.
1907   Rebuilt Peebles Hotel Hydro opened.
1914   Start of the First World War I. Peebles becomes a major military training centre.
1922   County War Memorial in courtyard of Chambers Institution dedicated on 5th October.
1923   Visit to Peebles by King George V and Queen Mary, the first royal visit for 321 years.
1939   Start of World War II. Peebles Hotel Hydro requisitioned as a hospital.
1942   Prisoner of war camp built in Caledonian Road.
1947   Visit to Peebles by King George VI, Queen Elizabeth and Princesses Elizabeth and Margaret.
1965   Tweedside Mill destroyed by fire.
1967   Closure of Damdale Mill.
2013   Visit to Peebles by Queen Elizabeth II.
2015   Closure of March Street Mill.

Author's Note

My wife and I married in July 1963. Our first home was in Kirkland Street, on the north side of Peebles and the Royal and Ancient Burgh has been our home ever since. Anyone coming to live in the town is known as a "Stoory foot" and that is what we are. Those born in the town are "Gutterbluids". Both our sons qualify for that accolade and one of them remains in the town, where he in turn has married and has a daughter and son. So Peebles has a very special place in the hearts and minds of the Ireland family.

Over the years since we came to Peebles it has changed dramatically, expanding its boundaries north, south, east and west from its historic core. Its origins are ancient. It is one of the original royal burghs of Scotland. Its history is diverse and the town has played host to a significant number of the great characters who have strode the stage of Scotland throughout its long history.

Living here for more than 50 years has given me much that I cherish and in writing this book I hope I may give something back in return. I make no claim to academic prowess but have tried to tell the story of the town to the best of my limited abilities.

There have been a number of attempts over the years to tell the story of the long life of Peebles. Those have largely focussed on the domestic life of the town itself and its surroundings. While I have taken account of the work of all those writers, I have tried to tell the story of the Royal and Ancient Burgh with a broader canvas, setting its life in the context of contemporary events in Scotland, starting with the Roman occupation. The life of Peebles over the centuries mirrors the life and development of other Scottish burghs. Its story tells something of the life and times of Scotland itself, particularly in the medieval period.

The history of Peebles for the years 1850 until 1990 have been well documented by Joe Brown and Ian Lawson whose edited history of the town covered that later period. Apart from it, no attempt has been made to draw together the earlier sources to tell the history of the town in the centuries prior to the nineteenth and this book is an attempt to rectify that omission.

In all the works of the earlier writers there is an abundance of detail, which I have not sought to copy. Rather, I have been selective of the events, personalities and anecdotes, true or fabled in order to tell an evolving story of the development of Peebles, its peaks and declines and above all to try to present a picture of the everyday life of the town and how it has been affected by national events.

In writing this book I have researched from a wide range of sources. Wherever possible I have gone back to original publications, sources and documents and put my own interpretation on them, rather than simply accepting the interpretation of earlier writers.

In summarising my thoughts and feelings about the writing of this book, I could not do better than echo the words of the Rev Alex Williamson, who in 1895 in his introduction to his own history of the town *Glimpses of Peebles,* wrote the following :

'The author is perfectly well aware of the defects of the volume he now gives to the public, but he trusts these may be overlooked, and his sincere desire alone remembered, which is to give to the inhabitants of Peebles, and those connected with it, some information they may not possess regarding the town and neighbourhood. He has written the following pages in leisure hours, and the work has been a labour of love. Such as it is he offers it for acceptance.'

For my own part I hope that this book may have an appeal to a wider audience as it attempts to tell the story in the context of the evolving history of Scotland, reflecting the lives of ordinary folk through the centuries.

Peebles
August 2021

Acknowledgements

No published book is the sole preserve of the author.

I am indebted to a number of people without whose help and guidance, publication would not have been possible. To Rosemary Hannay and Liz Hanson for reading my original draft, correcting errors and giving helpful advice and recommending publication; to Geoffrey Hamilton for giving it the seal of approval on behalf of the Tweeddale Society; Douglas Millar for endorsing it on behalf of the Peebles Callants Club; Steve Dubé for his helpful advice on a range of associated matters; Chris Sawers for help in identifying images and sourcing information and some of the illustrations; Ian McLeod and Ruth Lowe of Elmbank Print for their design input, which has made publication possible and their patience with the physical production of the book.; Anne Solamito for providing the Index and my granddaughters, Sophie for designing a logo for *The Loaningwood Press* and Annabelle, for taking charge of publicity.

I am also grateful to Ann Goodburn for allowing me to include her translation of Blaew's description of Tweeddale; Lady Elizabeth Benson for allowing me to include an image of *The Siege of Neidpath* painted by Jack Roney; The Traquair Charitable Trust for allowing the inclusion of the portrait of John Stuart, 1st Earl of Traquair and to Professor Sir Tom Devive for allowing me to include a quotation from his book, *The Scottish Clearances*.

I am indebted to Peebles Callants Club for meeting the cost of those illustrations which are subject to copyright and for which payment has had to be made.

Last but by no means least, my wife Margaret for her support, helpful comments; guiding my wayward grammar; correcting the manuscript and generally being there.

The Peebles Mural

Early in 2010 a small group of people in Peebles met to consider the idea of creating a mural which would reflect the long history and culture of the Royal and Ancient burgh.

Michael Jessing, an internationally recognised artist, who lived and worked locally, was commissioned to produce a design. The location ultimately chosen was the wall of the Bakehouse owned by St Andrews Leckie Parish Church in Pennel's Close, off the High Street.

Assisted by local historians and other organisations, Michael Jessing prepared a series of drawings which were put on public display. Those received a very positive response from the people of Peebles. The project was led by the Community Council of the Royal Burgh of Peebles, which led a successful fundraising campaign. Preparatory work, involving the artist and various others, was started in August 2015 and was completed by Michael Jessing in October 2015, followed by an official unveiling on 18th November of that year.

It seems to me that the mural encompasses everything that this book is about and I am indebted to the late Michael Jessing and the Community Council for allowing me to use an image of it as the front and rear covers of this book.

Sadly, Michael Jessing died shortly before this book was published.

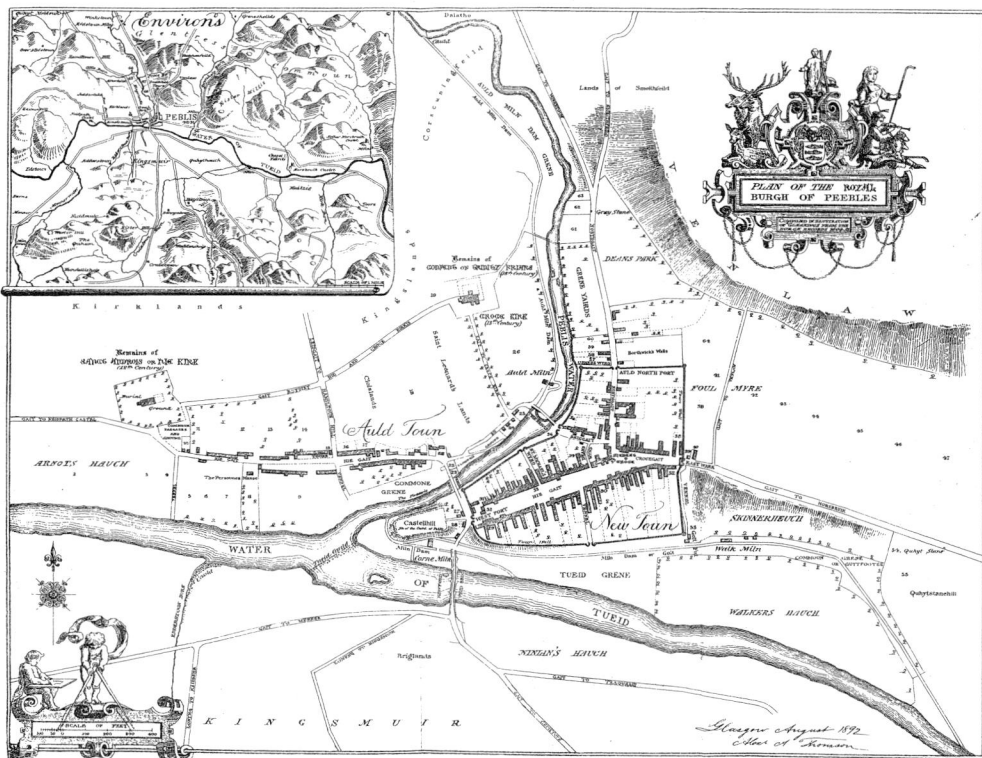

Plan of Peebles, c 1609 -52 as drawn by Alex A Thomson, 1892,
From *THE BURGH OF PEEBLES: GLEANINGS FROM ITS RECORDS, 1604-52*
By Robert Renwick 1907

Introduction

To the casual visitor to Peebles, and today there are many, it may seem a very attractive, yet ordinary place, not untypical of many an old Scottish burgh. Its High Street has an air of architectural variety and quality which speaks of a past Victorian and Edwardian era, but gives little indication that it has been a place of habitation for nigh on two thousand years. Although its origins are shrouded in the mists of time, there has been a settlement at Peebles, at least since Roman times and the beginning of the Christian era.

Like many a major centre of human population and endeavour, Peebles has seen its star rise and fall, only to rise and fall again, before emerging into the modern era and the industrial age. At least since the twelfth century, it has caught the attention of the crowned heads of Scotland and from time to time the depredations of monarchs of the neighbouring kingdom of England. From the fourteenth to the seventeenth centuries, it featured strongly during the reigns of a succession of Stewart monarchs. Writing towards the end of the eighteenth century Captain M J Armstrong observed, 'That the town of Peebles has been a Royal Residence, is very evident, from the walls, ports, and other remains of regal security : several decayed buildings & etc. still retain the names of their possessors in office; as the Dean's house, Usher's wynd, Borthwick's walls, King's house, Castle hill, King's orchards & etc', while the Agricultural Survey of Peeblesshire of 1802 recorded that 'Peebles would appear to have been often used as a hunting residence by our Scottish Kings. Money would seem to have been coined in it; an house still retaining the name Cuinzee Nook.'

The later eighteenth century saw it descend into a gentle decline. Lord Cockburn, the eminent nineteenth century Edinburgh judge and observer of his times, remarked, when describing another particularly dull and lifeless place that 'it was quiet as the grave, or Peebles'. That was before the town was lifted again to greater prominence by the industrial revolution and the resurgence of a textile industry driven by the demands of an increasingly affluent society, the advent of new technology and not least the coming of railways.

To present a true and cohesive picture of the town is no easy task. There is little archaeological evidence of the town's earliest years and little to document the centuries at least until the fifteenth. There is certainly rumour and possibly fable, but apart from the Chambers Brothers, the most substantial body of evidence for the burgh's past comes from the work of Robert Renwick and Dr Clement Gunn, although Walter Buchan later added to their work. The name of the Rev Alex Williamson, whose work appeared at the end of the nineteenth century, is less well known, but he also made his contribution to the story. Because of their national prominence, the Chambers brothers, born in Peebles at the beginning of the nineteenth century, merit a chapter in this book, while information about the other writers can be found in Appendix I.

Inevitably the style of writing of these writers has all the formality and pedantry of their era and this present book, while recognising an indebtedness to their work, is intended to provide the story of Peebles in the language and usage of the twenty-first century and with an eye to a more modern interpretation of the available evidence.

Since their time a number of archaeological investigations have been carried out in the town, the most recent in 1979, when the site of the former castle of Peebles was investigated shortly before it was developed as the site of the Church Centre of the Old Parish Church. While those investigations have yielded little of real substance, probably because later developments have obliterated what past evidence there might have been, there is no doubt that such evidence as there is, confirms the ancient origins of the town.

There remains quite a large body of evidence of iron age activity and population in the immediately adjacent countryside and quite close to the burgh boundary, while to the west and within four miles of it, the presence of a Roman fort and temporary camp, has been clearly established, but the first documented evidence of a recognisable town does not occur until the twelfth century.

The earliest description of the Tweeddale countryside is by Blaew in 1654, but first hand descriptions of the town do not appear until 1715, when Alexander Pennecuik of New-Hall, wrote his *Description of Tweeddale*, which was published with additional notes by Robert Brown of Newhall, in 1815. Captain Armstrong has already been mentioned. In 1775 he published his *Companion to the Map of Tweeddale* and again as previously mentioned, *A General Review of the Agriculture of the County of Peebles*, was published in 1802 by the Rev. Charles Findlater, the minister of Newlands. Both of these writers include some descriptions of Peebles. Then in 1794 the first *Statistical Account of the Parish of Peebles* by Rev William Dalgleish was published, to be followed in 1842 by a *New*

Statistical Account of Scotland, compiled in respect of the Parish of Peebles by the minister, the Rev A M Elliot.

A number of maps have been produced to show the layout and extent of the town at various times in its history. Those include one showing the town in 1569, which appears in William Chambers' preface to *Charters and Documents and Extracts from the Records of the Burgh of Peebles, 1165-1710* and one as it might have been in 1609-52, by Alex A. Thomson, published in 1892, which appears in Robert Renwick's *The Burgh of Peebles : Gleanings from its records 1604-52*. Both of these are conjectural, although possibly quite accurate. In 1752, William Roy produced a Military map of the Lowlands of Scotland. This gives the first reasonably accurate representation of Peebles and the surrounding area. The first accurate map of the town itself is a *Plan of the Burgh of Peebles* published by Armstrong in 1775 at the same time as his *Map of Tweeddale*. This was followed in 1823 *by A Plan of the Town of Peebles from Actual Survey* by John Wood.

The end of the Roman occupation of southern Scotland, is normally taken to be about 410 AD. From then on and until the twelfth century, the history, not only of southern Scotland, but much of the rest of Britain and Europe, is obscured by a lack of firm evidence not only in the written word, but also in the absence of the remains of physical structures. Consequently, those are known as the Dark Ages. There is a common view that following the departure of the Romans and their organised system of government and society, there was a descent into chaos and a return to barbarity. It does seem true that in certain parts of continental Europe at least, Barbarian hordes swept away much of the urbanised development which the Romans had created, but this may not necessarily have been the case in northern Britain, where there was and probably remained, a society which was more pastoral. In recent years, there have been finds of coinage and jewellery and other artefacts of gold and precious stones, not only in England but in central Scotland too, which indicate a quite sophisticated society, possessing considerable skills and craftsmanship. Those treasure troves, which seem to relate to burials of the great and powerful, indicate a society with a structure and a hierarchy.

The absence of significant finds of houses and other buildings from that time can be explained by the fact that many people were still semi-nomadic and that the materials used were mainly timber and animal hides and would not have been of a permanent nature. These were easily constructed, but though easily destroyed by weather or militant enemies, they could be quickly restored.

The written word is almost entirely absent. The earliest writings which remain, date from the eighth century and include the *Lindisfarne Gospels* and the works of the Venerable Bede, both emanating from Northumberland.

It has been suggested that Peebles had little significance in the life of the monarchs of Scotland, but the records suggest otherwise. Several of the early medieval Scottish monarchs left their personal mark on the town. The later Stewarts from James I onwards, were regular visitors to Peebles and Tweeddale until James VI&I took himself off to England. With his departure in 1603 any direct link with the subsequent reigning Kings of Scots ceased for 320 years until the visit of King George V and Queen Mary in 1923. Since then there have been a number of visits by the present Queen, the most recent in 2013.

Is Peebles a Border town? Some would say, 'no'. Yet it shares many of the features of its near neighbours. Like Galashiels, Melrose, Selkirk, Jedburgh, Hawick and Duns, it has an annual celebration, "The March Riding and Beltane Festival". In its present form it is an invention of the late nineteenth century, but so are those of Galashiels, Jedburgh, Melrose and Duns. Those of Hawick and Selkirk do stretch back many centuries, but then "The Play" of Peebles has even older origins, as has the Beltane Festival, which was certainly in existence in the reign of James I in the early fifteenth century. The town shares with Kelso, Melrose and Jedburgh in the destruction of the Border Raids, the "Rough Wooing" of the sixteenth century, a fact recognised by James VI&I in his Charter granted to the burgh of 1621. He calls to remembrance 'the ancient erection of our burgh of Peebles, the great benefits, memorable and agreeable services performed by the Provost, Bailies, Burgesses and community............performed and manifested, as well in peace as in war, not only in defending the country against foreign enemies, but also by exposing their persons to open and evident oppression, as well as struggling on the borders of England as of Scotland............... the city often being spoiled, burnt, laid waste and desolated, lying contiguous to the said borders.'

It also shares the textile trades with many of the Border towns, the Websters or Weavers Guild being one of the oldest and certainly the most prominent in the town. An echo remains today in the form of the Guildry Corporation of Peebles. Like those other towns it drew the raw material of wool from the flocks of the surrounding hills. Where it differs, is in its connection with the political power centre of Scotland, Edinburgh. Unlike the other Border towns, as well as looking south, it has long looked north and west. Its ecclesiastical links lie with Glasgow and its central location a day's journey by horse and carriage from Edinburgh, made it a favourite stopping off point for the Stewart monarchs, *en route* to the southern Borders, at least up until the Union of the Crowns. The attraction of the hunting Forest of Ettrick, almost on its doorstep was a further incentive to the attentions of king and courtiers. In the seventeenth century the activities of the Covenanters of the Killing Times, who were most active in the neighbouring counties of Lanarkshire, Dumfries, Galloway and Upper Tweeddale, had their influence.

Throughout this book there are quotations from the original records. Where appropriate and in order to give an authentic flavour, these appear in the Scots language of the time, some with modern English alongside where necessary in the interests of clarity.

The works of the earlier writers referred to above contain a considerable amount of detail, some of it relating to the minutiae of life. Anyone looking for details of financial records of the time, including such as burgh revenues and payments by the authorities of the day, will not find it here, unless included to illustrate a particular point. This book also attempts to paint a broader picture, focusing on events, serious, amusing and sometimes tragic, which give a picture of the life of Peebles over the centuries, which tell the story of this ancient and fascinating town. From time to time it takes in the contemporary national scene as a backdrop. One example is the Civil War of the seventeenth century which had such a major impact on the whole of the British Isles and had consequences which had a direct affect on the life of Peebles, as it did on communities throughout the land.

What seems beyond doubt, is that Peebles was numbered among the sixteen Scottish towns which were in existence in the twelfth century during the reign of David I and given the status of "Royal Burgh" by him. For that reason alone, its story deserves to be told.

PART I

From the beginning to AD 1200

1.

The Origins of Peebles

The Royal Burgh of Peebles lies in the cusp of the Tweeddale Hills and astride the River Tweed, where it is joined from the north by Eddleston Water. The town is dominated on the north-east by Venlaw, a wooded hill which forms part of Glentress Forest. From the summit viewpoint the expanding settlement spreads out towards the hills south and west. From this viewpoint the High Street and the streets and vennels on its flanks are clearly visible. What lies before you is a medieval town, its central footprint virtually unchanged for seven centuries. Yet, Peebles is much older than even this implies. There has probably been a settlement of some kind here for two millennia. So, when and what was or were the origins of Peebles and its people? As the well-known song from *The Sound of Music* says, 'Let's start at the very beginning, a very good place to start.'

The Roman invasion of Southern Scotland took place in 79 or 80 AD and little is known of the peoples who occupied the lands which today comprise the Scottish Borders, including Tweeddale, before that time. The natural topography meant that Peebles, in the centre of the Southern Uplands, was among the last areas of Southern Scotland to be colonised by a number of tribes.

At the time of the Roman invasion, two tribes dominated the area. The Selgovae had arrived from the west and from Cumbria, by way of the Clyde valley. In the east, the Votadini moved north from Northumberland by way of the east coast and the Tweed Valley and those tribes were bordered on the north by the Damnonii. As time went by the last two came together to form the states of Strathclyde and Gododdin, while the Selgovae seem to have been absorbed into a kingdom centred on Carlisle called Rheged. All these peoples have been classified as Britons and they probably spoke a similar language. Many local place names owe their origin to Cumbric, or derivations of it, which seems to have been the principal language of peoples stretching as far south as Wales.

Following the initial invasion of Britain in 44 BC, the Romans had gradually spread north, but the wilder terrain and equally wild inhabitants of what is northern England and southern Scotland, proved something of a challenge and in AD 79 the Roman general, Agricola, started out on a full scale attempt to subjugate these northern territories. In this he largely succeeded, but in the subsequent decades, marauding tribes still remained a problem. In an attempt at some containment, the barrier known as Hadrian's Wall was built from the Solway to the Tyne by his successors in AD 118, to be followed 25 years later by the Antonine Wall, stretching from the Clyde to the Forth.

There is a great deal of archaeological evidence of the Roman occupation to be found near to Peebles at Lyne and Eshiels and it is likely that this dates from about that time. It is generally recognised that the Roman military establishments were often to be found in close proximity to pre-existing native communities. The presence of Roman settlements is perhaps evidence that by that time there was already an established settlement at Peebles.

After the Roman withdrawal, two kingdoms dominated southern Scotland. In the east Bernicia, which included the earlier kingdom of Gododdin, stretched from Northumberland to the Forth and in the west Strathclyde, which covered an area from Cumbria northwards through Galloway, Ayrshire, Lanarkshire and as far north as Dumbarton and separated from Bernicia in the east by the great forest of Ettrick. These were not really "kingdoms" in the territorial sense, with defined boundaries. Rather they were defined by the tribes who occupied them.

With the departure of the Romans at the beginning of the fifth century, what is today modern Tweeddale had begun to be infiltrated by tribes and peoples from further afield, moving inland along and up the major river valleys of the Clyde and the Tweed. But the picture is a confused one, not least because this was a period when a semi-nomadic tribal society prevailed. Established tribes were increasingly challenged by newer arrivals. It was a time of great movement of peoples. Those arriving were literally searching for pastures new.

Following the Roman withdrawal, four different tribal groups have been identified as occupying or colonising the land which would eventually became Scotland. These were the Picts, Britons, Scots and Angles with later additions from Scandinavia. As each migration progressed, they fought and ejected their rivals only in turn to have to defend against later arrivals. In time they intermarried and settled.

The name, "Picts" is widely and often erroneously used as a generic name for all the inhabitants of Scotland prior to the Roman invasion. It is probably more correctly applied to the northern tribes, particularly those who lived north of the Antonine wall. Where they came from is not known, but they were firmly established in the far north and north east, although by the time of the Roman occupation and certainly immediately thereafter, they had moved further south and west and there is evidence that they may have occupied parts of Strathclyde and Galloway. They seem to have been formidable and aggressive in their attempts at expansion as evidenced by the Roman efforts to arrest their progress by building a physical barrier between the Forth and Clyde.

The Picts and the Britons were already established by the time of the Roman invasion, but the Scots and the Angles who complete this group of four did not arrive on the scene until about the time when Roman control was beginning to fade at the beginning of the 5th century.

First there were the Scots who were already well established in the north of Ireland. They were a Gaelic speaking people and by the 4th century they had started to expand across the seas to the west coast of Scotland, into Argyll, Cowal and Kintyre, eventually establishing a "capital" at Dunadd, south of Oban. They would expand further in the coming centuries and establish a significant kingdom covering much of the west including the southern Hebrides, County Antrim in Northern Ireland and bounded in the south by Strathclyde. This was the Kingdom of Dalriada and it was the Scots of that kingdom that gave Scotland its name.

Among the later arrivals were the Angles. Those newcomers were originally Germanic and had first arrived by sea along the Yorkshire coast, before spreading north and west. By the seventh century, those immigrants (for that is what they were) had pushed north, through modern Northumbria, Roxburghshire, Berwick and the Lothians. Their progress to the west was less rapid as the Kingdom of Strathclyde seems to have resisted the advance.

The situation in Tweeddale is not at all clear. While there is ample evidence of the Anglian colonisation of Berwickshire and the Lothians to be found in the names of places such as Oxnam, Coldingham and Haddington which all derive from that source, there is no similar evidence to be found in upper Tweed. Why this is so is something of a mystery. Perhaps after establishing themselves in the wider and more gentle lands of the lower Tweed valley, the less hospitable uplands of the Upper Tweed, much of it covered by thick forest, posed something of a challenge, not least as they would have been easier to defend by the indigenous tribes, established in their Iron Age forts of which there are many in the vicinity. In any event it seems that the Angles did not settle in Tweeddale until as late as the 9th century.

So who were those early inhabitants of Tweeddale? Perhaps they were Picts, but although there is evidence that they may have occupied parts of Strathclyde it is unlikely that they would have moved into the Upper

Clyde valley and into Tweeddale. The answer is that probably Tweeddale was occupied by various tribes of Britons who, as time passed became increasingly intermarried with new arrivals from east and west as the new migrations gradually spread through and up the valleys of Tweed and Clyde.

The valleys of the River Tweed and the Biggar Water provide a natural route linking Lauderdale in the east with Clydesdale in the west and there is evidence that in Roman times these routes were important and formed part of the Roman road system. A settlement at Peebles, situated at the junction of these routes, would have benefited from them.

Where did Peebles name come from? There is no completely definitive answer to that question, but the modern consensus is that it derives from the Welsh word, "pebyll", which means a tent or tents. That word in turn is derived from the Latin *papilio* which means *butterfly*, a Roman soldiers' slang for temporary buildings and tents. This is quite consistent with what is known of the area at the time of the earliest Roman occupation, as in all probability there would have been a semi- permanent encampment in or around the site of the present town. Permanent buildings of stone were virtually unknown prior to the arrival of the Romans. The "Welsh" origin of the name is also consistent, bearing in mind that Cumbric or close variations of it was the common language of much of southern Scotland, Cumbria and as far south as Wales.

From the time of the Roman withdrawal, at least until the end of the 9th century, Tweeddale was probably controlled, albeit loosely, by Northumbrian Bernicia. The lack of Anglian names already referred to does however, suggest that the Angles of Northumbria did not settle in Tweeddale and that its settlers continued to be Britons.

Since the departure of the Romans the many tribes in what became Scotland gradually coalesced and evolved into four kingdoms. Those were Pictland, which covered most of the north and northeast as far south as Fife and the Forth and had its centre, first at Forteviot in Strathearn and then Scone in Perthshire; the Scots kingdom of Dalriada based on Argyll and the southern Hebrides with its capital at Dunadd; Strathclyde which included Galloway, Ayrshire, Lanarkshire and Dunbartonshire, with its capital at Dumbarton and the Northumbrian kingdom of Bernicia.

In AD685 at Nechtansmere, in Angus an army led by the Pictish king, Brude defeated the army of Egfrith, the King of Bernicia and pushed Pictish domination southwards into Fife. The 8th century saw a merging of Pictland and Dalriada. First it was the Pictish kings who dominated their western neighbour, but in time it was the Gaelic speaking kings of Dalriada who eventually gained the upper hand. The enlarged kingdom became Alba.

Towards the end of the 9th century Northumbrian influence, already severely reduced after Nechtansmere was further diminished by the Viking invasion of parts of Yorkshire and also Cumberland and Westmorland, with the result that Strathclyde was able to expand southwards towards Carlisle and beyond. At the same time the Northumbrians of Bernicia were under attack from Scots of Alba from the north and were forced to withdraw from Lothian and eventually from the whole of southern Scotland. Tweeddale then became part of Strathclyde which in turn, both by conquest and dynastic marriages was under threat from Alba. By the 10th century the Scots of Alba largely dominated Strathclyde and even much of Lothian. There is evidence that while Tweeddale was now part of Strathclyde it was increasingly coming under Gaelic influence. The Royal Commission on the Ancient and Historical Monuments of Scotland has commented that twice as many place names in Tweeddale are derived from Gaelic as those from Cumbric. They include Romanno, Garvald and Fingland. A Gaelic Kingdom of Scotland was emerging, under the MacAlpin kings who would eventually control and merge the four ancient kingdoms.

Gradually, both Cumbric and Gaelic died out in southern Scotland to be replaced by a language which in turn developed as English and in due course diverged into Scots. There was of course a significant intrusion in the form of Norman French starting in the early 12th century.

* * *

If the origins and earliest history of Peebles and Tweeddale remain a mystery with little tangible evidence of what went before, then the history of religious development is somewhat less opaque, although it has to be said that what has come down to us over the centuries is probably as much a mixture of fable as of fact.

Christianity has played a significant role in the life of Peebles since its earliest days. Even in the Roman period there is some reason to suppose that if the military garrison at Lyne had among its numbers some from continental Europe, they may have been Christian. It is not unreasonable to think that they might have come from Roman Gaul[1] where Christianity was established by the third century AD.

There is the story handed down by John of Fordoun, the medieval Scottish chronicler, writing in the 14th century, of an ancient cross being found in Peebles, which he claimed may have been buried by Christian faithful in AD296, to avoid a Roman purge against Christianity at that time. If this story is true, then Christianity most likely came to Tweeddale with the invading Romans, as it was not until the fifth century that the first recognised Christian missionary, St Ninian, made his way northwards from Whithorn in Galloway. It has been suggested that in any event, his mission was more an evangelising of already established Christian communities, which had their roots in the Roman invasion which, like many Christian communities before and since, had lapsed into a degree of paganism.

One of the fascinating aspects of the history of those ancient times is the movement of peoples over great distances and in the present days of ease of rapid transport from one end of the British Isles to the other, such journeying seems remarkable. It was a time when whole populations were on the move and static villages, let alone towns and cities were only just beginning to be established. Territorial boundaries hardly existed. Where communities became established, places of worship also became established and it seems that there was some sort of Christian centre at Peebles at least from the time of Ninian. This gives further credence to the probability that there was indeed a settled community there by the fifth century, but no credible evidence survives in the form of archaeological remains, let alone documentary evidence.

What we do know is that a church had been established on the outskirts of the town by 1195 AD. This became in time St Andrew's Parish Church, which was probably built on the site of an earlier building. Its remnants, in the shape of a tower, partially restored by William Chambers in the late nineteenth century and a fragment of wall still stand today within the town's cemetery.

The early Christian Church in southern Scotland is dominated by three names, Ninian, Kentigern or Mungo and Cuthbert all of whom at least indirectly had some influence on the formation of a Christian church in Peebles. In *The Book of the Peebles Church*, published in 1908, Dr Clement Gunn gives a lengthy description of the early church and its antecedents. To the names of Saints Ninian, Mungo and Cuthbert, he adds two more, Gordian and Nicholas.

---

[1] Modern France

According to Dr Gunn, in the 4th century, Gordian was Deputy Governor of the Roman province of Gaul. He had become a convert to Christianity, but in AD362, during one of those periods of religious persecution which the Roman Empire went through from time to time, he and members of his household were killed for their Christian beliefs, Gordian himself being beheaded in Rome. He is commemorated by a monument which stands on the road leading to Kirkhope, in Manor Valley, a few miles south west of Peebles. Quite how this strange connection between Roman Gaul and an obscure Scottish valley came about is a mystery. Dr Gunn gives a plausible explanation, which is that in the Roman garrison at Lyne, as already mentioned, there could very possibly have been some of the occupying troops who came from Gaul. It is known that many of the forces of the Roman Empire, particularly in those parts furthest from Rome itself, came from other conquered territories and indeed it is also known that soldiers recruited from the native British population may have served on the continent of Europe. So, it is quite likely that there were those at Lyne who came from Gaul or had been to Gaul and knew of Gordian's martyrdom. Dr Gunn goes on to suggest that perhaps those based at Lyne who were Christian, may have wanted to find a quiet and secluded place where they could hold Christian worship and as Dr Gunn says, 'they established their little sanctuary in the hills.'[2] At a later time a church was built on the site dedicated to St Gordian and it has been claimed that it became the first pre-Reformation Parish Church of Manor. However, the writer, John Buchan strongly disputed that this was ever the parish church. Whatever the truth may be, there does seem to be evidence that there was a Christian establishment of some sort in the vicinity, which is further endorsed by the name of the farm lying close by, which is Kirkhope. The supposed site is today marked by an ancient stone cross erected in 1873. This seems to be the same cross which was seen by Armstrong in 1775, at that time standing at the road junction between Manor Kirk and Hallyards. There is no other known church or monument in Britain dedicated to Gordian and if Dr Gunn's story is correct, it is a rare link with the very earliest Christian activity in Scotland.

If little is known about Gordian, equally little is known of Nicholas. John of Fordoun, tells the story of the discovery of a stone urn found in AD1261 at the site of what became the Cross Kirk in Peebles. According to him, it contained the bones and ashes of a man and on the lid was carved "Locus Sancti Nicholai Episcopi" (Tomb of the Bishop St

---

[2] *The Book of the Church of Peebles AD 1195-1560* p2

Nicholas). The urn and its contents were discovered at about the same time as 'a stately and venerable cross' was discovered at the same spot and the combination of these two events turned Peebles into a place of pilgrimage for centuries to come. Nicholas, however remains one of the many mysteries of the early Christian church. He was certainly not the St Nicholas, known to most of us as the origin of Santa Claus. That St Nicholas was the 4th century Bishop of Myra in Greece and there is no record of his having travelled to Britain, let alone Peebles. According to John of Fordoun the cross which was discovered in 1261 may have been buried in about AD296 when there was a Roman purge of Christians during the reign of the Emperor Maximian. Dr Gunn says that Nicholas was a missionary, although he adds that nothing is known about him and he makes no suggestion as to how he came to be a "saint"[3] If he existed and unfortunately neither the cross nor his burial urn seem to have survived, as there is no mention of them in the records after 1261, that may be a further indication that a form of Christianity was being practised in Tweeddale during the Roman occupation.

The man who is generally recognised as the first evangelising Christian missionary in Scotland is Ninian. Exactly when he lived is uncertain. Dr Gunn gives his dates as AD360-432, but later historians suggest that he was active rather later in the 5th century. Much of what is known about him comes from the Venerable Bede writing in the early 8th century. It seems likely that he was a Briton and according to Bede he was a bishop. That suggests that rather than being a pioneering missionary, carrying the Gospel to pagan tribes, he was more of an evangelist, reviving a faltering Christianity which had survived from its earlier Roman introduction. He probably had contact with Roman Christianity in Cumbria and further south. Bede says that he may have received training in Rome itself, not impossible given the *Pax Romana* which gave Roman citizenship to all within the Empire and allowing freedom of travel throughout its dominions.

His base was Whithorn in Galloway where he is credited with establishing a church called *Candida Casa* which means the "white house" as it was believed to have been built of a white stone. It stood where Whithorn Priory stands today. From there Ninian and his disciples carried their mission to the Picts of Galloway and Strathclyde and may have reached far further north, even into Fife and the Lothians, although this is

---

[3] the name "saint" in English appears regularly in history applied to "holy" men and is more probably a corruption of the Latin word "sanctus", meaning "holy", rather than implying canonised sainthood

conjectural. If it is true it is unlikely that this was achieved during his lifetime, but if true then there is every possibility that the mission moved north through the valleys of the Nith and Clyde and into the basin of the Tweed and joined up with the Christian enclaves that remained after the Roman withdrawal, although no tangible evidence remains.

If the mission of Ninian and the immediate generations of his followers was as described, it may have taken a further century to complete, by which time the next great Scottish evangelist, Kentigern or as he is better known, St Mungo, was established as Bishop of Glasgow. He had earlier been forced to escape persecution and had gone to Wales[4], but when he returned he started the task of reviving and nurturing the faltering seeds of Christianity. Settlements had begun to be established with primitive churches attached to them and it is generally recognised that a church was established at Peebles at this time, although whether or not the good saint actually visited Tweeddale is unknown.

Early churches were invariably dedicated to a particular saint. The church in Peebles has always been associated with St Andrew as it is to this day, although it might have been expected to be dedicated to St Ninian or St Mungo as are many in those places which benefited from their missions. So although the church in Peebles may have originated from the mission of St Mungo, there must be a reason why it is St Andrew who became its patron saint.

Robert Renwick gives a possible explanation. According to him, one of the earliest known dedications of a building to St Andrew is to the monastery of Hexham in Northumberland at the end of the 7th century, which was then in the bishopric of York. Its bishop, Acca, apparently acquired relics of the Apostle, but towards the middle of the 8th century he was expelled from his see for reasons that are not known (it was a time of many doctrinal disputes). In any event Acca is said to have departed taking the relics with him. The story goes that he eventually reached a place in Fife then called Kilrymont and there he built a church, which he dedicated to the saint. Today that place is called St Andrews. It is a far cry from Peebles, but Renwick points out that Acca stayed at a number of places on his way from Hexham and that those visits are commemorated by churches dedicated to St Andrew. As Renwick says, 'it is not improbable that Peebles formed one of the group. A peculiarity of the churches modelled on that of Hexham was their combination with chapels dedicated to St Michael and the Virgin Mary, and this characteristic is observable in the case of Peebles church, two of its earliest altars being

---

4   Yet another example of the common language link

so dedicated.'[5] As possible further evidence of a visit of Bishop Acca to Peebles, Buchan notes that the name, Acrefield, near Rosetta is a corruption of "Acca's field".

What also is known, is that a St Andrew's day fair on the anniversary of the saint's day was already established at Peebles before the town's first charter was granted. In the later town records of 1652, it is referred to as existing 'thes mony aiges bygaine'.

So, by the end of the 8th century, there was an established church in Peebles. Nothing of it remains, but as earlier noted it is thought that it stood where the ruins of St Andrew's are in the Peebles cemetery today.

* * *

Communities were first established by family groups. Then new families arrived who, initially at least, formed part of the same tribe. The process continued and the group enlarged. There was conflict, but also intermarriage. As we have seen, Britons were joined by Angles and then by Scots and then of course there was the arrival of the Romans, so that by the time the Romans departed, there was already a complicated mixture of blood lines in the community which now became settled at Peebles.

The location of communities does not happen by chance and in those early centuries, in addition to access to the basics of water and food, there was a need for defence. The first settlement of Peebles was on the north bank of what today is Eddleston Water and on the higher ground rising beyond, where the "Old Town" is today. This gave access to water and potential grazing for livestock beyond. It might be thought that the spur of land which today is the High Street with the Castle Hill at its western end, where the Old Parish Church stands, would have provided a better defensive position, but the narrowing of the raised spur between the Tweed and the Eddleston Water would have blocked easy escape from any attack from the east, from which it was most likely to come. By contrast, the Eddleston Water formed an initial barrier to the Old Town, while the land to the north was an avenue for escape. The presence of some form of church nearby also gave it a focus.

It is impossible to date the expansion into what became the "New Town" which in time would become the main centre of the community, but it does seem probable that it was in being by the 12th century and it is to that century we must now turn, because that is when the first documented evidence of a Royal Burgh at Peebles comes into sight. By

---

[5] Renwick : *Peebles in Early History, 1903,* p11/12

then it is clear that after the centuries which followed the departure of the Romans, what had been initially little more than the centre of nomadic tribesmen near the confluence of the River Tweed and the Eddleston Water, was now a permanently established community, with a church and shortly to follow a royal castle. Its buildings would still be mainly of wood, hide and thatch, but a fixed social order was also in the making and within the next century it would be recognised by the monarch of the day and would evolve a structure and form of local government, which would remain the basis of good order for centuries to come.

2.
Medieval Peebles

It is generally accepted that what was known as "the Dark Ages" was the period after the end of the Roman occupation until the beginning of the 12th century, when the first tangible evidence of our past begins to emerge.

As we have seen, from a number of disparate "kingdoms" based on tribal allegiances, the four ethnically based kingdoms of Pictland, Dalriada, Strathclyde and the northern part of Bernicia, had themselves gone through a process of amalgamation. In those Dark Age centuries Scotland had evolved to a point where by the 11th century it had become a recognisable nation state, with a single ruler, the warlord, Malcolm II at its head and recognised as the King of Scots. However, the future of the Scottish monarchy and nation was far from settled. The MacAlpin/MacMalcolm dynasty had several branches and succession was not the settled affair which it would later become. The first to succeed Malcolm was his grandson, Duncan. This is the Duncan of Shakespeare, but far from being the venerable and seemingly popular monarch portrayed by him, he was young, incompetent and unpopular. He was indeed killed by Macbeth, but in battle and not by a wife-inspired clandestine murder. Macbeth may well have had a better claim to kingship than Duncan and what is more, "Lady Macbeth" was in fact Gruach who, as the grand daughter of one of the earlier MacAlpin kings, Kenneth III, probably had a stronger claim than either. Macbeth reigned as King of Scots for seventeen years and was eventually defeated and killed in battle, not at Dunsinane, but at Lumphanan in Aberdeenshire. The victor at Lumphanan in 1058 was Malcolm, the son of Duncan, who became King of Scots as Malcolm III, known as "Canmore" or big head, although this seems not to have referred to the size of his head, but rather that he was recognised as the great chief. He would marry an English princess, Margaret and their union established a line of monarchs who ruled without a break until the death of Alexander III in 1296.

Malcolm was very much the "warlord" and during his reign he tried on more than one occasion to expand his territory into both Cumbria and Northumberland. Fixed national boundaries did not exist. Territory was acquired through conquest and occupation. It was also during his reign that one of the most significant events in British history took place. In

1066 William, Duke of Normandy, William "the Conqueror", invaded England. The Normans had arrived. By 1072 William had extended his power northwards. Shortly before that, Malcolm had made one of his several incursions, firstly into Cumbria and then eastwards into Northumbria, but this ground to a halt outside Durham. The result was an attack into Scotland by the Normans which reached as far as the Tay. William and Malcolm met at Abernethy where Malcolm seems to have given William assurances of his future peaceful intentions. Whether or not this included Malcolm accepting himself as the "vassal" of William is unclear although it may have laid the foundations of later claims by English monarchs.

The woman whom Malcolm married[6] was Margaret, an Anglo Saxon princess, of the royal house of Wessex. She had been born in Hungary, while her father had been in exile there. The family returned to England but the events of the Norman invasion overtook them. They moved north to Yorkshire and when the Normans arrived there in 1070 she and her mother took refuge in Scotland, where she caught the eye of the widowed Malcolm, who clearly saw advantage in linking himself to Anglo Saxon royalty even if it had now been displaced by the Norman conquerors.

All three sons of Malcolm and Margaret would reign in succession as King of Scots. The youngest of the three was David, who reigned as David I. He was largely brought up at the English court of Henry I, who had married his sister, Matilda. Although his blood line was Pictish/Scots on his father's side and Anglo Saxon on his mother's, he was brought up as a Norman. While his mother spoke only Saxon English, his father had been bilingual, speaking Gaelic and Saxon English. David, although initially brought up to speak the languages of his parents, became fluent in Norman French which would become the language of the Scottish Court.

David became King of Scots in 1124 on the death of his brother Alexander II. Some years before then he had been made governor of Southern Scotland by his brother. He also fulfilled the same role in the north of England on behalf of his brother-in-law, Henry, so that by the time he became King of Scots he was already an established figure of power with, as it were, a foot in both the Scottish and English camps. In addition, by marriage to the daughter of the Earl of Northumbria in 1114, he also became Earl of Northampton and with it went the lordship of Huntingdon. With his years at the English court he had developed as the classic Norman knight. When he came north to take charge of the northern territories he brought with him Norman feudal government and, as his

---

[6] His second wife

45

supporters and companions, a number of Norman knights and retainers from his English properties to act as his stewards of his Scottish estates. Those families would in time form a significant element in the Scottish aristocracy. Among the Anglo-Norman families who put down their roots in Scotland at this time were the Lindsays, Morevilles and not least the Bruces and Stewarts.

David I can be said to have introduced settled government to Scotland for the first time. In a gradual process through intermarriage (and coercion) between the new Norman incomers and the indigenous Celtic families, the old order of the MacAlpin/MacMalcolm kings and their supporting mormaers[7] and great lords, was replaced by the feudal system under which all land was in the first instance vested in the king, who then might grant lands to the principal families. There was however, a quid pro quo. In exchange, the recipients had to pledge allegiance to the king and acknowledge that he was their "superior" and they his "vassal". In addition they would be required, when necessary to provide military manpower to support the king. Vassals in turn could grant parts of what they had received to others who became their vassals and they in their turn could make grants to lesser vassals and so on. At the lower levels of minor lords, or lairds as they would become, allegiance to the superior would remain the principal obligation, but in an agricultural population, this might be a specified proportion of their produce in place of the need to provide military manpower. In time this evolved into a system of cash payments, which in turn evolved into a system of leasehold and rent payment.

It was during the reign of David I that the feudal system was established. Essentially it was the primary means by which the king could exercise control over the nobility many of whom before had really been minor kings. These were the Celtic aristocracy and David, who was himself part Celt, although thoroughly "Normanised", was careful to see that the more significant of them were given feudal right to their traditional lands, which until then they had held by tribal occupation. Those Celtic lords may well have felt that this was no more than their just entitlement, rather than the "gift" of a king to whom they felt obliged. There was a balancing element, the Norman knights and retainers who had come north with David. In the main David and his immediate successors granted lands to them in the Lowlands and south Scotland leaving those west and north of the Forth much as they had been. To the Bruces he gave lands in Annandale and to the Stewarts lands in Renfrewshire and

---

[7] Pictish regional rulers

Ayrshire. From his reign onwards there is a recognition of settled communities which would come to be recognised as burghs. The name derives from the Saxon word *burh* and means a place of defence or a fortress.

A major feature of the land grants to the great lords was the need to create a system for defence and control. Those grants established obligations due by vassal lords to the king and in addition to vassalage, those lords were required to build defences at strategic locations. These were motte-and-bailey castles, which were relatively simple structures consisting of a wooden palisade, built on top of an earthen mound, sometimes surrounded by a ditch. Within it there might be little more than an encampment, although some of the more important might contain permanent buildings and even a tower, but these would also be of wood.

Throughout southern Scotland the sites of well over one hundred of these primitive structures have been identified and it would be a century later before some of the more important of them began to be constructed of stone and lime, becoming the much more formidable defences which would be a feature of the later middle ages. While a great many of these "castles" were erected by the great lords, others were erected by the king and remained royal possessions and the castle of Peebles was one of those. It was almost certainly a palisaded enclosure, which possibly extended eastwards, part way along what is now the High Street. Excavations in 1979 uncovered evidence of post holes on the Castle Hill which would probably have been for the main supports for the palisade structure. There would have been further protection from the converging Tweed and Cuddy or Eddleston Water and possibly a ditch running between the two along the line of the Port Brae/Cuddy Bridge where the west end of the present High Street takes a downward slope. The natural feature of what is today still called the "Castlehill" provided an elevated site. Whether there were permanent buildings within the palisade is not known, although as it was a royal castle and remained in being for perhaps two centuries, it is likely there would have been buildings to provide for the needs of royal visitors and a garrison. There was certainly a chapel which was endowed with a ploughgate of land[8]. This is later referred to as being granted with its endowment to the abbey of Kelso by King David, which was confirmed by his grandson William I and by Josceline, the Bishop of Glasgow

The establishment of a castle gave further impetus to the development of the town. It was probably also encircled by a palisade connected at its

---

[8]   Just over 100 acres - Kirklands, now occupied by the Peebles golf course and by Kingsland School

western end to the castle defences. While the burgh, as it had now almost certainly become, was independent of the castle, the protection which it afforded encouraged trading, merchants to became established and artisans to set up their places of work. Both would construct homes and a permanent community came into being. It is now that a more formal structure for the regulation and management of the burgh begins to emerge.

There is little direct evidence for the way burghal society and government developed in the 12th and 13th centuries and it is not until the late 14th and early 15th centuries that firm evidence of the structures which had emerged becomes available. In the case of Peebles, burgh records only appear for the first time in 1456. However, it is possible from these later records, to gain some idea as to how those structures had evolved, as they often refer to laws and practices as "long established".

In the years before he became king and while he ruled southern Scotland on behalf of his brother, David I instigated an investigation to establish what lands, churches and other properties, belonged to the See of Glasgow. This is known as *The Inquest of David* and Dr Gunn dates this as 1116 AD and gives a detailed description. Among the properties listed are five in Peeblesshire including as Dr Gunn says, 'Pobles, now Peebles. Here there were 104 acres of land and a church.'[9] Renwick says that the earliest document which mentions Peebles, is a charter granting certain lands to the monks of Durham which is dated at "Pebles" in 1126.

There is a debate as to whether David I or David II granted Peebles Royal Burgh Status. Chambers,[10] says David II constituted it a Royal Burgh by a charter, dated 24th September 1367. He seems to have relied on George Chalmers, who in his *Caledonia* says:

David II granted Peebles a charter, dated 20th September 1367, which made it a royal burgh, and which was confirmed by a charter of James II, and by another from King James VI in 1621.[11]

However, Renwick in his Preface to *Extracts from The Records of the Royal Burgh of Peebles 1652-1714* refers to this as an 'inconsistent and

---

9   Gunn, The Book of the Church of Peebles, p35
10   History of Peeblesshire, page 67
11   George Chalmers (1742-1825)– *Caledonia, or, A Historical and Topographical account of North Britain from the most ancient to the present times.*quoted from New Edition, Volume IV, 1889. Chambers would have been referring to an earlier edition, as he was writing in 1864. Although there is a small difference in the dates, he is clearly referring to the same document.

erroneous statement.' And goes on to say, 'Evidently Chalmers had not seen the charter of 1367, as he gives an entirely wrong indication of its contents. It was granted not to the burgh of Peebles but to the chapel of St. Mary within the burgh, and is not confirmed by the charter of James II, though it is described and confirmed by the charter of James VI, before which time the chapel and its endowments had been transferred to the community. Unfortunately, Dr William Chambers, in his *History of Peeblesshire*, adopted the misleading statement contained in *Caledonia*, and having also repeated its in gazetteers, guide books, and similar works, the story has gained a hold and established an impression which it will be difficult to eradicate'[12]

Buchan[13] agrees and says, 'The latter statement is not only inconsistent but wrong in fact' he adds, 'It is for the following reason that we know definitely that the town was a burgh when David I reigned. One of the distinguishing features of a Royal Burgh was the payment to the king of a rent in respect of the lands occupied by the burgesses. This rent was first collected direct, but it soon became the practice for the bailies of the burgh to farm the rent and customs for payment of a fixed sum annually – the surplus going to the common good of the town. Now, towards the end of the twelfth century, William the Lion confirmed to the monks of Kelso the Chapel of the Castle of Peebles, with a ploughgate of land pertaining thereto, and with a rent of 10s from the "ferme" of the burgh, which rent King David his grandfather had assigned to the Chapel for the celebration of divine service therein. Chalmers knew of this endowment, for he refers to it, but it escaped his notice that the fact of that endowment was in itself sufficient evidence that Peebles was a royal burgh when David I was king.'

Relationship between Crown and Burgh is further explained by Renwick again in the Preface to *Extracts from The Records of the Royal Burgh of Peebles 1652-1714,* when he writes :

In the twelfth century, when Royal Burghs first came to notice in Scotland, one of their distinguishing features was the payment to the King of rent in respect of the lands occupied by the burgesses either severalty or commonty, such lands having previously formed part of the royal domain. These rents, along with customs levied in the burgh market, were probably at first collected by the King's bailies and handed over to his chamberlain direct,

---

[12] The text of the charter is printed in the Appendix and is No.II at page 205 of *Extracts from the Records*

[13] *History of Peeblesshire*, page 4

but eventually it became the practice for the bailies, "chosyn thruch the consaille of the gud men of the toune," to farm the rents and customs for payment of a fixed sum, any surplus accrueing to the common good fund of the town. From an early period the burgh revenues or "fermes" formed a convenient source from which the annual allowances were paid by royal authority. The earliest preserved account of the burgh of Peebles, rendered in exchequer, is dated 8th February, 1327-8, and shows that the fixed rent then payable by the burgh to the King amounted to £23 6s 8d.

Renwick adds that there is evidence that two hundred years earlier a similar payment was being made from the burgh's revenues which shows once again that Peebles would have been a Royal Burgh during the reign of David I

What also seems certain is that by the time David I became King of Scots, there were perhaps as many as sixteen settlements in Scotland with the essential elements of a "castle" and a church, which had been formally recognised as "burghs" by the king. Peebles, with its castle and church had at least developed sufficiently to have the trappings of a burgh and it is generally recognised that it would have been included in the original group. Those burghs became in turn the centre for defence, for the regulation of trade and the collection of taxation due to the crown and governance of the surrounding countryside.

There is no evidence that David actually granted a Charter as such to the town. The earliest extant charter document, is the one granted by James II in 1451-2. During David's reign the first burgh laws were enacted by what was called the Court of the Four Burghs. That body comprised the burghs of Edinburgh, Berwick, Stirling and Roxburgh. What was decided by that court was applied to all existing burghs and it is thought that this made separate charters to each burgh unnecessary at that time. To quote Buchan again,[14] 'The most reasonable assumption is that when he (David I - Author) began his reign, he would find there a more or less organised community which had been in existence for a considerable period, and possessed large tracts of ground land in the vicinity as "folcland". It was his wish to develop such communities, and doubtless Peebles would receive her share of royal protection and benefits.'

As part and parcel of the feudal system, the king appointed a personal representative to act on his behalf in maintaining law and order over specific areas of the country, with a burgh as its base. Local government was undertaken by the neighbourhood feudal magnates who were

---

[14]   *History of Peeblesshire*, Vol.II, page 5

appointed as Sheriffs. It was a system which was already well established in feudal England, but was now introduced to Scotland by David and by the end of his reign many sheriffdoms or shires had been established. At what stage a sheriffdom of Peeblesshire came into being is not known, although Renwick records that the first mention of a Peebles sheriff occurs as early as 1184, just 31 years after the death of David I and a further indication that the town was by that time recognised as a "Royal Burgh". This was during the reign of William I and Renwick goes on to say that the sheriff in question was "Symon , the son of Malbeth", who is described as sheriff of "Travequeyr" rather than Peebles. The reason for this may be that because William usually stayed at Traquair, Symon took his title from there, although in practice this was synonymous with Peebles. In 1227 there is a reference to "John, sheriff of Peblis", although who this may be is unknown. Some time later in 1259 there is a reference to Sir Gilbert Fraser, on one occasion as sheriff of Traquair and on another as sheriff of Peebles. His son, another Symon, is called sheriff of "Peblys" in various charters dated between 1260 and 1266. While up to this point there does not seem to have been any mention of a local "magnate", it would suggest that these are early references to the Fraser family who in time became the Frasers of Neidpath.

David I introduced his own coinage, the first King of Scots to do so. The minting of coins usually took place in centres which were frequently visited and used as regional bases by the monarch. It is interesting to note that at some point in its history, Peebles did have a royal mint, which was situated where Veitch's Corner is today, at a point still known as Cuinzie Neuk,[15] although there is no indication whether or not it was in existence as early as the 12th century.[16]

As already noted the original settlement of Peebles was located in the area still known as the "Old Town". It probably never grew beyond a single street, although there may have been an area at its centre which allowed space for a market. When the settlement expanded into the "New Town" is uncertain, but there may well have been buildings there before the twelfth century along the line of the east-west route, the long established route of the Romans from Lauderdale to Strathclyde and its intersection with a highway from the Lothians to the north. The junction

---

[15] Cuinzie meaning "coin"

[16] The use of the word "coin" has a common derivation with the French word "le coin", meaning a corner. When metal coinage first came into use as a means of trading, the first coins were in fact cut from the corners of sheet metal, hence the term.

of these routes would have been a natural focus for such trade as there was and Renwick says that a market cross was erected at that point.[17] The royal grant of privileges to a burgh would include the right to hold a market. Indeed it seems that the producers from within the shire were required to bring their goods to Peebles for sale in the official market. As Renwick records, 'there need be no doubt that so soon as the royal burgh was founded, and the market for the whole shire was established at the cross, booths of merchants and craftsmen as well as their dwellings would spread over the vacant ground'. Another early development in the town's evolution, in addition to the establishment of a market, was the collection of revenues on behalf of the king.

To begin with there was a separation between the people of the town and the garrison of the castle. Ancient burgh laws made a clear distinction between the two. The governor of the castle was appointed by the king and while he had responsibility for military affairs of the shire, he could not hold any civic appointment in the town.

The more privileged class of inhabitants of the town were the "burgesses". To qualify as a burgess it was necessary to own land extending to one rood (quarter of an acre) with a street frontage of 20ft. Those who became burgesses, took an oath of loyalty to the king and in Peebles, admission was sometimes granted in exchange for a monetary payment or by supplying services to the burgh. Among their privileges was the right to elect "bailies", who in turn elected twelve burgesses to regulate the laws and customs of the burgh. They were often known as the "dousson" and evolved in time into the town council. As yet the position of provost did not exist.

Burgesses were granted special rights to trade and practise their crafts, but that and the evolving of a system of local government took some time and probably did not reach a settled state until the fourteenth century.

During the reign of William I, The Lion, (1165 -1214),[18] a law was passed which required all wool, skins, hides and, as Renwick records 'sic like merchandise' produced in any shire, to be brought to the market cross of the shire burgh and to be sold to the merchants of that burgh, 'and the custome tharof salbe payit to the King'.[19] This form of taxation or customs dues, was payable on all goods bought and sold in the burgh.[20] At first it

---

17 *Peebles in Early History* – R Renwick 1903 p.20
18 So called because he adopted the symbol of a lion on his shield, which subsequently became, the Lion Rampant on the royal standard
19 *Peebles in early History* – Renwick p22
20 An early VAT?

was paid direct to the King's officers, but in time it became the responsibility of the bailies, who collected it on behalf of the burgh. They in turn paid a fixed annual amount to the king. Any surplus over and above what was due to the king was retained as burgh funds. In a further complication and extension of the system, the bailies sub-let the collection of customs dues to "tacksmen".[21]   When this system was first implemented is unclear, but the burgh records from 1457 onwards, regularly record such arrangements.

---

[21]   The term survived into the twentieth century where feu duties are payable in respect of land comprising several properties, the feu duties being "allocated" to each of the individual properties. The collector of the allocated payments is known as the tacksman.

Part II
AD 1200 to AD 1400

3.

The Great Cause

The 13th and 14th centuries have a very special place in the story of Scotland. It was the events of that era which are at the heart of what today we perceive as the nation of Scotland. From the perspective of the 21st century, has emerged the romanticised notion of Scottish patriotism as seen through the image, or perceived image of a small but vibrant nation, threatened by a mighty and avaricious neighbour, intent on hammering it into submission, yet defended by great leaders of the common people. This is the era of William Wallace and Robert the Bruce, and the Declaration of Arbroath, eventually culminating in the Treaty of Edinburgh in 1328, which established the right of a Scottish nation to freely exist as a sovereign state, ruled over by its own, unique monarchy.

William I, The Lion was succeeded on his death in 1214, by his son Alexander II and then by his grandson, Alexander III, who ruled as King of Scots, until his untimely death in 1286. It was his death and what followed which set in motion the struggle for Scottish sovereignty which developed into the Wars of Independence. Before that however, it is worth pausing to look at the reign of Alexander III and in particular at an event which had a lasting significance for Peebles. It was to give the town a special prominence which lasted for three centuries.

Alexander III succeeded his father in 1249 at the tender age of seven. Like his immediate predecessors since the advent of the MacAlpin kings, he was crowned at Scone, seated on the Stone of Destiny, the last Scottish king to be afforded that dignity. The succession of a monarch in his minority, which was to become a regular feature of the later Stewart dynasty, was something of a novelty and it was during the time until he reached his mature years of personal rule, that three great families began to emerge as the power brokers in Scotland. Those were the Comyns/Balliols, the Bruces and the Stewarts. The first two of these were in time to have a part in the early history of Peebles, while the later Stewart monarchs would come to have a regular place in the story of the town.

Scottish nationhood progressed during the reign of Alexander III. Chroniclers of the 14th and 15th centuries have portrayed it as a "golden age", when Scotland was ruled over by a model king, encapsulating all the virtues of medieval kingship. Mythology has a prominent part in the history of nations and Scotland is no exception. Modern historians have however, taken a rather more sanguine view than the early chroniclers. The reign of Alexander did see a period of relative peace and an improving economy, with the beginnings of trade ties with Continental Europe. His second wife, Yolande was the daughter of the Count of Dreux in France. The use of coinage was on the increase and the established burghs continued to develop, albeit slowly. It was a case of slow but positive progress, rather than a great leap forward.

While the general line of the national boundary between the states of Scotland and England was fairly settled by 1237, it was not finally fixed until 1551. For centuries it was a matter of dispute. Indeed as late as the sixteenth century large swathes of the territory, now part of Cumberland and the valleys of Liddel Water and the Esk around Langholm, Gretna and Longtown, were known as "the Debateable Lands". The town of Berwick on Tweed changed hands on 13 occasions after 1147 before being finally ceded to England in 1482.

Since the reign of David I, there had been connections with the English throne and in those connections lay the seeds of the dispute which ultimately resulted in the Wars of Independence. The question was, did those connections signify feudal homage by Scottish kings to their English counterparts? There were common roots through intermarriage. The 12th and early 13th centuries had seen many incursions and skirmishes across a border not yet settled. On more than one occasion, a Scottish king submitted in homage to the English monarch, although continuing to deny that this signified acceptance of the feudal overlordship claimed by the English crown. It was certainly a claim made by Henry III, but perhaps the marriage of his daughter, Margaret to Alexander, as his first wife, may have muddied the waters. Henry claimed to be "Principal Councillor" to the King of Scots, whatever that might have meant! None the less in 1278, when Henry's successor, Edward I demanded his presence, Alexander seems to have made the journey to the English court in response, once more sowing seeds which would one day reap a bitter harvest in Scotland.

One of the most positive steps of Alexander's reign, was territorial expansion into the isles of the west, which were then part of the kingdom of Norway, long disputed by the Scottish crown. Alexander's father, Alexander II had embarked on an expansion of the western boundaries and a conquest of the Hebrides in 1249, following a failed attempt at acquisition by diplomacy. Although he made some progress in Argyll, he died on the island of Kerrera, near Oban, during an abortive attempt to advance into the Hebrides. His son took up cudgels again on reaching the age of personal rule. The battle of Largs in October 1263 saw his forces defeat an invading force of Haakon IV of Norway, who then retreated to Kirkwall in Orkney where he died shortly after. Alexander III continued to expand Scottish conquest of the islands and by 1265 his forces had taken control of all the Western Isles and the Isle of Man. Magnus, son of Haakon IV sued for peace and in 1266 a treaty was signed at Perth which ceded all the Norwegian possessions except Orkney and Shetland to the Scottish crown for a payment of 4000 crowns and an annual sum of 100 merks. Peace between the two kingdoms was further cemented by the marriage of Magnus' son, Eric II to Alexander's daughter Margaret, who died giving birth to a daughter, Margaret, the Maid of Norway. The death of the Maid in 1290 was to precipitate the crisis which led to the Wars of Independence.

While Hebridean conquest and English machinations may have dominated Alexander's reign, an event in Peebles was to thrust the burgeoning town into the spotlight, at least in ecclesiastical affairs. The story is told by the Scottish chronicler, John of Fordoun in the late 14th century :-

On the 9th of May, 1261, in the thirteenth year of King Alexander, a stately and venerable cross was found at Peebles, in the presence of good men, priests, clerics and burgesses. But it is quite unknown, in what year and by what persons it was hidden there. It is however, believed that it was hidden by some of the faithful, about the year of our Lord 296, while Maximian's persecution was raging in Britain. Not long after this a stone urn was discovered there, about three or four paces from the spot where the glorious cross was found. It contained the ashes and bones of a man's body – torn limb from limb, as it were. Whose relics these are no one knows as yet. Some, however, think they are the relics of him whose name was written on the very stone wherein that holy cross was lying. Now there was carved on that stone outside :- "Locus Sancti Nicholai Episcopi" (Tomb of the Bishop, Saint Nicholas). Moreover, in the very spot where the cross was found many a miracle was and is wrought by that cross; and the people poured and still pour thither in crowds, devoutly bringing their offerings and vows to God. Wherefore the King, by the advice of the Bishop of Glasgow, had a handsome church made there to the honour of God and the Holy Cross.[22]

---

[22] Fordoun's Chronicle, Skene's edition as quoted by Dr Gunn

The church which Alexander ordered to be built became the foundation of the Cross Kirk, whose ruined remains still stand in Peebles. In the 15th century it would become the centre of a monastery.

It is difficult from today's perspective to imagine the impact of such a find on the medieval mind. What is clear is that the Cross Kirk became a major place of pilgrimage as its fame spread throughout Scotland and northern England. There is no firm record or detail about the cross which was found. In Fordoun's account it is merely described as 'stately and venerable'. There is no later description of it, although it seems still to have been known about during the reign of James V. In 1529, in letters confirming the grant of a house of religion in Dunbar and its revenues to the Minister and Brethren of the Cross Kirk, he refers to it as being "quhair ane pairt of the verray croce that our Salvatour was crucifyit on is honorit and kepit". The passage of time and perhaps added mythology had now elevated the previously anonymous cross to something of a much higher status. If all the pieces of the "verray croce" spread throughout Europe were gathered together, it would no doubt represent quite a forest of timber! What of course is significant is that it enhanced the status of the church and monastery, which in turn brought travellers and trade to the town, an early example of tourist initiative!

There is one other reference to the direct involvement of Alexander in the life of Peebles. In 1262 there was a dispute between the burgesses of Peebles and Robert Cruik, whom they accused of cutting peats and also of damaging peats belonging to others and impounding a horse and a load of heather which he claimed were illegally on his land. For their part the burgesses claimed that Cruik had built a house on common land and ploughed part of the common grazings known as the Moss of Waltamshope. The dispute must have been referred to the King because in October 1262, he issued a breve or brief[23] in the following terms, instructing Eymour de Macisuuell, his sheriff of Peebles and the bailies, to hold an inquest or enquiry into the matter:

We command and firmly enjoin that ye cause inquisition to be diligently and faithfully made by honest faithful free and lawful men of the country whether Robert Cruik has deforced our burgesses of Peebles of our moss of Waltamshope granted to them as they say by our father Lord Alexander, King, of good memory, and afterwards by us, and whether the said Robert has tilled or in any other way unjustly occupied our land and the common pasturages of our said burgesses; and that ye cause the said inquisition

---

[23]   A legal instruction.

diligently and faithfully made to be sent to us as speedily as possible under your seal, together with the seals of the others who make the said inquisition, and this brieve. Witness myself at Lanark the seventh day of October in the fourteenth year of our reign.'[24]

It appears that a number of local burgesses and landowners were duly appointed to the inquisition. Such disputes regarding rights relating to the use of the common lands of the burgh, do however, occur from time to time throughout its history.

Alexander III died on 19 March 1286 in tragic circumstances. A few months previously he had married his second wife, Yolande of Dreux, after the death of his first wife Margaret. He must have been infatuated by her, because after a day of deliberations with his council of state in Edinburgh, followed by an evening of feasting and drinking, he determined to join her in Fife at his castle of Kinghorn. The weather was foul, as is often the case in Scotland in the month of March and although efforts were made to dissuade him from travelling, he insisted in making the journey, setting off for Queensferry with attendants. By the time they reached the ferry, the storm had increased and showed every sign of continuing, so much so that the ferryman refused to set sail across the Forth to the northern shore. Alexander, either over indulged in alcohol or over anxious to join his beloved bride, refused to be put off and demanded that the ferryman take him over to the other side. They did arrive safely, but in utter darkness and with a gale to contend with. The route to Kinghorn led along the high cliffs which bounded the shore. A little way short of his final destination, whether on account of the darkness or by a sudden gust of wind, his horse lost its footing and he was pitched over the cliff. His body was found on the shore the following morning.

In spite of two marriages, Alexander had no direct heir to follow him. The two sons, borne by Margaret had pre-deceased him, while his second wife was childless and his daughter, Margaret, who had married Eric of Norway had also died, but left a daughter, Margaret, the Maid of Norway, who was now the heir to the Scottish throne. In Scotland this was a time of uncertainty. The Norwegian princess, was the rightful heir and although still only three years old, she was a very eligible royal bride. The English king, Edward I of England, who had already demanded allegiance from Alexander III, saw her as an excellent match for his son, the first Prince of Wales. Scotland and Norway were broadly in agreement, although

---

[24] Translated from Latin as appearing in Chambers *Charters and Documents and Extracts from the Records of the Burgh of Peebles 1165-1710*

possibly naively unaware of Edward's ruthless pursuit of territorial dominance. In any event it was agreed that Margaret should come to Scotland and in 1290 she set sail but never reached her kingdom, dying in Orkney. What to do now? There was more than one claimant to the Scottish throne (there were in fact sixteen) and Edward stepped in ostensibly to act as arbiter in what became known as the "Great Cause". Arbiter, Edward may have been by invitation, but he saw it as an opportunity to pursue his own ambitions.

In the end it boiled down to a straight choice between the representatives of two families the Balliols and their associated Comyns and the Bruces. To cut a long story short in 1292, Edward came down in favour of John Balliol, one of the most unfortunate men in Scottish history, his character, perhaps unfairly summed up in his nickname "Toom Tabard".[25] Edward demanded submission from him and he was frequently summoned to the English court to hear Edward's demands.

By 1296 it was clear that Edward intended to impose his claimed rights as Overlord of Scotland by physical means. In March of that year he brutally attacked and sacked Berwick. In a feeble effort at resistance, in April, Balliol announced that he would no longer pay homage to Edward. The response was swift and devastating. The hammer descended on Scotland. Within a very short time Edward's forces had defeated a Scots army at Dunbar and the castles of Roxburgh, Edinburgh and Stirling were occupied by the English. Edward himself advanced as far north as Elgin. On his return journey he took with him the Stone of Destiny and had the Great Seal of Scotland destroyed. Balliol himself surrendered at Strathcathro in Angus and thereafter suffered the humiliation of having the trappings of kingship removed from him in the most humiliating circumstances. He was thereafter taken to London, but a few years later was allowed to go to France to the estates of his Norman forbears to live out the rest of his days in ignominy.

On 28 August, 1296, the leading Scottish landowners, churchmen and burgesses were summoned by Edward to Berwick to swear allegiance to him. The document which they were made to sign became known as the "Ragman Roll" because those signing fixed their seals on it to which ribbons were attached. On the document appear 71 names listed as residing in the burgh or county of Peebles. Among them are John, Vicar of the Church of Peebles and Friar Thomas, Master of the House of the Holy Rood of Peebles. There are also names that emerge in the later history of the burgh, such as William de la Chaumbre, bailiff and burgess of Peebles

---

[25] Empty coat

and William le Vache.[26] All those names are further proof of an established burgh and church by that date.

Scottish pride had suffered the severest of hammer blows, but within a year, although seemingly subjugated and leaderless, the seeds of revolt had begun to emerge. It was led not by the great magnates, but by smaller landowners or lairds, in the north by Andrew de Moray and in the south by William Wallace the son of a Lanarkshire Laird. National mythology has elevated Wallace to the pinnacle of patriotism. Great patriot he was. His leadership in reality was less successful. He was above all a guerrilla fighter, initially successful in local harassment of the English intruders, often from his base in Ettrick Forest. He did however move north, gathering an ever increasing army, eventually joining up with Moray who had been successful in recovering a number of the northern castles from English occupation. In the meantime an English army was advancing from Berwick into central Scotland. It was met by the Scots at Stirling Bridge, where the tactics of the Scots overcame the far larger English army in a famous victory. History has generally given Wallace credit for this victory, although just as much of the credit is due to Moray. It was in fact Wallace's one and only victory in a set piece battle, in which Moray was wounded, dying of his wounds some weeks later in November 1297. None the less it left Wallace as sole commander of the Scottish army and recognised early in 1298 as "Guardian of the Kingdom of Scotland". From then on Wallace was on a downward path. Although he had some success in incursions into the north of England, this further provoked a backlash from an England smarting under the humiliation of Stirling Bridge. In the summer of 1298 an English army heavily defeated Wallace's Scottish army at Falkirk. He escaped to France, taking little direct part in the continuing resistance thereafter.

During that period Robert Bruce, Earl of Carrick had become increasingly active in the struggle against Edward, as had John, the "Red" Comyn and after the departure of Wallace, they were appointed Joint Guardians of Scotland in his absence. Each represented one of the two great families claiming the Scottish crown. Together they had led an unsuccessful attempt to dislodge the English from Roxburgh Castle and with the leading Scottish lords and their forces, it was to Peebles that they returned to re-group and plan their continuing strategy. There was a great deal of frustration and ill feeling amongst them and according to a report by an English spy, there was a disagreement between Sir David Graham and Wallace's brother about lands which belonged to William Wallace.

---

[26] Chambers and Veitch

Robert Renwick appears to refer to this occasion and records that 'On 20 August 1299, Sir Robert Hastings, then the English sheriff of Roxburgh, reported to King Edward an inroad by the Scots on Selkirk forest, in Sir Simon Fraser's custody, the meeting there of the bishop of St. Andrews, the earl of Carrick and others, the dissensions among them regarding the division of Sir William Wallace's lands and goods, "as he was then going abroad without leave", and the final agreement under which the bishop of St. Andrews, the earl of Carrick, and Sir John Comyn were to be guardians of the realm, the bishop having custody of the castles. It is then related that all the parties "left Pebbles" going to their respective territories and the bishop remaining 'at Stubbowe'. [27] [28]

The report of the English spy records the "dissension" referred to by Renwick in some detail:

At this the two knights gave lie to each other and drew their daggers. And since Sir David Graham was of Sir John Comyn's following, it was reported to the Earl of Buchan and John Comyn that a fight had broken out without their knowing it; and John Comyn leaped at the Earl of Carrick and seized him by the throat and the Earl of Buchan turned on the Bishop of St Andrews, declaring that treason and *lese majeste* were being plotted.

Bruce could have been killed, but somehow, after the altercation Comyn agreed that he would support Bruce's claim to the throne, provided that Bruce would grant his lands to Comyn. The bargain was not kept by Comyn with almost inevitable fatal consequences. After tracking him down to Dumfries, Bruce killed Comyn in the Church of the Greyfriars where Comyn had sought sanctuary. Such a crime on consecrated ground led to Bruce's excommunication, but the removal of his principal rival, never the less helped pave his way to the Scottish throne.

Edward I himself is recorded as having been in Peebles on at least two occasions. On the first in August 1301, on his way from Berwick to the west of Scotland, he stayed for several days, bringing with him an army reputed to be 6800 strong. According to Renwick, he brought a portable chapel with him on the campaign trail and records that there was an entry in the accounts which makes reference to a payment of 7s on 4th August 'in his chapel at Pebles'.

---

[27] Stobo
[28] *Peebles in Early History* – R Renwick 1903 p.31

Following his departure, one of his retinue called William de Durhame was left in charge of the castle (clearly in existence then). He seems to have remained for a time thereafter. Renwick notes that in August 1302, 'he had with him ten men-at-arms; and from a list of officers and garrisons in Scottish castles it is ascertained that on 20 September, 1302, Sir William of Durhame, sheriff of Peebles, has for his keeping four men-at-arms'.

Dr Gunn[29] has more to say about Durhame and quotes the following entry in the records, 'To Sir William de Durhame, knight, whose horses and armour were carried off at Werk by Sir Simon Fraser at the time when he joined the Scots against the King, to buy a charger for himself, by the King's gift and his own hands, twenty merks.' This probably relates to one of the many cross border raids led by Bruce and his supporters during that period. Fraser had been sheriff of Peebles until he was presumably replaced by Durhame.

Although Sir William Wallace had largely dropped out of sight, he had returned to Scotland from France. He was a fugitive with a price on his head. Dr Gunn has an interesting entry referring to him at this time :

A.D. 1303-4. In Stobo parish did Sir William Wallace find refuge; for in King Edward's accounts for the year 1303-4 is found the payment of forty shillings to the messenger who brought Edward news of the defeat inflicted by Sir William de Latimer, Sir John of Segrave, and Robert of Clifford upon Sir William Wallace and Sir Simon Fraser at Happrew.

It was not long after, that Wallace was captured, taken to London, where on 23 August 1305 he was executed in gruesome circumstances. In the following year Fraser suffered a similar fate on 6th September.

Edward was again in Peebles in August 1304, while returning from an expedition to the north. He had been at Holyrood on the 16th of the month, at Pentland on the 17th and at Eddleston on the 19th. Dr Gunn says that there is a letter still preserved in 'The State Paper Office' in London which was sent by Edward to his Chancellor from Eddleston. The following day he made his way south through Peebles, Traquair and Selkirk to Jedburgh.

It seems that Edward was effectively in total control of the government of Scotland and it was his officers who collected taxation due to the crown. There are few Scottish records of the time, but the contemporary English accounts are a source of information. Renwick mentions a number

---

[29]   The Book of Peebles Church- AD 1195- 1560

of examples of rents paid in the period 1302-4, such as 'the sum of 40s.' collected 'of the farm of the town of Pebbles'; 'Wester Kailzie, which William of Hopkeliou held of the king, yielded 30s.,' and the following sums were received for lands described as "the King's demesne" : - Edrikestone, 13s. 4d.; Bondington, 10s; Esterschelis, 6s. 8d.

Renwick records many others too numerous to mention here, but one is of interest, '20s. from the farm of the vicar of Pebbles' land, a rebel.' Not every one it seems, followed the example of those who, for whatever reason, had signed the Ragman Roll!

Regardless of the fact that nominally at least John Balliol was still King of Scots, Edward was clearly in charge. He it was who granted the burgh and mills of Peebles to Aymar de Valence, in addition to the castle of Selkirk, the manors, desmesne lands of Selkirk and Traquair and the forest of Selkirk. [30]

De Valence and his heirs also were appointed as heritable sheriffs of the counties of Peebles and Selkirk. He was a cousin of Edward and was born about 1270, coming from a long established Norman family with extensive lands in France, Wales and Ireland as well as England. On the death of his mother in 1307, he inherited the Earldom of Pembroke. He was the first great territorial magnate to control Peebles and extensive lands in the Upper Tweed.

After some years of skirmishing and guerrilla activity, Robert Bruce had become sufficiently strong to make a final move to take the crown of Scotland. He went to Scone, near Perth, the ancient site where Scottish kings had been crowned and there, on 25th March, had himself crowned as Robert I, King of Scots. Many of the Scottish nobility were at that time in English hands, and those who attended the coronation were small in number, but significantly, they included the bishops of St Andrews, Glasgow and Moray. The crown was placed on his head by the Countess of Buchan, deputising for her husband the Earl of Fife, who was imprisoned in England.

Although now king, Bruce was far from being in control of Scotland. He still had not won over the mass of the Scottish people, many of whom were suspicious of him. After all, a few years before he had given Edward an oath of allegiance, although it may have been as much pragmatic as genuine. It would be some years before he could draw together the many strands of Scottish power which allowed him ultimately to achieve his great victory at Bannockburn in 1314.

---

[30]   Ettrick Forest

For now the tide was running against him. He had been excommunicated and of course aroused the ire and fury of Edward, who swore that he would never rest until he had conquered Scotland and issued orders that anyone who supported "King Hob" as the English derisively called him, should be slaughtered. In his present state the odds were against Bruce and in one of the earliest battles after his coronation, his small army was heavily defeated at Methven Park, near Perth by Edward's army led by none other than Aymar de Valence, Earl of Pembroke – and sheriff of Peebles.

The rise to total domination of Scotland by Robert Bruce need not concern us here. Suffice it to say that from the time of Bannockburn onwards, he was in full control for the remainder of his reign. His only actually recorded visit to Peebles, is the one already mentioned, when he quarrelled with John Comyn. There may have been others and there is certainly evidence that he had knowledge of the Royal Burgh. Although no trace of it remains, it seems he granted it a charter giving the right to hold fairs. Renwick records an entry in the town's accounts, which he says were given to the exchequer in 1327.[31] This says that, 'the sum of 4s. is allowed for the privilege of a mill lade through the land of James Spotis, and 40s. are given to John, son of Adam Spotis, for his sustenation at the schools by the will of the King', which, as Renwick says does indicate an interest in the burgh's affairs on the part of the king.

In May 1328, the Treaty of Edinburgh[32], between Bruce and Edward III, the grandson of his great enemy, finally recognised Bruce as king of an independent Scotland. The English king also undertook to intercede with the Pope to recognise the legitimate sovereignty of the Scottish monarch, but Bruce was now a sick man and died the following year on the 7th June, just six days before the Pope issued a bull allowing the coronation of a King of Scots by the Bishop of St Andrews.

In his last years in spite of his earlier excommunication, Bruce had become reconciled to the church and had vowed to go on a crusade. Ill health had prevented him, but he had asked his friend and great supporter James Douglas, to take his heart with him to the Holy Land. Douglas did as he was asked, but he himself never returned. He was killed while in Spain on his way to the Holy Land, although the heart of his king which he had carried so dutifully, was saved and returned to Scotland where it is said to rest in the grounds of Melrose Abbey, not so far from Peebles.

---

[31] It is not clear what these were, bearing in mind that Renwick has also reported, as have others, that the burgh records only start in 1456
[32] It is sometimes called, "Northampton"

The king now in control of England was Edward III. Unlike his weak father, Edward II, who was defeated at Bannockburn, he inherited the warlike aggression of his grandfather and Peebles and Scotland were to suffer as a consequence in the decades to come.

Robert Bruce was succeeded by his son David who was then only five years when he was crowned King of Scots. In the same year there is a recorded visit by him to Peebles.

As so often has happened in the medieval period in Scotland, the vacuum created by the succession to the crown of a minor, sparked off internal conflict. The rivalry between the Bruces and Balliols, submerged during the reign of Robert Bruce, now re-emerged and in 1332 Edward Balliol, the son of King John, landed with a sizeable force at Kinghorn and had some success in defeating a Scots army led by the Earl of Mar at Dupplin near Perth. He then had himself crowned at Scone, but he had limited support in Scotland, although he gained the support of Edward, by promising to hand over Berwick, which was then in Scots hands, although besieged by the English. A Scots army led by Archibald Douglas was heavily defeated at Halidon Hill, while trying to relieve the disputed town in July 1333, which fell to the English. The next year Balliol acknowledged Edward as his liege lord, at the same time ceding large areas of land in the south of Scotland to the English king. It was a time of desperate danger for the Scots, with the warlike Edward, threatening invasion. Although still a child David had been married to the sister of Edward in 1328 as part of settlement under the Treaty of Edinburgh when he was aged four, while she was three years older. In the unstable and vulnerable situation in which Scotland found itself, the young couple were sent to France in 1334 where they stayed at the Chateau Gaillard, which lies on the River Seine, between Rouen and Paris, remaining there until their return to Scotland in 1341.

As part of submission to Edward and granting of lands in the south of Scotland to him, on 12th June of that year, Balliol also granted him "Villum at Comitatum de Pebles".[33] There is no mention of the "castle". In the case of all the other places named in the grant including Edinburgh, Roxburgh, Jedburgh, Dumfries and Berwick, their castle is specifically referred to, which suggests that the castle of Peebles no longer existed. Dr Gunn, says that after 1327, there is no mention of the grant of ten shillings annually to the Chapel of the castle of Peebles and that this is further evidence that it had ceased to exist by then. It may have been destroyed by

---

[33]   The town and county of Peebles

Edward I or possibly by Robert I, who had adopted a policy of destroying any fortification which could have been of use to the English enemy.

Dr Gunn records that on 29th December 1334, Edward Balliol was at Peebles at the behest of the English king. Edward had been preparing to march north into Scotland. Scottish forces under the Earl of Moray were preparing to meet the challenge, but he died at Musselburgh before preparations could be completed. Peebles was among other towns in the south which were left virtually undefended. Unlike his grandfather Edward I, whose policy was to occupy and govern the lands of Scotland conquered by him, Edward III adopted a scorched earth policy, burning not only buildings but also the surrounding countryside to deny the people their means of support. Along with large areas southwards towards Carlisle, the town and district was laid waste. This would be the first occasion when those acting on behalf of an English king would inflict devastation on Peebles. It would not be the last.

The reign of David II lasted until his death in 1371. His career as king was chequered to say the least. He returned to Scotland in 1341 to take up his personal rule and to a country suffering from the ravages of war. He was much influenced by his time in France where he had established close links with the French crown. What Scotland needed was a peace to rebuild a shattered country, but in 1346 at the request of the French king, Philip VI, who was then engaged in a struggle with England,[34] he invaded England. Although, he had spent a lot of time in France practising knightly arts of war, he was a poor commander and the Scots were heavily defeated at Neville's Cross, near Bishop Auckland. He himself was wounded and captured and spent the next eleven years in English custody. He was eventually freed in 1357 in exchange for the payment of a ransom of 100,000 marks, payable over ten years. The Scotland he came back to was at a low ebb. Not only had it suffered from almost constant warfare, but the Black Death had arrived, carried north from the English neighbour.

After the defeat of Neville's Cross a meeting of the Scottish parliament is supposed to have been held in Peebles. Parliament Square off the High Street is the alleged site. However it is much more likely to have been an emergency meeting of the Council of magnates, rather than a representative body.

It was during the reign of David II that the royal burghs began to play a part in the political life of Scotland. It seems likely that by 1340 there was an established Scottish parliament which was attended by their representatives. Taxation was a major issue, increasingly so after the

---

[34]   The start of the Hundred Year's War.

return of the king in 1357 when the problem of the ransom payment had to be addressed. The royal burghs are recorded as being represented at the General Council held that year and in 1366, both of which were mainly concerned with taxation. Peebles would certainly have been included and Renwick says that Peebles joined with the other fourteen royal burghs, 'in an obligation for the King's ransom in 1357'. Buchan[35] tells us that Peebles sent two commissioners to the 1357 parliament and named them as, "Nicholas the son of John, and John the son of William." Renwick mentions that in 1343 during the first period of the personal reign of David II, there must have been contact between the burgh and the royal court as there is a record of 30 shillings from burgh funds being given to the queen's tailor.

The burgh's loyalty in its contribution to the ransom payment seems to have been recognised, because on 8th March 1362 David issued letters assigning an area at the west end of the High Street for the erection of a chapel dedicated to the Virgin Mary. Before then there had been a Chapel of the castle of Peebles. It had in all likelihood been destroyed along with the castle. Dr Gunn refers to the whole ecclesiastical situation at the time in Peebles in some detail :

It has been stated that before this time the Chapel of the Castle of Peebles, which David I had established, had probably now ceased to exist. Still there were two ecclesiastical fabrics in the town each with its staff of clergy – (1) S.Andrew's, the Parish Church; and (2) the Cross Church, which does not seem to have possessed a monastery as yet, though it was an institution of preaching and itinerant friars. Once more was the burgh to benefit under Royal patronage, and an addition was about to be made to the places of worship in the burgh. Letters by King David II were sent charging the community of Peebles to assign a stance in the Common Muir to build a Chapel. This was exactly a century after the founding of the Cross Kirk by King Alexander III, and a hundred and sixty-seven years from the dedication of the Church of S.Andrew. The new foundation was to be dedicated by the name of the Virgin Mary, and was to occupy what in later years was to be the west end of the High Street, but was at that time the Common Muir.

The financing of church establishments relied heavily on revenues from property and endowments. Dr Gunn records that, 'in 1365-6 oblations[36] and offerings to the "Church" were granted by John, Vicar of Peebles, to the Chapel of S.Marie of Peebles, near the Castle. (he seems to have

[35] History of Peeblesshire, Vol.II 1925 – p10
[36] In modern usage - Offerings to God.

forgotten his earlier view that the castle no longer existed!) Two silver shillings were to be paid yearly to the Church for the oblations. In this manner did the new foundation receive encouragement'.

Further encouragement was given in 1367 by the king who granted the revenues of the mill of Innerleithen to the Chapel. The relevant charter dated 20th September 1367, reads in the translation from Latin[37]:-

David, by the grace of God, King of Scots: To all good men of this whole land, clerics and laics, greeting. Know ye that we, moved by divine charity and for the weal of our soul and of the souls of all our ancestors and successors, Kings of Scotland, have given, granted and by this our present charter confirmed to God and the chapel of Saint Mary newly founded within the burgh of Pebyls, and to the chaplain celebrating and to celebrate divine service there for ever, our mill of Innerlethane, with the whole multure which formally used to pertain to our mill of Traquair, on the north bank of the water of Twed from the town of Horsburk to Gatehopburne. To hold and have to the said chaplain in the said chapel celebrating and to celebrate divine service for ever as aforesaid, for his sustentation for ever, in pure and perpetual alms, as freely, quietly, fully, wholly and honourably as any rent in any other place within our kingdom of Scotland is most freely, quietly and honourably, in pure and perpetual alms given or granted. In testimony whereof we have ordered our seal to be appended to our present charter.

The witnesses to the charter include the bishops of St Andrews and Brechin, Robert, Steward of Scotland and the earls of Douglas and Strathern.

There is little more to say about the remainder of the fourteenth century concerning Peebles. There is only one further incident of interest worth noting from Renwick's Early History. In 1363, the effects of the increased taxation raised to meet the king's ransom approved by the parliament of 1357, had become an increasing source of unrest, not least because the large sums collected had been used by the king for his own personal expenses, rather than meeting the ransom instalments. A group of nobles led by Robert, the Steward and the Earls of Douglas and March rebelled, but were soon brought to heel. David II although twice married, had no direct heir and the next in line as heir to the throne was the Steward,

---

[37] Appendix to Chamber's Extracts from the records of the Burgh of Peebles, 1910 – p 205

whose father had married Marjory, the daughter of Robert I, so that his part in the rebellion was hardly likely to endear him to his uncle the king. During the course of it, the Steward was in Peebles. Renwick[38] records that, 'The rising was promptly quelled by the Royal Forces in or before May, 1363, but in the course of the military movements the Steward appears to have been in Peebles. On 20 May, 1363, he granted to Laurence Govan of Cardrono "a hostilage, house and inn in the town of Peblis", where the said Robert resided in the time of hosting or muster.' Buchan[39] adds to this story, saying that the hostilage was on the site of what is now the "Cross Keys Inn" in the Northgate which he says has a 'respectable antiquity' and that it may have belonged to the abbot and convent of Arbroath, which was founded and endowed by William the Lion. In addition to extensive areas of land, the king also granted a "toft"[40] in each of his burghs, so that the convent became the owners of a building and land in Peebles, which they subsequently granted in 1317 to a burgess of Peebles called William Maceon. In addition to an annual payment, Maceon was required to provide hospitality to the abbot and others associated with the Arbroath convent 'as often as they should need it, each according to his station'. What he had to provide for his "guests" was set out in detail. He was to 'provide them with a hall with table, tressles, and other furniture, also sleeping chambers and a stable for their horses. Fuel was also to be supplied, and white candles of tallow of the kind commonly called Candles of Paris, straw or rushes for the hall and chamber and salt for the tables.'

It is also worth noting that before the century ended, yet another ecclesiastical establishment appeared close to the town and associated with it. This was the hospital or hospice of St.Lawrence. The first reference to it occurs in 1395. It lay close to Horsburgh Castle at modern day Eshiels and was a wayside refuge and almshouse for travellers. Some years later the name of St.Leonard was added to its title. So Peebles now had four religious establishments, making it a significant religious centre as the fourteenth century drew to close.

In 1371, David II was close to entering a third marriage with Margaret Drummond, whose family had become one of the most powerful families at court. David was still only forty six and could yet have produced an heir, which would have changed the course of Scottish history, but he died suddenly that same year before the marriage could be arranged. In spite of

---

[38] Early History p.38
[39] History of Peeblesshire p.10
[40] An old Norse word for a house

the opposition of the Drummonds and his part in the insurrection of 1363, Robert, the Steward, became king as Robert II. The Stewart dynasty had been founded.

Robert, the grandson of Robert I, succeeded to the throne at the then fairly advanced age of fifty four. He died in 1390 after a relatively uneventful reign, to be succeeded by his son John, Earl of Carrick, who took the title of Robert III. He was a feeble king. In his own words he was 'the worst of kings and most miserable of men'. Partially crippled and ineffectual, his reign, which lasted until 1406, was dominated by his two brothers, Robert, Duke of Albany, who installed himself as regent for much of the latter part of the reign and the other, Alexander, Earl of Buchan, better known as "the Wolf of Badenoch".

At the close of the fourteenth century, while Peebles was a long established royal burgh, with an ordered community and a large ecclesiastical establishment, its castle no longer existed and its defences were limited. There was no full defensive wall as there would be in the sixteenth century. Such defences as there were, probably consisted of no more than a joining up of the "head dykes"[41] linking adjacent burgess properties. The last two decades of the century were a time of disorder, uncontrolled by two successive weak kings. Much of this was in the north where the Wolf of Badenoch carried out a campaign of devastation culminating in burning the town of Forres and the destruction of Elgin Cathedral.

In the south of Scotland border skirmishing continued, interspersed with brief periods of peace. The Second War of Independence initiated by Edward III and his attempts to establish Overlordship of his northern neighbour was continued by his successor, Richard II, who led an English army reputed to be over 14,000 strong, penetrating north as far as Edinburgh and burning Melrose on the way in 1385. The Scots had retaliated by mounting a largely unchallenged raid into the Western March towards Carlisle, while at the same time James, 2nd Earl of Douglas led a Scots army into Northumberland carrying out the usual tactic of burning and laying waste the countryside, which was such a common feature of border raids by both sides at the time. In 1388 he was met by an English force led by Lord Percy at Otterburn, some miles south of the border. Douglas was killed but the Scots won the day, or rather the night as the battle took place in the late evening. It was the last set piece battle of the thirteenth century Wars of Independence.

---

[41] Stone wall at the end a burgess's land

It seems that Peebles did suffer from the incursion of Richard II and other English raiding. The bailies, who were responsible for the collection of taxes, were sometimes relieved of the annual tax payments due by the burgh 'on account of occasional disasters'. Between 1388 and 1392, no charge was made because the greater part of the town, including the mill, had been burnt. A raid by Sir Robert Umphraville, the vice-Admiral of England is mentioned by both Renwick and Buchan when he attacked Peebles and burned it. The raid took place on a market day, when the local merchants had their stalls and booths set up at the market cross. As Buchan says, 'His methods were not according to market customs, and he caused his men to measure out the cloth with their bows and spears, thereby acquiring the name Robin Mendmarket' He goes on to quote from a poem of unknown origin relating to the event.

> *At Peebles....*
> *He brent the toun upon their market day,*
> *And mete their cloth with spears and bows sere*
> *By his bidding without any nay;*
> *Wherefore the Scots from henceforward ay*
> *Called him Robin Mendmarket in certain*
> *For his measure so large and plain.*

Dr Gunn in his History of the Church of Peebles, sums the fourteenth century very well:

Thus closes the fourteenth century. Meagre indeed is the contemporary documentary history of Peebles for the period. This is accounted for by the disturbed state of the Borders at the time. The early years of the century were ushered in amid the Wars of Scottish Independence, when there was no king; its closing years saw the kingdom in the hands of a regency, and the King, Robert III, a ruler of feeble will. Border wars filled up all the intervening years. Peebles, although farther up Tweed than most of the Border towns, must have suffered severely and frequently; hence the absence or destruction of public documents. But the church of Scotland had steadily gained ground; and the end of the century saw Peebles possessed of the Parish Church of S.Andrew, the Cross Kirk, the Chapel of S.Mary and the Hospital of S.Lawrence and S.Leonard.

The next two centuries would see a steady increase in the prominence of the Royal Burgh both politically and ecclesiastically, with the rise to dominance of the Stewart monarchs all of whom, at least until the Union of the Crowns in 1603, would have a place in its history. It would also be a time of change, culminating in the Scottish Reformation with all its consequences and the town would not escape from further suffering and destruction at the hands of 'our auld enemy of England'.

PART III

1400 – 1600

4.
Emerging from the Mists of time

At the beginning of the fifteenth century, there had been little change in the community and structure of Scotland since emerging from the Dark Ages. The population remained much as it had been 200 years earlier in the reign of David I. There had been growth in the population, but the arrival of the plague and pestilences of the fourteenth century had severely reduced its numbers. A second war of independence, instigated by Edward III had burned and destroyed much of the south of Scotland and it had been the cause of widespread famine. The chronicler, John of Fordoun says that nearly one third of the population of Scotland died in 1349. Thereafter there was again a gradual increase in the next fifty years.

As the fifteenth century progressed there was a great deal of change. Perhaps most significant was the development of the larger urban centres, none more so than Edinburgh, established as the nation's capital towards the end of the century, during the reign of James III. Prior to its loss to England in 1330, Berwick was the principal trading port in the south of Scotland and the focal point for the main Scottish exports of the time, wool, skins and hide, much of it produced in the pastoral lands of the Borders. The loss of that vital trade outlet gave Edinburgh and its port of Leith an unrivalled opportunity, which its merchants duly exploited.

The beginning of the fifteenth century also marks a significant milestone in the development and life of Peebles. Written records become increasingly available. The early medieval period still has about it a degree of mystery, but now previously shadowy figures begin to emerge from the mists of time. The town of Peebles and its people start to take on a human face. Family names which are familiar to modern ears begin to appear and recur over the centuries which follow. Chambers and Veitch, with their antecedents in Norman French[42] have already been mentioned. Others have a clearly identifiable source in the names of places where they lived and some are derived from their occupation. There are also some which seem to have come about because of a specific event. "Horsburgh" is one, a name that lives on today not only as a family name but also in the names of Horsburgh Castle, Nether Horsbugh and Horsburgh Ford, which lie a mile or so down the valley of Tweed from the town. The story of how the

---

[42]   de la Chambre and de la Vache

name came into being is told by Robert Chambers in his *Picture of Scotland*.

According to him, an un-named King of Scots and some of his nobles were out hawking one day along the banks of the Tweed, a short distance to the east of Peebles. The king's hawk, following its prey, flew across Tweed. The river was in flood and the King and his retinue could not follow the bird and to make matters worse, they were unable to recall it. This particular bird seems to have been a special favourite of the King, who was upset by its impending loss. However, the predicament was solved unexpectedly by a local farmer. He was ploughing land on the other side of the river and as he knew the depth and flow of the river, whose banks he had cultivated for many seasons, he unhitched his plough and with one of his horses, came across the river and returned the hawk and its prey to the King. As a token of his gratitude, the King, instantly granted him all the lands, north of the Tweed, which could be seen from his plough.

Tradition adds that as he was crossing the river, the king, anxiously watching, called out 'horse bruik weel' by which he meant 'I hope the horse carries you safely.' From that time on, the lands and their new owner became known as "Horsbruik" and in time this became "Horsburgh". The remnants of Horsburgh Castle can still be seen today, close to the main Peebles/Galashiels road, just after the entrance to Glentress and the surrounding lands still retain the name. The un-named king was likely to have been either James I or II, because by the second half of the 15th century the name "Horsbruk" appears quite frequently in the records. For example "Alexander of Horsbruk" is mentioned as being made a burgess in July 1473.

While this was a period of evolution in local society, the problems of national government, which were unresolved at the end of the previous century continued to cast their shadow. The old and increasingly ineffectual king, Robert III was still on the throne as the new century opened, but for all practical purposes, the kingdom was ruled by his brother Robert, Duke of Albany. Tragedy further blighted the king's final years. His elder son, David, at the age of twenty, had been created Duke of Rothesay in 1398 at the same time as his uncle was made Duke of Albany. The rivalry between the two was intense and one which King Robert was quite unable to control. In 1399 Rothesay, the heir to the throne was appointed Lieutenant of the Kingdom, while his father retired to Rothesay Castle on Bute. It was an appointment which was for a fixed term of three years. Rothesay for all that he had seemed to have the attributes of leadership his father lacked, was little more successful in his governing of the kingdom and when his three year term came to an end in 1402, Albany, taking advantage of the general dissatisfaction with his nephew's rule, had him arrested and imprisoned in Falkland, where he died in suspicious circumstances less than two months later. Although never proven, it has been alleged that he starved to death and that his uncle was responsible. In any event Albany was restored as the effective ruler of Scotland when he was appointed once again as Lieutenant of the realm.

King Robert suffered a further blow in 1406. His remaining son James, then aged ten, was sent by his father to France, which was now a close ally of Scotland. It was supposedly so that he could be educated at the French court, but more probably because Robert feared that the young prince's life might be in danger, a clear possibility bearing in mind the fate of his brother. In the event it proved to be a disastrous decision. The arrangements for travel went wrong from the outset. First the boy had to spend a month in winter on the Bass Rock, awaiting a suitable vessel, hardly a comfortable or auspicious beginning. Eventually he was able to board a ship from one of the Hanseatic ports sailing from Leith with a cargo of wool and skins bound for the continent, but it was attacked by English pirates near Flamborough Head in March 1406. The young prince was delivered into the hands of the English authorities and he was soon in London in the Tower. It was the final calamity for Robert, this "worst of Kings" and within a few weeks he died. So the reign of James I started with him as captive of the English king Henry IV. It would be eighteen years before James returned to Scotland to take up his personal rule.

He returned to Scotland in 1424, with his Queen, Joan Beaufort, whom he had married while a prisoner in England. There is every reason to suppose that Albany had made no effort to have the King returned to Scotland and it was only after his death in 1437 and the succession of his son Murdoch as regent, that negotiations with the English crown started, largely as result of the growing power and influence of the Black Douglases and the unpopularity of Murdoch's rule. This is not the place to discuss the wider issues of national politics, but suffice it to say that James returned to Scotland determined to revenge himself against those whom he saw as conniving in his capture and detention in England. His short and swift campaign very soon removed his principal adversaries from the scene.

James could be said to be Scotland's first Renaissance king. He had learned a great deal at the English court. He was highly intelligent, an accomplished musician and poet. His best known work is the

Kingis Quair, or at least there is some agreement that it may be his work. There is a manuscript copy in the Bodleian Library dating from the latter part of the sixteenth century, some time after his death. The content of the poem does appear to refer to events during James' English captivity, which have been authenticated, which gives some credence to the story.

Peebles claims to hold a special place in his reign. There is actually little evidence of his presence in the royal burgh, although doubtless he did visit it. The phrase "Peebles at the play" is certainly attributed to him, although the origins are disputed. It appears in two completely different poems. The first is *"Christis Kirk of the Greene"*.

> *Wes nevir in Scotland hard or seen*
> *Sic dansing nor deray*
> *Nouthir at Falkland on the grene*
> *Nor Pebillis at the play.*

The other poem which has the title *Peebles at the Play* is also attributed to James I by William Tytler. Writing in the eighteenth century, he claims that it was written by the king during one of his visits to Peebles, when he may have stayed at St Leonard's Well, the hospice some one and a half miles downstream of Peebles. Tytler claimed to be the discoverer of the *Kingis Quair,* but the evidence of the authorship of this later work is somewhat hazy. However, whoever wrote it must have had a personal knowledge of Peebles and the surrounding district on account of the place names which appear in it. In any event it is a lengthy poem of some twenty-six stanzas, but the following extracts give the flavour of it : –

> *At Beltane, when ilk body bounds*
> *To Peebles to the play,*
> *To hear the singing and the sounds,*
> *Their solace, sooth to say*
> *By firth and forest forth they found,*
> *They graithit them full gay ;*
> *God wait that wald they do that stound,*
> *For it was their feast-day,*
> *They said,*
> *Of Peebles at the Play.*

> *All the wenches of the west*
> *Were up ere the cock crew ;*

For reeling there might nae man rest,
For garray nor for glew."

The poem then goes on to mention a number of places where some of the revellers are to be found : -

Hope, Cailye, and Cardrona,
Gatherit out thick-fald,
With "Hey and Howe, rohumbelow,"
The young folk were full bald.
The bagpipe blew, and out they threw
Out of the towns untald ;
Lord, sic ane schout was them amang,
When they ower the wald,
There wets,
At Peebles at the Play.

There is a description of a tavern where inevitably, there is a quarrel and a fight :-

They thrang out of the door at ance
Withouten ony reddin ;
Gilbert in ane gutter glayde,
He gat nae better beddin.
There was not ane of them that day
Wad do ane other's biddin ;
Thereby lay three-and-thirty-some,
O draff,
At Peebles at the Play.

Little changes in five hundred years!

The twenty-sixth stanza brings the poem finally to a close : -

By this the sun was setting fast,
And near done was the day :
There men might hear shookin of chafts
When that they went their way ;
Had there been made of the sang,
Mair suld I to you say ;

> *At Beltane, when ilk body bounds*
> *To Peebles to the play.*

William Chambers seems to have no doubts about the poem's authenticity. Writing in his *History of Peeblesshire*, he says, 'James I was crowned in 1424, and his poem of *Peebles to the Play* was in all probability suggested by his visits to Peebles during the ensuing ten years. The date of the piece may be referred to about 1430, as by which period the ecclesiastical establishments of Peebles were in their glory, and the town was rendered attractive by a famous anniversary of rural sports on Beltane-day, or on the 1st of May.'

In the Notes introducing his book *Select Scottish Ballads* published in 1783, John Pinkerton, is in no doubt that *Peebles to the Play* is the work of the king, but he ascribes *Christis Kirk of Greene* to James V. Other authorities ascribe both to "Anon" and that may be the safest conclusion, although the more romantic notion may be that James was indeed the author and thus well acquainted with Peebles.

Opinions differ as to what the "Play" of Peebles might have been. Williamson records that, 'For centuries the annual recurrence of "Beltane" had drawn crowds from all quarters to witness the games – horse-races, archery, feats of strength and agility – and to participate in the boisterous festivities which marked the celebration of that ancient and famous fair, the scenes of which had been sung by at least one Royal Poet'.

Chambers has the following description :

> The festivities of Beltane originated in the ceremonial observances of the original British people, who lighted fires on the tops of hills and other places in honour of their deity Baal;[43] hence Beltane or Beltein, signifying the fire of Baal. The superstitious usage disappeared in the progress of Christianity, but certain festive customs on the occasion were confirmed or amplified and the rural sports of Beltane at Peebles, including archery, and horse-racing, with much holiday fun and jollity, drew crowds not only from the immediate neighbourhood, but from Edinburgh and other places at a distance.

It would probably have been held on the day of a fair. Possibly there would have been some competitive events and in addition to those mentioned by Chambers, it has been suggested that there might also have been some form of football game. If the quoted poem is anything to go by it was certainly a day of celebration and conviviality.

---

[43] Beal or Beil, the Celtic god of light

The freedom of James from English custody had been achieved at some cost to the people of Scotland. There was a substantial ransom to be paid and this was to impose a considerable burden of additional taxation, much of it coming from customs dues which were of course collected by the burghs as a tax on local trading, as well as from import dues.

The future of the Stewart dynasty was still by no means assured and until the birth of a male heir in 1430, James could have been succeeded by the Earl of Atholl. The marriage of his eldest daughter in 1436 to the Dauphin of France enhanced his position as a European monarch. With a new found confidence and authority and after the years of his captivity, James was anxious to impose his authority on the country, which brought him into conflict with powerful landowning interests who had supported his uncle.

Like David II before him, taxes raised to meet ransom demands may well have been used for other purposes, while at the same time revenues were falling and the king now had to resort to extracting funds from the nobility. It was a recipe for unrest and opposition and when an expedition led by him to recover Roxburgh Castle, still in English hands, failed ignominiously and he attempted to reduce the powers of the nobility, his popularity plunged. A plot was planned by Sir Robert Stewart, his own chamberlain of the royal household and grandson of the Earl of Atholl. It resulted in the king's murder at the Dominican Friary at Perth on 21st February 1437.

In the absence of any solid proof as to the king's associations with Peebles, Chambers, commenting on the king's death, once again seems to be in no doubt as he says that :

> …it is pleasing to know that its accomplished commentator, (here he is referring to *Peebles at the Play*) James I, was long retained in grateful remembrance by the community of Peebles, as is evidenced by their endowment to say mass daily in the parish church for the soul of the royal poet, who was barbarously murdered at Perth 1437.

However, it may be that Chambers is confusing this with a later endowment commemorating the life of James V, a century later. When the Parish Church of St Andrew was made into a Collegiate church in 1543, there is a story that among those to be remembered in the services was 'James Fifth, our dearest father, of good memory.'

The king who succeeded James I, was his son, James, a mere child of seven years, who was crowned at Holyrood on 25th March, 1437. Once again Scotland was in the hands of regents who ruled during the little king's minority. Inevitably that was a time when the great lords flexed their muscles and vied with each other to be the principal power in the land. It was the time when the great House of Douglas dominated, in spite of attempts by their rivals to oppose them. One conspicuous example was the famous "Black Dinner" in Edinburgh Castle, when the young William, sixth Earl of Douglas and his younger brother David, were entertained by the boy king, who was then effectively under the control or guardianship of Sir William Crichton and Sir Alexander Livingstone. They were in attendance. The story goes that a black bull's head, a symbol of death was placed on the table. In spite of the king's attempts to prevent it, the two Douglas brothers were dragged out and summarily executed.

It was some years before James, at the age of nineteen finally personally took the reins of power as King of Scots in 1449. He had married Mary of Gueldres earlier that same year, cementing the long standing alliance with France.

The early years of James' personal rule saw the power struggle between the crown and the House of Douglas reach a climax. William, the eighth earl was five years older than James and for a time mounted what was an armed rebellion. James, to his credit did what he could to reach an accommodation with the earl, who acted as if he was an independent power. In the end it was James who prevailed, although the final chapter is wrapped in controversy. William was invited to meet with the king at Stirling Castle and there in the heat of a quarrel the king stabbed him to death. This episode has been held against James as an act of treachery, but the eventual outcome was the eclipse of Douglas power, which that house never recovered.

Those events passed Peebles by, but the reign of James II was not without its influence on the Royal Burgh. James proved to be an effective and successful king. During his reign the concept of a government as a partnership between monarch and parliament developed and the various meetings of the Estates as the Scottish parliament was called, presided over by the king, introduced widespread legislation which was to effect the organisation and conduct of the burghs. The centre of power became firmly focussed on the national as opposed to local authority. The apparatus of local government was now to be determined by the central, which for example, decreed that a form of small debt court be set up in each burgh, which would quickly provide justice for the weaker ordinary folk pursuing debts against their stronger adversaries. It was to consist of twelve men appointed by the Privy council to deal with all claims of less than £5, which were to be settled within a week.

It was still a time when the threat from south of the border remained real. The parliament of 1458 had much to say about local defence. Burgesses however, were only to ride out 'in feir of weir' with the king or his officers. Archery was to be encouraged and boyers[44] and flatchers[45] were to be established in every county town. Butts were to be built at the parish church and archery practice was to be held every Sunday after worship. Every able bodied man aged between sixteen and sixty was required to shoot a minimum of six rounds. Any absentees were to be fined at least tuppence and the proceeds were to be used to buy drinks for those who complied with this law. Wapinshaws, which were a show of arms were to be held regularly. Conversely football and golf were to be banned. In Peebles butts were built on the Tweed Green 'betwex the wateris in the Common Hauch'. In 1484 one of the burgesses was required to "mak a but at the north end of the toun at the Lang Aiker", while in 1486 another burgess had to 'big a gud sufficiand but at the north end of the toun on the Venlaw syde'.

As warning of the approach of hostile forces a system of beacons was set up from the Tweed to Fife, with each beacon in sight of the next. At each location there were four beacons. If one was lit it was a warning that a hostile force of some sort might be on its way; two beacons lit at the same time indicated that it was definitely coming; all four lit at once was warning that the hostile force was coming in considerable numbers.

By the end of the fifteenth century, the burgh was firmly established. It was governed by a town council, with 3 bailies and twelve councillors chosen from the burgesses, but as yet no provost.

James II granted a Charter to the town on 5th February 1452. Except for the one granted by Robert I, which related only to fairs, this is the earliest known charter granting rights and privileges to the burgh by the monarch. It records that previous charters and deeds giving legal possession by his ancestors as King of Scots, had been destroyed by war and fire and this charter shows the extent of burgh possessions at that time. On the north Hamilton Hill, together with Jedderfield, Edston and Upper and Nether Kidston, were burgh property, as was Venlaw and the lands of Glentress on the east. On the south side of the Tweed burgh lands stretched out towards Manor Water, including Kingsmuir and Cademuir and in time they became the common lands of the burgh.

An essential element in any burgh, was the corn mill, where grain from the surrounding lands was ground. They belonged to the crown in the first

---

[44] Bow makers
[45] Arrow makers

instance, although they were sometimes let to individual tenants or tacksmen. A corn mill at Peebles is first mentioned as early as the reign of Alexander III, when he made a grant of meal from it to the Hospice of Soltre[46], but that was cancelled by him in 1263. In later years between 1388 and 1392, when the town was subjected to English raids it was burned, but must have been rebuilt because in 1395, Robert III granted the mill to Alexander of Eshiels and his wife who continued as tenants until 1425, when it was leased to the burgesses. That was confirmed in the 1452 charter, when they were granted a feudal title in perpetuity.[47]

There were two further mills in the town which feature around that time. Those were the Rood Mill and the Waulk Mill. The first reference to the Rood Mill appears in 1461. It was so called because the tenant was obliged to pay two merks annually to provide for services at the Rood Altar in St Andrew's Church. It was situated on the south side of the hill which had been the site of the castle and at that time the mill was probably still under construction. Some years later, in 1476, it was tenanted by one Robert Myller who was required to build a "fulling" or "waulk" mill. This was a mill which formed part of the process of woollen cloth making and involved cleaning the wool to remove impurities including dirt and oil and also making it thicker. The mill was at the east end of Tweed Green where Walkershaugh is today, a "waulker" being the name given to those who worked in such a mill. Three years later the mill became the property of the burgh. A lade connected the two mills. It ran along the north side of Tweed Green. It was called the "gott" or ditch and this gave its name to the land adjacent to Walkershaugh, today called "The Gytes". The existence of a waulk mill is a clear indication that the weaving of cloth was already an established industry by that time. In its introduction to *Peeblesshire - An Inventory of The Ancient Monuments*, the Royal Commission on the Ancient and Historical Monuments of Scotland, quotes Andrew Halyburton's *Ledger* of 1493-1503, which describes the transport of wool and cloth by pack horse, from Peebles to Edinburgh, Leith, Berwick and other centres for export from Scotland. This included a type of cloth known as "Peebles white" which was sent to Antwerp, where it was dyed red.

The site of the Rood Mill had remained crown property after the demise of the castle, but a charter granted by James IV, dated 24th July 1506, which set out the burgh properties, included a grant of the mill by then built on the Castlehill.

---

[46]   Buchan - *A History of Peeblesshire* Volume II p14 – presumably "Soutra"
[47]   The site of that mill is modern day Damdale

At least one of the two bridges across the Peebles Water (or Eddleston Water) is known to have existed at this time, built of timber. There is certainly evidence from modern excavation and reconstruction of the Tree Bridge, as it is called, which connects the Bridgegate and Damdale, being built of oak beams. A record of 8th May 1488 includes the following :

Item, Adam Smeith for twa tries gevin to the brig at the tolboith ende, and sal pay vs. at the wil of the toun; plege for his dewities[48] his awne land.

This was probably a payment in kind on his being admitted as a burgess, the pledge of his own land no doubt required to ensure that he did not fail to meet this obligation. There is an interesting footnote. In 1982 when the present bridge was built, the foundation excavations unearthed several large pieces of oak which dated from that time.

The second bridge joining the Old Town with the High Street, may well have been built in the fifteenth century and there is evidence of repairs to it being carried out in 1495. Prior to its construction it is likely that there would have been a ford across the Peebles Water.

When the bridge across Tweed was built is not known. Originally there may have been a timber bridge and before that a ford connecting the routes from the town's common grazings on Hamilton Hill on the north and those of Cademuir on the south, linking up with the ford crossing the Peebles Water. The first mention in the records occurs on 2nd February 1465 when seven were chosen as 'bryg masteris'. This must have been a "committee" given the responsibility of managing and overseeing the maintenance of the bridge. As it is the first reference to the appointment of a management committee, this may suggest that the bridge had been recently completed. The entry goes on to say that the 'nychtburis'[49] which presumably refers to those living near the bridge, agreed that whenever called upon by the bridge masters to come and work on the bridge they would be paid for a day's work at the rate of 6 pence. There is no specific mention of materials used for construction or repair at that time, but later entries relating to repairs certainly indicate the use of stone and mortar.

It is not known who designed or built the bridge, although there is an interesting sidelight on this. The Tay Bridge in Perth is thought to have been built about 1440 and 1465. The master mason who undertook the work was known as John of Peebles, so that it is very possible that he was

---

[48] Duties/obligations
[49] Neighbours

also responsible for the Tweed Bridge.[50] Although twice reconstructed in later centuries the outline of this ancient medieval bridge can still be seen today.

The layout of the principal streets forming the core of the New Town was by that time established and the foot print would remain, virtually unaltered for three centuries and still in essence remains today. The main thoroughfare, the Highgait (now the High Street) ran eastwards from the Castlehill to the market cross and continued on into what was then known as the Crossgate, although now known as the Eastgate, which ended at the East Port. The main route to the north, towards Edinburgh, branched from the cross and from it the Briggate descended to the Trie (or Tree) Bridge over the Peebles Water. On the other side of the water stood a house called Brighouse. The higher ground beyond was called Brighouseknowe from which the modern name "Biggiesknowe" is derived.

The earliest record of the proceedings of the burgh appears in 1456. The date is the 4th of October and it reads as follows :

The hed curt of the burgh of Peblis, halding Mononday the ferd day of the monath October the yeir of God m cccc l and vj, the suttis callit, the curt effirmit, ilk absent in amerssiment.
(The head court of the burgh of Peebles, meeting Monday the fourth day of the month October the year of God 1456, the assise called, the court affirmed, anyone absent fined.)

It was a meeting of the town council and the business of the day included the appointment of John Madour, John Dekysoun and Wyl Mouat as bailies for the following twelve months. Also appointed were four members of the council as "flesh pricers" and four more as "ale tasters". All those appointments seem to have been made annually during the first week in October.

This is an early indication of the control the council exercised over much of the minutiae of daily life and much more becomes evident in the reports of meetings of the council around that time. For example in April 1464 the council ordered that no-one was to go outside the gates of the town to buy hides, skins, dressed skins or lamb skins, or any other goods that should have been brought to be sold at the cross and market, either on a market day or on any other days. The penalty for that offence was eight shillings. It did not apply if they happened to meet the vendor while they were going to church or on 'another needful errand'. The reason for this

---

[50] See RCAHMS Tweeddale 2 p341

was in all probability that all goods were required to be sold at the town's market where they were subject to taxation. There was clearly a "Black Market" even in those far off days!

An entry of 30 September 1471 sets out in some detail how the market should be regulated. Fish, meat, butter, cheese, fruit, salt or any other goods which were brought to the market were to be sold only at the market cross. No one was to keep any goods, which would damage or prejudice the reputation of the burgh and they would be fined if they did.

Naturally the cleanliness of the streets was of concern to the council. In the main streets there would have been a single gutter or shallow ditch running the length of the street. It was the common practice and remained so for centuries to come, for the detritus of both households and livestock alike to be dumped into the street where it formed mounds or "middens". They inevitably caused a blockage from time to time and it seems that that is something which was of continual concern to the council. Typical is the council record of the 25 June 1459:

Item, ilk day it was concordit be the balyeis and the hal cort that ony man that layd medyn on the causa and liti for days sal pay, vngefyng, viij s.[51]
(Item, that this day it was agreed by the bailies and the whole court that any man that put down a midden on the causeway and left it lie four days shall pay, unforgiving, 8 s.)

The problem seemed to be a persistent one, because a few years later in October 1462, we find the council again trying to deter the offenders by imposing a penalty, this time to be paid to the street cleaners :

Item, that ilk day, thai have statut and ordanit that na mydyngis ly on the calsay[52] *langer than viij, vnder payn of chet*[53] *to the calsay dychteris.*
[54]

Another problem was uncontrolled livestock and in October 1470 we find the council ruling that pigs should not be allowed outside or causing damage. Any found would be slaughtered wherever they were encountered. The same applied to geese.

---

[51] From the fourteenth to the seventeenth century, when Roman numerals are used, the letter "j" is the equivalent of "i". Thus viij would after 1700 be written as "VIII")
[52] Causeway
[53] Forfeiture
[54] Cleaners

Rules for the sale of fresh food did not escape the attention of the authorities. In October 1466 anyone who cut up red fish to sell it, must also sell the skin of the fish with it, while those who cut meat must sell it with its joint. Health and Safety was alive and well five hundred years ago!

The price of ale was fixed by the council and any brewer who failed to keep to the price was to lose a gallon of ale for the first offence, two for the second, three for the third and if a fourth occurred was to pay 8 s. Much the same system applied to the price of bread and again any deviation from the established price carried significant penalties. The price of a measure of wheat was fixed by the bailies, as was the weight of each loaf. Any "wyf" who deviated from the stipulated weight was to have two loaves taken from her for the first offence; for the next offence, four loaves; for the third offence of loaves 'wantand of the wecht of the lafe', six loaves to be taken and given to the poor; and anyone found to at fault four times was to be 'clossyt of bakking' for a year and a day.

During that period there are many entries recording the admission of burgesses and the payment in cash or in kind which they were to make for the privilege. On the 2 November 1456 Dic Patonson was admitted and was required to pay half a mark 'for his freedom'. On 15 November 1456, 'was mayd burges Thom Fyldar' who was to pay ten shillings, 'at thwa termis, that is to say beltain the ta (one) and Bartylmes the tothir half.' Sym Patonson was made a burgess on 27 May 1470. His contribution was to be the cost of building a dyke on Venlaw from 'the tentour (top) ryk (right) doun to the east nowk.'

Among the more unusual are the admissions in March 1462 of John Scot, Rechert of Geddes and Wyllem Gybsoun, who were each required to give a bow and a sheaf of arrows. Burgess status was not confined to men. On 29 October 1459 'was made burges Meg Wodhal' who was to meet the cost of a rood of causeway.

The maintenance of law and order was also the preserve of the council and there are numerous entries which deal with public disturbances. It was quite common for the money gathered from fines to be used for a specific purpose. For instance on 11 October 1462, the bailies met in the tolbooth, with members of the public present and ordered that if there was any fighting or quarrelling, either by night or day, which caused a disturbance in the town, as was said 'for gret peryll of ill doyng', anyone found to be in the wrong, was to be fined and the proceeds were to go towards the cost of the road to the parish church. Another entry shortly after said that anyone found disturbing the town by fighting, scolding or quarrelling was to be fined two shillings The proceeds in that case, were to go to the cost of buying the town clock. There are other cases at that time where the fine was to go towards the cost of bridge repairs.

The records also show that for the purposes of collecting cess, or local taxation, the town was divided into four quarters, corresponding to the main streets, the Highgait, Crossgait, Northgait and Briggait.[55] Each had a quartermaster[56] overseeing it and two quartermasters were appointed to the district 'beyond the water', namely the Old Town.

The municipal centre was the tolbooth, which was the meeting place of the town council and also housed the court house and burgh jail. When any major issue of common interest to the townspeople arose, it was to the tolbooth that they would be summoned. It was probably built about the middle of the century, as there is a record of a payment in July 1458 of ten shillings by one Andrew Cady towards the cost. This was the subject of a pledge or security, given on his behalf by John Lilley. Over the centuries its location changed but at that time it stood at the foot of the Briggait. In the years 1985-87, archaeological excavations were carried out at the site before it was redeveloped for housing. This uncovered the foundations of the tolbooth itself and the adjacent buildings.[57]

As already mentioned, the Chapel of St Mary had been built on "the Common Muir", at the west end of the Highgait. Adjacent to the Chapel was the Steeple, built sometime between 1488 and 1496 and close to it was the West Port or gate which closed that end of the Highgait. The castle had long since ceased to exist as a place of defence, but defensive ports or gates, probably had been in existence from earlier times. As well as the West port, the North Port was in existence by that time. At the eastern end of the main thoroughfare was the East Port guarded by a building which came to be known as the "East Wark". The foot of the Briggait, where it met the Peebles Water, was protected by a barmkin, which was a form of defensive wall with a gate or doorway set in it.

The defences surrounding the town still remained little more than a series of walls connecting individual properties known as head dykes, which their owners were obliged to maintain at their own expense. It would be a further century before full fortifications were constructed. In the light of the havoc and damage caused in the fairly recent past, this may seem surprising, but perhaps the growth of a sizeable religious community, which was by that time reaching its zenith, may have acted as

---

55 Gait is the old Scots word for a road or track.
56 The name is used more broadly today.
57 *Bridgegate, Peebles, 1985-87* by PJ Dixon and D R Perry

93

some deterrent to marauding Englishmen, having a care for their immortal souls. Certainly from now on and for a further century until the Reformation of 1560, the place of the religious community would have a major impact on the life of the burgh.

By 1460, James II had succeeded to a large degree in bringing stability and a measure of prosperity to Scotland, although a constant threat remained from England. The parliament of 1458 had introduced legislation for the regulation of the countryside, including a number of acts which encouraged agriculture and dealt with land tenure, giving farmers greater security. There was to be support for the planting of hedgerows and trees and rules were introduced for muirburn. There was to be protection of wild birds during the nesting season, although crows and predators, such as wolves were exempted and their extermination encouraged. Close seasons were introduced for ground game such as hares and rabbits and also for fish. All of these have a curiously modern ring, more than five centuries ahead of our time, as has the commission set up to investigate hospitals, including checking that their original foundation documents were being complied with. This would have included the Hospice of St Lawrence and St Leonard at Eshiels. Laws were introduced for the regulation of uniform weights and measures and any gold work was to be the subject of inspection by the Dean of Guild.

There was a renewed prosperity. The king was encouraged to continue along the road of progress. The nobility were able to dress in some degree of finery, although laws were enacted which decreed who could wear what. Silk and Marten's fur and scarlet garments were to be worn exclusively by the nobility and denied to the common folk. An exception was made for the bailies and burgh officers as a sign of their rising status. When at work labourers were to wear grey or white although there was a dispensation on holidays when they were permitted to wear colours such as red, light blue or green.

The English problem continued to engage the king. There was rebellion in England with the half mad Lancastrian King Henry VI, fending off Yorkist rebels. The castle of Roxburgh remained in English hands, the last stronghold north of the border to do so and seeing an opportunity when attention was focussed elsewhere, James decided the time was ripe to recover it once and for all for Scotland. He laid siege to the castle supported by the earls of Huntly and Angus and John of the Isles. James had long had a fascination for artillery and had brought up a number of siege guns, one of which split its barrel on firing, killing the king who stood close by. Scotland had lost an able and successful king, whose memory still is recalled in the charter he gave to his royal burgh of Peebles in 1452.

James III, the son who succeeded him was eight years old when his father was killed, an accident which he personally witnessed. Whatever calm James II may have brought to Scotland, under the surface the old forces of a restless nobility were not far beneath, ready to burst out once more. A lengthy minority hardly augured well, but for the first few years the Queen Mother, Marie of Gueldres, ably and wisely guided by Bishop Kennedy of St Andrews, presided over a period of relative calm, but after Marie died in 1463 and Bishop Kennedy in 1465, the young king was effectively captured by Lord Boyd who was thus able to dominate the government of the kingdom until James himself was able to personally take control in 1469. He married Margaret of Denmark in the same year and the Boyds lost their hold on power.

Unlike his father and grandfather, James III lacked their strength and political skills. He was more interested in the arts than in conflict. Consequently as his reign progressed, his control of affairs descended into chaos and a state of rebellion by a group of the most powerful magnates, which culminated in his murder by a still unidentified assassin in 1488. The tragedy was further marred by the role played by his fifteen year old son. He had been persuaded to support the rebels, something he was to regret throughout his subsequent reign as James IV.

5.
Alms, Friars and Priests

James III does have a place in the story of Peebles. During his reign, there were two significant building developments, one directly attributable to the intervention of the king and his queen. Those were an almshouse and the other the Conventual Monastery of the Holy Cross.

The Chapel of the Virgin Mary, built at the west end of the High Gait on part of the then Common Haugh, had stood for a hundred years. It was now decided that an almshouse should be built as an addition to the chapel. There was already an almshouse or hospice and chapel at Eshiels, but there seems to have been ever larger numbers of pilgrims coming to the area probably intending to visit the Cross Kirk and its relics. The numbers were especially large at the two annual feasts of the Finding of the Cross and the Exaltation of the Cross. It is likely that the Eshiels Hospice of St Lawrence and St Leonard were unable to cope with the number of pilgrims who now came from far and wide to visit the shrine. Both the Master of the Cross Kirk and the Procurator of the hospice appear to have had an interest in the proposed new building which indicates that it had a direct connection with the pilgrim visitors. The hospice at Eshiels would also have provided shelter for the poor and no doubt the new almshouse would have provided additional facilities for them.

In any event, in October 1462 the scheme to establish a new almshouse was under discussion. The earliest reference to it appears in the Burgh Record for 25th October in that year, when an area of ground at the west end of the burgh was handed over by Sir William Gibson to the bailies who in turn passed it to Sir John Smayle[58]who was to hold it on behalf of 'the pur folk', to provide 'harberry and beddying'. Because it was given to the poor, the chaplain of the Chapel of St Mary was to be in charge of the almshouse. It seems to have taken some time for the scheme to be finalised, because in October 1464, two years later, the Master of the Cross Kirk, Friar William Gibson and someone called William of Peebles, appeared before the court or council to ask that a piece of ground, between

---

[58] Senior clergy often had the title "Sir", but it was a courtesy title and did not signify knighthood. Those who were sufficiently educated to have a university degree of Master of Arts, could use the title "Magister" or "Maister"

the West Port and Castlehill, be given for the building of the almshouse, so that 'with the help and supple of cristyn pepyll mychte byge apon it a Hous of Almus for tyl harbry in it pur folk.' The council granted the request. The site of the Chapel and almshouse was approximately where numbers 82 & 84 High Street stand today.

In 1473 Sir William of Fyllop, was granted some land on the west side of the hospice free of charge, on condition that if he built a house on it, on his death it would revert to the hospice.

There is no direct reference to the almshouse thereafter, but there is reference to "the old almshouse" in 1549 when land and property owned by Master John Smith of Smithfield was inherited by his son in October of that year. The land is described as lying outside the West Port and the adjoining property, referred to as 'the almous hous and yarde' is described as being bounded on the north by 'Peblis Water' and on the south by 'Our Lady Chapel'. That would suggest that the actual site of the almshouse was in what is now the ground behind the former Bank House running down to Eddleston Water and also that it had ceased to be used for 'the pur folk' or pilgrims. By then religious activity in the burgh had sharply declined.

There is one further reference in October 1564, some four years after the Catholic Religion had been supplanted by Protestant Presbyterianism, when an old priest called Sir James Davidson is to be allowed to stay in the 'almshouse connected with St. Leonard's', which was of course situated at Eshiels. However the entry goes on to say that John Hay, master of the hospital, came to the almshouse of the hospital, 'situated within the burgh' and arranged for the old priest to take up residence. As will be seen later, in the years immediately after the Reformation of 1560, there was a period of transition and in Peebles at least, there seems to have been some sympathy for the clergy of the former order. It may be that the house in question, was the one which was to be built adjoining the almshouse in 1473 by Sir William of Fyllop for his personal use, which is mentioned above.

The parish church of St Andrew had been established as long ago as 1195. Sometime before 1427, a local benefactor called John Geddes, who owned extensive lands to the west of Peebles around Broughton, Kirkurd and Ladyurd, gave money for the erection of a chapel to be built at St Andrew's. It was dedicated to "the Blessed Virgin Mary". Modern excavations have not confirmed the exact location, but it seems likely that it formed an extension on the north wall of the church. What may have been the connecting doorway can still be seen in the north wall of the church, which is all that remains of the first parish church, apart from the tower.

A second church had been established by King Alexander III in 1261, close to the site where a 'magnificent and venerable cross' was found together with a stone urn thought to contain the bones of a bishop of the early Christian church, called Nicholas. That was the Cross Kirk which became a place of pilgrimage. John of Fordoun, writing towards the end of the fourteenth century says that as a result of many miracles attributable to the cross, 'the people poured and still pour thither in crowds, devoutly bringing their offerings and vows to God'. It seems that the popularity of the Holy site was undiminished in the second half of the fifteenth century.

The original building established by Alexander III, was a plain rectangle measuring 114ft by 33ft externally, with walls 3ft thick. On the north side was a small extension, which is thought to have been a vaulted sacristy. There was no tower at that time, nor were there any permanent monastic buildings. The ruins which remain today, include the original nave, but the chancel, has gone, demolished some time after the reformation in 1560, when the Cross Kirk, became the parish church of Peebles.

From its inception, the ministry of the church was in the hands of an order of friars, not to be confused with monks. Monks spent their whole life within their monastery, living a life of contemplation, prayer and praise, often solitary. That apart, they engaged solely in the life of the monastery which was self-sufficient in its feeding and physical comforts and although a monastery might from time to time provide food and shelter to those outside or passing by, they generally did not engage in the wider life of their neighbourhood.

Friars by contrast, engaged with the community at large. Many were itinerant preachers, travelling the countryside, spreading the Christian gospel. They were not allowed to own any personal property and survived by begging. There were never monks in Peebles. The friars who made the Cross Kirk their base belonged to the Order of Trinity Friars, who wore a white gown or habit with a red and blue cross on its back. They became known as "Red Friars". Their origins went back to the Crusades of the early thirteenth century and their Order was founded to give relief to Christians who had been captured by the Saracens and in the case of Peebles there are examples of their raising money for that cause. This order of friars seems to have been the custodian of Cross Kirk and its relics from its earliest days. It would occupy the site and have a leading role in the life of Peebles until the Reformation of 1560

The importance of Peebles and its Cross Kirk relics had clearly become greatly enhanced by the middle of the fifteenth century and in 1473 a Conventual Monastery was established at the site. On 3rd of February that year a letter was sent from the Monastery of St.Mathurin in Paris, which had been the headquarters of the Trinity Friars since 1228. It was from the head of the order, Brother Robert and explained that he had received a petition from James III, King of Scots and his queen, Margaret of Denmark, with the support of King Louis XI of France. The king and queen wished to build a Conventual Monastery for the Trinity Friars at the Church of the Holy Cross of Peebles. It was to be supported by substantial endowments so that divine service could be celebrated there in all time coming. The House of the Trinity Friars at Berwick had been destroyed by English raiding and the royal couple also asked that the whole of its revenues should become the property of the new House of the Holy Cross of Peebles.

Brother Robert duly agreed and in addition to Berwick, the parish church of Kettins[59] and its revenues, which had belonged to Berwick, was added to Peebles[60]

The existing church building was to form the centre piece of the monastery. Unusually however, the new buildings were constructed on the north side of the church, contrary to the normal practice which placed them on the south side. The layout with the church on the north side was so arranged to provide shelter to the living quarters from cold northerly winds. The layout at Peebles, meant that the living quarters were in shade of the higher church building for most of the time as well as being exposed to the north. The reason seems to have been that the shrine containing the famous relics was situated within the south wall, presumably because that was supposed to be where they had been discovered in 1261 and could not therefore be disturbed, whatever discomfort that may have caused to the inhabitants.

An extensive exploration and survey of the site was carried out by the then Ministry of Works in 1923 and the results can be seen in the *Inventory of the Ancient Monuments of Peeblesshire,* published by The Royal Commission on the Ancient and Historical Monuments of Scotland.

---

[59]   Now in Perth and Kinross

[60]   Ecclesiastical establishments in the middle ages were generally supported by revenues from property and it was common for larger establishments to be supported by others, often at a considerable distance from them.

Those clearly show the probable extent of the monastery complex which covered a large area, all to the north of the church. It is likely that beyond those limits there would have been additional buildings associated with it of which no identifiable traces remain, possibly because they may have been of a less massive or permanent construction.

What the survey shows is that a rectangular range of buildings, possibly two storeys high, enclosed a central cloister. It also seems that the tower at the west end of the church was built at that time. It was somewhat higher than the remnant remaining today. Dr Gunn mentions that Dr Dalgleish, the last Protestant Minister of the Cross Kirk had claimed that the tower was built only after the Reformation. However, Dr Gunn disputes this. He is somewhat dismissive of the good Dr Dalgleish, who he says was 'no antiquary'. He points out that on the south west corner of the tower, there is a niche projecting from the stonework about ten feet above the ground which probably held a small statue, which he says may have been of St Nicholas. He goes on to say that in all probability this statue was destroyed at the time of the Reformation when Calvinist and Puritan forces carried out a campaign of iconoclasm against what they considered to be Popish idols. Whatever the merits of Dr Gunn's theory, which in fact seems not unreasonable, his conclusion has been confirmed by RCAHMS[61] who firmly date it to the late 15th century and the time of the construction of the monastic buildings.

By the time the new monastery was completed at the end of the century, with the parish Church of St Andrew, the Chapel of St Mary and the Hospice of St Lawrence and St Leonard and now the monastery itself, religious activity, and the religious community must have dominated the town. Chambers suggests that there may have been 70 friars based in the conventual monastery alone. Add to that the numerous clergy of the parish church and St Mary's Chapel. If Chambers is correct there must have been upwards of 100 in Holy Orders of one sort or another. Writing of the situation as it was sometime later in the first half of the following century, Dr Gunn says that there were so many of the clergy in Peebles, that they formed a distinct group in the burgh and that the part of the town in which they lived was effectively an ecclesiastical quarter.

He adds that there would have been a constant flow of clerical traffic between the Parish Church and the Cross Kirk, which were connected by Cross Road, while there would also have been a regular contact with the "New Town" across the Eddleston Water by the Tree and Peebles bridges. There would have been frequent ringing of bells, summoning the faithful

---

[61]   Royal Commission on the Ancient and Historic Monuments of Scotland

to the morning service of matins and evensong at the end of the day. The many altars in both the Parish Church (there were eleven in it alone) and in the Cross Kirk as well as those in St Mary's Chapel, would each have some act of worship, all summoned by bells of one sort or another.

The whole town was dominated by the religious community for a period of 100 years, leading up to the Reformation. It embraced not only the spiritual life of the town, but the intellectual life also. The clergy had a virtual monopoly of learning, which extended to municipal affairs, at a time when the ability to read and write was to all intents and purposes the preserve of the clergy. The town clerk was a priest on account of his literary skills. Even the winding of the town clock was the preserve of a priest. The notaries or lawyers were also priests and together the church was able to exercise a dominating influence on the governance of the burgh. Such was their influence that Holy Church was able to accumulate enormous wealth in property rents, legacies and donations from townsfolk seeking to secure their immortal souls. Of course that was no more than what was happening throughout Scotland and Europe, but the situation in Peebles with such ecclesiastical dominance was particularly evident.

Of course it did not stop there. Such a large body of clergy would need the support of local craftsmen and tradesmen and would be dependent on the local agricultural community for food, although doubtless the friars of the Cross Kirk monastery would largely provide for themselves. The area on the west side of the town which is still known as "Kirklands", would have been a source of produce. As a place of pilgrimage there would have been a constant stream of visitors to be accommodated, fed and watered. Many would have been put up in the Monastery of the Cross Kirk, but this early example of tourism, must have benefited the town and surrounding countryside which would provide for their needs.

Pilgrimage to Peebles had been a feature ever since the discovery of the ancient cross and burial urn of St Nicholas in 1261. It seems that those holy relics were kept and displayed in part of the Cross Kirk set apart for the purpose. The original relics were described by John of Fordoun as being, 'a stately and venerable cross', but he adds no further description. It has been assumed that it was made of timber, but it could have been of stone.

Sometime after the original find, it seems that the relics included a "fragment of the True Cross" on which Christ was crucified. Whether it was the cross found in 1261 or a later addition is not known. The presence of the fragment held at Peebles seems to have been an accepted fact. As earlier noted, King James V was apparently convinced and it was sufficiently significant for it to form the basis of two annual festivals, the Feast of the Finding of the Cross and the Feast of the Exultation of the Cross.

On one notable occasion in 1474, what was described as a "miracle", occurred during the Feast of the Finding of the Cross which was held at the beginning of May. The annual Beltane sports were also held at about the same time. The town was filled with visitors from far and near to see the games, which included horse racing and archery, as well as taking part in the religious celebration. It was nothing less than a tourist "Tour de Force".

As usual, large crowds had gathered in the grounds of the Cross Kirk to see the Relics displayed. At the point when the 'holy fragment of the True Cross' was about to be elevated, there was a sudden commotion in the outer reaches of the crowd which quickly spread through the whole company. The eyes of the waiting pilgrims were diverted from what was happening in front of them. Beyond the Kirkgait[62] and the Eddleston Water, thick black clouds of smoke were billowing from the Briggait, followed by flames shooting up into the sky. It was clear that some poor soul's house was well on fire. Before long, the word was that it was the house of one, John Scott.

In the meantime, no doubt somewhat disturbed by the crowd's lack of attention, the Friars, assisted on this occasion by the priests of the Parish Church of St Andrew, all dressed in their regalia, had begun the procession which culminated in the actual Elevation of the Relic. Accompanied by the singing of the choristers, the procession continued round the boundaries in spite of the interruption and then returned to the church. There was a rectangular aperture in the south wall of the church and the leading clergy, as was the custom, now unveiled the Relic to the awaiting crowd through this. Just as they did so there was a murmur in the crowd and turning again to look towards the Briggait, it was seen that the smoke was dispersing, the flames were gone; the fire was out! It had apparently stopped at the very moment when the Holy fragment was elevated! It could only be a miracle! If there had previously been any doubt about the sanctity of the Relic, here was proof of its power. It was the way the medieval mind worked. Modern minds might have thought somewhat differently. Indeed there were those present who noted a sudden change of wind, but anyone that day who had voiced such a cynical view could expect to find himself in deep trouble. It was none the less, quite a coincidence!

---

[62] Now Old Church Road

One man who had no doubt, was John Scott, the relieved house owner. On the 18th July following, he and his wife, Alison undertook to make an annual gift to the Holy Cross of twelve pence from his lands in the Briggait on the North Row, 'for the Grace of Almighty God and the Holy Cross, that the said John Scott's house was kept from burning with fierce fire from the time forth that the Holy Cross was showing.'

It was during the reign of James III that an old poem of unknown authorship known as *the Tailes of the Thrie Priestis of Peblis*, was thought to have been written. It has been suggested that it was in fact written later during the reign of James V, but William Chambers gives a convincing argument in favour of the earlier date. He points out that there is a reference in the poem to one of the kingdoms which later became Spain, being at that time "heathen", to use Chambers' word. Presumably he meant that it was during the time of the occupation by the Moors of North Africa. The significance of that is that it must have been before 1492 when the Moors were sent packing by the forces of Ferdinand and Isabella, the king and queen of Aragon and Castille.

The poem relates to the meeting of three priests in a hostelry in Peebles, where they spend an evening of couthy conviviality, during the course of which each of the priests, Maister Archibald, Maister Johne, and Sir William tell a tale of politics and morality, which are full of references to the current state of the country. Whether they were actual priests living in Peebles at the time is uncertain, but Dr Gunn notes that at that time St Michael's altar in the Parish Church was the responsibility of one Master Archibald Dickson and Master John Houston was chaplain of St Martin's altar. Both the chaplains of St Lawrence Altar and of the Chapel of the Virgin Mary in the High Street, were called Sir William. It certainly seems a coincidence!

Two of the priests, Master John and Master Archibald, had travelled abroad and were Masters of Art in an age when universities were something of a novelty. In Scotland, only St Andrews and Glasgow had been founded by that time, although there were older establishments in continental Europe. Sir William, however, made no claim to having gained a degree or to have travelled abroad.

The opening lines of the poem are:-

> *In Peblis toun sum tyme, as I hard tell,*
> *The foremost day of Februare, befell*
> *Thrie priestis went unto collatioun,*

Into ane privie place of the said toun.
Whair that they sat richt soft and unfute-sair;
Thay luifit na rangold nor repair
And gif I sall the suith reckin and say,
I traist it was upon Sanct Brydis day.
Whair that thay sat full easilie and soft ;
With monie lowd lauchter apoun loft.
And wit ye weil, thir thrie meid gude cheir ;
To thame thair was na dainties than too deir ;
with thrie caponis on a speit with creis,
with monie other sundrie meis.
And thame to serve thay had nocht bot ane boy ;
Fra companie thai keipit thame sae coy.
Thai lufit nocht with ladry nor with lown
Nor with trumpouris to travel throw the town,
Bot with themeself quhat thai wald tell or crak ;
Umquhyle sadlie ; umqhuyle jangle and jak ;
Thus sat thir thrie beside ane fellounfyre,
Quhil thair capons war roistit lim and lyre.
Befoir them was sone set a Roundel bricht,
And with ane clene claith, fielie dicht,
It was ouirset ; and breid was laid.
The eldest than began the grace, and said,
And blissit be the breid with Benedicite,
With Dominus Amen, sa mot I thee.

The first priest's tale starts after they had begun their meal and they had 'drunken about a quarte'. It asks why the wealth of merchants is never passed on to the third generation, but is always squandered by the second generation. Another tale questions why the clergy are no longer able to work miraculous cures in the way that seemed to have been common in the early church. It suggests the reason is that the clergy no longer observe purity of living, knowledge, or spiritual graces –

> *Sic wickedness this world is within,*
> *that symonie is countit now na sin.*

If the poem is a true reflection of the times, it does indicate, that good living among the clergy was the order of the day and those in Peebles seem to have been no exception. Within the next fifty years, that, together with the general corruption of Holy Church would be the cause of the Reformation.

6.

A Great King and "the Flowers of the Forest"[63]

Apart from his promotion of the Monastery of the Cross Kirk, James III, does not feature prominently in the history of Peebles. The monarchs who followed him, however have a significant place in the life of the burgh, fully justifying its "Royal" status.

James III died in 1488 at the end of a period of all out rebellion led by the earls of Angus and Argyll as well as the Humes and the Bishop of Glasgow, all of whom he had alienated in one way or another. At their head, in name at least, was the young heir to the throne, Prince James, then aged fifteen. The king had his supporters, many of them from the Highlands and after attempts at compromise failed, he raised an army. James III, unlike his father and grandfather, was no military leader and when the two opposing forces met at Sauchieburn, near Bannockburn, his army was destroyed and James himself fled the field. Although there is no firm evidence to support it, the story goes that some way from the battlefield his horse threw him, just outside a cottage. He was badly injured and may have been taken into the cottage by the sympathetic occupant. What happened thereafter, is pure conjecture. He may have been pursued, but in any event, he was found stabbed to death. The government mounted an enquiry, which reached no conclusion other than that the King 'happinet to be slane'.

Fifteen days later, on 26 June his son was crowned at Scone as James IV. It was of course the traditional crowning place of Scottish kings, but had not been used since 1424. Unlike his father and grandfather, both of whom had succeeded as mere boys, James IV was already at an age when he could command respect and allegiance. His immediate predecessors had each suffered significant failings. James IV was different. In spite of his ultimate failure 25 years later at Flodden, he goes down in history as certainly the greatest Scottish king of the medieval era. He cultivated the art of kingship, was charismatic and a regal presence. He dressed as a king in rich and sumptuous clothing and was a brilliant communicator. Not only did he dominate his court, but he could also be a man of the people,

---

[63] A reference to the Battle of Flodden

approachable and as much at home in the company of the common folk as the great and the good of the court. He was a king constantly on the move throughout his kingdom, dispensing justice north and south. In a relatively short space of time he was able to unite what had become a disunited kingdom, so much so that when he assembled the great army which marched to Flodden, almost every part of the kingdom was represented. He spoke several languages and was probably the last King of Scots to be fluent in Gaelic, something which helped him to pacify the Highlands and bring the Lordship of the Isles, so long the private fiefdom of the MacDonalds, under the crown. On the European stage he was no less dominant and seen as a powerful ally, not least by France and throughout his reign he played a significant role as European peacemaker. He built a fleet of warships which rivalled and even eclipsed that of England. His flagship the "Great Michael", built on the Firth of Forth, was the largest and most powerful of its day.

He was a frequent visitor to Peebles. Strangely the "Extracts" from the Burgh records for the period of his reign make no reference to him. There is in fact a complete gap between the years 1511 and 1531 for reasons which are not clear. On the other hand at least six documents registered during his reign are recorded in the National Archives as issued at Peebles.

Dr Gunn is in no doubt that he was a frequent visitor to the burgh, his principal source being the Accounts of the Lord High Treasurer. The first visit he refers to is on 5th November 1488, less than six months after the murder of his father. The story that James wore a circle of iron around his waist, in penitence for his part in his father's demise, is well known. Dr Gunn has it that this visit to Peebles was as a pilgrimage to 'the Holy Relic of the True Cross' at the Cross Kirk and that this was a further act of penitence. He apparently made an offering of 18 shillings.

He was in Peebles again on 2nd June 1497. The accounts show that a payment of £5 3s 4d was made to the Master Cook for 'the King's expenses'. Also included is a payment of 2 shillings for half an ounce 'of white silk to sew the King's sarks', 6 pence for black silk, 'to the collars of them'.

Between 1504 and 1508 visits by the king are recorded on at least twelve occasions. They nearly always included a visit to the Cross Kirk as regular offerings were made by the king. One of the popular sports of the time was heronry. It involved releasing falcons against herons flighting back to their heronry. Two falcons would be released to attack and if successful, kill a single heron. James was an avid participant and on at least one occasion, in 1504, he paid fourteen shillings to a man bringing herons from the laird of Dawyck, which was well known for the quality and speed of its birds. In the same year he again paid fourteen shillings, this time for two 'fair hounds', brought to him from Dawyck.

On 5th March of 1505 the usual offering of fourteen shillings is made to the Cross Kirk and the following day one Sandy Law was paid the same amount to search for a hawk and another fourteen shillings is offered to the Cross Kirk the very next day. He was back in Peebles a few days later after a brief visit to Dumfries. The visit must have lasted several days during which he made two offerings of the usual fourteen shillings to the "Holy Cross of Peebles", as well as twenty eight shillings paid to the priest for his sermon. The laird of Dawyck once again receives a payment, this time nine shillings for a hound. The king paid forty two shillings for his lodgings on that occasion.

In 1507 he decided that the Cross Kirk should have a cross of pure gold and in April of that year he commissioned the goldsmith, Matthew Auchleck to make the cross and a silver base for it. The cross, which weighed four ounces and a quarter cost £3 10s to make in addition to the materials, which cost £10 7s. It weighed seven and a half ounces. Auchleck was paid a further £5 5s 3d for the silver base which weighed four ounces and a quarter. No trace of that valuable ornament remains. No doubt it did not survive the Reformation, but whether removed, stolen or simply melted down is not known.

On the 24th July 1506, James IV granted the burgh a Charter of Confirmation and Novodamus. It effectively renewed and restated all the lands, rights and privileges which had been granted by James II in 1452.

What until then had been a glorious and successful reign came to an abrupt end on the 9th September 1513 on Branxtonhill, a few miles south of the River Tweed and the boundary with England. The battle of Flodden has been portrayed as a tragic mistake by an otherwise accomplished monarch. Trouble from south of the Border had been brewing for some time. The king's brother in law, the arrogant and belligerent Henry VIII, had been threatening his northern neighbour, while at the same time threatening France. James had made strenuous efforts to act as peace maker in a troubled Europe, where powerful alliances were preparing for war. Scotland, for all her relative smallness, none the less carried significant political weight. At that time she probably had the most powerful navy and Scottish soldiers were a familiar presence on the continent. As a counterbalance to the threat from England, to which both France and Scotland were subject, the Auld Alliance between the two was strengthened by a binding agreement that in the event of either being attacked by the English, the other would act in support. Invasion of France would precipitate an invasion of England by the Scots. James, the Renaissance king, was a man of honour and when Henry attacked France, he responded accordingly. It is a mark of the loyalty throughout Scotland that James had built up and his charismatic leadership, that when he called for the people of Scotland to take up arms and follow him, he assembled the greatest fighting force ever seen in Scotland, coming from every part of the kingdom.

It is very probable that Peebles was well represented, although there is nothing in the records to confirm this. After all, this was a town which had been shown particular favour by the king and if the whole nation, as seems the case, was represented in the Scottish host, it is very unlikely that Peebles would not have contributed its fair share. We do know that among those who perished at Flodden were, the sheriff of Peebles, John, the 2nd Lord Hay and according to the burgh accounts of 28th October 1513, Patrick Gillis the burgh Treasurer also lost his life, as the record says, 'deceissit in the Kingis host.' Doubtless there were others too.

7.
The Poor Man's King

The monarch who now succeeded to the throne as James V was only 13 months old. The huge losses among the nobility at Flodden, which included nine of the twelve earls who took part in the battle and James IV's illegitimate son, the Archbishop of St Andrews, as well as a great many of the sons of the nobility, created a vacuum. It led to more than a decade of troubled times as the remaining magnates and not least Margaret, the Queen Dowager and sister of Henry VIII, grappled for power. In practical terms it meant control of the boy king.

The troubles extended not only to warring magnates, but also to a general breakdown in public order. As an example Peebles was fined £10 for its failure to submit accounts for the years 1521-3, but the bailies pled that they were heavily engaged in pursuing thieves and attempting to recover stolen goods which had prevented them from preparing the accounts and having them audited. Their arguments seem to have been convincing, because in due course the fine was remitted.

In the years between 1513 and 1524 when James started his personal rule, the records of Peebles are virtually silent on all matters except for a few instances of donations to the parish church of St Andrew made for the setting up of altars. The process entailed making a direct financial contribution or the grant of land or property and the income from it, which was to provide for services of mass being said at the altar, very often for the eternal soul of a departed relative of the donor.

James seems to have had a particular affection for Peebles and its surrounding forests, to judge by his many recorded and perhaps many more unrecorded visits to the Royal Burgh. His first recorded visit was in August 1525. He was 15 years old and was brought to Peebles probably by the Earl of Angus, who was then his 'guardian'. There is an entry in the accounts of a payment of twenty five shillings being made by the Lord High Treasurer for his 'portmanteau' to be carried to the town, where he seems to have stayed, together with his Lords and Council. Where they actually stayed is not known. There was of course no longer a royal castle in the burgh. William Chambers has, probably wrongly, described Neidpath Castle as 'the castle of Peebles' and it might have provided suitable accommodation. However it is more likely that the king and his sizeable entourage enjoyed the hospitality of the Minister and Brethren of the Cross Kirk or possibly the hostlery of Arbroath Abbey in the Northgate, both of which would have provided more spacious accommodation, than the rather more cramped conditions of Neidpath. Wherever it may have been, on the evidence of the food and drink purchased and consumed, there must have been a sizeable company present because on that one occasion in a single day, 157 loaves of bread, 1 bullock, ¼ calf, 17 sheep, 72 poultry, 9 capons, 8 plovers and large quantities of barley, eggs, pears, apples, butter and mustard, not to mention 46 gallons of ale were needed to sustain them. The next day they moved on to Selkirk!

James was back again the following year from 17-19th July, at a time when he was still under the forcible fostering and tutelage of the Earl of Angus and the Douglas family. He made his escape from the Douglas' clutches in 1528 and from then on, although still only eighteen years old, he was able to be very much his own man.

The household accounts for the spring of 1529 disclose the first of several expeditions aimed at re-asserting royal authority in the Borders. James was at Peebles on 20th and 22nd April. The Border country had long been lawless and difficult to control. It was populated by many extended families or clans who were constantly feuding and damaging each other's property. During the minority of James, after a period of relative stability during the reign of his father, James IV, lawlessness had gone unchecked. The great magnates who might have maintained some control were more concerned by the pursuit of their own interests, which centred on the struggle for power and for control of the boy king. Consequently little attention was paid to the feuding of minor Border lairds and the whole area had descended into a state of virtual anarchy.

In March of 1529, the Lords of the Council had announced that Justice Ayers[64] would be held in Lauder, Jedburgh, Selkirk and Peebles. So as to bring some semblance of order to the region, various local magnates were given the responsibility for the conduct of law and order. The system was simple. If they failed to maintain order and punish wrong doers, they themselves would be punished by warding or in the last resort forfeiture of property. Thus on 25th June, at Peebles, Patrick Hepburn, 3rd Earl of Bothwell, gave a bond for good rule in Liddesdale.

On his first mission to quell the Borders, it was from Peebles that James set out in the spring or possibly the autumn of that year. It seems that about that time or shortly after, an event took place which has become

---

64 Circuit courts for trying criminal offences.

part of the folklore of the Borders, on account of a story, *The Ballad of the Border Widow*, which Sir Walter Scott included in his *Minstrelsy of the Scottish Borders*. It concerns one Parys Cockburn of Henderland. He was typical of many of his contemporaries who were in constant conflict with each other, raiding their properties, stealing their livestock, burning and destroying. They were the Border Reivers and it was their accepted way of life.

Cockburn's base was Henderland Tower, situated in the Forest of Ettrick on the Megget Water, not far from where it flows into St Mary's Loch. He had decided to make a raid on the property of his near neighbour, Adam Scott of Tushielaw. As usual it was to be carried out under cover of darkness. James had determined to bring order to the chaos of the Borders and planned to deal with Cockburn as an example to others of his kind. So it was that he set out from Peebles in the early morning, to ride over the hills to Henderland. The route would have taken him by way of Manor Valley and then from Manorhead, up and over the hills, then down into the valley of the Megget Water. As it happened, the previous evening at dusk, Cockburn had set out on his raid to Tushielaw. One of Cockburn's former retainers had been in Peebles that evening and heard of the King's intentions. He set off to warn Cockburn and arrived at Henderland some time after he had left. Cockburn's wife, Marjory, was wakened and told what the king planned. Earlier in the day when she heard of Cockburn's planned raid, she tried to dissuade him. She had a premonition of danger and remembered an old prophecy, said to come from Merlin the Wizard. It ran:

> *On Cockburn's elm, on Henderland Lee,*
> *A Cockburn laird shall hangit be.*

Cockburn had brushed aside her concerns and full of bravado and in spite of a rising storm, had set out on his mission of theft and destruction, but when the messenger from Peebles arrived with news of the king's approach Marjory sent him after Cockburn to warn him not to return to Henderland. Cockburn had other ideas. His mission to Tushielaw completed, he none the less set off back to Henderland. Perhaps through arrogance and a disregard for higher authority, he thought he could deal with this young and untested king. He could not have been more wrong. In the meantime James and his forces, which ominously included a hangman, had reached Henderland and demanded entry and to know the whereabouts of the laird. The frightened gatekeeper eventually told the king that his master had left around midnight to revenge himself on Adam Scott, who had raided Henderland a few weeks earlier, driven off many head of cattle and injured some of Cockburn's retainers. The king was unsympathetic and as soon as Cockburn returned he was seized and ignominiously hanged from the buttress of his own house.

The ballad tells that while preparations for the laird's return and execution were being made, Marjory fled to the nearby woods until she heard the sound of the king's cavalcade departing towards Tushielaw, where they intended to serve similar justice on Adam Scott. She returned to find the body of her husband hanging from his own house.

So Parys Cockburn was not hanged from the elm tree as Merlin's prophecy had said, but in a final twist, the tale relates that during the storm of the previous night, many trees had blown down, leaving standing alone the great elm of the prophecy. It is said that Marjory never recovered from the trauma of that day and died of a broken heart three years later.

A rather different version of this story is that James did indeed set out from Peebles on his first mission to bring order to the Borders and that both Cockburn of Henderland (although named in the records as William, not Parys as of folklore) and Adam Scott of Tushielaw were apprehended and taken to Edinburgh. The following year they were charged with various offences and executed by beheading. There is no doubt that at an early age (he was still only 19 years old) James was intent on making it clear who was master in Scotland.

Whatever the truth of these differing versions, there is a gravestone which can still be seen in Henderland churchyard. Carved on it is the inscription, "Here lies Parys Cockburn, and his wife Marjory".

The destruction of the two Ettrick lairds, was not the only occasion when Peebles was the starting point for an expedition of pacification in the Borders. While most visits combined the pleasures of hunting with State administration, some continued to be part of the drive to rid the Borders of its warring clans. Most notorious were the Armstrongs. They were not just common Border reivers. They set themselves up as lords and masters of much of the area of Liddesdale and more besides. Their activities recognised no national border and dominated what became to be known as "the Debateable Lands". They recognised no authority other than their own, and certainly not that of the King of Scots. That was something which James could not tolerate. The story of his pursuit, capture and destruction of the chief of the clan, Johnnie Armstrong of Gilnockie and his cohorts, has become part of Border legend. It was from Peebles on a July day in 1530, that James and his followers set out on the expedition which was to destroy the power of the Armstrongs and finally bring him control of the southern borderlands of his Kingdom. He summoned Armstrong to meet him, granting him safe passage, but as soon as the reiver and his supporters were met by the king and his force they were overpowered and to a man hanged from the nearby trees. The story may not do James the greatest of credit, but it sent a potent message to any who thought to oppose his authority.

James personally presided over Justice Ayres held in Peebles of 25th June, 1529. They were circuit courts, held from time to time in the main burghs of Scotland and were often attended by the king himself. As well as dealing with specific crimes, it also provided an opportunity for settling local disputes and gave an opportunity for the lower ranks of society to seek redress against repressive landlords. The dispensing of justice was something which James encouraged and developed. The Court of Session, which remains today the highest court of Scotland, was established by him. Perhaps it was this sense of justice for all which earned him the title of "the poor man's king".

Following the Justice Ayres, James and his party left to hunt at Cramalt and Meggetland in Ettrick Forest, not far from Henderland. It became a favourite hunting venue and was an added attraction to the pleasures of Peebles nearby. He returned to Peebles and from there rode to Edinburgh on 1st July. That particular visit is marked by letters given under his "privie sele at Peblis" when, as previously noted, he confirmed the grant of a house of religion in Dunbar and its revenues to the Minister and Brethren of the Cross Kirk 'quhair ane pairt of the verray croce that our Salvatour was crucifyit on is honorit and kepit' Perhaps he had quite often enjoyed hospitality of the Minister and Brethren and this was just reward. He would of course have been familiar with stories of his own father's many visits and donations to that place of pilgrimage.

The affairs of State and pursuit of the pleasures of the chase were very much intertwined. Like his father James IV, his reign demanded that he be a peripatetic monarch, in days when the only way to communicate with distant subjects and to address the problems of the day, was by personal visitation. The frequency of visits to Peebles may be due to a combination of circumstances. Not only was it a pleasant place, with loyal and agreeable townsfolk, but also its geographical location, a day's ride from Edinburgh, made it a convenient stepping off point for excursions into the wilder and more distant Border lands. Its location on the edge of the Forest of Ettrick, with its unrivalled hunting, was a bonus.

There are a number of further recorded visits to the Royal Burgh. 1529 saw several. He rode from Linlithgow on 2nd July with his Lords and Council and was at the town the following day. From there he rode to Douglas Water on the 4th July and returned on the 13th. He was at Cramalt hunting on the 15th and back in Peebles on the 18th, before returning to Linlithgow on the 20th. It was during a period when Linlithgow rather than Edinburgh was the centre of State business because there was an outbreak of the plague which seems to have been rife in the Capital at that time. It is noted that in September of that year, that the Lords of the Council, meeting in Peebles, agreed that their next meeting should be held in Edinburgh 'geif it be clene of the pest' failing which it was to held in Linlithgow.

He returned to Peebles some six weeks later, on 14th September and after hunting at Cramalt on the 15th, he was back in Peebles on the 16th and 17th. Regular visits to the Royal Burgh continued although later records are more sparse. His interest and affection for it is confirmed by his renewal on 27th November 1539, of Royal protection for the citizens and by letters issued under his Privy Seal on 12th October 1541, confirming the market privileges of the burgh. There are Crown charters dated "Peblis 10 July 1542."

Towards the end of November 1542 James visited Peebles and spent the night in the burgh among the folk he clearly regarded as his loyal burgesses. It was to be his last visit. James has sometimes been portrayed as something of a tragic king. The immediately preceding years had been a time of illness and disappointment. In April 1541 both his young sons died, leaving no Heir to the Throne. He had become embroiled in a war with his English neighbour and uncle, the arrogant and avaricious Henry VIII. His attempts to muster a Scottish force to oppose him were largely a failure, a failure which culminated in the defeat and humiliation of his army at the hands the English at Solway Moss, which finally broke his spirit. On 8th December a daughter, Mary, was born to his wife Mary of Guise and a few days later, on 14th December, only three weeks after his sojourn in Peebles, at the early age of 32 James V died at Falkland. Whether or not he uttered the words 'it came with a Lass and will pass with a lass' as he turned his face to the wall is a matter for conjecture.

In the end there may have been failure, but James had done much to bring law and order to Scotland and to protect its weaker citizens. There are tales of him travelling the countryside, supposedly to find out how ordinary folk fared, disguised as a figure who became known as "the Guid Man o' Ballengeich", although that may also have been a cloak for amorous adventures! None the less the folk of Peebles seem to have remembered James V with some affection. When in 1543 the Parish Church of St Andrew was made into a Collegiate church, one of those to be remembered in the services was 'James Fifth, our dearest father, of good memory.'

It was during the reign of James V that an event happened which was to change the course of history and in time would also change much of the character of Peebles, where for centuries the Church of Rome had had a dominating influence. On 31 October, 1517, a German Augustinian friar called Martin Luther pinned a lengthy document to the door of the Schlosskirchen of Wittenburg. It was a declaration against the sale of Indulgences, by which the Pope, Leo X, hoped to raise vast sums of money from the faithful, to replenish the coffers of Rome, emptied by the extravagance of a succession of Popes. In an age of scientific ignorance those indulgences promised the purchaser automatic entry to Heaven. For Luther, who had long been dismayed by the corruption of the Church of Rome, that proved to be the final straw and declaration that day was to signal the start of the Reformation.

It was some 50 or more years before the old Roman Catholic order in Peebles was replaced by Calvinist Presbyterianism. In those intervening years much else was to take place which was to have a devastating effect on the town.

8.
Our Auld Enemies of England

The fortunes of Scotland and France have been intertwined for centuries. As far back as 1295, John Balliol, the ill fated King of Scots of the day, entered into a treaty with Philip IV of France, for their mutual defence against their rapacious neighbour, Edward I of England. Little good it did Balliol, who eventually ignominiously surrendered to Edward, precipitating the Wars of Independence. For all that, the bonds between France and Scotland, the "Auld Alliance", became firmly established from that time and somewhat romantically, if not practically, can be said to remain to this day. It was an alliance which was to cause suffering to the Scots. It was an alliance that precipitated the disaster of Flodden, but it also had dynastic consequences.

James V married two French princesses in succession. In what might seem a somewhat romantic pursuit of the first, but was equally political, he spent nine months at the French court of Francis I and won the hand of the King's daughter Madeleine, marrying her in the cathedral of Notre Dame in Paris on 1st January 1537. They returned to Scotland as King and Queen of Scots in May of that year. Sadly Madeleine was suffering from tuberculosis. Hardly had she set foot in her new kingdom, but the disease attacked and she died on 7th July. She is buried, as is James, in the choir of Holyrood Abbey.

A dynastic marriage with France was still James' aim, but there were no longer any eligible royal princesses. Instead his choice fell on the Duchesse de Longueville, who was a young and attractive widow and a daughter of the House of Lorraine and Guise, whose dukes were closely connected to the French royal house. She is better known to us as Mary of Guise.

James and Mary were married in the cathedral of St Andrews in June 1538. Mary was intelligent and able. In the years following the death of James in 1542, she was to become a dominant force in Scotland. She was of course the mother and in her early years the protector of Mary, Queen of Scots, born at Linlithgow Palace on 8th December 1542, just six days before the death of her father.

Of all the monarchs of Scotland, Mary Queen of Scots perhaps ranks highest in the popular mind, not because of her success as a monarch, because ultimately she failed, but rather because hers was a life of Shakespearian tragedy, but a romanticised one, which has left a legacy for which the tourist industry of Scotland can be duly grateful.

Her reign had a significant impact on Peebles, not just through her direct connections with the town and that of her dissolute husband, but also because of the damage and destruction which it suffered during the years of her childhood and adolescence in France, when Henry VIII and those acting on behalf of his successor Edward VI carried out raids on the Borders from which Peebles did not escape.

Henry VIII of England was her grand uncle and one of the most unattractive crowned heads in the history of Britain. Taking advantage of what must have been an uncertain situation following the death of James and an untested regency, he wasted little time in staking his claim to be Overlord of Scotland and to try to dominate his weaker neighbour. For the people of Peebles, those early years of the child queen Mary's reign were a period when terror and destruction by the forces of that arrogant tyrant caused death and deprivation.

It started, not entirely unreasonably, with Henry's proposal that his son and heir Edward and Mary should be joined in marriage. The result, had he succeeded, would have been to unite the two kingdoms in time. Following the death of her husband, Mary's mother, Mary of Guise, now the Queen Dowager, had effectively become Regent of Scotland. She was a formidable lady and although ultimately she would lose the support of most of the great magnates, at that time she had the support of the Scottish lords and together with them she rejected Henry's overtures.

The Scots had entered into a Treaty in 1543,[65]which would have ended the conflict which had marred the last years of the reign of James V. It had provided for the marriage of Mary to Prince Edward, when she reached the age of eleven. Henry, for his own reasons delayed the ratification of the treaty. At that time the Auld Alliance with France was being strengthened, mainly due to the influence of the Queen Mother's family, the Guises, who were becoming a powerful force at the court of King Henri II of France. The old and now traditional friendship with France seemed infinitely better than domination by England.

Henry's prevarication gave the Scots time to reconsider the serious implications which it would have brought. Whatever the advantages the treaty might have held for Scotland, it was inevitable that the proposed marriage would, at long last, confirm English domination and it was not a happy prospect. The Queen Dowager and her Scottish lords for their part,

---

[65]   The Treaty of Greenwich

eventually rejected Henry's proposal. Not one to take "no" for an answer, Henry reacted by demanding that the Scots think again and meet his wishes. The Scots declined and Henry, never one to be thwarted by anyone, sent the Earl of Hertford north, with orders to enter Scotland and to lay it waste by fire and sword. Peebles did not escape.

It was the time which was to become known as "the rough wooing" Not long after the accession of the baby Queen Mary, twelve Border towns were robbed and damaged by raiders from Liddesdale, acting on the orders of the English Warden of the Marches. The Warden's specific instructions were that they should go as far as Peebles, which he noted was some 28 miles from the border, a slight underestimate as it happens.

In 1544, there were more serious incursions by English raiders. One raid led by Lord Evers and Sir Brian Latoun caused widespread destruction. As many as 200 towns and settlements were reportedly burned or destroyed, leaving 400 dead, with 800 more taken prisoner and as many as 1000 cattle and 12,000 sheep stolen and driven back over the border to England. The effects would have been devastating to an area which depended on cattle to sustain the local population and sheep for the wool trade with continental Europe which was the mainstay of its economy.

There is no direct evidence that the raid affected Peebles, but it does seem likely that the burgh and its surrounding shire felt the effect of the marauding English. At that time the defensive walls of the town, were rudimentary and little more than a linking together of the "head dykes" which joined the stone walls, marking the boundaries of the properties which descended on either side of the High Street to the Eddleston Water on the north and the banks of the Tweed on the south. Even the fortified houses of the local lairds and the bastel houses of the towns folk who could afford them, would have been unable to withstand a major onslaught.

After that initial raid on the Borders and following his appointment as Lieutenant of the Borders, the Earl of Angus, brought a detachment of his army to Peebles, where they met with the earls of Angus, Glencairn and Cassels, who brought a troop of men from the west. The assembled army was camped in the town for two nights. The local laird, Lord Hay of Yester, was a kinsman of the Earl of Angus, so it is probable that a contingent of Peebles men under his command were also added to the main force.

Robert Scot of Wamphray, who was an English spy, reported the departure of the force to the Warden of the West March and that 'they lap onne Sunday night at ane of the clok and rayd furth of Pebles ane thowsand men by cariages.' Wamphray also reported that Earl of Angus had been instructed by the Governor General, James Hamilton, 2nd Earl of Arran, to make for Coldingham in the Merse.

It was the start of a counter offensive, which culminated in a heavy defeat of the English invaders at Ancrum Moor in February 1545, in which the Peeblesshire contingent of Lord Hay played its part. It caused the invaders to retreat beyond the Border for some time, but revenge was not long in coming. Later that year a further incursion by the Earl of Hertford saw the burning and destruction of the abbeys of Kelso, Jedburgh, Dryburgh and Melrose, which have never since been rebuilt.

That was not the end of the raiding. Although the detestable Henry VIII died in January 1547 it did not bring a halt to English aggression. In March of that year, there was a brief respite which allowed the Scottish Privy Council to a try to re-establish its own authority over the Border country, which had been so disrupted by English marauding. It had also encouraged a general descent into lawlessness in the area, with thieving and reiving by the Border clans once more becoming virtually uncontrolled.

With a view to bringing the area back under control and to prepare for any further major incursion by the English, the Privy Council assembled an army under the command of the Governor General Arran, to meet at Peebles, with sufficient provisions for twenty days. Word had reached Scotland that an invasion by land and sea was planned, with the stated intention of laying waste the countryside by burning and inflicting death and destruction on a population already suffering from the effects of the earlier raids.

The expected invasion by forces led by the Earl of Hertford duly arrived on 10th September, which became known as "Black Friday". Arran was a weak and ineffective leader and the Scots suffered a severe defeat at Pinkie Heuch in East Lothian. Lord Hay, who had succeeded his father as Lord Yester in 1543, was taken prisoner and as commander of part of the force which included the Peebles contingent, it is likely that some of the Peebles men were also taken prisoner.

At the same time it appears that the townsfolk of Peebles, at a safe distance from the battle, were showing some support for the English and continued to do so for about fifteen weeks thereafter, until saner influences prevailed! For that treacherous and almost treasonable behaviour, a fine of £200 was imposed on the burgh, which seems modest in the circumstances. In mitigation, it can perhaps be said that the people of the town and their leaders had merely adopted a pragmatic approach, because the Duke of Somerset,[66] the Lord Protector of the English Realm and Regent for the young king Edward VI, had effectively occupied most of the East of Scotland with headquarters at Haddington. Thus the whole area was at the mercy of the English and in submitting to them, the burgh probably had little choice. In spite of their apparent support for the English invaders, for the people of Peebles worse was to come.

The continued English aggression posed considerable risk to the five year old child queen, Mary. The Earl of Arran was nominally the Regent of Scotland. Never an effective leader, his position had been further weakened by his total failure at Pinkie. The Queen Dowager, Mary of Guise, was already the major power and influence in the Privy Council and that gave her the opportunity to strengthen the already strong ties with France at a time when the English invasions were a very present danger to her and her daughter. By that time, England was at least nominally Protestant, but there were stirrings of reformation in Scotland and while the country was still predominantly Catholic, Mary of Guise was determined to resist the rise of Protestantism in Scotland and protect its Catholic monarchy. She appealed to France for help. and in response the French king, Henri II, encouraged by her powerful Guise relations at the French court, was happy to support her.

In the aftermath of the Battle of Pinkie the child Queen Mary had been taken with some of her companions to the safety of the island Priory of Inchmahome on the Lake of Menteith. She was then moved to the safer haven of Dumbarton Castle. The English policy of seeking to unite the Scottish and English crowns if necessary by force, merely produced a totally adverse effect. The Scots Parliament finally decided that enough was enough. No doubt aided by the French party of the Queen Dowager and influenced by her powerful French relations, the Guises, it was decided that Mary should marry the Dauphin, the heir to the French throne. In July 1548 a formal treaty was entered into which provided for French troops to be sent to bolster the beleaguered Scottish forces in exchange for the hand of the Queen of Scots. A French fleet and a large contingent of soldiers was sent to Leith, to assist the Scots in dislodging the English from the large area of south east Scotland which they effectively occupied by that time.

For her continuing safety, education and enlightenment as the future Queen of France, as well as of Scotland, the French King Henri II insisted that Mary should be brought to France and live under his benign and

---

[66]   Formerly the Earl of Hertford

fatherly eye at the French court. The French sent a fleet of ships to Scotland by way of the Irish Sea. Mary left Dumbarton and set sail for France, the fleet again taking the route through the Irish Sea. After days of storms and rough seas, avoiding marauding English ships, the fleet reached France and Mary landed at Roscoff on the 13th August 1548.

The five year old queen had left her native Scotland for an unknown country, leaving behind her mother, Mary of Guise who had been her close companion, guide and guardian since birth. True she had with her the "Four Marys"; Beaton, Seton, Livingstone and Fleming, who had been her companions in Scotland, but although she had some knowledge of French from her mother, Scots was her first tongue and she knew nothing of the country to which she was bound. Yet the next thirteen years were for Mary perhaps the happiest of her life, safe in the hands of a powerful and stable regime, solidly in the sphere of the Church of Rome. For Scotland and Peebles things would be somewhat different.

The departure of Mary, even although it signified an end to any question of an English marriage, by no means deterred the English from pursuing their campaign of carnage and destruction. It is true that much of it was encouraged by a deep divide in the Scottish body politic and that divide was centred on religion. The Kingdom of England, now firmly Protestant and severed from the Church of Rome wanted to ensure that its northern neighbour was also separated from the Roman Catholic Church. The raiding and marauding continued unabated and although in due course the combined Scots and French forces succeeded in finally driving the English invaders back beyond the border, it was not before the English made a final attempt to implement a "scorched earth" policy throughout the area. Peebles did not escape!

The town, which was virtually unprotected, suffered near catastrophic destruction in 1549. It was no random attack. In July of that year, one of the English commanders, Sir Thomas Halcroft wrote : "I trust your grace shall hear that we will burn Peebles, and other things which we never burned, to welcome Monsier de Termes[67] to the country." A less confident Halcroft wrote again on the 25th September to report that mounted forces under Buccleuch were at Selkirk and Peebles and that seems to have been a temporary deterrent, but not for long and in November or December there was a major attack.

It is difficult to imagine the horror of such a raid! There were no permanent defences or town wall at that time and it was not until 1569 that a protective perimeter wall was built as a permanent fortification, although

---

[67]   The French commander

some buildings would have been individually fortified. Peebles was a defenceless town, largely populated by unarmed citizens, living in houses which were mainly built of timber with thatched roofs and thus tinder boxes. The mounted attacking force, even if no more than 100/200 strong would have presented a formidable and awesome spectacle as it relentlessly approached the East Wark and then charged through the town, throwing lighted torches of tar onto the thatched roofs. How many died or suffered injury is not known, but it is unlikely that all escaped death or injury.

There is no direct record of the attack, but later records give some indication of the damage which must have resulted. The East Wark, which was then a fortified steeple at the eastern approach to the town, was destroyed and considerable damage was done to the buildings in the Northgait and Briggait. The Church of St Andrew was badly damaged and never to this day rebuilt, while the Cross Kirk was damaged as well. The town's Rood Mill situated near the Castle Hill also suffered major damage. The records show the rent as falling into arrears for some years thereafter, presumably because it had been so seriously damaged that it could no longer operate.

The ordinary citizens suffered a great deal of material and financial hardship and in the subsequent years there are many references in property dispositions, to sales of fire damaged properties which the owners had to dispose of in their damaged state. In March 1550 there is reference to a couple being forced to sell their damaged property, 'a burned land of theirs' sold 'in their great need and necessity'. In April of the same year there is reference to 'a property lying on the north side of the Briggait and the east side of the Almshouse…….. as then being burned by our auld enemies of England, it being sold on account of its owners great necessity and need for a certain sum of money in gold and silver.' In May George Paterson and his wife Christian Smyth 'passed their land burned by our auld enemies of England', lying in the Northgait, and sold the same in their 'great necessity and need.' There are many more similar examples which show that great economic as well as personal destruction was caused, as it was intended to do and as so often is the case, it was the defenceless and innocent who would have suffered.

The child Mary Queen of Scots, was no doubt untouched by the affronts to her kingdom and subjects. She was by then safely established at the French court and it would be thirteen years before she returned to Scotland. The country she returned to in 1561, was very different from the one she left. In the intervening years the whole fabric of Scottish society and life was changed by a religious revolution. Peebles, which for three centuries had been a religious centre, was to change dramatically in those years as the Scottish Reformation took hold.

9.
Reformation

At about 11 o'clock on the morning of the 11th December 1560, Gilbert Broune, of the Trinity Friars and Minister of the Cross Kirk of Peebles for the past eight years, handed over the keys of the outer door of the church to the bailies of the Burgh of Peebles, in response to a demand by them, which they said was made in the name of the parishioners. So ended the power, influence and pastoral care of the Church of Rome, which had ruled in Peebles since the days of St Mungo and had dominated the town for three centuries past.

To understand how that came about, we need to go back to an autumn day in the year 1517, when Martin Luther climbed the steps leading up to the Schlosskirchen in the German town of Wittenburg and pinned his great document to the main door. There had been earlier attempts to reform the Church of Rome. Discontent with the conduct of its hierarchy and its lower orders of clergy had shown itself as early as the fourteenth century when John Wycliffe, the English philosopher and theologian had spoken out against the materialism of the church. He suffered martyrdom for his trouble, but it inspired Jan Huss to start a movement for reform in the early fifteenth century in Bohemia, now part of the Czech Republic. He was burned as a heretic at Prague. In Scotland too, there were stirrings. James Resby, a follower of Wycliffe was burned as a heretic at Perth in 1407. Paul Craw, a follower of Huss made his way to Scotland and openly preached Hussite doctrine and like other heretics before and after him, was burned at the stake.

The Reformation had a considerable significance for Peebles. For the better part of three centuries, since the finding of an ancient cross at the site of the Cross Kirk in 1261, the Royal Burgh had been a place of pilgrimage and Holy Church had long dominated the town. As already noted earlier, Dr Gunn has said that there were so many clergy in Peebles, that they formed a distinct group in the burgh and that there was a whole area of the town in which they lived which was almost exclusively ecclesiastical. All that was changing. The holy men of Peebles were not immune from the charge of materialism, but before looking at the failings and fortunes of the priests and friars of Peebles it is helpful to look at the wider European scene, where the Church of Rome was in turmoil.

There is little doubt that religious development, particularly from the twelfth century onwards, was generally a force for good. The monastic movement especially, provided for the spiritual and pastoral needs of many communities such as Peebles. In addition it was a refuge and a support to the needy. By the fourteenth century however, it had progressed from the spiritual to the material and the political. It was a change that started at the very top, with the Papacy, but its effects would filter down in time to the lowest levels of the clergy.

Three Popes in particular represent the Church's worst excesses. Perhaps the most corrupt and dishonest was Rodrigo Borgia, Pope Alexander VI. He was "elected" Pope in 1492. Most of those who voted for him were bribed or otherwise intimidated. His election elevated materialism in the papacy to new heights. Alexander was acquisitive and certainly not celibate. His daughter was the notorious Lucretia Borgia and his son, the infamous Cesare Borgia.

Alexander was succeeded after a brief interval by a man whose policy was to demonstrate the power of the church and of the Papacy by military conquest and the acquisition of material wealth. His name was Guiliano de Rovere, who was elected Pope in 1503 and took the name of Julius II. Like the Borgia Pope, he came from one of the great Italian families. He believed in the political dominance of the Church and wealth as the symbols of spiritual power. It was he who commissioned the rebuilding of St Peter's Basilica in the form it is seen today, the painting of the ceiling of the Sistine Chapel by Michelangelo and the Papal apartments of the Vatican by Raphael. He was known as the "soldier Pope", because he personally led the Papal army to the defeat of Venice and halted the military incursion into Italy by France. He also amassed a huge fortune for the Papal coffers.

The third of these Popes was Giovanni de Medici, a member of the great Florentine dynasty. He was elected in 1513, taking the name Leo X and followed directly after Julius II. He was intelligent and well educated, but quickly succumbed to the pleasures of the flesh and personal indulgence. During his papacy he managed to run through much of the fortune so carefully gathered by Julius II.

As a result of his profligacy coupled with the enormous cost of continuing the building of St Peter's, Leo X had to find ways of raising new money. It had long been the practice in the Church, for those seeking its services to make a financial contribution. It was not always for the immediate offices of prayer and worship, but also as a way of easing the path to eternity for themselves and their families and the souls of the departed. Now a new and highly profitable, but questionable scheme for filling the Papal coffers was devised. That was the sale of Indulgences. It was a document signed by the Pope which guaranteed the purchaser entry to heaven. In an age when superstition dominated much of religious belief, sales throughout Europe soared. It was what brought Martin Luther to the point of no return. The document he had pinned to the door of Wittenburg's Schlosskirchen was a "Declaration against Indulgences".

There is no doubt that while Luther may be seen as the final piece in the jigsaw which ushered in Protestantism, the corruption of the Church was wide spread throughout Europe and it permeated down through every level of the clergy. Its primary concern seemed, not the pastoral care of the people as it should have been, but money and materialism with little regard for its true purpose. Correspondence between the Scottish hierarchy and the Pope in Rome dealt almost exclusively at that time with money matters and in particular the enjoyment of benefices. Rarely if ever did it deal with spiritual affairs.

In Peebles, while undoubtedly the church must have played a significant role in the welfare of the community, similar attitudes are all too evident. The Church records are littered with examples relating to material matters and there is little reference to questions of pastoral care or the conduct of worship.

Robert Chambers comments :-

It may here be mentioned, that the burgesses of Peebles were as liberal, in proportion to their means, to the clergy of the Catholic church, as any of their contemporaries. Their donations of houses and rents for *sawl-heill*, or soul welfare, during the fifteenth century, were very numerous ; one of them is in the following terms :- 'On the 12th day of February 1473, William of Peebles, burgess of that ilk", resigned his "foreland, under and aboon, by and on the Conyhe (*maison de coin*, the corner house – the place is now called Cunyie Neuk), neist the North Gate, to Sanct Lenard's hospital, for his sawl, his wyff's sawl, his bairnis sawlls, and for all the sawlls that the said William *had ony gud wrangously of*, in bying or selling, or ony enterchangyng.'

As already noted, at the beginning of the fifteenth century there were four places of worship in the town or nearby. In Peebles itself, were the Church and Monastery of the Cross Kirk, the Church of St Andrew and in the High Street, the Chapel of St Mary. The Chapel of the Hospice of Saints Lawrence and Leonard, at Eshiels was only about a mile outside the town.

In each of them was a number of altars, with one or more clergy assigned to each individual altar. William Chambers[68] refers to a royal charter granted on 8th June 1543 by the Earl of Arran, then the Regent of Scotland during the minority of Mary Queen of Scots. It constituted the parish church of St Andrew as a collegiate church. It states that the staff of the church was to consist of a provost dean, twelve prebendaries,[69] each assigned to one of the twelve altars which were dedicated to :- The Blessed Virgin Mary of Childbirth; the Holy Rood; St Michael the Archangel; St Mary Major; the blessed Peter and Paul; St Mary of Geddes Aisle; St Andrew; St James; St Lawrence; St Martin and the twelfth, to St Christopher. There were also to be 'two young persons having a youthful voice to chant divine service with the provost and prebendaries'.

The foundation charter of the collegiate church made provision for each of the twelve prebendaries to have a room and a yard in the Old Town, adjacent to the house which in 1543 belonged to Alexander Dick, the archdeacon of Glasgow, who occupied it for part of the year in his capacity as *ex officio* parson of Peebles

They were supported by endowments which might be payments given by individuals or the revenues of properties given by them. That was in addition to the local hierarchy and the Trinity Friars of the Cross Kirk, all of whom were supported by the contributions of the people, often in the belief that their generosity would ensure their remembrance and perhaps a more comfortable life in the world to come.

The endowments usually arose from land or property, granted or gifted in former years and were a source of considerable revenue.
According to Dr Gunn:-

...the wealth of the church, even in a burgh like Peebles was enormous. There was hardly a piece of land or a tenement which did not pay something to the revenues of the Church. Besides which the Church possessed much property herself. All the altarages were endowed, some more, others less : and their incomes were constantly increasing. As Magistrates were officially patrons of most of them, it has been seen how Burgess fees went toward the upkeep of the Altars and the Services of the Parish Church.

---

[68]   *Preface to Charters and Documents and Extracts from the Records of Burgh of Peebles 1165 – 1710,* p xiii
[69]   A prebendary is a senior member of clergy in a collegiate church normally supported by the revenues from properties and parishioners

Dr Gunn lists the endowments of the altar of St Mary Major in detail. That altar alone had endowments from twenty four different sources. They included:-

An acre of land lying on the north side within the lands of of St Mary of Geddes Aisle.

A rood[70]of land called St Mary's Rood lying on the east of Dalatho.

Eighteen shillings and fourpence from the land of David Robison in the Briggait.

Four shillings and eightpence from the land of John Johnstoun lying at the east end of the burgh on the south side of the highway.

Two shillings from the tenement called Caverhill in the Old Town of Peebles opposite the tenement of the Archdeacon, together with the whole tenement of Caverhill.

Six shillings of annual rent from the land called Gledstaneland[71]lying on the north side of the highway near the lands of SS Peter and Paul.

Two shillings from Small Island in the Old Town of Peebles on the south side.

How many clergy there actually were in the town is not recorded, but what with Trinity Friars and the army of altar chaplains and others it must have been a considerable number! As Dr Gunn goes on to comment :

A.D.1543. The clergy in Peebles formed a sufficiently numerous body to be a caste or a cult by themselves. Their residences and lands in the Old Town rendered that locality the ecclesiastical quarter. The position of the Parish Church and of the Cross Church, connected with each other by the Cross road, added to the tone of the neighbourhood ; and constant intercourse between both the Churches and the New Town across Eddlestone Water was ensured over two bridges. Night and morning the church bell rang to Matins and Evensong ; and the smaller bell summoned the devout to the other altar services throughout the day. The Church dominated the town intellectually as well as spiritually. Almost all scholarship was confined to the clergymen..............In municipal matters it was the same ; the Town Clerk

---

[70] Quarter of an acre
[71] Gladstone Place

had to be a priest, as priests almost alone knew how to write. What an influence the Church could exert upon the burgh through this official! The notaries were priests also ; hence the accretion to the Church of annual rents, legacies, and bequests from pious burghers. The town clock was wound by a priest. The Church was so wealthy that there was hardly a property or piece of land in the parish which did not pay an annual charge to the Church, or actually belonged wholly to it : and this enormous aggrandisement of the ages formed a potent factor in the downfall of the Church ; for all those who clamoured for reform were not actuated by a love of truth and purity of doctrine ; there were others who groaned under the burdens and extractions borne by their lands as annual charges to the Church.

By the sixteenth century financial pressures on the Church generally and the personal greed and indulgence of the clergy, resulted in many of the properties and land from which the endowments were derived being sold or alienated for cash. For example on 15th June 1554:

Sir John Bullo, Chaplain of St Martin's altar in the Church of St Andrew, passed waste land on the north side of Briggait pertaining to him in patrimony by virtue of Recognition, led thereupon by the late Sir Gilbert, Chaplain of St Martin, predecessor of Sir John. And there Sir John resigned the property in the hands of a Bailie, who gave sasine to Thomas Hoppringle. The feu duty payable to the chaplain being 10s.

Or again on the 23rd October 1554

Sir Thomas Purves, Chaplain of Our lady Altar in the College Kirk of St Andro, passed to a land of the late John Gledstanes of Cocklaw, on the north side of Hie Gait, and resigned all right to the land by delivering earth and stone in the hands of the Bailie James Robeson. Sasine given to Walter Gledstanes. Annual of 7s payable to the chaplain.

Ever since Martin Luther had set in motion what became the Protestant Reformation, his teachings had spread throughout Europe with remarkable speed in an age when the communication of new ideas could only be achieved by personal contact. Scotland with its close contacts with continental Europe had already been touched by earlier teachings of James Resby and Paul Craw and only a few years after Luther's momentous declaration, books spreading the new Lutheran doctrine, began to find their way to Scotland. In 1525 the Scottish parliament passed an Act which banned the importation of those books. It was repeated in 1535.

Patrick Hamilton, who had been the titular Abbot of Fearn in Ross-shire was probably born in Lanarkshire. He went to study in Paris, completing his studies there in 1520. While he was there he learned of the teaching and writings of Luther and became a firm follower. After a further period of study at Leuven, under Erasmus, he returned to Scotland in 1525 and began to preach the Lutheran doctrine of Justification by Faith. It was seen as extreme heresy by the Church of Rome which maintained a dominating role not only in spiritual affairs, but also in the political. In 1528 Hamilton was declared to be a heretic and was burned at the stake in St Andrews. It is perhaps an indication of how far the new Protestantism had spread its influence that this act produced a wave of public sympathy and revulsion against the church.

James V had begun to take a grip of the government of the country and it raises the question as to where he stood. He was greatly influenced by two men who had been his tutors and mentors during his minority. The first of them was David Beaton, who by that time was Cardinal Archbishop of St Andrews and the Primate of Scotland. He was the arch Catholic conservative and utterly opposed to any criticism of Holy Church or its practices, something he would carry over into the reign of Mary Queen of Scots as the principal advisor of Mary of Guise. The second was Sir David Lindsay of the Mount, Lord Lyon King of Arms. He seems to have been a man with what were for the time, quite liberal ideas and certainly an understanding of the failings of the Church. He is best remembered for his play *Ane Satyr of the Thrie Estaites*, which is still performed to this day, perhaps most memorably at the Edinburgh Festival of 1973.

The play is a devastating critique of a nation and church seen as corrupt and uncaring of the poor and needy. No part of the "establishment" is spared and certainly not the church. What is remarkable is that when it was performed at Linlithgow Palace in 1540 before James and Mary of Guise and the whole court, James seems to have accepted its message. Had such an event happened at the court of his uncle, Henry VIII, heads would have rolled, literally. Instead, it was said that when the performance ended, James turned to the bishops and senior churchmen present and told them in no uncertain terms that they should mend their ways and that if they failed to do so, he would send six of them to London to be dealt with by his uncle, who would be unlikely to show them similar tolerance. It seems that it had little effect and little changed. In the final two years of his life James had other pressing concerns.

Following his death, Mary of Guise, now Queen Dowager and strongly supported by David Beaton, was determined to see the Catholic tradition maintained. Mary was an intelligent and able ruler, at least for a time. She had powerful support from France where her family dominated the royal court. Her brother was the Cardinal Archbishop of Lorraine in a country where the Huguenot Protestants were engaged in a sometimes bloody battle with the strongly Catholic French crown. Here it is perhaps worth mentioning that following Luther's great 'revolution' the question as to whether or not Protestantism should replace Catholicism, would become as much a political as a theological matter. The kingdoms, dukedoms and palatinates of Europe more often, though not always, made their decisions concerning state religion on the basis of power and influence, rather than a genuine belief in one form of Christianity or another. Perhaps the extreme example was England, where Henry VIII, unashamedly parted from Rome, making himself Head of the Church, even giving himself the title Defender of the Faith, in order that he might divorce his first wife, Katherine of Aragon and incidentally destroying the monasteries and acquiring their undoubted wealth for himself. In the following century that was to be the cause of a civil war, the death of a king, an invasion of Scotland, which had direct consequences for Peebles and later in the seventeenth century led to the "Killing Times" and at least one local martyr.

In Scotland, it was the dissatisfaction with Rome, encouraged by the contacts which Scottish scholars and theologians had with their continental contemporaries, which was the main influence and driving force. Scottish scholars wanting to expand their learning, frequently became students at universities such as Paris, Leuven and Heidelberg where they were exposed to the teachings of Luther and his followers. Perhaps most prominent among them was George Wishart, who had become a follower of Luther after studying at Leuven. After graduating there in 1531, he returned to Scotland where he taught in Angus, but he was accused of heresy and fled to England spending some time studying and teaching at Cambridge and in Germany and Switzerland. During that time he translated the *The First Helvetic Confession* into Scots.

In 1543 the Estates, the Scottish parliament, agreed to allow the reading of the Bible in Scots and Wishart returned to Scotland that same year. For the next few years he was an itinerant preacher. He was well aware of the risk he was taking in preaching a doctrine which the Church saw as heretical, so when he preached in public places, he was always accompanied by a friend carrying a two handed sword. He mainly preached in the Dundee area, but ventured south into East Lothian. At Haddington his companion in arms was a local lad by the name of John Knox. It was while he was in East Lothian that he was taken prisoner in January 1546 by Lord Bothwell, acting on the orders of Cardinal Beaton, to whom he was handed over. Following what was a 'show trial', he was burned at the stake in St Andrews on 1st March, in front of the cardinal's palace, the cardinal a spectator, something he would come to regret. He was murdered in his own palace a year later by a group of his many enemies, who, probably motivated by wider political concerns, none the less could see it as vengeance for the life of Wishart.

On to the stage now steps the dominating figure of John Knox. It would however, be some years after the death of Wishart that he finally came to the prominence which has gained him the reputation as the greatest figure of the Scottish Reformation. His story is well known. Taken prisoner at the siege of St Andrews Castle; a French galley slave; freed at the instigation of the English authorities; personal chaplain to King Edward VI; travels to France , Germany and then to Geneva; returns to Scotland briefly in 1555; back to Geneva where he is recognised as one of the great figures of the reformation, along with Calvin, Beze and Farel (acknowledged by his presence with them on the memorial standing in the Parc de la Reformation in Geneva); while in Geneva writes his *First blast of the Trumpet against the Monstrous regiment of Woman* and returns to Scotland in 1559.

By the time of Knox's return, the conflict between the Church of Rome and the reformers had reached its height. In an unsuccessful attempt to preserve the old order, the Scottish Privy Council had tried to ban the printing of Reformist literature and to stop books of that kind being imported. Then in 1559 a number of nobles supporting the Protestant cause came together under the name of "The Lords of the Congregation". They produced a document called "The First Covenant". It was after this that Knox, preached a sermon in Perth which was to prove to be the final blow against Catholicism. In his sermon he denounced the worship of the Roman Catholic Church with its statues, relics, altars and images as evil symbols of idolatry, fit only for destruction. A riot followed during which those symbols in the church were destroyed. The mob then made for the Abbey Church and monastery nearby and carried out so much destruction that only the walls survived. In the meantime Knox had departed in safety, but his sermon that day had set alight a flame which would not be extinguished and throughout Scotland a campaign of destruction and iconoclasm followed, during which many of the artistic treasures of Scotland were lost for ever.

This rather long narrative may seem to have little direct relevance to a history of Peebles, but without some understanding of what went before, it is difficult to appreciate how a cataclysmic change in a short period of only forty three years since Luther made his Declaration, could completely transform Scotland and Peebles, with its long association with Roman Catholicism. As will be seen, the transition in Peebles, probably as in much of Scotland, was far from smooth and divided loyalties would persist for many decades. Although the rise and ultimate ascendancy of Protestantism had been achieved in less than half a century, it would be a further one hundred and thirty years before the Church of Scotland was finally constituted in the form we know it today.

On the first of August 1560 the Scottish Estates or Parliament, met in Edinburgh. It is perhaps one of the most significant days in the history of Scotland, because on that day the religious character of Scotland changed for ever. and within three weeks it had passed an Act endorsing a Confession of Faith, largely drawn up by John Knox. In addition, Acts were passed removing the authority of the Pope in Scotland. Any act of worship not conforming to the Confession of Faith was to be illegal. The celebration of the Mass was made an offence, with a succession of punitive measures culminating in death for the third offence. The sacraments were reduced to two, Holy Communion and Holy baptism.

Although Lord Borthwick, who owned property in the Northgait of the town and Lord Yester were in attendance at the Parliament, together with a Commissioner from Peebles, whose name is unknown, it seems that the burgesses of the town were divided, some prepared to accept the new order while others still supported the old. There had been signs of dissension in the spring of the previous year when a group of Protestant soldiers had occupied the town, clearly anxious to persuade the townsfolk to support the Protestant cause. The town council had other ideas and on the 5th May 1559 ordered the 'sojarries and allegit men of weir' to leave the town immediately.

Sometime later, in March 1560, two of the bailies declared their intention to remain in the Catholic faith 'and obedience to thair Prince bearand authorite for the time', that is to say, Mary Queen of Scots, still represented at that time by the Regent, Mary of Guise. They disliked the new style of worship, where the old liturgy was replaced by common extempore prayers and preaching. However, they were somewhat ambivalent. Although supporting the status quo, they clearly did not want to be seen to oppose the general movement for reform and said that their views were held 'in na contemptioun of the lordis of the congregatioun.'

It is perhaps understandable that the people of Peebles were divided and confused. Although the access to information and opinions which are taken for granted today, was not available then, there were merchants and other travellers who brought, news, rumour and gossip by word of mouth, particularly from Edinburgh. Any new arrival reaching the town would attract a ready crowd of listeners. Reports of the preaching of Knox in Perth and its aftermath would soon have reached Peebles. Who should the townsfolk support, the long established and familiar if flawed Church of Rome, or Knox and the Lords of the Congregation? Peebles had been a place of pilgrimage and retreat for the faithful to "Haly Kirk", since the establishment of the Cross Kirk in 1261. For nearly one hundred years, since its inception in 1474, as the Conventual Monastery of the Trinity Friars, the convent and monastery of the Holy Cross of Peebles, had been a dominating influence in the town and its surrounding country. Although the numbers of its occupants had dwindled, in spite of all their faults and there were many, the master or minister and the brothers would have been a source of some good.

Shortly before the end of March 1560, the Master of Maxwell with a detachment of troops, claiming to be acting on behalf of the Lords of the Congregation, entered the town and took possession of the Cross Kirk. As a result, on 30th March Brother Gilbert Broune, who was the Minister of the monastery appeared before a Notary Public, Sir John Allan. Brother Gilbert is described as 'a venerable and worthy man'. He was clearly also a pragmatist. He explained to Sir John that when Maxwell and his men, had taken possession of the church and monastery, because he feared for his life and also the safety of the buildings themselves, he had quickly taken off his white friars habit and changed into a 'gray keltour goune' and had put on a 'howe black bonet', but only out of fear and not because he supported the Protestant order. He asked the notary,[72] to give a written statement confirming that he still adhered to the Old Religion.

In May, an officer acting on behalf of Lord Borthwick, visited the minister and warned him to remove himself, his goods and his family from the lands and property belonging to Lord Borthwick adjacent to the monastery. Venerable and worthy the good Brother Gilbert may have been, but the reference to 'his family' might suggest that even he may have fallen from grace as far as the opposite sex were concerned, unless of course "his family" is to be construed as referring to the brotherhood of

---

[72] Who would be a priest and therefore sympathetic.

friars. Brother Gilbert protested that the actions of Lord Borthwick were illegal, because he had paid all rents due timeously and had not had sufficient notice as required by law. However, it all seems to have been to no avail.

None the less, it does seem that for the moment at least, Peebles still inclined to the Church of Rome, but the tide was beginning to flow strongly in favour of the reformed order and pressure was mounting against the old.

The meeting of the Estates in August 1560 finally brought that order to an end. In the context of Peebles and having regard to the actions of Lord Borthwick in seeking the removal of Brother Gilbert from his property, it is curious that his lordship was one of only five commissioners who objected to the Acts effectively abolishing the authority of the Church of Rome and protested that they would 'believe as our fathers believed'. Perhaps like many, his was a confusion of mind in what must have seemed an apocalyptic situation or perhaps in his dealings with Brother Gilbert he was merely being opportunistic!

The news of the events which took place in Edinburgh during August, travelled fast and on the day after the Confession of Faith was adopted, the somewhat quaintly named Dionysius Elphinston of Henderstoun, standing in the porch of what remained the Church of St Andrew, publically announced to anyone listening, that 'no ministration of the Common Prayers to the parishioners of Peebles was performed in the place where it ought to be done' in accordance with the newly approved Confession of Faith, either by the rector or anyone acting on his behalf.

In practical terms, public worship in the centuries old Parish Church had ceased and the parishioners were without a place of worship. Dionysius seemed to have become the leading advocate of the Reformed cause in Peebles, in contrast to his fellow landowner, Lord Borthwick who still hankered after the old order. Elphinston went on to announce that until such time as the rector or someone acting on his behalf, preached the Gospel to the parishioners in accordance with what was the new order, he would not feel obliged to make any payments of teinds to the rector or his factors.

In the general confusion, many of the former clergy in order to protect themselves from the risk of confiscation of the properties, which they relied on as a source of income, took steps to dispose of them. For example, the Dean of Peebles, who enjoyed the revenues of the Deanspark sold off the property in exchange for an increased feu-duty payable in perpetuity.

Peebles was now without a minister and the Ordinances of the Church and on 20th November 1560 it was decided that the town's baillies should go to Edinburgh, with the request that the Lords of the Congregation provide them with a preacher and minister. They seem to have met with instant success, for only a week later on 28th November, the magistrates met in the Tolbooth to appoint John Dickson to the Kirk of Peebles. John Dickson was thus the first Reformed minister of Peebles and the sole representative of Church authority.

In theory at least, the authority of the Pope in Peebles, was at an end, as elsewhere in Scotland. Any remaining clergy, who clung to Catholicism were removed together with Mass books and altars, which were probably destroyed. As Dr Gunn records:

> The work which had for centuries carried on in the Parish Church, with its eleven Altars by dean, rector, curate and twelve chaplains, and choir of men and boys and at St Mary's Chapel was now abandoned. The minister alone was to discharge the sacred office, and carry on the whole religious duty of the parish. To enable this to be done a service of a very much simpler form was necessary ; or rather, because the new Order was of so simple and severe a nature, one clergyman was considered sufficient to perform its offices.

The congregation essentially remained the same, the "common weal" of Peebles. They were however, without a proper place of worship. The parish church, the Church of St Andrew, was a ruin, as it had been since it suffered from the destruction of English invaders in 1549 and in December 1560, the town council presented a petition to the Lords of the Congregation on behalf of the burgesses and townsfolk asking that the Cross Kirk be granted to them as the Parish Church. The petition explained that St Andrew's could not be rebuilt at reasonable cost or in reasonable time. They were in urgent need of a church where they could hear the Word of God preached and have the sacraments administered. They also pointed out that the Cross Kirk, the church of the Trinity Friars, was in good order, spacious and very suitable as a Parish Church. They would however, require to refurbish it and remove all traces of idolatry. It was perhaps at that time that the statue which Dr Gunn thought might have stood in the niche at the south west corner of the Cross Kirk may have been destroyed.

The petition was granted on 7th December and it was a few days later when the bailies and town council went to the Cross Kirk to meet with Brother Gilbert Broune, who, as yet, was still the Minister of the Trinity Friars. They read the petition to him and the letter confirming the grant.

The compliant Brother Gilbert (he had little option!), seems to have accepted the situation with such grace as he could muster and agreed to give possession of the church to the bailies acting on behalf of the parishioners, but he said he did so on condition that the current annual rents and profits receivable by the monastery and convent, would continue to accrue to him and the monastery and convent, as opposed to the church itself. It was clearly his intention that the former friars should continue to occupy that part of the building. It was apparently agreed and confirmed in a document witnessed among others, by Dionysius Elphinston, who somewhat strangely, in view of his participation in the agreement with Brother Gilbert, then put forward a petition on behalf of the landward parishioners, refusing to accept the Cross Kirk as their Parish Church, not withstanding that it was to be acquired at no cost. The petitioners also demanded the appointment of a minister or deputy to provide the service of Common Prayers and the Sacraments, in accordance with the custom and practice of the Church of Scotland, as now established. Although he appears to have been wholly unqualified for that role, Dionysius put himself forward, because he was unaware of the appointment of any suitably qualified minister by the Lords of the Congregation or the parishioners.

It is difficult to understand what was behind the petition. St Andrews was a ruin and likely to remain so, while the actual distance between the two churches was negligible and the Cross Kirk was only a little further from the landward areas. It does however, show that the situation was far from settled. The list of witnesses to the petition document, including the dean and the Master of Yester, does indicate that the leaders of the old order had now accepted the Reformed order. There is also a suggestion that personal interest was involved, and that the Master of Yester was acting on behalf of his father, who claimed to have an option on the property of the Cross Kirk, which would be prejudiced by its transfer. In any event, on the same day, he made a public protestation to the bailies, in the tolbooth of Peebles, claiming that if the Cross Kirk become the Parish Church of Peebles, it should not prejudice a prior agreement made with Brother Gilbert Broune. The role of Dionysius Elphinston is even more obscure, although he may have been secretly persuaded to act in the interest of the Hay Family interest in property adjacent to the Cross Kirk.

It was on the orders of the Lords of the Congregation that the Magistrates received the keys of the outer door of the Cross Kirk from Brother Gilbert Broune on that day of 11th December 1560, thus finally completing its transformation as the Reformed Parish Church. Although there was no doubt a confusion of minds and conflict of allegiances on the part of many, the first part of the Reformation in Peebles, as in much of Scotland, was at least officially now complete.

That is not the end of the story. In the immediate aftermath, there was much to settle and quite a lot to dispute. There were those who naturally, tried to preserve their former position, at least in regard to their material and financial well being. Among them, not least were the few remaining incumbents of the former monastery of the Cross Kirk. Then there were those who sought to take advantage of the opportunity to acquire property and revenues previously payable to the various religious institutions in the town. They were doing no more than many in Scotland who saw a great opportunity for personal aggrandisement. As we have seen, perhaps in anticipation of an inevitable change, Brother Gilbert Broune and the Master of Yester had already come to an accommodation, although it was one which would later be disputed and only finally settled during the reign of James VI.

The situation in which Brother Broune and his brother friars found themselves at the beginning of 1561 can hardly have been comfortable. Of course they would have been well aware of the increasing influence of Knox and his followers, supported by the Lords of the Congregation. They would have been aware that magistrates of the burgh were in touch with the Reformist authorities in Edinburgh. They would have been aware that more than twenty years earlier, following the passing in England of the Act of Supremacy in 1534, King Henry VIII had himself replaced the Pope as Head of the Church in England and between 1536 and 1541 had conducted a campaign of suppression of the monasteries, convents, priories and friaries. More immediately they had been forewarned by the visit of Lord Maxwell and his armed retinue and also by the emissary of Lord Borthwick. None the less when the final blow came, it must have been traumatic. They were men and possibly women, who had been sheltered, fed, clothed and nurtured both materially and spiritually, by an all embracing Church which had determined every aspect of their lives. So what were they to do? On the evidence of the records it would seem that they were not accepted into the new faith, certainly not in any clerical capacity. They no longer conducted worship or the ordinances of religion. It was now the sole preserve of the minister, appointed by the Lords of the Congregation. Those were difficult times!

In the meantime the effects of reformation were beginning to bite throughout Scotland. In Peebles the final act of the destruction of Papal authority and the establishment of the Protestant Church of Scotland in accordance with the Confession of Faith, had been the handing over the keys of the outer door of the Cross Kirk to the magistrates of the burgh by Brother Gilbert Broune.

The very next day, some corn lying in a yard in the Old Town, which belonged to the former archdeacon and rector of Peebles was removed by John Dickson, now appointed as minister of Peebles. He claimed that it was so he could sell it and use the proceeds as part of the stipend to which he was entitled as the Minister of the reformed church. The corn was the most readily accessible of the goods belonging to the former Roman Catholic Church. However, Dickson had acted a little too hastily. Two of the towns' burgesses, who must have sympathised with the former clergy in their predicament and probably still supported the old order, came forward and acted as surety for the value of the corn, which was returned to the former owners.

The appointment of John Dickson as "minister" was short lived. Within a matter of days the bailies were instructed to approach the Lords of the Congregation to appoint a new minister 'to shew the true word of God', which would suggest that he was not sufficiently qualified or perhaps, it was just that as an incomer he did not go down well with the folk of Peebles.

It took some time to resolve, but on 5th February 1561, what was effectively the first kirk session of the parish of Peebles was appointed when the magistrates and community elected ten elders and eight deacons. The kirk session in turn, then elected John Allan (also spelt Allane) as minister, his admission being confirmed by John Willock, Superintendent of Glasgow. It is noteworthy that they also sought the endorsement of the appointment by John Knox, Superintendent of Edinburgh.

John Dickson, does not disappear from the scene, because a year later he was admitted as "reader and exhorter" by John Willock. That was effectively a role as assistant to the minister, able to conduct ordinary worship, but not the sacraments. It probably is confirmation that his earlier replacement was due to his lack of appropriate qualification.

February 1561 was a time of great activity and iconoclasm. The symbols of Roman Catholicism, altars, images and vestments were removed or destroyed. Centuries later the ancient pre Reformation stone font, which is now in the Old Parish Church, was unearthed when the foundations of the Tweedside Mill were being excavated in the 1920s. Although its original location is not known, it is likely that it was removed and dumped at this time.

As St Andrews was no longer the Parish Church the bailies and council instructed the town treasurer to arrange for its two bells to be removed. One was re-hung in the Cross Kirk, while the other was laid up in the Tolbooth and eventually sold in 1564. In March the same year, it was decided that all the remaining vestments should be sold by auction, with the proceeds to be distributed among the poor of the town. Bearing in mind the number of clergy and others who would have worn them, it would have amounted to a sizeable quantity. A "committee", headed by one, James Tweedy, and seven others was formed to draw up a list of those most in need. The money raised was to be distributed at their discretion. The linen cloths which had been used in the former Roman Catholic services had already been taken to the steeple and on 16th October 1562 the council ordered James Wilson and John Dickson to give these to poor people to be used in any way they wanted. This is probably the same John Dickson who had been appointed "reader and exhorter"

In his *Glimpses of Peebles*, Rev Alex Williamson mentions that as late as 1564, there were still ornaments, jewels and vestments in "Chapelhill", in which Brother Broune and several of the Trinity Friars had an interest. Dr Gunn also seems to have been aware of this. It may be that there never was a "chapel" as such there. It seems probable that in the twelfth century what became known as Chapelhill formed part of the endowment of the chapel of the castle of Peebles. There is evidence that the chapel, together with the land at Chapelhill was granted by David I to the abbey of Kelso in whose hands it remained until the mid sixteenth century, about the time of the reformation. The Royal Commission on the Ancient and Historical Monuments of Scotland makes reference to the building which was by then in place at Chapelhill, about one kilometre north of Peebles, being where 'ornimentis, westmentis and jewellis' belonging to the Cross Kirk may have been stored, which broadly accords with what Williamson recorded. It does however appear likely that the building in which they were stored was a small tower house, built at about that time which was later incorporated into what is now Chapelhill farmhouse.

A short time later on December 10th, 1563, the council decided that one of the chalices which been placed for safety in the tolbooth should be melted down and sold and that the proceeds should be used in what ever way the bailies might decide best.

Brother Gilbert Broune did not retire gracefully. On 13th February 1562, John Dickson, now Reader and Exhorter, appeared before the town's baillies to report that he had summoned Brother Gilbert to appear before the newly established kirk session the following Thursday for an examination of his life and doctrine. Brother Gilbert had refused on the grounds that the kirk session were not his masters and had no jurisdiction over him. Dr Gunn comments that it was ironical that the ex-minister of the Cross Kirk and Monastery had been summoned by a Protestant kirk session.

He does however, seem to have appeared before the bailies, sitting as the Burgh Court where he alleged that John Dickson had "back bited" him, to which Dickson responded that Brother Gilbert should show proof, failing which he should be punished for his error.

Brother Gilbert did not have his troubles to seek and was even at odds with his fellow friars. He had granted the income from a tack (or feu-duty) to Robert Murray, who was a burgess of the town, without the agreement of his brethren. They complained that Brother Gilbert had undertaken to ensure that no action was taken which reduced the income to which the brethren were jointly entitled and it had come to their ears that Brother Gilbert had entered into a contract with Robert Murray without their consent. The contract related to the lands of Burnfoot, known as the Third of Milkiston, which had belonged to the Convent, as they said "beyond the memory of man". They protested that, they were entitled to possession of the land and that they would seek a legal remedy. The following year when Brother Gilbert received a payment of £20 Scots from Adam, Bishop of Orkney, redeeming an annual feu-duty for land on the south side of the Tweed at Bridgelands, it was with the consent of the remaining brethren. In May 1564 Brother Gilbert gave an undertaking that in future he would consult with the Brethren 'in all their affairs, pleas, and disputes'. More particularly it related to endowments of the church of Kettins, which had long been a source of income. He agreed that no income or "Fruits of the said benefices, and especially of the vicarage and parsonage of Kettins" should be let to anyone without the consent of the brethren and that if it was, it would be null and void.

As the years went by, Brother Gilbert had further troubles. He was probably still living in part of the cloisters of the Cross Kirk and on the 28th May 1565 he accused John Wille of cutting down some of the ash trees which grew in the grounds, with a saw borrowed from William Kelle, who was a weaver. The charges were strongly denied by both, but Brother Gilbert had somehow obtained a copy of a written statement from one of the baillies which confirmed that the baillie had found evidence of ash tree wood in the house of John Wille. Brother Gilbert alleged that this was the same which had been removed from the Cross Kirk grounds. It seems that no action was taken, possibly because of a lack of sympathy towards the former minister.

On a more positive note, the Privy Council had decided that former Catholic clergy should retain two thirds of their benefices, with the remaining third shared between the new Protestant ministry and the Crown. In the circumstances that was a generous settlement. It seems that in addition to Brother Gilbert, only four former friars remained. He met them in the Cross Kirk on 20th July 1564, to discuss the matters of outstanding pension payments and other related matters. Brother Gilbert must have now been on better terms with his Protestant successors. There remained the ornaments, vestments and jewels at Chapelhill. Brother Gilbert had arranged that the brethren would benefit from any profit arising from their sale and that if the share of benefices due to the Queen was reduced in any way, they would benefit from that also. The caveat was that they were to co-operate with the authorities in future.

Brother Gilbert Broune is last heard of in 1580 when he is named in a charter of 28 July in that year. Dr Gunn, in a final commentary on his life says this :

> ...this is the last of the Last Minister of the Friars of the Cross Kirk. All his life-rents were now terminated. His lines had fallen in stormy times, and his sorrowful destiny had been to witness the downfall of the Romish Church of Scotland, and the Dissolution of the Monastery of which he was the last Romish Minister. There is no record whether Gilbert ever conformed to the New Faith; probably he never did. He did not yield his charge and possessions without a struggle, and when his death came, he does not appear to have left any successor of his own race. He is an interesting historical figure, over whom the distance of time along with his misfortunes have cast a glamour of pathos and of compassion.

An interesting character indeed!

10.

Peebles in the Time of Queen Mary

It is rare for the built environment of any town to come about in a structured way. Development is largely "piece meal" and at any given time what a town or village looks like depends on a process of evolution, often over a long period. That is certainly the case with Peebles. By the mid sixteenth century the town had come a long way from the tents and skin and timber of Roman times. The majority of houses would still be fairly rudimentary, with timber and thatch the principal materials, but there are likely to have been a number of more substantial buildings. There is evidence that there were a number of "bastel" houses[73] in the town. As many as fifteen to twenty are recorded by Chambers as still being in place at the beginning of the nineteenth century.

Those were built of stone, certainly on the ground floor. They were designed to provide protection against intruders, especially raiders attacking the town. The better of them, might have two storeys of stone, with an internal stair, but most two storey houses would be stone on ground level, with the upper storey built of timber and accessed by an outside stair. This form of construction became familiar in the town in later centuries, the last recorded still standing in the high street in the late nineteenth century, the earliest era recorded by photography.

Where did stone come from? Stone quarries? Not from the former castle as suggested by Chambers. All the available evidence suggests that it was mainly constructed of timber. Some perhaps came from Venlaw, which certainly was the source of material for buildings of the eighteenth and nineteenth centuries.

Although there are a great many property transactions recorded in earlier histories, those detailing the actual buildings sold are few and far between. Usually the recorded deeds give little more information than "land and bigging" or "tenement".[74] Renwick does give one or two examples of sales which are recorded during the reign of Mary Queen of

---

73 Partly fortified houses with a vaulted ground floor.
74 Renwick – *Peebles During the Reign of Queen Mary*, pp141/142

Scots and give some idea of the buildings included. One recorded as taking place on 15th July 1555 describes the property as,

> half land and bigging of umquile William Stensome' (half the land and building of the late William Stensone) which included, 'ane chalmer, with ane sellare thair under, land nixt the for houses, with ane hall and keching lyand contigue, done throuch thairto, quill it come to the nether hall, the borne under the said nether hall fra the over cheik of the windo done to the yard, and half the yard thairof, with the pertinentis.
>
> (a chamber or room, with a cellar beneath, land next the houses in front, with a hall and Kitchen adjoining, with access to it, until it reaches the lower hall, the barn under the said lower hall from the corner post of the window down to the yard, and half of the yard)

This is clearly a substantial property. Renwick also quotes the transfer of a property on the south side of the 'Crocegait[75] from Patrick Gowane to his son and heir, James Gowane, on 1st June 1557. This is described as extending to 'Tuede Grene' and comprising :

> the haill foirhous, the haill bitlare, byris, stabill, bernis and yard on the eist side of the clois, corse berne and yard on the fut of the clois, and the new chalmer on the west side of the clois,......with fre ische and entre up throw and done throuch the clois.
>
> (the whole of the front house, the whole buttery, byres, stable, barns and yard on the east side of the close, cross barn and yard at the foot of the close, and the new chamber on the west side of the close,..........with free exit and entry up and down through the close.)

Again this is a sizeable property and what both these descriptions show is that although situated in the centre of the town, there is clearly an element of agricultural activity involved. This can still be seen today in many rural villages, large and small, throughout continental Europe, through rarely now in Scotland.

The word "Sasine" first appears in the records during the fifteenth century. It is the Scots equivalent of the Middle English "seysen" which in turn has its origins in Old French and essentially means "to set". It appears first in a document dated 9 November 1456 as "sessyng". From then on it continues to be used in all references to the transfer of feudal property from one party to another. In common with the practice throughout Scotland, in due course it came to refer to the actual document

---

[75] Now the Eastgate

or deed relating to transfers of property. In 1617, a Register of Sasines was created by an act of the Scottish parliament for every county. It remains in use to this day.

Before 1617, it was usual to complete the transfer by passing "erd and stan" to the new owner. It was literally a handful of earth and stone from the property, which was given over as the symbol that the transaction was completed. Those transfers of property were arranged normally by the bailies. The current owner would pass the property to the bailie, who in turn passed 'erd and stan' to the new owner. The reason for that would seem to relate to the Feudal System. All the land and property in Peebles was originally granted to the burgh by the monarch. In turn, the bailies acting on behalf of the burgh would grant any land and property to individual burgesses. When a property was to be sold or transferred, it was in theory returned to the burgh who then granted it to the new owner.

An early example of one of those transactions is recorded on 18th January 1456 :

It is to remember, the Tysday the xviiij day of the monath Januar the yer of God m cccc and vj, that Mechal Forest has ressyngit with erd and stan a sartan of his land liand on the South Rau anenttis the cors, that is say vp fra the hos that Roben Johnson beget to the He Gat, fra hym and hys arris, liand bethwen the land John Hau on the west part on the ta part and the land of Gyb Darlyn on the est part, on the tother part, in Wyl Mouat hand than beand balhye, and than the sayd balhye gayf grund sessyng with erd and stan of that sartan land and just feftment with half the yard fra the kel don to Sym Conno and Besse hys wif and to the langar leuar of them bath vp throu and don throu. Ther witness, the balyhe Wil Mouat, John Lillay.......
(This is to confirm, the Tuesday the 18th day of the month January the year of God 1456, that Mechal Forest has given up with earth and stone a part of his land lying on the South Row opposite the cross, that is to say up from the house that Roben Johnson built in the High Gait, from him and his heirs, lying between the land of John Hau on the west side on the one hand and the land of Gyb Darlyn on the east side, on the other hand, into Wyl Mouat's hand then being a baillie, and then the said baillie gave the ground sasine with earth and stone of that piece of land and formal title with half the yard from the kiln down, to Sym Conno and Besse his wife and to the longest living of the two of them in all time coming?. Their witness, the bailie Wyl Mouat, John Lilley......)

By the mid sixteenth century, property transactions are commonplace. A number have already been mentioned, particularly examples of those which took place after the accession of Mary Queen of Scots, following the English raids of the "Rough Wooing". By that time the arrangements had become more formalised. While it was still one of the bailies who conducted the transfer arrangements and made the symbolic delivery of earth and stone, the town clerk, who was a notary and normally a priest before the Reformation, attended in his official capacity to record the proceedings in the "Common Book" and to give the new owner a notarial instrument, which was his or her title deed.

One unusual transaction took place on 11th March 1559. A midden "steid"[76]at the Briggait port was to be rouped[77]by public proclamation. Robert Murro wanted to see who would bid the most for the benefit of the common good.

Following the Reformation there appears to have been a formal process for the appointment of those qualified to hold the office of town clerk. Prior to that, the town clerk would have been a priest by virtue of his ability to read and write. In modern times, town clerks, while still in existence as they were until 1975, required to hold a recognised legal qualification, so it is interesting that the appointment and qualifications of one of the first to be appointed as Town Clerk of Peebles is recorded.

He was Sir John Allane (Allan) and had been a chaplain in the former Catholic Church in Peebles. An Act of Parliament required that he undertake an examination to qualify him for the post and on the 29th February 1564 he appeared before the examiners of notaries in Edinburgh. There he produced a document called an "instrument of creation" and also what was called his "protocol book", which seem to have satisfied the examiners as he was admitted and authorised to practise as a notary by the Lords of Session, acting under royal authority. According to Renwick, his admission is recorded in the official register. There he is described as 'notare publict, and commoune clerk of the burgh of Peebles' of 45 years of age, unmarried, born within the burgh of Peebles, within the 'diocy of Glasgow' and that in November 1546 he had been appointed as a notary public, under papal authority. Thereafter he took a prominent part in the affairs of the burgh.

As well as transfers of ownership as such, borrowing against the security of property was quite common. In the present age when this is commonplace, it may come as a surprise that the practice is in fact an ancient one. The procedure was somewhat different, however. Instead of there being one deed, conveying the property to the lender, with provision for re-conveyance once the loan is repaid, two documents were involved.

---

76   A walled dung heap
77   Sold by auction

The first conveyed title of the property absolutely, while the other bound the lender to renounce his title on payment of an agreed redemption price. In days when major financial transactions are made electronically, the method of repayment may seem somewhat bizarre. Before the Reformation, the lender would be required to deposit the redemption payment on a specified altar of one the town's churches.

In one case in 1546, Edward Gawane had borrowed from James Gawane and was required to deposit the sum due on the high altar of the Chapel of St Mary, at the west end of the High Street. He was required to do so on the appointed day "betwixt the sone rising and ganging to of that ilk". Provision had to be made against the possibility that the lender failed to come to collect what was due to him, so the deed of redemption stipulated that in the event that James Gawane or his representatives failed to collect it, after he had received due notice, Edward would none the less be entitled to full restitution of his property and the money deposited would be passed to the safe keeping of one of the baillies, who would account to James for the amount paid and any interest which accrued thereafter.

There was a bit of a difficulty following the Reformation, because of course, the altars which might have been specified, no longer existed and so could no longer be used as a depository. Old habits die hard and in practice the former arrangements continued, although the deeds would specify a church, but no longer a particular altar. There was a further problem in respect of contracts entered into before the Reformation where redemption became due after. That was further complicated in the case of redemptions due to be made on one of the altars of St Andrew's Church. Since December 1560 it had ceased to be the parish church, which was now the Cross Kirk. St Andrews did continue to be used by some members of the community, although it had fallen into a fairly ruinous state. An example as to how it was dealt with appears in the protocol book of John Allane, the town clerk It records that on 31 March 1564 a representative of Dionisius Elphinstoun, had warned someone with a right of redemption to appear in the Church of St Andrew 'in the place where the altar of St Andrew, the apostle formally stood', to receive the payment of 100 merks due to them. Perhaps, as earlier noted, that is why Dionisius was keen to retain an interest in the ruinous building?

Not much is known about trade and industry in Peebles at that time. Many of the burgesses are described as "merchants", but merchants of what? The population of the town itself was probably about 1000/1200 and would have remained at that level since it recovered from the plagues of the fourteenth century. As well as the towns folk themselves there was a sizeable rural population and the whole parish of Peebles probably amounted to some 1500 souls. The majority would have been involved in agriculture to some extent at least. Most households would have owned some livestock; a cow to provide milk, a pig or two to provide pork or ham and almost certainly hens. The better off might also have had a small flock of sheep and a few cattle for beef and hide. Burgesses were entitled to graze their sheep and cattle on the town's common grazings which were extensive. Livestock would also be found within the town itself, often ranging freely through the streets and vennels, to the consternation of the town council, who waged a constant battle to have hens and pigs in particular controlled by their owners. Severe penalties were imposed on the owners of offending animals, including confiscation and slaughter. Most of the livestock was kept primarily to sustain the families of their owners, but sheep did provide products which would have had a wider value and be a source of trade.

There is little hard evidence as to the quality of cattle and sheep or what they might have looked like. The improvements through selective breeding which have produced the animals we know and take for granted today lay far in the future. The first eyewitness accounts of agriculture in Tweeddale appear in the middle of the seventeenth century, but do paint a picture of a pastoral landscape, with good grazing and sheep that are long lived. Cattle are not mentioned, although there were clearly cattle of one sort or another in the vicinity.

One interesting item appears in an extract from Sir John Allane's protocol book which records a valuation of farm stock on 23 April 1557. It relates to the value of stock 'assigned in steilbow' from Robert Hoppringill to Thomas Hoppringill, his son. "Steilbow" was a system whereby the livestock on a tenanted farm was the property of the landlord. An incoming tenant would pay his landlord the value of the stock at the beginning of the "tack" or lease and at the end of the tack would be paid the value of the stock at that date by the next incoming tenant. The system is still in use in modern times. The valuation is usually undertaken by several local farmers or someone suitably qualified. In that case there were six, five of whom were local farmers, all the occupants of farms some of whose names are still familiar; 'George Elphinstone of Mann island' (Mailingsland), 'Alexander Wod of Wormistoun' (Wormiston), 'John Wilsone of Adamland; Thomas Lowys of Haltoun and John Thorbrand of Hairhope' (still as named). The sixth, Arthur Johnkensone is described as a 'burgess of Peebles'. The valuation in question was of 48 Hoggs, at 8s each; 5 score (100) ewes with lambs, at 12s 6d each; 6 plough oxen, at £4 8s 6d each; 6 cows at 5 ½ merks each; 40 bolls (a measure of grain of six bushels – 1 bushel = 8 gallons) of seed oats, 17 bolls of croft oats, at 16s each; 4 bolls of seed barley, at 36s each. For the time it represents a sizeable farming enterprise, but with sheep the predominant part. Note that the valuation included "plough oxen". The working plough horse had still to make its appearance as the regular power for cultivation.

The social history of the town and its inhabitants at that time is little recorded. How did people dress? Earlier during the reign of James II, laws had been introduced which limited more exotic materials such as silk and marten's fur which were the exclusive preserve of the nobility. There is an interesting entry in Renwick's *Peebles in the Time of Queen Mary*, where he records an extract from Sir John Allane's Protocols, describing a bequest of clothes in 1559, which had belonged to Marion Tuedy. Thomas Tuedy acknowledged that under the terms of the bequest and last will of the late Marion Tuedy he had received from John Dicksome, the husband of Marion and her executor, the following items of clothing :

ane pe (gown) begardit (trimmed) with velvet, tua Franch (French) blak kirtillis (a close fitting under garment), bordourit (edged) with velvet and stumpet (finished) with velvet; and pair of blak velvet slevis, lynit with herne (course cloth); ane velvet patelot (ruff), ane uter half of ane worset kirtill without lynyn, ane aprone of lilies (Lille) worset, and silk hat, tua colleris of Holand (Dutch) claith, ane collar of hame maid claith, ane reid crammay (crimson) stomak (breast piece), thre schort fret cursayis (net head dresses), tua sarkkis (Shirts).

Marion and her husband must have been people of some stature in the community as the inventory includes many costly items unlikely to be worn by the common folk. Bearing in mind the earlier reservation of the use of silk and scarlet garments to the nobility or the bailies and burgh officers, the inclusion of a silk hat and crimson stomacher, would suggest that her husband was a bailie, as he indeed was at that time. Note also that they included materials from France and Holland.

While Marion and her husband may have been a cut above their fellow inhabitants, their possessions could not match those of a gentleman of the upper class. When Thomas Hay of Smithfield, the grandson of Lord Yester died at around the same time as Marion, the inventory of his possessions included the following contents of one cabinet:

ane chakker (chessboard) with table men, an hat pasmannit (decorated) about with wyre gold ,ane lynnying sark, ane dowblat (jacket), of canves, ane Franche quhingare (?), ane bag to the pestilat (pestle), ane sward belt, ane payre of bufale hois (buffalo hose), ane pair of blak hois lynit with blew, ane freis cot frenzeit (ringed), ane ledder dowblat, ane payr of yello hois lynit with quhite, ane blak sating dowblat, ane velvet bonet, ane blak takhat dowblat, ane payre of doune velvot schone, ane black freis clok, ane payr of black stemmy (woollen) hois frenzeit with grene silk poyntis, ane tyn lavar, ane basing, ane maryskin cot (coat of Morrocan leather), ane blak ledder, ane payr of blak hois stokkit with velvet, vij (7) yello silk poyntis, ane corten frenzies for curtingnis (curtains), ane dossone of new Franche powder plaittis, ane dossone of cunter futtis (pieces of metal used in counting money), ane dossone of trynseouris (?) …. Ane bufill cot, ane payr of quhite hois, ane grey hud, ande blak riding pe ane pair of slevis of plait.

By contrast an inventory of the possessions of a burgess recorded some years later are rather more mundane. He owned a young horse, a cow and a calf. His clothes a cloak, a coat, breeches, stockings, shoes, garters, a belt, a ruff, a bonnet, a mutch, a napkin and a doublet. He also had a bed complete with sheets, pillows, blankets and bolsters. His furnishings and utensils included a table and table cloth, a dozen serviettes, ten wooden platters, a dozen plates, a dozen spoons, a pint wine measure, a quart measure, a salt vessel, a knife and a cup. Other items included, a cupboard, another table, a meal ark (storage box), a tub, a grape (digging fork), a foot spade and a peat spade, two saddles, a pair of bridles, with a halter and a tether, a sledge, two creels (baskets) for fuel, two creels for refuse, two creels for coal, a harrow and weapons which included a sword and a winger (a short sword).

The magistrates made rules and regulations covering the hiring of servants. It was an offence to contact another person's male or female servant without the express permission of their present employer. If anyone committed that offence, he or she was to be warded[78] for as long the bailies might determine. There is a reference to particular cases in October 1559 when the magistrates declared that it applied specifically to Adam Balkesky, the servant of William Bannerman and to Johne Williamson who was the servant of William Kid. The magistrates were making it clear that their employment by their current masters was to be protected. Once again it is an example of how the public authorities exercised control over much of the minutia of community life and in effect

---

[78] A form of house arrest

provided much of the legal framework which today we expect to be legislated by national government.

The town council did exercise some social welfare. In June 1561, James Douchell was instructed to hand over the keys of the west vault under the Tolbooth to the burgh officers, so that it could be made available to receive 'pure folkis' and those who were decrepit and bedridden. The instruction added that Douchell was to 'red his holis[79] that the ledder[80] in the said holis may be esy tane forth oof the same'. This last part of the instruction is interesting as it seems to suggest that there was a tannery close to the Tolbooth. That seems entirely probable assuming the Tolbooth was at that time still in the Briggait, as it is known that there were one or more tanneries beside the Eddleston Water which flows past the foot of the Briggait.

Although little or no information exists about trade in the burgh, a reference dated 5 February 1561 records that the council instructs the "wobstaris" to annually elect a Deacon. This is the first reference to a weaver's guild which is recognised as being the oldest in Peebles. What it shows is that by that time there was an established industry in the town of sufficient standing to have a special place in its affairs. In later years the Weavers or Websters Guild would earn the right to nominate its Deacon as a member of the Town Council. Earlier in this book, reference has been made to to the "fulling" or "waulk" mill which was established towards the end of the fifteenth century at the east end of Tweed Green, now known today as Walkershaugh. That mill was used to clean and remove impurities as part of the process involved in the making of cloth, so there was clearly an established cloth industry of some sort active in the town by that time. It is likely that most of the final products would have been a fairly course material called "keltour" which was a sort of course woollen cloth, used for everyday clothing by the common folk. Some of the woven cloth no doubt would have been of better quality. Worsted material did exist as the inventory of Marion Tuedy's wardrobe shows. It is likely that the town's merchants, of which there seem to have been a number, would have traded woven cloth further afield.

The presence of tanning facilities suggests that there would have been workers in leather active in the town. There is a reference to the council granting part of the burgh's common land 'lyand betwixt Peblis water and the Auld Mylne dam contenand in lenth and breid saxteen futtis.' in April 1549 to a burgess by the name of James Douchell for a lime pit and a bark

---

79   Vaults
80   Leather

pit which were used in the preparation of hides for tanning. From that brief description, the location would have been on what is now Damdale. Tanneries existed nearby in the vicinity of Cuddyside as late as the nineteenth century. The resulting leather would have had a wide range of uses, not least by cordiners or shoemakers who were quite frequently referred to in the context of market rules, although their trade guild was not officially recognised in the records until 1669.

There are a number of references about that time to malt kilns and their associated works, in documents relating to burgh property. While the more affluent might drink wine, usually imported from France, it is well known that ale was the normal drink of the common folk, because of the health hazards of drinking untreated water. Ownership or access to "kilns" was therefore an essential feature of town living. Many people brewed malt for their own use and had their own kilns. They might hire them out to neighbours, while for others who did not have their own, there were common kilns. Although described as "kilns", they were more likely to be vats which were heated by a fire underneath. One would be used to brew a mixture of grain and water and next to it would be another for drying off the grain which could be used as animal feed. The ground on which they were built was usually burgh property and annual rents were payable to the town's Common Good.

It was during the period when the child queen Mary was in France and her mother, Mary of Guise had been appointed Regent, that a new charter was granted to the town. It is dated 17th December 1554 and was granted and subscribed in the royal burgh by members of the Privy Council, who must have been present for this purpose.[81] It is possible in the circumstances that Mary of Guise, herself was also present.

After referring to the long history of the burgh and the occasions when it had been burned by English raiders, as well as pillage and plunder by thieves and criminals, all the former privileges and freedoms were confirmed. The right to hold two additional fairs each year was granted and all those privileges and freedoms were to be enjoyed in the same way as they were in Edinburgh or any other royal burgh. Previously the one fair authorised by earlier charters had been held on 24th August which was St Bartholomew's Day. The two new fairs were to be held on the 29th

---

[81] Those signing were, John, archbishop of St Andrews; Archibald Earl of Argyll; Gilbert Earl of Cassilis, the Treasurer; Donald abbot of Cupar, Keeper of the Privy Seal; James M'Gill of Rankeiloure Nather, Clerk of the Rolls; John Bellenden of Auchnoule, Clerk of Justiciary and Alexander Levyngstoun of Donypace, Director of Chancery

June, which was the day of St Peter and St Paul and the second on 9th October which was St Dionisius Day.

The charter also confirmed the powers granted for the government of the burgh. Those were the election of a provost, bailies and burgh officers. "Bailies" appear in the records from the earliest times, but the "provost" seems to have come into being comparatively late in the history of many towns. In the case of Peebles the first mention of the name "provost" occurs in a document dated 10th February 1552, but no name is given. The 'provost, bailies, consale and communite' are referred to again on 27 July 1553 and in 1555 John, Lord Hay of Yester, the Sheriff of Peeblesshire is referred to as "the provost". It is probable that he was elected following his return from captivity, after he had been taken prisoner at the Battle of Pinkie Heuch in 1547, together with a contingent of his followers from Peebles. He is generally recognised as the first provost of the royal burgh.

The first record of an election is at Michaelmas on 30th September 1555 when, 'my lord provost was chosing of before be the baillies, counsale and communite, and maid his aith thairapone, conforme to the statutes and acts of the burro lawis.' Robert Renwick comments that the proceedings of the town council are worth noting as they show how jealously the municipal authorities guarded the privileges and freedoms of the burgh.

One of the main functions of a burgh and particularly a royal burgh, was to be a centre for the collection of taxes. Since at least the fourteenth century it had been decreed that all sales of goods and commodities must take place within the bounds of the burgh. However, whether due to lax supervision by the authorities, or a deliberate attempt by some citizens to act illegally, it does seem that some inhabitants of the town described as 'divers unfreemen (not burgesses), chapmen (pedlars), cowparis' (traders) and others, were trading outwith the town, with the result that the crown was losing revenue. In letters of authority granted to the burgh by James V, he recalls the problem caused by them, 'be bying and selling of woll, hidis, skynnis, irne lint (ironed linen), ter (tar), silkis, wyne, spicis, and uthir stapill gudis, and be pakying and pelying (claiming to be a burgess) thairof at kirk mercats and uther places to landwart within the boundis of youre fredome.' The king reiterated that any 'unfreeman' should not 'mak ony privat mercat' anywhere outside the burgh, but must bring everything to the market in the burgh.

Taxes were levied on those goods. Purchase tax and VAT is nothing new. The taxes raised were a major source of the monarch's income. A fixed sum was levied on the burgh and remitted to the royal coffers and locally the magistrates collected the tax on local sales. Any surplus in excess of what was sent to the central treasury, was retained as part of the Common good.

Market days were therefore, an important feature of the town's life. They were busy affairs. The weekly market held in Peebles would be the meeting place for town and country folk. There is a description of one held on the 3rd May 1557, when there must have been a large crowd through which William Russell and his sister Marion had tried forcibly to make their way. This must have caused some resistance and possibly violence which resulted in William appearing before the magistrates where he:

> deponis be his greit aith that he, wes come fra the croce quhen he had bocht ane certane saip, and the mercat was thrang, and nocht knowand quha wes afor him in the mercat, to mak him fre passage and gait, put furth his hand, egling to mak himane gait and for displesour of na ma, nor for violence, bot to thring himself throw the mercat because it was thrang as said is, and culd na utherwayis evaid untuicht, and his sister folland him, sayand – I pray yow get ws rowme that we may haif fre passage for breking of the pig and saip was in hir hand.
>
> (Gave evidence on his great oath that he, had come from the Cross after he had bought some soap, and the market was crowded, and not knowing who was in front of him in the market, in order to clear a way through the crowd, put out his hand, intending to make a path for himself and not meaning to harm anyone, nor intending any violence, but to push himself though the market because it was crowded as already stated, and could not otherwise avoid this without contact, and his sister followed him, saying – I pray you give us room so that we can have a clear path to avoid breaking pig[82] and the soap in her hand)

Nor was it only the men of the town who might cause trouble. An entry in the records for 18 October 1559 relates to 'wives troubling the town'. William Johnsone and Andro Ra are to be put in the "chains", because they have come before the bailies to undergo correction for their wives who caused trouble in the town on the market day and disobeyed the bailies. They are to remain there at the bailies pleasure until they find caution 'that thair wiffis suld nocht truble the towne' or disobey the officers at any time in the future.

While one of the privileges of burgesses was to enjoy a monopoly of trade, their status also brought with it certain obligations. They were required to contribute financially to the Crown, both in times of peace as well as war. In addition in times of national emergency, they could be

---

82   An earthen ware vessel.

called on to provide supplies and provisions for the army and also to take part in the defence of the town itself and be prepared with arms to fend off any attack.

Scotland did not have a standing army at this time, but every able bodied man was potentially a soldier. Training and "wappinshaws"[83] took place regularly and we have already seen that the town was provided with butts for archery practice. There is a report in the records for 1572 of a 'vesying[84] of the wappynis', when 161 men of the town, all of whom are named, turned out on parade, to have their weapons inspected. They included spears, lances, swords, staves and even domestic axes and forks. There were also primitive firearms including matchlocks and hagbuts. Every man was in possession of at least one weapon. The report also lists six bows and a bag for arrows. Thirty men were supplied with helmets and one was fortunate enough to have a shield. It was however, a requirement that every man had a spear and those who could not afford one, were supplied with one by the town. All the inhabitants, whether young or old, capable of carrying weapons were required to be ready to parade in defence of the town and in an emergency, to march to what ever part of the town they were required to do so by the bailies.

Prior to 1569, when a proper encircling defensive wall was built, burgesses were required to keep their outside boundary dykes in good order. They were connected to each other so that a continuous fortification of sorts was in place, although clearly insufficient to keep out a major attacker. There were by this time gates or ports at the town's several entrances, which could be closed against an attack. It is probable that at least three of them would have been fortifications from which weapons could be fired.

At that time and subsequently, the town council made arrangements for the manning of the somewhat limited fortifications. In March 1559 it appointed Patrik Gowane as captain of the watch. He was required to walk round the town to check its defences at nine o'clock in the evening and on through the night until daylight. As watchman he was to accept only the principal householders or an able bodied man standing in for him and to be responsible to the baillies, the council and the community for anyone he appointed. The town treasurer was instructed to 'content him for his panis ane boll of malt, ane burges siluer and tua vnlawis'. In the event of his being absent, he was to provide another man as a substitute until he

---

[83] Parade and inspection of weapons
[84] Inspection

returned and if he failed to do so, he would be required to pay the town double the payment he had received.

The Old Town seems to have remained largely unprotected, possibly because the major buildings were of a religious nature and at that time it was still a religious settlement although then in decline. In any event any major attack would be likely to come from the east, where the New Town stood in its path.

11.
Mary Queen of Scots - Trials and Tribulations

The nineteen year old Mary was now a widow, her sickly husband having died of an ear infection in December 1560. She had been Queen of France (as well as of Scots) for only seventeen months. She was no longer welcome in her adopted country and in any event she had a duty to her own kingdom and returned from France in August 1561.

The country to which she returned was vastly changed from the one she had left as a child of five, thirteen years before. Her mother, Mary of Guise had died the previous year. Together with Cardinal Beaton, who was also now dead, she had fought a rearguard action against the Protestant reformers led by John Knox and the Lords of the Congregation. The Scottish parliament had outlawed the Catholic Church and its practices. The whole body politic of Scotland had changed radically. Whereas before her departure, the Church of Rome was still able to dominate the political as well as the religious spheres, a very different order now prevailed.

The religious authorities still exercised a major influence, but now the Church was a democratic body, with at its head, not an infallible Pope, but a General Assembly composed of representatives from throughout Scotland, many of whom were also members of the Scottish parliament. The financial power of the Church and its ability to accumulate wealth, by honest belief and less honest superstition, was vastly reduced. It was no longer in possession of large and lucrative estates. They were now in the hands of the Crown and the magnates and lairds. Society was more secular, but the Protestant Presbyterian Church of Scotland still commanded huge influence at both national and local level, particularly in matters of morality.

Although it ended in chaos and disaster, the early years of Mary's personal rule were relatively successful and the young queen was generally supported by the people of Scotland, although in those early years there were parts of Scotland, particularly in the north, where she encountered opposition.

In the summer of 1563 she turned her attention to the Borders, when she undertook a progress throughout the south of Scotland. If the records are anything to go by she was a less frequent visitor to Peebles than many of her predecessors, although her son would become a more frequent visitor and supporter of the burgh. Her first recorded visit to the town was on 27th August 1563, when she stayed overnight, probably at Neidpath Castle. The next day she followed the practice of James II and his successors, by granting letters of protection to the burgesses. They were reportedly written in her own hand.

In July 1565, Mary married Henry Stuart, Lord Darnley, who was the son of the Earl of Lennox. It was against all good sense, although perhaps all too characteristic of her and before long she came to regret it. Initially, she seems to have been infatuated by him. He was several years her junior, but behind his youth and handsome appearance was a weak and self indulgent character. By marrying Mary he thought he should have the title and privileges of "King". Mary, for once applying some sense, never granted him the Crown Matrimonial, but in the Scottish court he was referred to as the "King" and accorded the due deference which that title implied, little though he deserved it.

In time he became a more frequent Royal visitor to Peebles than Mary herself, although not necessarily for the best of motives. For Darnley, Peebles became a frequent bolt hole to escape the ire of his increasingly disenchanted wife. He found court life tedious and restricting, but in the country round about and in Peebles itself, a day's ride from the capital, he could indulge in his almost continuous pastimes of hawking, hunting, drinking and wenching together with a dubious band of friends and fellow travellers. "Peebles for Pleasure" is nothing new!

Towards the end of 1565 Mary was pregnant. The birth of an heir would give the child precedence over him and that was something he must have found difficult to accept. He met the queen at Linlithgow at the beginning of December. It was not a happy meeting and shortly after he left for Peebles for yet another round of hunting and carousing.

George Buchanan, the contemporary Scottish historian and in due time the boyhood tutor and tormentor of their son, James VI, inferred that she had deliberately sent the king to Peebles in the depth of winter with only a small retinue and that he nearly died of starvation as a result. Buchanan was one of the greatest critics of the Queen and the royal household. He rarely missed an opportunity to cast her, her husband and those about them in a poor light and his account is probably far from objective. The thought of "King" Henry's discomfort in Peebles no doubt gave him some doubtful pleasure.

Captain Armstrong quotes an extract from Buchanan's history of Scotland:

> Lord Darnly[sic] with his attendants, retired to Peebles, to avoid the fury of the Queen's jealousy, and courtiers envy; but throws an illiberal reflection on the country, which, Buchanan says, was so infested with thieves that King Henry was obliged to remove. Peebles, with its environs, has been particularly adapted for a hunting seat

Robert Brown's Notes to Pennecuik's Works include this apparent apology for the state of Peebles:

> The real, unbiased, state of these facts seems to be, that King Henry, being fond of hunting and hawking, went to his *Royal Hunting Forrest at Peebles*, near which, as we have seen, the hawk used in falconry breeds, in *Glendean's-banks*, as a place much resorted to for sport, to enjoy his favourite amusements; to which he was, even according to Buchanan, so much addicted as to neglect public affairs on their account; taking with him but few attendants, that he might be at ease with himself, and less burdensome on the town. It being a very severe winter; the town being altogether unprepared for his visit, even with the small retinue he had; a quantity of snow happening to fall on his arrival, so as, probably, in a great measure to cut off, in so highland a district, convenient access to their flocks, herds, and other supplies, and leave them exposed to the swarms of Moss-troopers, Gipsies, and Thieves, with which Peebles, of course, in common with all Scotland, was infested, and whose depredations would appear more numerous and heinous than usual from the apparent indigence of the inhabitants, and the want of fuel, and provisions amidst beggars, gipsies, free-booters, and mountains of snow; its pastoral people, thus embarrassed as to their own means of subsistence, it is likely enough, would be unable to entertain others. The King himself, "bred up at court, and used to a liberal diet", would, consequently, as in any other highland town in those days, have been very ill off, had it not been for the accidental arrival of the Bishop of Orkney, who, like a prudent and provident prelate, had taken care to provide against the poverty of the place, by carrying along with him, of the good things of this life.

Dr Gunn records one of Darnley's visits in 1565 which may well be the visit in question and quotes the following from an earlier source :

Darnley was in great hazard of wanting necessities, unless the bishop of the Orcades had casually come hither; for he knowing the scarcity of the place, brought some wine and provisions for his use.

Adam Bothwell was the son of an Edinburgh burgess. Before the Reformation of 1560, he was for a time parson of Ashkirk and one of the canons of Glasgow Cathedral before becoming Bishop of Orkney in 1558. He owned property in Peebles, and would have been well acquainted with the state of the town. The material privation suggested together with Buchanan's report of the lawlessness of the place, hardly paint a flattering picture of Peebles at that time.

Dr Gunn in the same extract, also gives a more likely reason for Darnley's visit at that time :

About Christmas time the Queen's husband was residing in Peebles. The weather is stated to have been exceptionally severe, and much snow fell. The object of the journey appears to have been for the purpose of effecting a meeting between Darnley and his father, the Earl of Lennox, who was out of favour with the Queen at the time. Here is a letter arranging the interview:

Sir, - I have received by my servant Nisbet your natural and kind letter, for which I humbly thank Your Majesty; and as to the contents thereof, I will not trouble you therin, but defer the same till I await upon Your Majesty at Peebles, which shall be so soon as I may hear of the certainty of your going thither. And for that the extremity of the stormy weather causes me to doubt of your setting forward so soon on your journey, therefore I stay till I hear further from Your Majesty, which I humbly beseech you I may, and I shall not fail to wait upon you accordingly. Thus committing Your Majesty to the government and blessing of Almighty God, who preserve you in health, long life, and happy reign, - from Glasgow, this 26th Day of December, - Your Majesty's humble subject and father, MATTHEW LENNOX.

This suggests that the true purpose of the visit was a meeting with his father and as the quoted letter implies this was something which had been envisaged for some time. It is however, further confirmation of Darnley's interest in Peebles.

At the time of the birth of her son James on 15th June 1566, there seems to have been unrest in the Borders. Mary was already heavily involved with the infamous James Hepburn, Earl of Bothwell and had appointed him to exercise royal authority in the Border lands. Following her confinement, on his advice, she decided to hold a series of royal assizes in the area in order to dispense justice and due punishment to the many troublemakers who were the cause of unrest. One was held at Peebles on 13th August, when she called on her subjects in the area to meet her in the Royal Burgh.

The royal couple were apparently reconciled for a brief period and visited Tweeddale, hunting in Ettrick Forest at Megget on the 14th of August and again on the 16th at Rodono and Cramalt. A large number of the nobility was in attendance and no doubt Peebles and its neighbouring villages would have felt the effect of their presence. The sport was poor, due to the scarcity of deer, which was so great that the queen ordered that they were not to be shot. The penalties for non-observance were severe! They then moved on to Traquair on 19th August before returning to Edinburgh by the 21st.

Darnley was murdered in February 1567, blown up by a massive explosion of gunpowder at Kirk O' Fields on the then outskirts of Edinburgh. Whatever loyalty or love the people of Peebles may have held towards the royal couple, his murder seems to have passed without comment. Perhaps in the light of their frequent experience of the debauched and wayward "King", the good folk of the town may have heaved a collective sigh of relief!

Mary's reign did not last much longer. Events moved quickly. In May she married the ambitious Earl of Bothwell. Once again, it was one of Mary's great misjudgements and caused a final rift with a large section of the largely Protestant nobility and not least her half brother, the Earl of Moray, who had earlier been one of her principal advisors. Civil war followed. The rebels led by Moray defeated a force led by Mary herself and Bothwell at Carberry Hill near Musselburgh. Deserted by Bothwell, she was captured by the Protestant Lords and taken to Loch Leven castle where on 24th July she was forced to sign a Deed of Abdication in favour of her infant son who was crowned King of Scots in the Church of the Holy Rude at Stirling just five days later. Moray was appointed Regent.

The story of her escape from Loch Leven is well known. Thereafter her forlorn attempt to regain the crown ended in final failure at the Battle of Langside on 13th May 1568, where her supporters, led personally by her (whatever else Mary may have been, she was no shrinking violet) were heavily defeated. Mary was forced to flee, heading south into Galloway, stopping briefly overnight at Dundrennan Abbey, before crossing the Solway Firth to England, capture and after long years of captivity, execution.

What of the attitude of the townsfolk of Peebles to Mary Queen of Scots? Loyalty to the monarch of the day has been a hall mark of Peebles throughout its history and no doubt the town remained loyal to her, at least for a time. The provost, Lord Yester was certainly a loyal follower of the queen as is surely demonstrated by his presence at Dunbar, when she rode there to be with Bothwell before their marriage and again at Langside, where he fought along side her together with his retainers, who must have numbered among their company some who came from Peebles.

The troubled and ultimately for her, disastrous reign of Mary Queen of Scots had opened with a religious order which had dominated the life of Peebles for many centuries. By its close, the Protestant religion had supplanted the Church of Rome and the spiritual and not least the moral welfare of the community was now in the hands of stern Calvinists. Otherwise life went on much as it had done for decades. Markets and fairs continued as before. The provost, bailies and town councillors continued to be elected annually. Rules and regulations were made, broken and duly punished. Weavers weaved, tanners tanned, cordiners made footwear and merchant burgesses plied their trade from Peebles across Tweeddale and beyond.

The reign of her son which followed would see the last monarch to visit the royal burgh for more than three hundred years. It also was to be a reign which recognised the past privations, but also the loyal service to the crown of the folk of Peebles.

12.

Law and Order restored

The monarch who succeeded Mary as James VI was a one year old child, yet he would become one of the most significant in the history of the United Kingdom of Great Britain and Ireland. James Stuart, the sixth of that name as King of Scots, would in time succeed to the throne of England, Wales and Ireland as James I.

The start of his reign was far from straight forward, following the enforced abdication of his mother. Throughout its long history, certainly since the days of Alexander III, the good people of Peebles and their leaders, had been loyal servants of the Crown, but there continued to be a struggle for power between those who still supported the deposed Queen and those who supported her son. To all intents, it was civil war. So, to which crowned head should that loyalty be given? The situation was further complicated because a succession of regents ruled over Scotland, from the time when James, metaphorically, ascended the Scottish throne in July 1567 (in later years he could not remember a time when he had not been king), until he assumed personal rule in 1578.

Not only had there been a traumatic transfer of royal power, but it came shortly after an equally traumatic and radical change in the governance of the Church and religious practice and belief. Minds were confused. The Scottish parliament had ratified the reformed Church of Scotland on 15 December, 1567. It was an uncertain time, when inevitably in those days national government had yet to evolve the structures which would bring order to society in later years. Lawlessness and near anarchy were once again taking hold on the Borders.

The Burgh itself was not immune to trouble and strife. As William Chambers commented :

Unhappily, while the whole district of country from the Merse to Dumfriesshire was a scene of disorder, the general dissensions were imitated on a minor but no less rancorous scale by the burgesses of Peebles, who among themselves scolded, quarrelled, and fought, used towards each other opprobrious epithets in open council, constantly disagreed about rights to common property, and at times, out of malice or an inclination for plunder, committed crimes which brought them to the scrutiny of the higher courts.

There were many family feuds, often involving local lairds, which resulted in violence, sometimes ending in the most serious consequences, if the protagonists happened to meet in the burgh. On a fine summer's day in July 1572, just such an encounter had a tragic end. John Dickison of Winkstoun was attacked and murdered in the High Street, yet no one saw the attackers or at least came forward as witness and no one was ever punished for the crime. There were five suspects, who were tried at the High Court of Justiciary held a few weeks later, but all were acquitted. Dickison and his father William had been in dispute with the burgh some years earlier over boundaries. John had actually become a well respected member of the community and had been elected as a baillie, but none the less he seems to have been a troublesome individual. The earlier dispute must have been revived and his resulting unpopularity was probably the cause of that somewhat extreme end to the matter. He is referred to at a much later time of violent trouble as the "provost" of Peebles, but there is no evidence to support this, as the provost at the time of his murder was William Lord Hay of Yester who had been elected in 1572. It is possible that he may have been the most senior Baillie and that he deputised for the elected provost on occasions.

There had been a long standing feud between the Tweedies of Drumelzier and the Veitchs of Dawyck. In June 1590 Patrick Veitch was set upon by a band of Tweedies and their associates, the Crichtons and killed as he rode home. He had been seen in Peebles by James Tweedy of Drumelzier who saw an opportunity to destroy one of his traditional enemies. Together with five members of his family, two Crichtons and one Porteous, he planned to ambush the unfortunate Patrick. They divided into two parties, one going ahead to block the route at the narrow pass opposite Neidpath Castle and the other to follow up behind. Nine of the Tweedy faction against one Veitch was hardly a contest. Although the Tweedies were imprisoned for a time, they were never brought to justice, but that was not the end of the matter. The Veitches, no doubt assuming that no action would follow, took the matter into their own hands. Four days after the murder, one of the assassins, John Tweedy, was walking in the High Street of Edinburgh, where he was met by two relatives of the murdered man. A fight broke out and Tweedy was killed. The long Mafia-like feud between the families continued for many years until the King, writing to Lord Dunfirmline and the Lords of the Privy Council in March 1611, demanded that they took action to stop the feud and enforce a reconciliation between the two warring parties.

In 1595 a somewhat remarkable duel took place at Edston Haugh, some two miles west of Peebles between Brown of Hartree and George Hepburn. They were both members of the household of James, Lord Hay of Yester. It appears that permission for the duel to take place was given by the king himself. Both men were mounted and armed with swords and spears. The winner was Hepburn, who had been the challenger. Brown was knocked from his horse and as was the custom on such occasions, Hepburn had his honour and reputation vindicated. Brown refused to admit any fault and Hepburn could have killed him, but was persuaded to spare his life. None the less, Brown swore he would be avenged and maintained his hatred of his enemy for many years thereafter until reconciled in 1605, only after he was summoned to appear before the Privy Council (it must have been a serious matter!) where Brown eventually said that, 'Albeit he had borne feud against Hepburn in time byegone he was content, in obedience to the council, to be reconciled with him, and gave his oath that from his heart he remitted Hepburn all rancour, and should never quarrel with him thereafter, and took him by the hand , and were reconciled together.'[85]

The Earl of Moray, bastard son of James V and half brother of Mary had been an exile in France towards the end of her reign, but returned before the final chapter was played out. He had been instrumental in persuading (or coercing) Mary to abdicate and had been appointed Regent. On 10 October 1567, he issued a proclamation that the nobility and civil authorities of the area should meet him at Peebles on 8th November of that year. That was primarily to deal with thieves and reivers causing trouble in Annandale and Eskdale. It was going to be a major visitation on the town. Moray ordered that the town should have ready bread, brown ale, horse meat and meat for men and all necessary provisions to be provided to the King's lieges at the crown's expense. Lodgings were also to be provided. All was to be ready by the 8th November. However, although everything required had been provided, the payment due seems to have been delayed, because in January 1568, one of the bailies accompanied by a burgess were appointed to go to Edinburgh, "for the silver" which was due.

Later in 1568 and again before Michaelmas in 1569, Moray wrote to the provost and bailies, urging them to use all their available financial resources to build a proper defensive wall round the town to 'resist the invasioun of thevis' . The town council complied shortly thereafter. There was a degree of urgency and on 2nd March 1569 it was decided that the work must be progressed and if the full council was not present when the

---

85   As quoted by Dr Gunn, Book of the Cross Kirk, p 48

final decision was made, then the decision could still be taken provided there were six councillors present. It appears that that Bailie Stene Robeson had previously offered to carry out the work but it seems that the council wanted to appoint someone else. Bailie Robene was the tenant of the town's mills and the council offered to extend his lease for three years and pay him sixteen pounds annually, by way of compensation. Even in those days, conflict of interest was recognised, because he was suspended from the council until such time as a final decision was made. In the event he must have accepted the offer, because the council then instructed Sir John Allane to draw up a contract with Thomas Lauder to undertake the necessary construction. Sir John has been mentioned previously as the first clerk to be appointed following the Reformation. He had fallen out of favour for a few years, but had now been reinstated. It appears that as well as acting in his capacity of clerk, he was also to be allowed to be a partner with Thomas Lauder.

The contract required that a wall should be built round the town and completed within four years. According to Chambers and Dr Gunn, it was to be four "ells" high. However that must be a mistake, because the name "ell" derives from an old Germanic source. It is a unit of measurement, representing the length from a man's elbow to the tip of his fingers, approximately eighteen inches or forty five centimetres. Four ells would therefore be less than two meters high, which seems unlikely. However, the word which appears in the original contract in old Scots is "elne". This is an old Scottish unit of measurement of about thirty seven inches or ninety four centimetres, which would make the wall height just under fourteen feet or four and a quarter metres, which seems much more probable. The breadth was to be three and a half feet or just over a metre. It was to have blockhouses or towers with shot holes at certain points.

In payment the two partners were to receive the profits of the two corn mills in the town and the waulkmill and associated land for the next thirteen years. The payment of the profits was to begin at Beltane (May). In addition the contractors were to receive 200 merks annually for thirteen years.[86] The town was to provide 200 loads of lime before Easter and a similar quantity each year for four years. As far as stone was concerned,

---

[86]   The merk was not a coin but a unit of value equal to two thirds of a £1 Scots. In the records of the time monetary values are usually quoted as merks or £1 Scots. At that time the value of the £1 Scots measured against £1 English had fallen from £4 Scots equalling £3 English towards the end of the fourteenth century, to £6 Scots to £1 English. It would decline even further to £12 Scots to £1 English by the beginning of the seventeenth century.

the new wall would have used material from the existing head dykes, but it would have had to be augmented from other quarried material, which the partners would have had to have provided. Fragments of the wall and the blockhouses remain today in the Eastgate car park and on the Post Office Brae.

Moray visited Peebles in person on 20th December 1569, when he gathered a force from the southern counties to oppose an army led by the earls of Northumberland and Westmoreland, who were in revolt against the English crown and were looking for a safe haven north of the border. Moray had had a great deal of support from Elizabeth I in his rebellion against Mary Queen of Scots and felt consequently obliged to support the English queen. His regency was fairly short lived as he was murdered on 23rd June 1570, in a street in Linlithgow where he was shot by a member of the Hamilton faction, which was still supporting the deposed queen. He was succeeded as regent by the Earl of Lennox, the grandfather of the young king, who continued to encourage the building of the town wall.

There was of course the question of cost. Following the Reformation, the disposal of the furnishings and other possessions of the former Roman Catholic Church was a matter of some controversy. It included some of the contents of the church buildings known as "kirk graith". Prior to his death, Moray had said that all the proceeds of this kirk graith should be used to meet the cost of building the wall and in a letter to the council of 11th September 1570, Lennox reaffirmed that. Steps were taken by the council to implement the instruction but the problem was that quite a significant amount of kirk graith had already been removed by means that were not entirely legitimate. So the council demanded that anyone who had acquired former church property in that way, should hand it over to the council for the Common Good. Among the culprits were John Horsburgh and Patrick Newtoun who were on the leet at the time for election as baillies. That produced a protest from William Dickison, who was also a candidate, who said that if either of them was elected, it would be in clear disobedience of the regent's instruction. As a result John Horsburgh, admitted that he had received part of a chalice from James Tweedy, the town's treasurer, but that he was prepared to pay for it. Quite what Tweedy was doing with it is not explained, although he did say he had been compelled to give it to Horsburgh as he was of greater seniority in the burgh. There seems to have been other offenders as well and finally on 24th May 1571, the council ordered that anything illicitly acquired should be handed back or paid for. That was finally successful, because on the 5th December orders were given to start construction of the wall the next day, to raise the existing head dykes and to complete the work as far as possible with existing materials, some of them coming from the ruined parts of the Cross Kirk. It may have included the original chancel which was probably removed at that time.

The immediate aftermath of Moray's death was a time of uncertainty, when once again cross border raids disturbed what was in any case a fragile peace. The Earl of Westmorland, who had rebelled against the English queen, Elizabeth, aided by the Border lairds of Buccleuch and Ferniehurst, had crossed the border and attacked forces loyal to the queen, with the usual fire and sword. In response, English forces retaliated, causing death and destruction in the Merse and Teviotdale. It alarmed the towns folk of Peebles and in February the town council ordered that there should be a watch kept each night. As the new wall was as yet incomplete, the head dykes were to be immediately repaired. All strangers were to be barred from entry to the town and if the town bell was rung, everyone was to assemble. In March those precautions were strengthened by the posting of watches outside the burgh bounds, who were to keep an outlook from 'glomyng' until sunrise. They were to be armed with a steel bonnet, a jerkin, a spear and a sword and buckler. Later in the month six gunners were to be hired.

Early in 1571 the town was ordered to raise men to provide reinforcements for the army which the regent[87] was raising in defence of the king's party. It was to assemble at Glasgow on 14th February. However, showing lingering support for the deposed queen and her cause, the bailies and townsfolk showed little enthusiasm and decided instead to apply to be relieved of that duty and be allowed to 'byde at hame'. As with the transition from Catholicism to Presbyterianism, it shows that the town might not as yet have been entirely supportive of the government of the day.

The following September, underlining that the struggle between the supporters of the deposed queen and her son was by no means over, in a raid on Stirling by a group of men still loyal to Mary, Lennox was murdered. He was succeeded by the Earl of Mar and an attempt was made to finally establish where the allegiance of Peebles lay. In September 1572 a deputation consisting of two of the bailies and three of the town's burgesses travelled to Leith, where they appeared before the Regent Mar and the Lords of the Secret Council and at least acknowledged 'the King's majestie for thair onlie Soverone'. They gave assurances that they would have nothing to do with 'traitouris and notorious rebellis'. The

---

[87] Lennox

provost was not a member of the deputation, which perhaps illustrates that loyalties in the town remained divided to a degree. However, it seems that the majority of the towns folk did approve the initiative and when the delegates returned the relevant document was endorsed by the council as confirmation of the town's obedience to the king 'as dewtifull subjects'.

Although Peebles had made clear where it stood, the wider conflict was by no means settled. The security of the town was still a major issue and as the threat of attack from either of the competing factions was still very real, steps were taken to further improve the town's defences. On 19th May 1572 every able bodied man in the town was called upon to appear, complete with armour and weapons in a great "wappinschaw". They were to be in possession of a spear and those who were too poor to own one, were to be supplied at the town's expense.

At the start and finish of each night and morning watch, 'the drum was to be struck by Robert Thomson, tavernour'. At any other time when the drum or "common bell" sounded, every male in the town able to carry arms, was to assemble at any place in the town which the baillies might decide upon and they were to do so in their 'best and most honest substantious manner'. The need to protect the town and its inhabitants from danger from whatever source was a very real concern. and as Dr Gunn records, on 28th May 1572:

Orders were made regarding the fortifications of the town. One man was appointed who was to shoot the artillery from the east Wark, and another to superintend the gunpowder. Another man was appointed to walk nightly upon the bartizan of the East Wark, and keep watch from thence. The east port to be closed from nine at night until five in the morning...............A new gate was to built in the new wall out of the readiest of the Kirk timber, beginning on the morrow. All through the summer these precautions were continued and in the autumn they were increased. The watches, both by night and day, were augmented, and men appointed to walk outside the north gate, at which the expected trouble might come....................The clock was to be made to strike nightly, and to ring curfew, twelve and six respectively. All the gates and their wickets were to be closed in daylight, and opened also at daylight in the morning; and the key of each to be in the keeping of a different man. All who leaped the wall were to be put in irons for twenty-four hours for the first fault; banished for the second ; executed for the third. All barn doors were either to be reinforced or else condemned under penalties. One man out of every house ordered to convene at seven in the following morning, and assist in heightening the wall.

Those precautions do not seem to have been wholly successful. The threat was not just from the warring supporters of the king or the deposed queen, but also from the many roving bands of robbers. Dr Gunn notes one example:

> Nothing certain is known now, but on January 6, 1572, they (the council) inhibited Harry Thomson for all time coming from being found within the liberties of the town of Peebles; because it was notoriously known that he was at the plunder of the town of Peebles on the 27th day of March last.

Mar had tried unsuccessfully to bring an end to what was civil war. He died in October 1572, it was said of a broken heart, 'because he loved good peace and could not have it.' He was succeeded by James Douglas, 4th Earl of Morton, one of the least pleasant characters in Scottish history. Morton was a "strong man", ruthless and competent, but also personally avaricious. He was recognised as leader of the Protestant faction and through force of character, unpleasant as it may have been, he was able to re-impose a measure of order in Scotland. Under his regime the civil war which had rumbled on for six years since the queen had been forced to abdicate, was finally brought to an end.

To achieve that, Morton needed the backing of a strong army. On 16th July 1574 he issued an order that all able bodied men aged between 16 and 60 living in the Sheriffdoms of Lanark, Peebles and Selkirk, were to assemble at Peebles on the 26th July. They were to come with food and provisions for four days and thereafter to accompany him 'and attend upoun service, under pane of tynsall of lyfe, landis and gudies', that is loss of life, lands and possessions. He was clearly serious about the matter. Morton, being the man he was, this was no idle threat!

Morton's regency effectively came to an end in 1581, when the young king, James started to rule in person. Not long after he was executed for treason in 1581. Although Morton had brought about a measure of peace and stability, the almost endemic lawlessness of the Borders was never very far beneath the surface and in 1583, four of the notorious Border clans, Johnstones, Grahams, Elliots and Armstrongs combined to carry out a raid on Peebles. They must have caused a great deal of damage, because a complaint was lodged by the town with the Convention of Royal Burghs, who in turn appointed commissioners to take the complaint to the king, which had been put before them 'be the toune of Peiblis anent the greit injuris done to theme' by the four named clans and sought 'quhat redres may be ressonabliest obtanit thairof.'

The first positive reference to James' presence in Peebles is in April 1585, when all the inhabitants aged between 16 and 60, were ordered to meet the king or his deputy there on 2nd May. Buchan described it as a 'formidable gathering' as it almost certainly would have been. It was called because of the continuing feuds between the Border families and crimes committed on the borders and especially by Robert Maxwell, natural brother of John, Earl of Morton and others. Over the years of his reign, James was largely successful in imposing his authority on the Borders. Peebles became a regular place of meeting and he was again in the town in 1592 and 1593, planning the pursuit, apprehension and punishment of those who flouted Royal authority.

In February 1587 the troubled life of Mary Queen of Scots came to an end when she was executed at Fotheringay Castle after long years of imprisonment by Queen Elizabeth of England. James reigned supreme over most of Scotland and not least the Borders. The age old loyalty of the Royal Burgh to the Crown was no longer in doubt. It was a loyalty which James would recognise and reward in later years.

In religious affairs the burgh had elected a body of elders and deacons in 1561, which in due time would constitute what was to become the Kirk Session. The General Assembly of 1580 had created "presbyteries" for the first time, but as late as 1582 none had been established in Tweeddale, which as the Assembly of that year noted, was due to the lack of qualified ministers within the shire, but in 1583 a new "synod" was created joining together Dunbar, Chirnside, Melrose and Peebles.

While there may have been a general lack of qualified ministers, that did not however, apply to Peebles. It has already been noted that following the decision of the Scottish parliament to remove the authority of the Pope and effectively outlaw the Roman Catholic Church, John Dickson had been appointed as the first Reformed minister of Peebles. His appointment was made by the Lords of the Congregation in Edinburgh, with the appointment subsequently endorsed by the town council of Peebles. However, the first minister to be ordained as the Minister of Peebles, was Thomas Cranstoun who was called to Peebles in February 1570. He had previously been the minister of Liberton and was inducted at Beltane 1571 and had the responsibility of conducting the sacraments throughout the whole of Tweeddale. His stipend was 200 merks annually, which was worth £134 Scots and £22 English. It would have been paid out of that part of the former revenues of the Roman Catholic church, which had been provided for in the Reformation settlement by the Privy Council which had decided that one third of the former benefices should be used to meet the stipends of ministers of the new Presbyterian order. In the case of Peebles that was confirmed when it was agreed in April 1571 that Cranstoun should receive one third of the parsonage of Manor and Peebles.

Prior to the Reformation, the church lands of Peebles, which were presumably separate from the parsonage, were held by the vicar of Peebles, who was entitled to the benefice or revenues from them. The lands comprised the Glebe and lay on the north west of the Old Town, adjacent to St Andrews Church. The area is known as "Kirklands" to this day. Although the Reformation had ended the practice whereby members of the clergy received revenues from church properties, it seems that some of the former Roman Catholic clergy must still have held property, because in June 1569 Master Thomas Archibald, at that time vicar of Peebles[88]sold the lands to John Wichtman, who was a burgess of the town. The lands which had been in the hands of the Church for centuries have remained in private ownership since then. An act of Parliament required that the manse, together with its outhouses, gardens and three acres of land should be retained. They were ultimately disposed of at a much later date.

A few years later there was a serious problem about the use of the Cross Kirk as the parish church of Peebles. It will be remembered that when it became the parish church in place of St Andrews in 1560, Lord Yester had attempted to prevent that, claiming that he had an agreement with Brother Gilbert Broune, that the property of the Cross Kirk should become his. At that time Yester did not succeed, but it seems that sometime thereafter he had obtained possession, by means fair or foul. As a result the congregation were now worshipping in the Chapel of St Mary in the High Gait (High Street), which had stood there since 1362. However, the presbytery, which had finally been established on 28th April 1597, instructed the minister of Peebles to stop conducting services in the Chapel and to return to the Parish Church[89]the following Sunday. That instruction was to be intimated to the kirk session. The Cross Kirk was used as the place of worship after that, so it must be assumed that Yester acquiesced or was thwarted. In any event the matter was settled by the king, who instructed the granting of a Charter in the same year, under the Royal Seal giving the Cross Kirk to the town as the Parish Church.

Our sovereign lord ordains a charter to be made under the great seal, in due form, making mention that His Highness, after his perfect age, and all

---

[88] An office which no longer exists in the Church of Scotland.
[89] The Cross Kirk

his vocation and the zeal His Majesty bears to the glory and service of God, and to the entertainment of policy and keeping of good order among His Highness' subjects, specially within His Highness' burgh of Peebles, where the Parish Kirk of the said burgh was burnt of long time bypast, in time of war betwixt His Highness' realm and that of England; with advice and consent of his lords of His Highness' secret council and exchequer, has given, granted and perpetually confirmed, and by the tenor hereof gives, grants, and perpetually confirms to the provost, bailies, burgesses, community and inhabitants of His Highness's said burgh of Peebles, and their successors, heritable, all and whole the Kirk called the Cross Kirk of Peebles, with the yards, place, and enclosure adjacent thereto, and all their pertinents lying within the sheriffdom and parish of Peebles, to the effect that the said provost, council, burgesses, community, and inhabitants of the said burgh, and their successors, may sustain, build, and repair, and use the same for the Parish Kirk of the said burgh of Peebles in all time coming. Which Kirk, called sometime the Cross Kirk of Peebles, sometime pertained to the friars of the said Kirk, called the Trinity Friars of Peebles, and their predecessors, and now pertain to our said Sovereign Lord, fallen and come into His Highness's hands, and at His Highness' gift and disposition, by the acts of Parliament and laws of this realm through the abolishing of the superstitions of the said friars.

Although the religious order had now been settled in favour of Protestantism, the years which immediately followed brought fresh controversy. What kind of Protestantism was it to be? Calvinism, with its emphasis on the Bible as the true word of God, or Episcopacy, largely developed in England, with its strong links to the former Roman Catholic liturgy and more importantly, its hierarchy of bishops? This would be a struggle which would not be settled until the end of the next century, when the Church of Scotland in its Presbyterian form we know today was finally established. In the meantime there was confusion as the various factions conducted a battle of ideas. Much of it was about land and territorial issues.

The first meeting of the General Assembly in 1560 had been a relatively small affair. In 1562 it set up Provincial Assemblies or Synods. Geographically they approximated to the former bishoprics. In the place of bishops were "Superintendents". John Knox became Superintendent of Edinburgh, while John Willock was appointed Superintendent of Glasgow. Peebles came under his jurisdiction. In January 1571 the Estates or Scots parliament passed an Act by which all former church property should be held by the Crown, but the major arguments were about governance and the remaining years of the sixteenth century would see the pendulum swing one way then another. In September, not withstanding the appointments made by the earlier General Assemblies, the Privy Council, without any consultation with the Kirk, appointed bishops to St Andrews and Glasgow. The General Assembly of the next year reluctantly accepted Episcopacy or rule by bishops, which was known as the "Concordance of Leith". That meeting was attended by the minister of Peebles, Thomas Cranstoun.

In practice the new bishops had very similar powers to the Superintendents whom they replaced. The significant point however, was that bishops were appointed by the Crown and not by the General Assembly. Politics and religion became inseparable and in the decades which followed, first James VI & I and then his son Charles attempted to dictate the religious as well as the political order.

So ended the sixteenth century which had witnessed, the greatest cataclysm in the history of Christianity. The power of the Church of Rome and its Pope had effectively been destroyed and in its place a church now stood in Scotland which placed the Bible at its centre, as the one and only true word of God and the template for its life and doctrine. Scotland under the rule of James VI, was at last a land of relative peace, able to move forward to a more stable economic future, or so it seemed.

Peebles was a place of ordered security, safe behind its now completed defensive wall. It had an established system of civic government, controlled by elected representatives of the burgess class, at its head a provost who was still of the landed aristocracy, although that would shortly change. It had established trading and marketing arrangements, firmly controlled by the town council. The spiritual and political integrity of the burgh was controlled by a local elite. Justice was dispensed in the King's name.

The century which followed would however be dominated by a political struggle between the Crown and the people, the ruler and the ruled, the "Divine Right" of kings and the rights of the citizen as expressed through parliaments, which would ultimately be settled in favour of the latter. It would also see the culmination of the theological battle between Episcopacy and Presbyterianism. Both those battles would have their effect on Peebles.

PART IV

1600 – 1700

13.
The Longest Century

The century commenced on January 1st 1600. This particular 1st of January was significant because since Roman times, each new year had started on 25 March, based on the Julian calendar, so called after Julius Caesar. In October 1582, Pope Gregory VIII introduced a new calendar that still bears his name. It was adopted in Scotland by an Act of the Scottish Privy Council of 17th December, 1599. 1st January, 1600 became the first day of the first year of the new calendar. The Gregorian calendar, was not adopted by England for another 150 years.

The new century was arguably the most dramatic and traumatic in the long history of the British Isles. It saw a King of Scots succeed to the throne of England, Wales and Ireland, while remaining the monarch of Scotland. It saw the publication of a book, the Authorised Version of the Bible, which is one of the most significant in history. It saw a constitutional and religious conflict, which became a civil war, culminating in the execution of a king and the establishment of a republican government in England, which then imposed itself on and occupied Scotland, bringing it for the first time in its long history into a single Commonwealth of all the territories of England, Scotland, Wales and Ireland. It saw the restoration of monarchy and an escalating conflict in Scotland between Episcopacy and Presbyterianism. Royal promotion of Catholicism brought a "Glorious Revolution", the demise of absolute monarchy and the establishment of a Constitutional Monarchy, subject to the will of an elected parliament. In Scotland with the establishment of the Church of Scotland, it brought an end to the religious struggles, which had dominated the past 150 years since the days of John Knox.

For James VI, the early years of the new century were the most successful of his life-long reign, in which he established himself as one of the most politically adept of all monarchs. Not only did his long Stuart ancestry give him unchallenged authority as "King of Scots", but through his great-great-grand mother Margaret Tudor, he also stood in line for the English throne as well. It was by no means a settled conclusion and England's current monarch Elizabeth I, unmarried and childless, declined to nominate her successor, but on 24th March 1603 Elizabeth died and James was proclaimed King James I, King of England, Wales and Ireland.

Later in that year he travelled to his new capital of London. Apart from a brief visit to his northern kingdom in 1617, he never returned to Scotland.

During the years which remained before James added the throne of England to his Scottish inheritance in 1603 and departed to London, the practice of calling together his subjects from the Border shires at Peebles had continued. The last recorded occasion was on 15th October 1602, when he was present at a Justice Ayre or court held in the town on that date. It was appointed by the king 'for trying and punishing, the many enormities and insolences which have been committed during several years bygone.' In addition to the court hearings, it was another occasion when there was still a threat of armed insurrection. The king and a number of his council were to be present in person and it was necessary 'that His Majestie be weel and substantiallie accompaneit by a force of his guid subjectis.' He therefore directed that all aged between 16 and 60 living in the shires of Peebles and Selkirk should meet him at Peebles 'ilk ane of them weel bodin in feir of war' and be prepared to attend on His Majesty for a period of fifteen days, 'under paine of tinsel[90]of life, landis and guids.'

Again that must have represented a sizeable gathering and would have strained the resources of the town to its limits. In practice, while the King's proclamation required all his subjects aged 16 to 60 to attend, in reality perhaps it related more to the men of influence and representatives of the people, rather than the whole population? It was to be the last visit by a King of Scots to Peebles for 345 years.

The population of the town at that time was probably still no more than 1100. 133 are listed as ratepayers in 1609, all of whom would have been burgess householders, owning their own property. The fortified town steeple, with its clock and bells, stood close by the West Port and formed part of the town walls at the west end of the High Street. It had several bells, each for a different purpose. There was a bell to signify the start and end of the working day and one to summon those who attended school. There was the Great Bell which was rung on the rare occasions when the townsfolk needed to be alerted to the approach of hostile forces. Facing the steeple on the high ground to the west there were a few isolated dwellings on the former Castlehill.

Most of the houses throughout the town would have been one storey, built of whinstone and thatched with heather or straw. The larger houses would have had an upper storey, built of timber, with access to the upper

---

90   Loss

floor by way of an external wooden stairway to a projecting balcony, again built of wood and lacking any protecting hand rail. The construction of all those dwellings made them very susceptible to destruction by fire. Some houses were beginning to see the traditional turf and thatch used as roofing materials replaced by slate on a small scale. That was certainly the case by 1624 when the burgh accounts show a payment being made for someone to go to Duddingston to collect slates. There is also a record of a payment for 'leiding five hunder sklaitis' out of the Cross Kirk, 'to the schappell.' They are likely to have come from the former monastic buildings rather than the church itself.

Turf and thatch roofs remained a favourite roosting place for poultry, many of which ranged freely through the town and often not owned by the householders on whose roofs they roosted. Turf and thatch were subjected to the scratching and scraping which is part of the life of poultry, but would have been detrimental to the roofs themselves. It became such a problem that the council introduced rules which allowed the owners of properties damaged, to kill the offending birds without payment to the owner. They went further some years later when the problem persisted and ordered that everyone owning hens or "capons" should tie a piece of wood to the foot of each bird, for sufficient weight to stop it flying. Anyone finding a bird without such a "cloige" was to be entitled to catch it and dispose of it as they saw fit.

As in the past some of the houses would have had a bastel door which could be barred and bolted against unwelcome intruders. Those were days which still saw unruly and felonious behaviour.

The High Gait or High Street was the centre of town life. Beneath the projecting stairs and balconies of the larger houses townsfolk would gather to discuss the affairs and gossip of the day. It was a wide open space and the market stalls of merchants and the suppliers of the bodily needs of the population would have been scattered about it. They would vary in number and position, regulated by the town council. That seems to have been quite difficult at times and the control of the stalls and where they stood and by whom they might be used, was a matter often on the agenda of their meetings.

The street was wider than it is today and many of the buildings forming the modern frontage have been built in front of earlier buildings. The alignment of houses was more haphazard, with no attempt to adhere to a common building line. The only defining features along the High Street frontage were open drain channels running down either side. There are many entries in the records about those drains which were frequently blocked by steadily growing middens, especially at the mouths of the wynds and vennels that ran north and south from the High Street itself (and still do). In days when sanitation was virtually unknown, straw would have been used as a floor covering in houses and also in the wynds and vennels. Most householders would have had livestock of one sort or another which also needed straw for bedding. That had to be removed from time to time to middens situated in the main street. The middens were a further source of concern to the town council, because they often built up and blocked the drain channels. Judging by the many entries in the council records, it made regular attempts to have the middens removed or reduced but the need for householders to be rid of their own and their animals' ordure was a constant problem.

On the north side not far from the West Port, the Chapel of St Mary still stood as it had for nearly three hundred years. Close by and also on the north side was the steeple which in a few years time would be joined by a new tolbooth, becoming the centre of the town's administration, meeting place of the magistrates and town council and place of incarceration for felons and those committed to ward or prison there by the council for various misdemeanours.

A plan compiled by Alex Thomson in 1892 from the Burgh records of 1609-52 shows the town as it probably was at that time. Few buildings stood outside the walls which encircled the town and had been reconstructed and improved in 1569 as previously mentioned. Most of those were situated in the Auld Toun, the original settlement of Peebles, which lay across the Peebles Brig and stretched westwards on both sides of the road leading to the Kirklands and the route to Neidpath Castle continuing westwards beyond. The walls themselves ran northwards from the West Port, until meeting the Peebles Water (the Cuddy), which they then followed in an easterly direction passing by a gate giving access to St Michael's Wynd and further on to a second entrance to the Briggait opposite the Trie Brig,[91]through a barbican. That bridge gave access to the Cross Kirk, some distance to the north and to the Auld Mill further along the Peebles Water, standing close by the river bank. From there it turned east along the length of Usher's Wynd to the Auld North Port at the end of the North Gate and continued east before turning south along the edge of the of common ground on the east of the town called the Foul Myre and then to the East Wark, which guarded the eastern entrance to the town from the road to Traquair and Selkirk. It was by then in a near ruinous state. From there it ran downhill southwards along the margin of

---

[91]   Tree Bridge

Skinnersheuch,[92] before turning west again along Tweed Green to rejoin the West Port. In the last section there was a further access to the High Gait (High Street) by way of a gate and vennel[93] which gave direct access northwards to the High Gait.

Just beyond the East Wark, a road branched northwards from the route to Traquair and beyond and led to the town's common pasturage on the south side of Venlaw and as will be seen later, the place of execution of witches. The main route east passed by the Qubyte Stane.[94] It was the custom for travellers to Traquair and more distant Selkirk and the eastern Borders to stop there and drink a stirrup cup to set them on their way.

On the north side of the town, property belonging to Lord Borthwick lay outside the walls beyond the Auld North Port. Opposite was an area next the Peebles Water, belonging to the town known the Grene Yairds. On the other side of the Peebles Water ran the mill lade feeding the Auld Mill which continued down to the Tree Bridge, beyond which lay the few dwellings of Biggiesknowe.

There were routes north, south, east and west out of the town. Those to the east and west and their destinations have already been noted. The route to the north led on to Eddleston and eventually Edinburgh, as it does today, but a further route branched off taking the route which still exists running up on the north side of Venlaw. Today this peters out to the north east of Mailingsland Hill and at that time would have been the access to the town's lands of Glentress, Shieldgreen and Easter Common. According to Buchan this was originally the principal route to Edinburgh and was superseded by the route northwards along the Eddleston Water to Leadburn which is the route today. He says this was not built until 1770, which seems unlikely as neither of the maps published by Roy (1752-55) and Armstrong in (1775), which are the earliest based on a proper survey of the area, show the Venlaw route. They would certainly have shown it if it had still existed at that time. It is likely that Buchan's suggestion was based on the Alexander Thomson plan, which showed Peebles and the surrounding area as it was in 1609-52. That plan, although probably accurate in many respects, was conjectural and it is more probable that the Venlaw route was a local one only.

The cost of maintaining the Tweed Bridge and the bridge over the Peebles Water was a source of concern at that time and in 1608 the town council approached the Convention of Royal Burghs asking permission to

---

[92] Where the Park Hotel now stands.
[93] Now the School Brae
[94] White Stone

levy a tax or toll on users of the bridges. In the following year their petition was granted. The proceeds were to be used for repairing the bridge and its approaches. For every load passing over the bridge, burgesses were to be charged 2d, while non burgesses were to be charged 4d. Every cow, ox or horse crossing the bridge on its way to sale was charged at 1d, while a score of sheep (20) cost 4d. The charges were to apply for nine years.

In July 1615, the Convention gave permission for revised charges to be levied for the following seven years. These were to be 2d for a horse, 8d for a score of sheep, 2d for pedestrians and 4d for horsemen. The proceeds were once again to go towards the costs of bridge maintenance.

There is every reason to suppose that Peebles lay on the route of the cattle droves which took place annually. It involved the movement of many hundreds of cattle from as far afield as the Northern Highlands, to the markets of northern England. It was a trade that was on the increase, now that the Union of the Crowns had achieved a measure of peace in the Borders, with a much-reduced threat from marauding reiver bands. Potentially it should have been a rich source of additional revenue. Peebles was a logical place at which to cross the Tweed.[95] Evidence of drove roads descending from the Central Lowlands to the north and continuing south over the Tweeddale hills still remain, but it is open to question whether the drovers would actually use the bridges or avoid the expense by crossing at some point up river where it could be forded, perhaps even as close by as Hay Lodge Park where an annual fording takes place during the modern riding of the marches, forming part of the Beltane Festival. If so it must have been a sore trial to the burgh fathers to see such a fine source of revenue pass them by!

It is difficult to paint an accurate picture of the social history of the town and its people in the seventeenth century. The records of the burgh and the writings of its earlier historians give a great deal of information about the ownership of property, the conduct of council business in the governing of the town, law and order and kirk discipline and while this last does document much about individual citizens, it is almost entirely a reflection of the negative aspects of life. So what would every day life in Peebles have been like for the ordinary folk of the town?

First of all there was the question of local government and the election of the town council, which affected the everyday lives of all the inhabitants. By that time the practice of electing the members by the

---

[95] It was the only bridge crossing of the river above Berwick until modern times.

burgesses of the burgh had been superseded. In 1469 the Scottish parliament, copying the   system used in France, had passed an act which completely changed that thoroughly democratic process. In future the new council was to be chosen annually by the old council. However, Peebles did not adopt the practice until a century later.

The "election" was held annually at Michaelmas, 29th September. In *The Book of Days*,[96] edited by Robert Chambers, he gives this rather whimsical account of the reason for this date being chosen. It follows a passage about angels and saints and their role in influencing and protecting mortal men:

> It will be learned, with some surprise, that these notions of presiding angels and saints are what have led to the custom of choosing magistracies on the 29th September. The history of the middle ages is full of curious illogical relations, and this is one of them. Local rulers were esteemed as in some respects analogous to tutelar angels, in so far as they presided over and protected the people. It was therefore thought proper to choose them on the day of St Michael and All Angels. The idea must have been extensively prevalent, for the custom of electing magistrates on this day is very extensive.

The constitution of the burgh, known as the "sett", made provision for the council to consist of a provost, two bailies, dean of guild, eleven councillors and one deacon, who was the deacon of the weavers, who were at that time the only recognised craft guild in the town. It does seem to have been usual for some of the councillors at least to be merchants and traders in the town, but the ordinary folk had no say in the election. They did have an opportunity prior to the election to say if they had any objection to any members of the council, at a public meeting called "the head court", a meeting of the townsfolk to which everyone was called to attend. In practice, the council was a law unto itself. The deacon of the weavers was chosen somewhat differently. The Weavers Guild nominated six of its members and then the magistrates[97] nominated a leet of three, from whom the whole council chose one.

Until that time, the provostship had been held successively by the Lord Yester of the day, but an Act of Parliament of 24th June 1609 required that in future the holders of the offices of provost and magistrates in a burgh could only be those who lived and worked in the burgh and "noblemen and gentlemen" were no longer allowed to hold those offices. In October

---

96   *The Book of Days* Vol. II p389
97   Provost and two baillies

1609, following the annual election of the council itself on 29th September, John Dickisoun was the first commoner to be elected to the office of provost. The influence of the Hays was not entirely at an end as the eighth Lord Yester, who became the Earl of Tweeddale, sat as an ordinary member of the Council for many years.

The charters and papers of the burgh were kept in what was known as the "Common Kist". It was a large chest kept in the tolbooth. It was also used to house items of value belonging to the burgh and from time to time, sums of money. The key was usually held by the provost of the day. During the time that various members of the Hay family held that office as they did almost continually for many decades up to the time when parliament debarred them, there were occasions when inevitably problems were caused when they were not in residence at Neidpath. In March 1571 the council instructed the bailies to write to Lord Hay asking for the key so that "the common buikis" and other documents could be examined. The problem still remained unresolved and a year later a further letter was written requesting Lord Hay to confirm that the key was in his possession. Unfortunately the key was still not produced and in desperation on 4th February 1573 the council instructed the bailies to write to or visit Lord Hay confirming that if he would not hand over the key, they would have a new key made with the approval of the king, because they had urgent need to inspect the town's official documents.

The council might well have regarded the holding of the office of provost by a peer to be a mixed blessing. The matter of the key was not the first occasion on which the council had fallen out with their aristocratic and often absent provost. On 18th March, 1572 they had written to him requesting him to come in person to help the council in their deliberations. They threatened that if he did not come they would discharge him from holding any office in the town in future, which they thought would be in the best interest of the townsfolk. It appears to have had little or no effect, because on 10th November they decided that when he next came to Neidpath they would seek assurance from him whether he would act in the best interests of the community or not and what he was prepared to do on its behalf.

That was not all. Lord Hay had borrowed a tent or pavilion belonging to the town, for use by him when he was inspecting the boundaries of his estates. The council tried to recover it and on 10th May 1572, William Kello, one of the burgesses, for some reason agreed to provide surety for its safe return. Sadly for him it was not returned. On 16th October that year the council ordered it 'to be brocht hame.' It was never recovered and from an entry in the records for 9th April the following year, it seems that the unfortunate William Kello was forced to pay the penalty specified in the surety bond. As Buchan comments, 'Thereafter he would not be likely to put his trust in princes.'

The council was an august body with wide ranging powers over its citizens. Magistrates and councillors were held in the highest esteem and any criticism or personal insult was regarded as a serious offence and subject to severe penalties. In 1621 John Baillie was censured for what was described as 'misusing the provost'. For the offence, he was ordered to go to the cross on the market day and get down on his knees to ask for the provost's forgiveness. He was also fined five merks which were to be given to the poor. That same year, one of the burgh officers, John Robene, lost his job after he was convicted of hitting the provost's wife and reproaching the provost himself. His wife was also involved. She, clearly a spirited woman, ended up in the stocks for slandering him. In 1624 Charles Porteous was banned from working in any freeman's trade because he called the provost and bailies 'a company of greedy gluttons'.

One of the principal functions of the council was to maintain law and order. There is a general perception that when James VI & I departed for London in 1603, he left behind a country largely settled and at peace. It is true that the nobility, so frequently feuding in the past, were now pursuing their ends by more civilised means. The Border lairds and reivers were largely under control. The union of the crowns had brought together the defenders of the Border marches in common cause. James wanted to see a real union between what were still two independent kingdoms, albeit sharing a single monarchy. Although his vision of a United Kingdom of Great Britain was not achieved until more than one hundred years later, he wanted to see the distinctions which to a large extent had fuelled the old cross Border feuds removed. Up until that time special laws and customs governing the Borders had been in place, designed to meet the special circumstances of what was frequently a lawless region. In the mind of James there were no longer any grounds for cross border raiding. As he said, 'now, by the happie conjunction in oure persone of boith the kingdoms, the caus of thes being removit, their aucht no langer continuance be of those former customes.' He went on to say that now that those parts of both kingdoms which had formed their marches or boundaries, had become, 'the mid center of the whole yland under our impyre' they should be subject to the rule of law of the whole land. The former Borders was to be renamed the "middle shires of Great Britain.' Ten commissioners, drawn from both kingdoms were appointed, who were given full powers to regulate the northern Counties of England, the Scottish shires of Annandale, Roxburgh, Selkirk and Peebles and the stewartries of Dumfries and Kirkcudbright.

The commissioners were responsible for preventing and punishing murders, theft, riots and all other crimes and disorders. They seem to have pursued their task with considerable force and success. At the end of the first year they reported that thirty two criminals had been hanged at Hawick, Jedburgh, Dumfries and Peebles; fifteen more had been banished and more than one hundred and forty had been designated as 'fugitive outlaws', who 'ought to be pursued with hue and cry wherever they have dispersed themselves.'

The principal citizens of the town were the burgesses, who held special privileges. Their status had been established as far back as the 12th century when Peebles was first recognised as a Royal Burgh. To qualify, it was necessary to own a quarter of an acre of land, with a street frontage of 20ft. Although by the seventeenth century they had lost the right to elect the council and the magistrates, they remained the dominant group in the town. By that time it was possible for someone who did not otherwise qualify to become a full burgess in certain circumstances, but he or she would be required to make a minimum payment of 40s to the town's coffers. However, someone could become a burgess at a slightly lower cost if he married the daughter of an existing burgess. For example on 7th November 1606 William Ellot was admitted. Because he had 'mareit ane burgeis air', he was charged only 33s 4d. Following that case, the council decided that 'all that sall be be admittit heirafter that mareis burges airis to do the lyk.'

Every new burgess was required to swear an oath of allegiance. It is impressive and is in the following terms :

Here I protest before God and your worships that I profess and allow with my heart the true religion which at present is publicly preached within this realm, and authorised by the laws thereof. I shall abide thereat and defend the same to my life's end, forsaking the Roman religion called papistry. I shall be loyal and true to our sovereign the King's Majesty and his successors, to the provost and bailies of this burgh. I shall keep and underly the statutes of this burgh. I shall obey the officers of this burgh, fortify and maintain them in the execution of their offices with my body and lands. I shall not colour unfreemen's goods under colour of my own[98]I shall not purchase

---

[98]   In other words would not sell goods which belonged to someone who was not a burgess as if they were their own

lordships or other authority contrary to the freedom of this burgh. In all taxations, watching and warding, and all other burdens to be laid upon this burgh, I shall willingly bear my part as I am commanded by the magistrates, and shall not use nor purchase any exemptions or privileges to be free thereof, renouncing the same forever. And finally, I shall not attempt nor do anything hurtful to the liberties and common weal of the said burgh; and so often as I break any point of this my oath I oblige myself to pay to the common affairs of the said burgh the sum of one hundred pounds, and shall enter and remain in ward[99] until the same is paid.[100]

The oath is interesting in number of regards, not least the reference to the religious order of the day, which at that time was Episcopacy and also the renouncing of Papacy and that this takes precedence followed by loyalty to the monarch of the day.

As well as the burgesses, there was also a less privileged class who were called "calsay burgesses". Their status does not seem to be defined, but probably they did not own sufficient property in the burgh to qualify for full burgess status. They had no rights of pasturage on the common grazings of the burgh and it is likely that the main reason for them becoming "freemen" was to allow them to trade in the town. The designation, "calsay" may well originate from them carrying out their trades from stalls standing on the causeway or "calsay", although there do seem to be examples of people who had no trade in the burgh being admitted to that group, possibly for reasons of non residence, but yet having influence with the council.

More than that of any of his illustrious predecessors, between 1603 and 1607, the government of James VI&I, was successful in bringing the former turbulence and lawlessness of the Borders under control. From that time on. the Borders effectively became part of the wider society of Great Britain. No longer were the marauding reivers seen as more of a threat to the peace of honest communities than foreign invaders. From now on they became part of the mainstream and as the years went by those who in reality had been no more than gangland thugs, became a romantic memory in the legends of the Border ballads and folklore

At a local level however, things were far from peaceable and petty feuding and violence was still very much the order of the day, not least in Peebles, although on the surface it was by now a place with an ordered

---

[99]   Effectively, prison
[100] English version adapted from the original Scots by the author.

and secure society. Disturbances of the peace were more often than not "stair heed" and bar room brawls fuelled by drink, rather than the clan warfare of former years.

The Privy Council was certainly aware that all was not always peace and tranquillity in the Royal Burgh, particularly on occasions when large numbers of people gathered together on festive days such as Beltane. It still included the annual horse races held on 1st May each year, but these gatherings often descended into drunken brawling. In his *Domestic Annals of Scotland*, Robert Chambers[101] records the concerns of the Privy Council:

'The great difficulty attending such festivals arose from the tendency of the people to mark them with bloodshed. Men assembled there from different parts of the country, each having of course his peculiar enmities, and the object of similar enmities in his turn; and when they met and had somewhat inflamed themselves with liquor, it was scarcely avoidable that mutual provocations should be given, leading to conflicts with deadly weapons. So great reason was there now for fearing a sanguinary scene at Peebles, that the Lords of Council thought proper to issue a proclamation forbidding the race to take place.'

The proclamation was as follows:

28th April 1608. Forasmeikle as the Lords of the Secret Council are informit that there is sue horse-race appointit to be at Peblis the [1st] day of May nextocome, whereunto grit numbers of people of all qualities and ranks, intends to repair, betwixt whom there being quarrels, private grudges, and miscontentment, it is to be feint that at their meeting upon fields, some troubles and incoavenients sall fall out among them, to the break of his Majesty's peace and disquieting of the country without remeed be providit; Therefore the Lords of the Secret Council has dischargit, and be the tenor hereof discharges, the said horse-race, and ordains that the same sall be nawise halden nor keepit this year; for whilk purpose ordains letters to be direct, to command, charge, and inhibit all and sundry his Majesty's lieges and subjects by open proclamation at the mercat-cross of Peblis and other places needful, that nape of them presume nor tak upon them to convene and assemble themselves to the said race this present year, but to suffer that meeting and action to depart and cease, as they and ilk ane of them will answer upon the contrary at their heichest peril.

---

101   *Domestic Annals of Scotland* - Reign of James VI 1603-1625 Part B

Violent disturbances were not confined to such occasions. It was common practice for citizens to carry swords or whingers, which inevitably resulted in injuries when tempers frayed. As a consequence, in May 1605 the carrying of those weapons was forbidden, except in special circumstances, subject to a licence being granted by the bailies. It would only be granted on occasions when, 'they carie the same for feir of invasioun of gentillmen without burgh being for the tyme within' - in other words strangers visiting the burgh who might pose a threat.

On occasions, blood could still be drawn during local disturbances. In October 1605, James Currie, Frances Murdo, Riche Leggatt and some others were involved in a fracas during night time in which a number were injured. They were ordered to appear at the next court sitting and be tried for causing injury and disturbance and be reported to the council. In early November, James Currie was convicted of night assault, resulting in blood injury and various other offences. He was ordered to be banished from the town. His is the only punishment recorded and no mention is made of the others who had been involved. Perhaps he was adjudged to be the ringleader or had a bad previous record and the others received lesser penalties.

The Festival of Beltane was still annually celebrated. In former times before the Reformation of 1560, in addition to revelry and entertainment, much of the emphasis had been on the religious festivities centred on the Cross Kirk and its holy relics, which drew large numbers of pilgrims from far and wide. Surprising as it may seem, there were still those who regarded the Cross Kirk as a place of pilgrimage as it had been for centuries before the Reformation. Whatever the private beliefs of individuals may have been, officialdom was totally opposed to any lingering manifestation of Roman Catholicism. The veneration of holy relics was anathema to Calvinist Presbyterians. In any event by that time most of the former monastic buildings were in ruins, their materials plundered for use elsewhere and the church building itself had been stripped of its golden cross, its altars, statues and other devotional symbols in the wave of iconoclasm which followed the Reformation. Clearly though, the Cross Kirk of Peebles and its miracles had not been entirely forgotten and travellers still came to the town to visit this holy place in search of salvation.

Before the Reformation the high point of religious observance had been the Feast of the Finding of the Cross, which was celebrated annually at the beginning of May, coinciding with the Festival of Beltane, held then on the 1st May rather than late June, when the modern festival of the same name takes place. It was a time of particular concern and together the church authorities and the town council took steps to discourage and if possible, prevent any so called "pilgrims" from visiting the Cross Kirk. In April 1601, the Presbytery called on the elders of every parish to appoint 'some gentlemen of their parish' to go to the Cross Kirk during the evening on Saturday the 30th, and the Sunday following to, 'prevent and stay the superstition' of those coming to it. This seems to have been fairly successful because two weeks later the minister and bailies of Peebles were able to report that 'at this Beltane there was no resorting of the people into the Cross Kirk to commit any sign of superstition there.' The Presbytery were duly impressed and 'rejoiced, exhorting them in like manner in all time coming to use like diligence that all abuse of the place may be avoided.'

That was not quite the end of the matter. Further visitations were still seen as a possible threat, because on 29th April of the following year the parson of Peebles was instructed 'to wait on such persons as superstitiously repair to the Cross Kirk at this Beltane, and endeavour to have them apprehended, and punished by the magistrate.' That however must have been successful as it is the last that is heard of illegal pilgrimage either by visitors to the town or townsfolk themselves and the centuries old practice appears to have finally lapsed.

14.
Fire, Plague and Episcopacy

The year after James VI&I left Scotland for his new capital of London, Peebles suffered a devastating major fire on 4th July. What caused it is not known, although fires were quite common at that time and were often serious bearing in mind the materials used for building, much of it timber and thatch.

There are no detailed accounts of the damage suffered or the extent, but it must have been an event of some consequence. An Edinburgh burgess, Robert Birrel, who was a well-known diarist of the day, recorded events in Scotland between 1532 and 1605. In his entry for 4th July 1604 he refers to 'ane grate fyir in Peblis toun.' The reference to a 'grate fyir' suggests that it was something out of the ordinary and a major conflagration which may have damaged or destroyed many of the town's houses and buildings. It was apparently sufficiently serious that the council asked the Convention of Royal Burghs 'for thair helpe to the re-edefying of the toun...brunt with sudden fyre.' The Convention, in response, asked all the Scottish burghs to consider contributing towards the restoration costs. The task of raising funds for the repair and restoration of the damage was not confined to the council. The Kirk authorities also added their weight and the presbytery sent a letter to other presbyteries asking them for their support.

While help was sought from the wider church, the presbytery also attempted to ensure that the local community itself did what it could. On 2nd August, 'The Lord of Newbottle, the laird of Traquair, the laird of Blackbarony, and other gentlemen, being present with divers of the Presbytery, condescended that publication should be made throughout the whole kirk by the brethren that the next day it is craved that every gentleman and honest man within the parish will declare and make manifest what they will do for the support of the town of Peebles.' On 9th August they went further declaring, 'it is thought good that the town of Peebles itself, with the bailies and the whole council, and the whole parish being called on to declare what they will do themselves for the supply of the portions of the town that are damaged by fire.'

The presbytery seemed to still have been concerned to encourage a generous response from the congregations within the presbytery. At its meeting on 23rd August, 'The brethren reported concerning the town of

Peebles as has been injured, they had intimated to all their parishioners the necessity and lawfulness thereof, and had willed them in that all of their flocks be feeling members, and to resort to the presbytery to make manifest their mind thereanent.' However, apparently few if any turned up and the Presbytery ordered that the members of all the kirk sessions should see to it that their congregations were informed where contributions could be collected. It was also agreed that a letter should be written by the sheriff and signed by the common clerk of the sheriffdom, to every congregation asking them, 'not to be negligent in kything (showing) of their charity in the Lord.'

The town records for the years 1573 to 1604 are missing or have been lost. It is very likely that they were destroyed by that great fire. Fire was not the only major hazard. From time to time outbreaks of the plague or "pest" occurred in Scotland as in the rest of Britain and Europe at intervals from the fourteenth century onwards. It is difficult to establish just what that might have been. There are various forms of the disease of which perhaps bubonic plague is the most common. This highly infectious and deadly form certainly seems to have afflicted the citizens of Edinburgh on a number of occasions and there are a number of references in the burgh records relating to those outbreaks. One has already been mentioned in 1529, during the reign of James V, when the king and the Lords of the Council used Linlithgow as their base rather than Edinburgh because of an outbreak. Following a meeting in Peebles in September that year, it was agreed that their next meeting would be in Edinburgh, if it was clear of the plague, otherwise they would meet in Linlithgow.

In 1604 and 1605 there were outbreaks of the disease and at that time Peebles was itself affected. In December of 1604 (clearly a bad year for the town, what with fire and now plague), the council ordered that nobody within the burgh should take in visitors, either during day time or night, during 'the tyme of seikness', without first notifying the bailies.

In spite of those precautions, in May 1605 the plague had none the less arrived in the town. By 29 May, three people were already dead. Stringent regulations were drawn up in the hope of preventing the spread of the disease. The quartermasters were instructed to inspect all the houses in their districts. Everyone was to stay in his own house and it was forbidden to visit any other house. Anyone who became sick had to report it. The penalty for failure was death, although death would likely have followed in any case. Cleaners were brought in to purge and purify infected houses. Although there is nothing in the records to substantiate it, the Rev Dr

Dalgleish[102]claimed that everyone who was infected was confined to the cells and cloisters of the Cross Kirk.

Some years later towards the end of 1624, rumours reached Peebles that the "pest" was again on the march across the country. The council were concerned about visitors coming to the town who might spread infection and on December 24th of that year, ordered that a watch should be kept at the four ports or town gates for as long as the plague continued in Edinburgh, Lothian or any other parts. The watch was to be kept from six in the morning until eight in the evening. There was presumably some sort of rota, as the watchers were to be four men who were the heads of their households or the principal servants of any widows. Anyone failing to appear when due to undertake that duty or be absent at any time during the appointed hours would be fined ten pounds Scots and be further punished as appropriate. It seems however, that on that occasion no "visitation" occurred, although the precautions were no doubt justified.

James VI&I now in London, famously claimed that he ruled Scotland with his pen. He had left his native land with the government of the Kirk something of a mixture between Presbyterianism and Episcopacy. Doubtless, his newly acquired first hand experience of the English Episcopacy had demonstrated to him the power to govern the church and the political advantages which went with it, which was in the hands of the sovereign. James was always canny. Unlike the son who was to follow him, he adopted a pragmatic approach to most things, never pushing policy beyond what was possible. Although in former years he had shown himself to be critical of the English Church, even saying in a speech to the General Assembly of 1590, 'As for our neighbour Kirk in England, it is an evil said Mass in English, wanting nothing but the liftings.' This last reference was to the Elevation of the Host, which formed part of the Roman Catholic mass but did not form part of the English Episcopal liturgy.

Now however, he found the English practice much more to his liking and pulling the strings of government in Edinburgh from far off London, he instructed his Scottish ministers to move further towards Episcopacy at least as far as the government of the Kirk was concerned. At a meeting of the Estates, the Scottish parliament, at Perth in 1606, which included the two Scottish archbishops of St Andrews and Glasgow, an act was passed which effectively restored the former bishops, complete with all their trappings of ancient revenues and privileges.

---

[102]   Minister of Peebles 1761-1807. The last minister of the Cross Kirk.

Later that year, James ordered a "Convention" to be held in Linlithgow in December. At that meeting it was decided that every presbytery should have a permanent chairman or moderator and that the role would be undertaken by bishops. It was also agreed that there should be permanent moderators of Provincial Synods as well. The meeting was not a General Assembly and the ordinary clergy were astonished to discover that the "Convention" was, none the less, to be regarded as a General Assembly, which technically was the only body which had the power to make such decisions. No longer was there independent control of the Kirk by presbyteries and synods and the clergy were now under the authority of the bishops and of course the bishops were appointed by the king.

In 1610, Courts of High Commission or Commissary Courts, were set up under the jurisdiction of each bishop. Those courts gave wide ranging powers to the bishops over the lives of ordinary folk. They could deprive non-conforming ministers of their offices and livings The General Assembly of that year approved all these changes, almost without dissent and in 1612, the Estates added its endorsement

Peebles was in the Diocese of Glasgow and an application was made to the Archbishop to have a Commissary Court set up in the town. The archbishop duly appointed an advocate called Henry Balfour to hold the office of "Commissar" for Teviotdale, Liddisdale and Tweeddale 'with full power to the said Mr Henrie to sit within the burgh of Peiblis, sua that the said commissariat in all tyme heirefter salbe callit the commissariat of Peiblis.'

In a letter to the council, the archbishop wrote 'I dout not as ye haif bene ernest to haif your toun the seat of that judicatorie, so ye will haif care to se the judges and thair memberis of courte well usit.' The council agreed to make the tolbooth available to the Commissar on those occasions when the court sat. The necessary arrangements were put in hand and all this seems to have been acceptable to the townsfolk as there is no note of any dissent.

15.
The Charter of 1621

Perhaps the most significant event in the life of Peebles during the reign of James VI&I, was the granting by him of a Charter of Confirmation and Novodamus in 1621.

The document itself, which is of considerable length, is written in Latin on a single sheet of parchment. At the time when William Chambers was writing his *History of Peeblesshire* in the mid nineteenth century, the various charters granted by a succession of monarchs of Scotland to Peebles, including this one, were thought to have been lost, but in 1863, the lost documents were discovered in the Town House. How they were discovered is described by Chambers in his later book, *Charters and Documents and Extracts from the Records Burgh of Peebles, 1165-1710,*[103] where he quotes Robert Renwick's description of the search.

Renwick, who is perhaps the most important source of information based on the historical records of Peebles, was at that time assistant to J D Marwick, who was Secretary of the Burgh Records Society. Together with Alexander Harris, who was another of Marwick's assistants, their searches of the various inventory of manuscript collections published between 1800 and 1813 identified transcripts of the principal Peebles charters. This was evidence that the original documents must have existed during that time. They included the MS Collection of General Hutton of documents transcribed by him.

Not surprisingly, it was thought that the most likely place where the lost documents would be found was in Peebles itself. An approach was made to Mr J D Bathgate, the town clerk of Peebles for permission to make a thorough search in the town house and other likely places in the town. As Renwick recorded:

> The permission was at once given, and it was arranged that Mr Harris and I should take advantage of our first holiday to make an investigation into every corner where there was any probability of coming upon the papers. Fortunately, our search was successful. Two presses in the Town hall, at Peebles, were found to contain large collections of papers ancient and modern, and amongst these we discovered a considerable number of volumes

---

[103] p xlix

of records of several descriptions, and all, or nearly all the papers which General Hutton had made use of..

Renwick goes on:

It is observable, from scraps of paper placed here and there as marks in some of the volumes of records, that they have passed through the hands of some person, within the last twenty years or thereabouts. It seems probable that the belief in their loss has arisen from the books not having latterly come under the observation of those qualified to decipher the writing; and, but for the conviction of their existence, founded on the knowledge derived from General Hutton's volumes, and the impulse derived from this publication, these valuable records would not at the present time have been brought to light.

The document itself and the steps taken to preserve it for posterity is described by Renwick:

'The principal charter, that of James VI, 1621, is not recorded in the register of the Great Seal. A complete and accurate copy is consequently of the greater importance. The original deed is written on the face of a large sheet of parchment, and in several places, particularly at the folds, the material has been entirely worn away. In others, owing to the action of time and apparently of damp, the writing has faded to such an extent as to be quite undecipherable. In these circumstances, Mr Marwick applied to the Town Council of Peebles for permission to endeavour to restore the faded writing by chemical process, so far as to enable it to be read, and this permission was at once accorded. The charter was thereupon placed in the hands of Mr Dickson, Curator of the Historical Department of the General Register House, by whom the faded writing was brought up sufficiently to allow him to complete the transcript..................The community of Peebles may accordingly, now be said to possess for the first time, an accessible and authentic copy of their most valuable Burgh Charter;'

The original copy of this historically important document is preserved in the National Archives of Scotland. The charter tells much about Peebles, its possessions, its governance, its privileges and its daily life. It is worth quoting the preamble in full.

JAMES, by the grace of God king of Great Britain, France and Ireland,[104] defender of the faith, to all good men of his whole land, clergy and laity,

---

104   The claim to the Throne of France may seem somewhat bizarre, but none the less the English monarchy still maintained its ancient claim. It could perhaps be said that James had a better claim than most of his predecessors, bearing in mind that his mother, Mary Queen of Scots, had been Queen of France.

greeting : Know ye that we, after our lawful full and perfect age, and all our revocations, as well special as general, considering the assiduous care and singular diligence which we and our most noble ancestors of most worthy memory have taken in the erection of royal burghs within our kingdom of Scotland, in the increase of which, the policy advantage and glory of our said kingdom consists, and is daily augmented and renowned, and we calling to remembrance the ancient erection of our burgh of Peebles, the great benefits, memorable and thankful services done and performed by the bailies, burgesses, and community of our said burgh of Peebles, without any suspicion, fault or crime in every past occasion, as well in peace as war, not only by defending the country against foreign enemies, but also by exposing their persons and estates in resisting open and evident oppressors, as well on the borders of England as of Scotland, and likewise the great prejudice and loss sustained by them thereby, both in punishing criminals and other breakers of the law within the marches of our kingdom, the town lying contiguous to the said borders being often sacked, burnt, laid waste and desolated, likewise calling to our remembrance that the said burgh of Peebles has always been a very convenient place where the administration of justice for the time might have a safe and secure residence and defence, for punishing malefactors at the particular courts of justice thereof, and has been always protected, preserved and supported from open invasion by the said burgh and inhabitants thereof: and being willing to defend the rights and privileges anciently granted to our said burgh of Peebles and to the burgesses and inhabitants of the same, that thenceforth a better opportunity may be given of continuing in their faithful office and service:

It then goes on to narrate the rights and possessions granted to the burgh in earlier times, mentioning particularly those granted by James II and James IV and re-confirms them. They included church revenues which passed to the burgh following the Reformation, the High and Cross Kirks and extensive landed properties possessed or to be possessed by the burgh which are listed in detail; the common lands of Cademuir, Hammildoun (Hamildean), Venlaw, the lands of Glentarss (Glentress) and Common Struther, the common grazing on the King's Muir. In addition were the corn mill, known as the Ruid Mill (or rude mill as it has previously been referred to) and the waulk mill built on the side of the Castlehill and the corn mill, known as the Auld Mill, which was on the north side of the Peebles Water (the Cuddy) together with the mill dams, multures[105] and houses and buildings built on the side of the Castlehill; waters, fishings of salmon and other fish, both in the Tweed and the Peebles Water, hawkings and huntings, which had belonged to James IV. It included the

---

[105]   Payments made for the grinding of corn

right to use and enjoy the hill lands and valleys of Cademuir, Homildon, Venlaw and Common Struther for grazing, ploughing and cropping. In the case of Glentarss, the right was of common grazing with free access between sunrise and sunset. Although there are no detailed records, it is likely that of the town's burgesses would benefit, as most, if not all, would have some livestock and grow winter fodder crops to sustain them.

It should perhaps be mentioned here that the number and type of livestock which an individual burgess could graze on the common grazing was regulated by a system known as "souming". There are many references to this in the records, often in connection with disputes. It seems to have been the responsibility of the bailies to decide on individual soums. The system still exists in the crofting areas of Scotland. In respect of all the common and mosses, the charter granted the right to pull heather and of digging and removing peats, turf, fuel and divots.

There is a list of further properties, described as the whole lands of Glentress in which the burgh had an interest in "commonty" only. That is to say that it was shared with other proprietors who claimed rights to various parts. They seem to have covered a very extensive area, although today it is difficult to define the overall extent, as many of the names have disappeared. Identifying these properties was a problem even in 1872, when Chambers comments, 'where the many possessions are, it would be painful to consider.'[106]Some names can however, still be identified. They include Dounrig (Dunrig), Cairnsman (Cairnsman Hill) Card (Cardie Hill), all within what is now Glentress Forest. Further afield are Homildon (Hamildean) to the west of Peebles and Gaithope and Hollielaw (Holylee) beyond Walkerburn. Even further afield is Glenlude lying on the road today known as Paddock (Paddy's) Slacks.

The charter confirmed the much earlier grants by King David II in 1367 of the Chaplaincy of St Mary in the High Street and of the mill of Innerleithen, together with the multures which belonged in the past to the mill of Traquair supplied with grain grown on the lands north of the Tweed between the village of Horsburgh (Eshiels) and the Gaithope Burn (at Holylee); the lands near the Traquair mill, known as Hillhouses and Thomashauch.

Those far flung properties and their associated interests suggest that the burgh had a significant interest in much of the old County of Peeblesshire, of which it was of course the principal centre. Taken together, these were

---

106   *Charters and Documents and Extracts from the Records Burgh of Peebles, 1165-1710* p lxxii

extensive properties with valuable income derived from them, in addition to the right of burgesses to use the common grazings.

Renwick enters a note of caution, when he writes:

> The extensive territory embraced in the charter is, however, misleading, unless it is borne in mind that Royal grants were always issued *salvo jure cujuslibet* (saving or reserving the right of all others). Indeed, crown donees could only look upon as theirs what could not be claimed by somebody else under prior or more satisfactory titles fortified by possession. Thus the great charter of Peebles gave burgesses a *prima facie* (at first sight) right to enter into legal contest with other competitors, but the final issue of these was largely dependent on extraneous evidence, and in the course of many prolonged law pleas, the pruning knife of the legal lords succeeded bit by bit in reducing the wide domain in the charter into somewhat modest dimensions.[107]

All the rights and privileges granted in the past in respect of the governance of the town and its markets and festivals are re-confirmed. Power is granted to the burgesses and community to create new burgesses, hold courts and punish transgressors within the burgh in the same way as other royal burghs in Scotland. The provost, bailies and councillors are given power to regulate trade, including the buying and selling of all types of merchandise, not only produced in the burgh but also outside. This extended to trade not just in the burgh itself, but also within the bounds of the whole sheriffdom (effectively the county) of Peebles. They were also entitled on behalf of the burgh to levy and collect 'petty customs and other duties' within those same bounds.

The burgh was given the right to have a guild of merchants, together with guild courts, council and members. The Guildry Corporation of Peebles survives to this day.

The right to hold weekly markets, according to the established custom was confirmed, as were three fairs each year. Those were Beltane Day, to be held on the third of May, which was to last for forty eight hours; St Peter's Day, to start on the twenty ninth day of June and again last for forty eight hours and lastly St Bartholomew's Day which was to be on the twenty fourth day of August and on that occasion last for eight days.

---

107   Robert Renwick -*Burgh of Peebles, Gleanings from its Records, 1604-52* p

In exchange, the burgh was required annually to pay the sum of 'twelve merks'[108] as rent and also 'twenty six shillings and eight pennies', to the Master of the Hospital of St Leonard, 'in the name of alms'.

Finally, the provost, bailies, councillors and community were required each year to make 'humble and daily supplications and prayers to God Almighty' for the preservation of King James and his successors. The charter was signed by James, witnessed and delivered at Newmarket on the 19th November 1621, which it notes is in the fifty-fifth and nineteenth years of his reigns (of Scotland and England respectively).

It is confirmation of the special relationship between the Scottish Crown and the people of Peebles and is James' reward for the steadfastness and loyalty of the burgh throughout the centuries. It was steadfastness and loyalty that was to be stretched to its limits and beyond during the reign of his son Charles I.

---

108   £8 Scots =13 shillings and 4 pence sterling

16.
Rough Justice

The charter of 1621 confirmed previous charters which granted to the provost, bailies and councillors power to sit as a court in judgement of those who broke the law and to punish offenders. The punishments which they might deliver ranged from the minor to the most severe. This included "pit and gallows", which meant capital punishment.

Robert Renwick claims that the use of capital punishment was exceptional and that there is only one case of the magistrates passing a capital sentence which appears in the records. While it may be the only case appearing in the town records, there are in fact rather more, as on occasions those convicted of capital offences were sent to Edinburgh for execution. An example is that of Thomas Horsburgh, who killed William Chisholme with his whinger 'under silence and cloud of night' and after he had robbed him of ten six pound pieces and white silver valued at twenty merks. He had also robbed his own mother of £22. For these offences the justiciary court sentenced him to be taken to the Castlehill of Edinburgh, there to be hanged and thereafter his head and right hand to be cut off. His head was to be 'set upoun ane pike upon the steepleheid of Peebles, and his richt hand to be put on the East Port thairof' and all his moveable goods were to be forfeited.

Dr Gunn records a number of other murders, around the turn of the century, including that of John Govanne in 1599; Dunkie Kaid and James Dickson in 1600; Duncan Kidd in 1602 Later are the murders of William Braid in 1619 and Robert Scot in 1623. Those appear in the records of the Presbytery of Peebles. The actual circumstances of the killings is not recorded, but more than likely the deaths occurred as a result of some sort of feud or fracas.

In each case the perpetrator was to be subject to excommunication, if he did not give satisfaction to the family of the deceased and receive a remission from the king. It is worth noting that in those cases the offenders were not subject to capital punishment. It would seem that such a crime could perhaps be mitigated by the payment of money. In the case of Duncan Kid, his murderer, John Crauford, 'signified his pitiful humiliation and willingness to satisfy parties, to whom he has made offers, and that he thirst earnestly to be reconciled with God, His Kirk, and all others whom he has offended, by his odious and scandalous act, for which in the Lord he is penitent.'.

It seems odd to modern eyes that such a major crime as murder should apparently be treated so lightly, while theft was taken more seriously. Perhaps it was because physical violence was common, both in situations of war and personal conflict. Killing in those circumstances was rarely premeditated, whereas theft almost always is. In the case of Thomas Horsbugh, theft was a significant element and that may explain why he was executed and in the case which follows, it was the only issue. The "exceptional" case to which Renwick refers is indeed worth noting. The actual punishment was grotesque in the extreme. The case related to the conviction of a Peebles weaver by the name of Thomas Patersone. He was accused of stealing two ewes from Aikerfield, belonging to Johne Dewar on the 8th December 1623 and of taking two more ewes and a 'dymmont sheip'[109] ten days later. Three days after that he was accused of having taken a 'smeiret' or marked ewe belonging to Dewar. In the meantime he had also taken a ewe from the cloister of the Cross Kirk which belonged to James Wylie, which also was 'smeiret'. That was unfortunate for Patersone because, after a search the carcase and the marked skin of the animal was found in his possession. The search had also found three heads and skins of the ewes stolen from Aikerfield and the skin of the marked ewe belonging to Dewar, all of which were produced in court when the case was tried.

The trial was held in the tolbooth on 22nd December. Patersone confessed to the 'steilling and away-bringing furth of the landis of Aikerfield' of four sheep belonging to John Dewar and the 'steilling and away-bringing furth of the cloister of the Croce Kirk' of the marked ewe belonging to James Wylie. He denied all the other thefts he was accused of, probably because unlike the ones he had confessed to, there was no physical evidence.

He was duly found guilty of the thefts he had confessed to. Sitting in judgement were the provost, James Williamson and Alexander Mure, one of the bailies. Their sentence was that he be taken to 'Peblis Water, bewest the brig theof and there before nightfall and be kept in the water until 'he be deid'. All his goods and possessions were to be forfeited. The record adds that 'dome was given be John Tempill, dempster'.

That exceptionally cruel and barbarous execution is thought to have taken place on the part of the Eddleston Water or Cuddy lying between

---

[109]   Two year old wether.

the bridge and the junction with the Tweed. Today this stretch of water is fairly shallow throughout its length, but at that time there was an inlet on the south bank of the Cuddy which fed a mill lade and it is likely that there was a cauld or some form of obstruction, creating a deep pool at the mouth of the lade.

The execution took place just the day after the trial. Justice was swift with little chance of a change of heart on the part of the authorities. Patersone was tied with four fathoms of rope supplied by John Tuedy, described as a merchant and he was kept in the water until he expired. The burgh officers and others who had been hired to carry out the sentence were given meat and drink for their trouble, while the official executioners named Cleirie and Makwate were given bread and three shillings each. Thus ended one of the most the most extraordinary events which Peebles had witnessed in its long history.

If the execution of Thomas Patersone was bizarre, then the treatment of those who were charged with the crime of witchcraft, was not only bizarre but rooted in ancient fears of the supernatural.

The idea of witchcraft has exercised minds throughout the centuries, at least since the Middle Ages. In times before the Age of Reason and before scientific discovery provided answers to many of the mysteries of life, the explanation for events was largely based on simplistic concepts of good and evil. Those events which resulted in positive outcomes were seen as the work of an Almighty God, while those which were negative and harmful were seen as the work of the Devil. The representatives of a good and bountiful God were the saints and the saintly, while evil was the domain of the Devil's disciples, of whom warlocks and witches were the primary representatives. Witchcraft had been recognised as a crime since the Dark Ages. In the fifteenth century, ultimately it was for the crime of witchcraft that Joan of Arc was burned at the stake.

In the sixteenth and seventeenth centuries the whole of Europe became obsessed with the notion that human beings, mainly women, could be invested with Satanic powers. There were indeed those who believed in their own ability to cause harm and even death to those who had displeased them and did so by invoking the help of the Devil, but there were countless others who were accused and usually convicted of sorcery and witchcraft. They were often no more than the unfortunate victims of the malice of their neighbours. Almost every illness, tragedy, misfortune or unexplained event, came to be attributed to "witchcraft". Those accused were rarely acquitted. It was a case of "guilty until proved innocent".

Denials were disregarded because as it was assumed in advance that as the accused was a "witch" they must therefore be lying.

In Scotland the fixation with witchcraft reached its zenith in the seventeenth century. Following the Reformation of 1560, which put an end to the dominance of the Roman Catholic church and established Calvinist Protestantism, what were seen as the "mystical" practices of the Church of Rome were regarded with suspicion. Central to the Mass was the belief that bread and wine became the actual body and blood of Christ, that miracles were possible and that saints, long dead could intercede on behalf of ordinary men and woman, to achieve a better afterlife or restore health and wellbeing. That was no longer accepted by the Reformed church. At a time when there was a strong reaction against those practices, it was a small step from that to thinking that anything which might be unexplained was surely "witchcraft" and perpetrated by those who were in league with the Devil. In 1563 the Scottish parliament had introduced a Witchcraft Act which made it a capital offence to practise witchcraft or consort with witches.

James VI&I, took a remarkable and almost obsessional interest in the whole idea to the extent that in 1597 he published a learned treatise on the subject called *Demonologie*. He was quite sure that 'Satonic powers' were a reality and that events such as violent storms at sea were the work of the Devil. This was enhanced when sea storms delayed the journey to Scotland of his future bride, Anne of Denmark and his own journey to Denmark to meet her and their eventual journey back to Scotland. In James' mind the spells and incantations of witches were the cause and were a direct attempt by the Devil to destroy him.

He had been present at the trials of a number of alleged witches, most notably that of Agnes Samson and the North Berwick witches and had personally interrogated those unfortunate women, who were subsequently burned at the stake for their "crimes" It was that trial which convinced James that there existed a "demonic pact" between the Devil and his supposed adherents.

James was not alone in his concern to punish and stamp out those who were alleged to practise "the dark arts". As late as 1643 the General Assembly decreed that there should be a purge of witches and set out specific instructions as to how that should be done. Further afield in America between 1692 and 1693 more than 200 citizens of the town of Salem were accused of the crime and some 20 were executed for it.

It was genuinely believed that warlocks and witches existed and could exercise a malign influence over their fellow men. Who were those "warlocks" and "witches"? In all probability they were the unfortunate few found in every age and in every community who were mentally afflicted or were nothing more than social misfits; the awkward squad. They were the sort of people who always attract a degree of fear and aversion from their fellow men. Those unfortunate enough to be accused of witchcraft were unlikely to have received a fair trial and so called "confessions" were extracted rather than volunteered!

According to Dr Gunn :

> To these causes also must be attributed the awful delusion of witchcraft..........which in this seventeenth century obsessed the Church like a hideous nightmare. Some of its victims were undoubtedly insane; others were the subjects of an aggravated hysteria which prompted them to confess to horrible practices out of a mere craving for notoriety; but very many suffered from false and vindictive accusations of their neighbours in order to afford the gratification of spite or revenge.........

Astonishing as it may seem today, witchcraft featured in Peebles. The punishment for this offence, varied from the mild to the extreme. For example, on 4th January 1627, a Peebles widow Margaret Dalgleish, was accused of witchcraft and "charming"[110], which she denied. The only thing which could be proved against her was that she had threatened someone with whom she had quarrelled. She confessed to that and asked for pardon, at the same time repeating that she did not practise witchcraft. It was a crime often associated with personal quarrels and disputes and no doubt in the heat of the moment, words were used and curses cursed, which were later regretted.

Margaret was lucky, escaping with an admonition. Less fortunate were the three women who perished for their alleged crime of witchcraft during 1628 and 1629. They were strangled and then burned at a place called the Calf Knowe. The site has never been positively identified, but probably lay to the east of the town, possibly on the lower slopes of Venlaw. Who they were or how they came to be condemned is not known, although a payment of 12s for the cost of a document recording a confession by Isobell Grahame against the rest of the witches, appears in the Treasurer's Accounts. Perhaps she was spared their fate as a consequence of her "confession" and as the record refers to it as being against 'the rest', it seems possible that confession led to compassion.

---

[110]   Having occult power.

To modern minds it seems extraordinary that such events could happen in a place like Peebles, where every inhabitant would be known, although it is likely that the three wretches in question were not popular in the community and were the subject of severe dislike. Possibly they were the victims of the sort of personal hatred which can still emerge in communities today when unpopular individuals can find themselves blamed for the misfortune of others. As Dr Gunn commented:

'These were terrible days of Church discipline. Much attention was paid to evidence of a merely hearsay character; the result being that opportunity was afforded to the envious, to the malignant, to the slanderous and the revengeful, either to pay off old scores, or to destroy the reputation of a neighbour.'

Those events were sufficiently important for the records to list in detail the associated costs of their execution, down to the smallest item. The apparently cold and matter of fact way in which this done is disturbing:

For making the gibbet £4. For the hire of the lockman £3 and for the amount drunk at his feeing 26s 8d. To John Robene, for five loads of peats, with a quart of ale he gave to the peatmen, bought to burn the witches, 32s 8d. Three loads of coals 36s. A load of heather, 9s. Three fathoms small cord to bind the witches hands, 30d. Four fathom of thick rope to hang them up with all, 6s 8d. Bread and drink fetched forth to the assytherees, 30s. Hangman' wages £10. To his son for being doomster, 12s.

In addition Alexander Dikisone was paid 3s 4d for carrying three tar barrels to the Calf Knowe, in which the witches were to be burnt. In a separate note of payments made by the provost there is one for £5, 16s for ten loads of coal for 'the burning of the last three witches'.

In 1644 there is another reference to the execution of witches. On the 8th January in that year, Alexander Lauder was instructed by the Council to go to Edinburgh or Musselburgh and to bring back an executioner to deal with witches who had been charged with the crime and were to be despatched on the following Thursday, the 11th of January (the number or names is not specified). It is possible that he had sympathy for the unfortunate women and had shown some reluctance to undertake the task, because, if he refused, the provost and bailie were to appoint someone else, but at Alexander's expense.

The following verses are attributed to Dr Gunn:

Outwith the burgh stands a grassy mound,
Oft kissed by smiling sunbeams of the morn,
And bathed by evening dews, but hallowed ground
To us, though to our sires a place of scorn,
To which were led old dames of friend forlorn,
To yield in lambent flame and pungent smoke
Their lives in martyrdom oft bravely borne
In name of justice, but too oft a cloak
For spite and jealousy of neighbour folk.
A redder glow than sunbeams fired it then,
The dew was human tears from spirits broke,
Hearts torn and robbed of hope by cruel men.
This mound thus takes to-day the form of passing eyes
Of one vast altar raised for human sacrifice.

In her book *Borders Witch Hunt,*[111] Mary W Craig writes that in 1629, twenty seven men and women of the town of Peebles were accused of witchcraft and put on trial and that twenty four were subsequently executed and burnt in tar barrels on the Calf Knowe. She refers to this as following the issue of a Commission by the Privy Council This seems an extraordinary number and the present author can find no evidence of such a large number in the extant histories of the town and county or extracts from the burgh records, but that may be an omission which fails to take account of those who may not have been resident in the burgh and parish of Peebles.

The Register of the Privy Council of Scotland records the Commission. It is addressed to the Sheriff of Peebles and his deputes, the bailies of the burgh of Peebles, the bailies of the regality of Dalkeith, the bailies of the regality of Glasgow, or any two of them and commands them to, 'search for, imprison and examine', the twenty seven whose names had been submitted by the Moderator of the Presbytery of Peebles who were 'vehementlie suspect' of witchcraft. The examination was to take place within fifteen days of the apprehension of any of the named and the results of their examinations were to be reported to the Privy Council, who would thereafter issue further orders.

---

[111] Mary W Craig, *Borders Witch Hunt*– The Story of the 17th century Witchcraft Trials in the Scottish Borders.

The twenty seven names recorded confirm Mary Craig's figure, but only three, Agnes Chalmers, Susanna Elphinstoun and Margaret Yerkine are actually from the burgh of Peebles itself. At first sight it might be thought that they may well have been the three "witches" whose death by burning was recorded in such detail. Of the remainder, Gilbert Hog is described as 'in Winkstoun' (Winkston), Patrick Lintoun, 'in Melingsland' (Mailingsland?), Katherine Mairshell, Marion Boyd and Margaret Gowanlocke from the parish of Athelstoun (Eddleston), Helen Beatie and Janet Achesoun, from the parish of Menner (Manor), Margaret Johnestoun from the parish of Traquair, Margaret Dicksoun, Kailzie, and Katherine Broun from Innerleithen. The rest come from various parts of the county of Peebles, six alone from 'Lintoun' (West Linton).

On 22nd December 1629 the Privy Council issued a Commission to William Burnet of Barns and another two selected from James Naismith of Posso and the provost and bailies of Peebles, to hold courts and try three of those listed, namely, John Grahame, Margaret Johnestoun and Susanna Elphinston for witchcraft. It has been previously assumed by the town's earlier historians, that the three witches whose burning was described in some detail were all women. The name of Susanna Elphinston appears in both Commissions. However, it seems likely given the relevant dates, that those were in fact the three "witches" referred to. Agnes Chalmers and Margaret Yerkine whose names appear in the first commission may have escaped the ultimate punishment or there may have been other burnings.

Witches and witchcraft were still an issue as late as 1651. In October of that year the accounts show a sum £2 for 'setting up the gallows to the witches'. The previous year, two women, Mariotte Watsone and Bessie Eumond, had been held in the steeple for more than six months suspected of practising the "black art". On 26th April the council decided to release them subject to each of them providing caution of 500 merks and on condition that they remained in their own houses 'in silence.' They were not to go to church or the market or to move from their houses. Also, if called on by the magistrates, they were to appear before them and their clerk, to be formally charged.

It does seem that the release of the two women may have been more a matter of economy than of compassion. The steeple of Peebles provided prison accommodation for the county as well as the burgh and the magistrates were finding it difficult to extract contributions to meet the cost of keeping the prisoners. In one example, the kirk session of Newlands had refused to what they were due arguing that there were 'only four witches in the prison and little watching needed'.

17.

The Tolbooth, Steeple and Weapons of War

The principal building in burghs and large towns at that time, apart from places of worship, was the tolbooth. The name derives from its original purpose which was the collection of customs taxes or tolls. In time it became the centre for all official business. It was the meeting place of the council and it was to the tolbooth that citizens were called to hear public pronouncements and to take part in public discussion and debates. It also served as the town prison.

For at least two centuries there had been a tolbooth in Peebles. The first recorded building was situated in the Briggait and as previously mentioned was built probably about the middle of the fifteenth century. As time passed it seems to have proved inadequate as a prison and at some time before the sixteenth century the building known as "the steeple", situated next to the Chapel of St Mary, began to be used for this purpose. It remained in use until near the end of the eighteenth century.

The whole question of suitable prison accommodation had become a matter of concern to the Privy Council who decreed in June 1605 that every burgh should have sufficient prison accommodation. The Privy Council further decreed that if within the next twelve months the tolbooth of any burgh was deemed to be failing to meet that requirement, the burgh would be fined £1000 Scots.

The facilities in Peebles were judged to be inadequate and on 25th October, the burgh became liable to build 'ane sufficient and sure tolbuith and prisone, able for kiping of all sic malefactoures and prisoneris as sall happin to be committed to ward.' According to Dr Gunn, Hector Cranstoun appeared before the Privy Council on behalf of the magistrates and council and undertook that they would build a 'sufficient and sure' tolbooth and prison within two years, complete with irons and stocks.

The question then arises is where was it built? William Chambers says that it was built in the High Street, opposite what he calls "the Old Town Hall".[112] Dr Gunn agrees, but Robert Renwick questions this. It does appear that the council acquired property at that location. In 1631 the

---

[112]   Also called the "Town House" and now the "Old Fire Station"

purchase of a tenement between the High Street and the Briggait is recorded and it may be that this was originally earmarked as the site. Building materials were ordered for 'the new tolbuith' and some costs were incurred, making alterations and carrying out repairs to the property, but a few years later it was sold.

An entry of 1632, relates to the appointment of John Robene as keeper of the steeple, the jail house and the tolbooth. So it is more likely that all three were located together at the west end of the High Street, adjacent to the Chapel of St Mary. The steeple already stood there and was used as a watchtower. It included a belltower and clock. Any new building would have formed an extension to it. There are references to the council convening for its meetings in the chapel, so it can be assumed that that group of buildings had now become the administrative centre of the burgh and continued until 1753, when a new town house (the Old Fire Station) was built at the top of the School Brae. There is a further piece of evidence appearing in the burgh accounts. An entry dated 24th July 1638 relates to payments made for repairs to the Tweed and Peebles bridges and to the *tolbuith*. What is interesting is that originally *Chappell* had been written, but this scored out and *tolbuith* written in its place. This would seem to indicate that in the mind of the town treasurer the two were associated.

The steeple was taken down in 1776 and around the same time the tolbooth and Chapel were also demolished, which is perhaps further evidence of the combined municipal use of that group of buildings.

Some indication of the extent, use and complexity of that group of buildings can be gathered from the considerable number of keys which were passed to John Robene at his appointment as custodian : the great key of the lock of the outer gate of the steeple; the key of the lock at the foot of the turnpike of the steeple; the key of the door of the house known as the 'cowmmoune' house or hall; the key of the house called 'Maile Grayes' house; the key of the door in the midstair or turnpike of that house; the key of the clockhouse door; the key of the lock of the outbuilding beyond the clock; the key of the bell house; the key of the door of the 'Brokisholl' and three 'hinging lockes' (padlocks) and their keys. Also listed as being passed to his charge were a long iron rod complete with rings and shackles attached to which prisoners were fastened as well as a pair of wooden stocks.

At around that time animals were slaughtered in the High Street (as the High Gait was now called). In November 1629 the council instructed John Thomson to inspect all the meat which had been 'slane on the Hea Streit.' The slaughtering of animals in the main thoroughfare of the town cannot have been a very satisfactory arrangement and two years later the treasurer was instructed to buy ten joists and twenty boards for the construction of a flesh market in the close of the tolbooth. The council instructed that in future all animals to be killed and sold within the burgh must killed in and sold from this new flesh market.[113]

Throughout his reign and particularly in the later years James VI&I had tried to establish peace. In his own kingdom of Scotland he had been fairly successful, especially as far as the Borders were concerned, where for centuries the rule of law had been largely ignored, at least in the landward areas. Cross border raiding from both sides had been almost endemic, but with his accession to the throne of England, he had been able to impose stability, so that what had previously been the ' Debateable lands" had been become "Central Britain" with a common interest in establishing law and order. Also, now that there was a common monarchy, the threat from "our auld enemies of England" was no longer an issue. As a result there was little incentive for the training of local militia and in Peebles that was certainly the case. It had been many years since there had been any serious preparation for the military defence of the town.

Yet war and threat of war was never far away and towards the end of James' reign there were stirrings of war in Europe, where once again Spain in particular was seeking to dominate the continent. Those were the early days of the Thirty Years War. James had a particular interest. In 1612 his daughter Elizabeth had married Frederick V, the young Elector of the Palatinate, which was the leading state in the union of German Protestant states. In 1618 the German princes elected Frederick and Elizabeth as King and Queen of Bohemia. That was immediately opposed by Frederick II, the Hapsburg emperor whose Imperial troops invaded Bohemia defeating Frederick and forcing him and Elizabeth to flee to the Netherlands. At the same time Spanish and Bavarian troops invaded the Palatinate. James was under pressure from English protestant hawks to intervene and restore his daughter and her husband, by force if necessary. It would have involved war with Spain, but James, the dove, the peacemaker, wanted to resolve the problem by diplomacy. The heir

---

[113]   It does appear that this flesh market was subsequently replaced. An entry for 30th January 1671, records the decision of the council that a flesh market should be built, "at the bak of Thomas Smyth, clerk, his yaird dyke upon the Bridgait". This is almost certainly the Old Slaughterhouse, the remnants of which still stand today adjacent to the Deans Wynd and the Bridgate.

apparent, Charles supported a military intervention in support of his sister, but although steps were taken to strengthen the navy, James could not justify the cost of a full-scale military adventure on the continent of Europe. None the less the threat of war aroused concerns throughout the whole country. Britain was an island, but it was a time when other nations, Spain and the Netherlands in particular, had substantial naval forces, which might pose a threat of invasion and throughout the country, local militias were once more being raised. Peebles produced its own response and on 24th August 1624, a 'general wappinschawing', the first for many years was held in the churchyard of the Cross Kirk. A "wappinschaw" was an occasion when townsfolk paraded with whatever arms they had in their possession. On that occasion, as was usual, the parade was supervised by the provost and bailies. There was a turnout of 100, including 25 from the "Auld Toun". 6 more were reportedly absent. Everyone present had his armour and arms inspected.

The majority of weapons carried consisted of swords, lances, hagbuts or muskets and spears. In addition there were a few who carried what Renwick calls "pistolets".[114] Two of those present had a bow and quiver of arrows in addition to a sword and spear. Among the whole company there were 86 swords, 69 spears, 16 hagbuts and 6 lances. As far as armour was concerned, 38 had 'steil bonnets' or helmets, 10 were dressed in suits of mail.

Although it seems a sizeable tally, only 37 of those present were passed as being satisfactorily equipped. As Renwick records, 'Thus, one appearing with sword and hagbut, is required to procure a jack and steel bonnet; another, having only a sword, is "unlauit" for wanting armour; another, with sword and spear, is to get a jack, steel bonnet, and hagbut; another, with an "auld sword", is to get a new one, and other arms and armour; and another, with sword and hagbut, is to get a "buffil coit."'

In most cases, it was possible to make good deficiencies, but one case, that of John Lausanne, who came on parade with a rusty sword and a spear "wanting the heid" was considered beyond redemption, so much so that the authorities were speechless and let him leave the parade without further comment!

In the two decades which followed, Peebles would be called upon to contribute men, money and materials towards the defence of Scotland, so that those martial preparations were not wasted.

---

[114] The original word refers to a type of bread found in Belgium, rather than a weapon of war. Renwick probably meant a type of small pistol

18.
A New King

King James VI&I died on 16th March 1625. The king who succeeded him was an of an entirely different character.

Charles Stuart was born at Dunfermline in 1600, the last King of Scots to be born in Scotland. As a child he was sickly and suffered from a speech impediment. When his father, James acceded to the throne of England and moved south to London, Charles, alone of the family, was left behind in Scotland as he was thought not to be sufficiently strong to make the journey. The following year he did join the royal family in London. It was 29 years later before he returned to his native land. Although he retained something of his Scottish accent, it is unlikely that he retained any memory of the country he had left behind and would one day come to rule over. In reality he knew nothing of it or its people or its social and religious attitudes.

He also had the disadvantage of being the second son. His older brother Henry was charismatic, sharing many of the intellectual characteristics of his wily and politically shrewd father. He was charming and extrovert, the very model of a prince. Charles, by contrast was shy and reserved. Henry, as the heir apparent was educated in the skills of politics and kingship. Charles, although well educated in a general sense, was not.

In one of those tragic events which might well have altered the course of British history, Henry died from an infection, thought to be typhus, at the age of eighteen. James had gone to considerable lengths to teach him the art of ruling and the pitfalls of court intrigue. Those had been instilled from an early age, but James seems to have been unable or unwilling to continue the process with his younger son. Towards the end of his life, James tried to give Charles some part in the government, (he was allowed to attend meetings of the Privy Council and Parliament) but when he finally acceded to the throne he was largely unprepared. He had already demonstrated a lack of judgement, when, aided and abetted by the Duke of Buckingham, his friend and the favourite of James, he had embarked on a madcap expedition to Spain, ostensibly to woo the Infanta Maria. They adopted a ridiculous disguise, with false beards, which fooled nobody. Their expedition, which James had been most unhappy about, ended in embarrassing failure.

Charles did return to Scotland on a number of occasions, the first in 1633 for his belated coronation as King of Scots and although he did visit Fife and other parts of the lowlands, he never visited Peebles. None the less the effects of his reign and its aftermath did have a significant influence on the town, although that would be some years in the future.

In Peebles, the early years which followed the accession of Charles I were fairly uneventful. There were the usual problems of regulating trade and at about this time some of the practices of traders were damaging the reputation of the town. The sale of all produce offered was supposed to be confined to the officially designated market areas, which were located in the High Street, but in March 1628, the council became alarmed by the amount of illegal trading which was taking place. It noted that there were many injuries, losses and damage being suffered by the burgh and its market as a result of the selling and buying of shoes and other market wares and merchandise. In addition, the buying and selling of meal on market days at a number of landward small holdings, as well as booths and houses within the burgh, was contrary not only to the particular laws of the burgh, but also of parliament. As the council minute says, 'thairby the mercat of this burgh is becum as it war little or altogider nothing, be the malignant dispositioun and deilling of sum malicious and evill-disposit persounes.' In order to exercise more control, the council set fixed times for the shoe market and the market for all other merchandise and 'merchant wairs'. Each market day was to begin at eleven in the morning, signalled by the chapel bell, while the market for 'vituals', that is meal, bere (an old variety of barley), malt, wheat, peas, oats and rye, was to begin every market day 'preceislie at tuelf houris in the day'. If anyone was found buying or selling at a landward farm toun or smallholding or in a booth or private house within the town before the goods were displayed at the market or sold anywhere outwith the market place, then the shoes and merchandise or the meal or other foodstuffs and the money taken for them would be confiscated and used by the town. The perpetrators would be punished according to the law.

A few years later there were still problems. In 1644 it concerned the sale of eggs by, 'certain avaritious and godless persons'. The preamble to an act of the Privy Council, passed in 1615 had complained that :

Amang the mony abuses whilk the iniquity of the time and private respect of filthy lucre and gain (little changes with the passing centuries!) *has produced within the commonwealth, thare is of late discoverit a most unlawful and pernicious tred of transporting of eggs furth of the kingdom....', carried out by people, 'void of modesty and discretion, preferring their awn private commodity to the commonweal, goes athort the country and buys the hail eggs that they can get, barrels the same, and transports the same at their pleasure.*

That created such a shortage of eggs and poultry, that it threatened to cause the complete loss of both throughout the country and the act forbade any further export of eggs and imposed severe penalties. The problem must have persisted or re-emerged in Peebles, because on the 26th February 1644 the town council ordered, 'that na eggis be transported furth of this burgh, and lykwyis na eggs salbe sauld within this burgh' by any inhabitants. If any did, the penalty was, 'warding of their persones during the magistraittis will; and quha salbe tryit to export or sell ony egges furth of this burgh', was to be banished. So it was a serious matter and may have been dealt with in response to renewed instructions to provincial authorities by the Privy Council, although clearly it may have been prompted by a local abuse.

It was not just a question of regulating how trade was carried out. There was behind it a more important issue and that was the question of taxation. For centuries one of the primary functions of a royal burgh was as a central point for the collection of taxes, ultimately as revenue for the Crown. By that time what was paid to the Crown was a fixed annual amount, but it was "farmed" by the burgh. In practice what that meant was that the burgh collected whatever revenue it could from what was effectively a local sales tax. The annual amount due to the Crown was paid from the total collected annually, but the burgh retained any surplus to be applied to its own needs as determined by the council. So, there was every incentive for the council to ensure that all goods of whatever nature were openly sold and bought within the burgh. It included produce from the landward area. Anything to be sold which was not brought in to the official market area of the town, was an offence.

A levy for certain commodities was also fixed by the council. In the case of livestock, all cattle, sheep, lambs and pigs were only to be slaughtered and sold in the new flesh market on payment of a levy. For a lamb, a burgess paid 2d and a landward owner 4d. For each sheep the levy was 4d for a burgess and 8d for landward owners; for cattle more than a year old, by a burgess it was 12d and by landward owners 2s; for pigs 12d each for a burgess and 2s for landward owners. Initially, the Council appointed two officials to collect what was due, but in 1632 it was decided to let the flesh market at a rent of £10 per annum, leaving the tenant to collect the levies.

The Weavers Guild had received official recognition by the council as far back as 1563 when its position was confirmed by a "Seal of Cause" granted by the provost, bailies and council in February of that year. It was a document or act recorded in the town records to which the burgh seal was attached, hence its name. At that time although formally recognised, the guild was not "incorporated". None the less it had been operating under an agreed set of rules and regulations. They included a requirement that all guild members used weights and measures which conformed to those used in Edinburgh. Similarly, the scale of payment for their work was also to be the same as those used in the Capital. It also included a requirement that a deacon be elected annually as was the practice in Edinburgh and Dundee. One of his duties was to collect a levy from the guild members of one penny weekly which was to be passed to the bailies, who in turn would distribute it to the poor.

On 29th of January 1629, John Edmond, the deacon of the Weavers Guild, presented a claim for incorporation to the council. It was granted and was the first formal incorporation of the guild in spite of its having been officially recognised for more than sixty years. It was also the first guild in the burgh to achieve that status. One of the results of incorporation was that the guild became entitled to have a seat on the town council represented by the deacon. Guild members chose a leet of six names from the guild membership. That was then submitted to the magistrates (provost and bailies) who reduced it to three from whom the guild members finally chose one. That arrangement continued until the terminated by the Municipal Reform Act of 1833, apart from a period of 30 years when the privilege was withdrawn because of the personal wrongdoing (unspecified) by a deacon of the day.

The production of cloth, as it would remain until the advent of the Industrial Revolution, was a "cottage" industry. Weavers would produce the cloth usually in their own homes on hand looms. The completed cloth then had to go through a process of cleaning to remove dirt, oil and other impurities. It also compacted the cloth, making it thicker. This was the process of fulling or waulking and was carried out at the town's Waulk Mill, the only one officially approved. It was situated at the east end of Tweed Green, where it had stood since the end of the fifteenth century. The area is today known as Walker's Haugh. The name derives from the process of "waulking" and not, as might be thought, from the name of a person. In 1632 it was leased by the burgh to a partnership of James Frank and James Tueddell. The terms of the lease required them to repair and rebuild the mill and to maintain it during the lease, for which they paid an annual rent of £32 Scots. They were also required to maintain the cauld from which water was taken for the mill. The terms of the lease not only covered the physical property, but also their employees. They were to employ enough qualified staff for, 'the working of their warkis and claithis honestlie and substantiouslie, pleasing the owneris thairof to their best and maist proffeit and commoditie, that na complaint be maid of thame nor ony of them.' The craft of waulkers or fullers of cloth was recognised as a separate trade. As with other trades in the burgh, the waulkers were protected from competition, with their monopoly position formally recognised as an entry in the records in December 1625 confirms :

It is statute be the hail counsel that quhasoever within this burgh sall tak ony wobbis to be walkit at ony uther walkmylne nor the walkmylne of this burgh, and be the walkeris thairof, they alwayis doing their dewtie, that the persone or persones quha sal happin to contravene this act sall pay to the saidis walkeris for their loissis fourtie pennies for ilk elne thairof, exceptand always furth of the present act sik claith as salbe littit and walkit in claith in Edinburgh.

Later another waulk mill would be established by the seventeenth century in what today is Damdale on the west bank of the Peebles Water (the Cuddy) on the site of what in the fifteenth century had been the corn mill.

The working day was regulated by the tolling of the town bell or sometimes by the beating of a drum in an age when timepieces were unknown to all but the richest members of the community. In 1634 there seems to have been a problem. Perhaps the bells were out of commission or no one was available to beat a drum, but in any event, in November of that year John Layng, the town piper was instructed, 'that he sall daylie and ilk day, at four houris at morne and aucht houris at evin, play through the toune with his grit pype till Martinmas 1635.'

Gypsies make their appearance in Peebles about that time. It was thought, quite wrongly, that they originated in Egypt and the name "gypsy" is thought to have come from that source. Renwick actually refers to them as "gypsies or Egytians" (sic). In fact they were a distinct ethnic group known as "Romani", who originated in North India and perhaps because of their swarthy skin they were confused with the people of North Africa and the Nile. Since the Middle Ages there had been wandering tribes of Romani people throughout Europe. They are first mentioned in Scotland at the beginning of the sixteenth century. The southern Borders, in particular Kirk Yetholm, near Kelso would become a major centre.

They seem to have been a source of trouble, because in 1630 the Privy Council issued an order for their suppression and when in 1634 a number of them arrived in Peebles, the town council took action against inhabitants of the burgh who associated with them. On 21 July, one of them, Walter Scott, was charged with associating with them (they are referred to in the records as "Egiptianes") during the previous three weeks and allowing two of them into his house on several days. Gypsies, as now, made a living from the sale of goods, but Scott denied buying anything from them. He was ordered to appear before the council to explain himself, as was John Pringill, who was charged with frequenting them for the past six weeks and that he 'playit at the pennie stane upone the Tuid Greine' with them, which he denied. The "pennie stane" was a flat stone used instead of a quoit (usually a metal ring) which was thown at a target. It was a game which was quite common in Scotland at the time and no doubt was played with accompanying bets being placed.

These are parochial affairs. Further afield greater matters were developing, which in time would affect not only Peebles, not only Scotland, but the whole of the British Isles.

19.
Prelates and Prayer Books

In 1633 Charles I arrived in Edinburgh for a belated coronation as King of Scots, eight years after he had inherited the throne from his father. It was his first visit to Scotland since he left the land of his birth 29 years before. It did not start well. Charles insisted that the coronation service should be in accordance with the Episcopal order, complete with clergy, bedecked with all the grand vestments which were seen by Calvinist Scotland as prelacy and the hallmarks of popery.

His entourage included William Laud, Bishop of London and soon to be Archbishop of Canterbury, a man full of his own importance and an arch enemy of Calvinist Presbyterianism. It caused outrage. Yet Charles' arrival in Edinburgh had been greeted with enthusiasm by the citizens who lined the streets of the Capital, but that would soon change. Not only was the coronation to be an Episcopal celebration, but with Laud's support and persuasive advice, the king also ordered that in future the services in the Royal Chapel and the High Kirk of St Giles, should be conducted in accordance with Episcopal liturgy. The capital city was created an Episcopal see.

The history of the Protestant religion in Scotland is a complicated one. The final eclipse of the Roman Catholic Church had occurred in 1560, when in August of that year the Estates of Scotland passed an Act which established a Calvinist Presbyterian order, based on John Knox's "Confession of Faith". It abolished the authority of the Pope and with it bishops and bishoprics. It set in their place a system of kirk sessions, presbyteries and synods under the overall control of a General Assembly, in which all congregations were to be represented. The Sacraments were reduced to two, Holy Communion and Holy Baptism. Each synod which roughly coincided with the former bishoprics, was presided over by a "Superintendent".

In England, the reformed Church established by Henry VIII, had taken a different path from Scottish Calvinist Presbyterianism. Bishops and bishoprics remained. Vestments and liturgy still retained many elements of the former Catholic order. It was called "Episcopacy", with the monarch at its head and in spite of retaining much of the previous liturgy, it was fiercely opposed to the church of Rome.

In Scotland changes began to emerge during the reign of James VI&I, who commenced his personal rule in 1578. From then on a struggle developed between those who supported Presbyterianism and those who supported Episcopacy. The debate, in which James played a prominent part, was not just about theology and liturgical order, it was also about ultimate authority. The authority of the Pope had been removed. Presbyterian doctrine claimed the General Assembly as the supreme authority, with the Bible, the Word of God, as the source of that authority direct from God. Episcopacy placed the reigning monarch as Head of the Church as God's representative on earth, the Divine Right of kings. The way the pendulum swung depended on which faction dominated the Privy Council, the Estates and the General Assembly.

In 1571 an Episcopal-dominated Privy Council held sway and bishops were restored. In 1581 a Calvinist Presbyterian parliament abolished them, persuading the young king to confirm the renunciation of Catholicism in a document which became known as the "King's Covenant", but in 1584 he was able to persuade the Scottish parliament to pass a series of Acts which introduced the principal that the king was the head of the Kirk and that General Assemblies could only take place if sanctioned by him. Bishops were restored once more, their appointment being a royal prerogative. In 1606 the parliament restored all the privileges of the bishops and finally in 1618 a meeting of the general Assembly meeting at Perth and packed by supporters of the king set out rules for the future of the Kirk. It lent heavily towards Episcopacy in respect administration and restored all the Sacraments and Holy Days, but in practice congregations largely remained Presbyterian. In many cases churches and ministers continued as before and some adopted a mixture of the old and the new. That then was the position when Charles arrived in Edinburgh.

It is not clear where Peebles stood in this confusion of religious governance, practice and belief. Renwick notes, that from what the records show, the changing situation was accepted without comment. Possibly the answer lies in the life and doctrine of the Rev Dr Theodore Hay, Minister of Peebles at that time, which gives a picture of a period of change and change again and the conflict between Episcopacy and Presbyterianism. Dr Hay was the third "Reformed" minister of Peebles. He achieved the remarkable feat of presiding over the Church of Peebles for a period of 38 years, until his retirement. He had had the honour of meeting King James VI himself in 1610, shortly after he began his ministry in Peebles on 20 April of that year.

1. The Edston Hoard of 290 Roman coins from about AD 222 found near a hill fort at Edston Farm, Peebles

   (Tweeddale Museum and Gallery Collection)

2. Roman copper alloy statuette of Jupiter, found on banks of the River Tweed and believed to have been brought by a Roman soldier visiting Eshiels, Lyne or Happrew

   (Tweeddale Museum and Gallery Collection)

3. St.Gordian's Cross, Manor Valley

(photograph by the author)

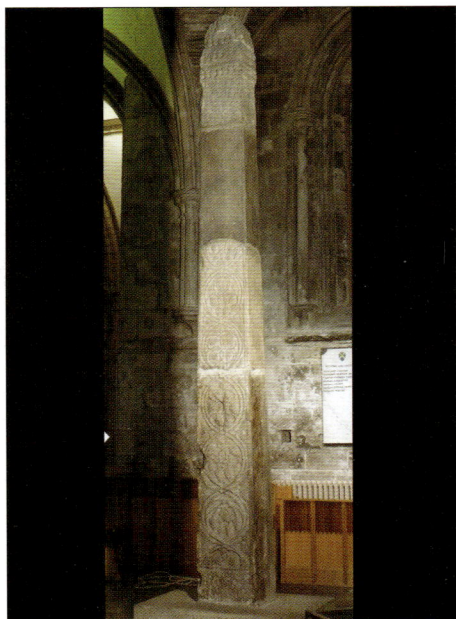

4. Acca's Cross.

*(photograph by Chris Britton,
copyright Hexham Abbey)*

5. Statuette of Alexander III

*(photograph by the author with
permission of the Kirk Session of
Peebles Old Parish Church of Scotland)*

6. Conjectural Image of Peebles Castle circa 1250
*(Watercolour by Gareth Hughes Design and Illustration,
reproduced with permission of Peebles Civic Society)*

7. Conjectural image of Peebles High Street, circa 1500, showing Chapel of St Mary
*(Watercolour by Gareth Hughes Design and Illustration,
reproduced with permission of Peebles Civic Society)*

8. The Cross Church before Reformation of 1560.

From drawing by Alex Blackwood

9. Cross Church and Monastery on north side

From drawing by Alex Blackwood

10. Cross Church Cloister and Garth and tomb of Earl of March 1560

From drawing by Alex Blackwood

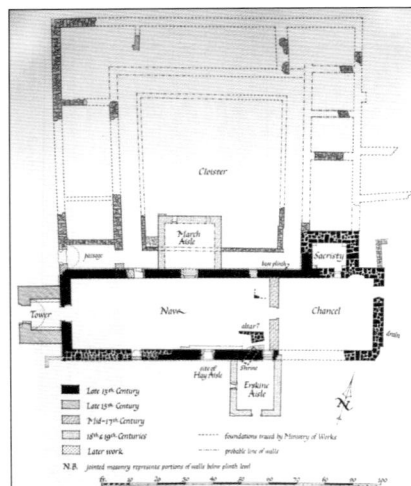

11. Plan of Cross Kirk

(© Crown Copyright: HES)

12. Portrait of John Stuart, 1st Earl of Traquair – School of George Jamieson

(by kind permission of the Traquair Charitable Trust, Photograph by Alasdair MacFarlane)

13. Siege of Neidpath: Watercolour by Jack Roney.

(by kind permission of Lady Elizabeth Benson, Photograph by Alasdair MacFarlane)

14. Portrait of Sir James Hay,
1st Baronet of Smithsfield
and Haystoun, 1586-1654
School of Sir Anthony van
Dyck

*(by kind permission the
Hon. Mrs Mary Coltman,
Photograph by Alasdair
MacFarlane)*

15. Rev. William Veitch. First Church
of Scotland Minister of Peebles,
1690 – 1694

*(With permission of the Kirk Session
of Peebles Old Parish Church of
Scotland)*

16. Falconry lure and hawk hood associated with James Naesmyth of Posso in Manor (1575–1658) who was appointed Royal falconer to King James VI.

(Tweeddale Museum and Gallery Collection)

17. Whisky toddy ladles carved from rowan wood at Gameshope, Tweedsmuir, 1763

(Tweeddale Museum and Gallery Collection))

18. 16th century wooden ball carved by a Flemish monk, showing the Shrine of the Nativity. Donated by Mrs Fergusson of Spittalhaugh in 1854

(Tweeddale Museum and Gallery Collection)

19. Detail of Nativity scene

PLAN OF
CASTLEHILL OF PEEBLES
1779

REDUCED FROM PLAN PREPARED BY
WM. OMAN IN CONNECTION WITH PROPOSED
SITE FOR NEW PARISH CHURCH

Lines dotted thus ·—·—·—· show site of
Parish Church in use from 1784 to 1885

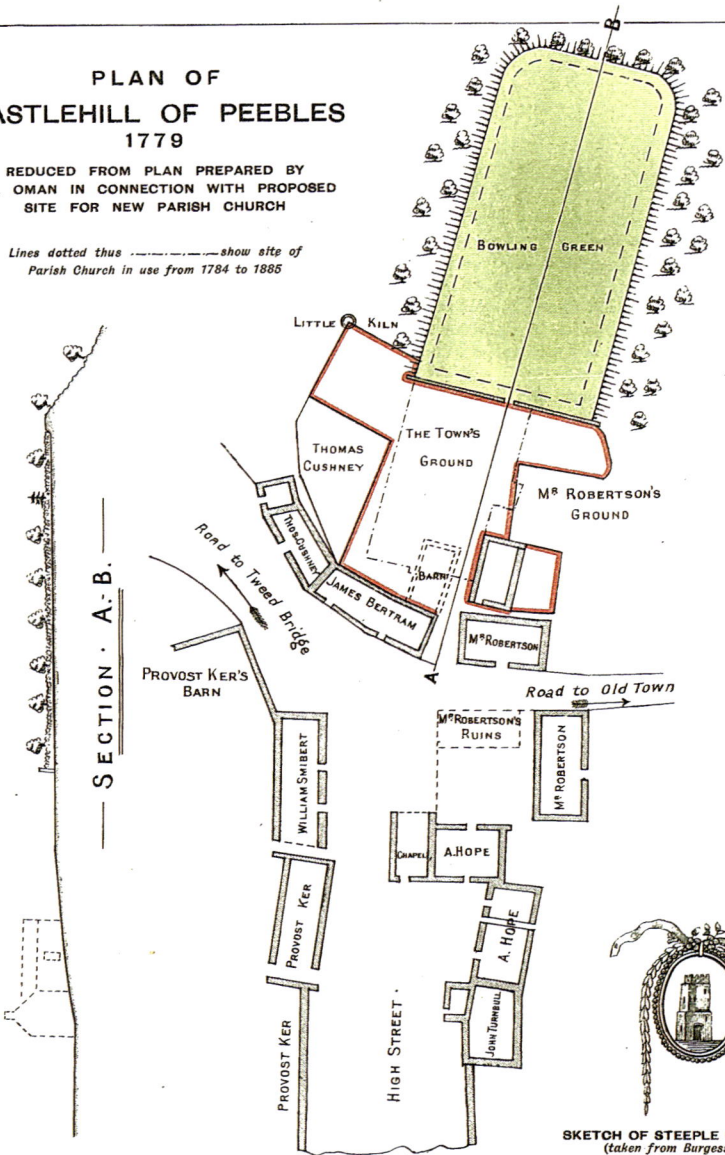

BOWLING GREEN

LITTLE KILN

THE TOWN'S GROUND

THOMAS CUSHNEY

Mʳ ROBERTSON'S GROUND

Road to Tweed Bridge

Thos. Cushney

JAMES BERTRAM

BARN

Mʳ ROBERTSON

PROVOST KER'S BARN

Road to Old Town

Mʳ ROBERTSON'S RUINS

Mʳ ROBERTSON

SECTION · A · B ·

WILLIAM SMIBERT

PROVOST KER

CHAPEL   A. HOPE

A. HOPE

PROVOST KER

HIGH STREET ·

JOHN TURNBULL

SKETCH OF STEEPLE OF PEEBLES
(taken from Burgess Ticket)

REMOVED IN 1776

| 100 | 50 | 0 | 100 | 200 |

— SCALE OF FEET —

W. & A. K. Johnston Limited, Edinburgh & London.

20. Plan of Castle hill 1779 from *The Book of the Parish Church of Peebles AD 1784-1885* by Dr Gunn (1917)

21. Print of St Andrews Church reproduced from *Antiquities of Scotland*
by *Francis Grose 1797*

22. Print of Cross Kirk reproduced from *Antiquities of Scotland*
by *Francis Grose 1797*

23. Hilt of Jacobite sword
    owned by Naesmyths of
    Dawyck and Posso 1745

    *(Tweeddale Museum and
    Gallery Collection)*

24. Engraving on scabbard

25. Municipal measures for liquid and dried goods, circa 1800

(Tweeddale Museum and Gallery Collection)

26. Portrait of Mungo Park by Atkinson Horsburgh

(Tweeddale Museum and Gallery Collection)

27. Mungo Park's surgery circa 1870

(Tweeddale Museum and Gallery Collection)

*28. Example of model ship of war made of bone, made by
French prisoners of the Napoleonic Wars 1810-14*

(Tweeddale Museum and Gallery Collection)

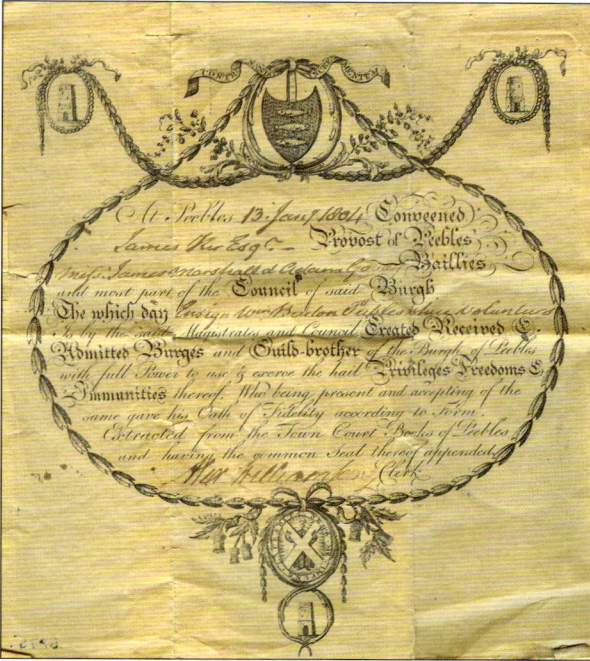

29. Burgess ticket 1804

(Tweeddale Museum and Gallery Collection)

30. Provost's chain first presented to James Kerr in 1823

(Tweeddale Museum and Gallery Collection)

32. Contemporary Wemyss Ware plate with image of house, Biggiesknowe, birthplace of Chambers brothers.

31. Portrait of William Chambers by John A Horsburgh

(Tweeddale Museum and Gallery Collection)

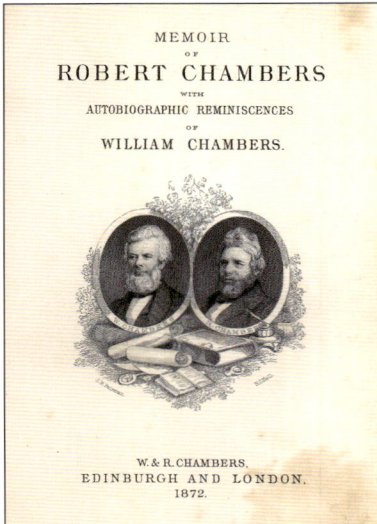

33. Frontispiece of *Memoir of Robert Chambers with Autobiographical Reminiscences of William Chambers*

34. Portrait of Robert Chambers by John Horsburgh

(Tweeddale Museum and Gallery Collection)

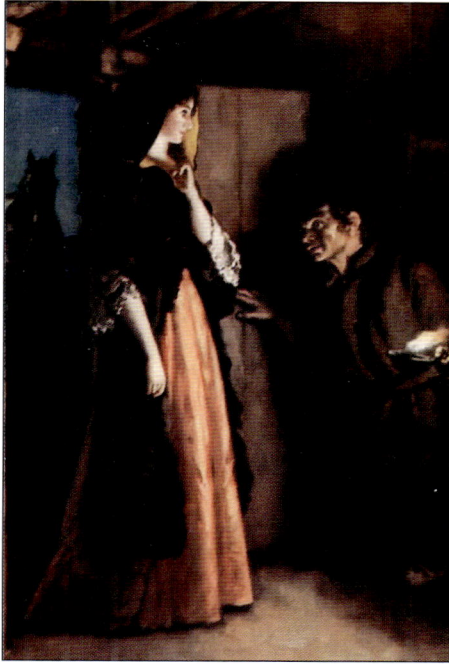

35. Miss Vere's visit to the Black Dwarf from *The Black Dwarf and a Legend of Montrose* by Sir Walter Scott *(Portrait edition Vol V – 1913)*

36. Statue of the Black Dwarf, Hallyards House, Manor

(Photograph by the author with kind permission of Mr & Mrs Michael Gush)

*37. Print of Church from south of River Tweed circa 1800
from lithograph by A & J Macpherson, Edinburgh*

*38. Tweed Green by Charles Blyth 1836
(Tweeddale Museum and Gallery Collection)*

Peebles was in the diocese of Glasgow, whose bishop John Spottiswoode, was a strong adherent to Episcopacy and the supremacy of the king in ecclesiastical matters. It is unlikely that he would allow the appointment of anyone of non-conformist views and it is probable that Theodore Hay was at heart an Episcopalian. This is further underlined by his being a member of the Court of High Commission for the diocese in 1615 and again in 1619. That would not have made him popular, as those courts were regarded with distaste and seen by many as an unacceptable tool of repression by unwanted bishops. He received the degree of Doctor of Divinity from St Andrews University in July 1616. It is later noted that in 1632, Dr Hay made a gift of 100 merks towards the cost of building Glasgow Cathedral college library, perhaps another indication of his support for the current order.

He was old enough to remember the initial struggle between the two forms of church government from 1572 until 1592, when Presbyterianism gained control, only to lose it again in 1610, the year of his appointment as minister of Peebles. It marked the start of the first proper period of Episcopacy, which continued until 1638, when Presbyterianism was re-established, albeit against the will of Charles I. In 1645 he had to further trim his coat to the discipline of the Westminster Confession. He had greatly disliked the resulting changes to the liturgy, which radical puritan elements had succeeded in imposing on the Kirk. Those included discontinuing the reciting of the Lord's Prayer and singing of "Glory to the Father" and even the reading of scripture. He lived long enough to witness the further disruption of the church in 1651, when conduct of worship became largely monopolised by protestant non-conformists.

Dr Gunn comments that:

'It is a curious thought that during all that time his name occurs with rare infrequency in the records of the day..........Whether Dr Hay was a dignified and scholarly man of peace, who made it his ruling principle to quarrel with no one, or was a lukewarm Laodicean[115], cultivating a Gallio-like indifference to all the changes going on around him, there is now no evidence to shew. But amid such stirring times it was surely no mean statesmanship which enabled this man to continue for so long a period as minister of Peebles and yet leave behind him no indications of his tastes, proclivities, principles, friendship, policy or ritual.'[116]

---

[115]   Those who following the Revelation of St John, believed in the doctrine of predestination.

[116]   *The Book of the Cross Kirk, Peebles A.D. 1560-1690* pp 150-151

Perhaps those omissions also reflect the attitudes of the town itself, which as will be seen, appear to be largely in tune with the changing political and ecclesiastical developments throughout the seventeenth century.

As further evidence that the religious affairs of Peebles and its minister were acceptable to the Kirk hierarchy, the town was visited in May 1636 by Patrick Lindsay, Archbishop of Glasgow. It was clearly treated as a significant occasion. The archbishop and his considerable entourage were met by a reception committee at Lyne Bridge. The accounts record a payment of 24 shillings as the expense of the meeting. There followed a reception in the town itself by the council which was held in the provost's chamber, where the party was treated at the town's expense to comfits,[117] ale and shortbread. The archbishop may also have been made a burgess on that occasion. Lindsay ceased to be archbishop in 1638 at the restoration of the Presbyterian order. By the time of the visit of Charles I to Edinburgh, Peebles was firmly established in the Episcopal fold.

---

[117] One of the oldest forms of confectionery comprising seeds, nuts or pieces of spice, coated in sugar

20.

Local Affairs

The records of the burgh for the years which followed the coronation of Charles I as King of Scots cover largely mundane matters. None the less it is the mundane which perhaps gives a true picture of the nature of life in a Scottish town in the mid seventeenth century. We read of the problems associated with the town's possessions, its buildings, bridges and common lands and the regulation of trade.

There is good reason to suppose that the defences of the town were in some state of disrepair. The defensive wall had been completed in 1579. The three main entries to the town were the West Port, Northgate and the East Port. The West and East Ports each formed part of a complex of buildings and were constructed so as to form part of the defences. The West Port was connected to the Steeple, which in turn was connected to the Chapel of St Mary. At that time they were fully in use and in good order. On the south side, the town wall ran above the Tweed Green, turning northwards about half way up the present Post Office Brae. There are remnants of the base of what would have been a tower set at the turning point of the wall, which is mentioned as being at 'Patrick Govane's yardfoot'. Across the main route eastwards from the High Gait (Street) was the fortified building known as the East Wark. It is first mentioned in the records in 1488. It was then known as the "New Wark". It was first occupied in 1494. It seems to have been a substantial structure. It is referred to as containing lofts and vaults which at that time were let to tenants. At its centre and bridging the highway was a gate made sufficiently strong to prevent intruders. The cost of building seems to have fallen on some of the burgesses and it is likely that it was at that time town property. Sometime before 1549, for reasons which are not clear, it came into the possession of the chaplain of the Rood Altar in St Andrew's Kirk. 1549 was the year in which the town suffered considerable damage at the hands of English invaders and there is evidence that it suffered in the resulting destruction. It also appears that at that time the building had been leased to John Stewart,[118] the then laird of Traquair at an annual rent of 4 merks by Sir James Davidson, who was the chaplain. The lease was to

---

[118]   The spelling "Stuart" seems to have been adopted in the latter half of the 16th century.

continue during Davidson's lifetime. The relevant deed is dated 26th March 1550. Some years later on 3rd May 1563, Davidson granted a new lease to Stewart for a period of four years at the same rent as before. The reason given for granting it was that he was unable 'to big and edify the samin, beand brint be our auld enemies of England'. Presumably it was on condition that Stewart carried the necessary repairs at his expense. It may well have also been because in the interim, the Reformation had significantly changed the previous order.

The granting of the lease of such a prominent building stirred up old jealousies. The Stewarts of Traquair and the Hays of Yester had been rivals for many years. The Hays were of course prominent in the burgh and had effectively been provosts since the office was originated. Before the second lease was granted, John Stewart, who is described as "knycht", undertook 'never to desyre to be provost, bailie nor burges within the burgh of Peblis, nor to haif no forther pre-eminence nor intormission within the said burgh nor he hes presentlie.'

Once this assurance was in place, the bailies, council and community agreed that Stewart could have the building in 'feu ferme'[119] always providing that the provost, at that time William, Lord Hay of Yester voted in favour. After he was re-elected the next year, which was hardly a surprise as the role of provost was effectively a Hay fiefdom at least until June 1609,[120] he vetoed the proposal and said that no one should be allowed to have title to the property and that the building should be repaired at the town's expense. Traquair had for the moment at least to accept his position as only lessee.

Eventually in 1579 Hay gave up his opposition to Stewart obtaining a title to the property and that year it was duly granted under certain conditions which included a reservation to the town of the port and a right of access by the town, their magistrates and officers, whenever the provost, bailies and council considered it necessary (for example when required for defence) and the payment to the town of four merks annually.

As more peaceful times became established, the old fortification gradually ceased to have a strategic importance and fell into decay. By the 1630s it was probably more of a hindrance to passing traffic than a deterrent to invaders. It did not survive long thereafter and was demolished 1656 when its title once again reverted to the town.

---

119   A feu disposition.
120   Parliament removed the right of "noblemen and gentlemen" to hold that office, which became the sole preserve of those who lived and worked in the burgh

The space between the West and East Ports, of which the High Street formed the principal part, sometimes provided the stage for punishing malefactors. One such occasion is recorded in April 1637 when the provost and bailies ordered that Issobell Stensone, wife of James Brodderstanes, described as 'sumtyme burgis' of the burgh, was to be taken to the "jogges"[121] and to be 'claspit, and stand thairintill during the space of tua houris.' Thereafter the poor woman was to be taken and beaten from the West Port to the East Port, before being banished from the burgh as she was a perpetual criminal. Her crimes, the "pyking"[122] and stealing six pieces of salt mutton, a quantity of beer and some peats. She was ordered never to be seen or found again in Peebles, 'under pane of death, ather be drowning or utherwyis, at the plesour of the magistrattis thairof.'

The maintenance of the town's three bridges had become an increasing burden on the burgh finances. All three bridges had been in place for the best part of 150 years. The original stone from which they were constructed had come from a variety of sources, none of them in the immediate vicinity of the town. Writing in 1864 in his *History of Peeblesshire,* William Chambers[123] has a section devoted to the geology of the county and says:

> Practical stone masons assure us that the blocks of sandstone used in building the bridge across the Tweed at Peebles, must have been excavated from quarries near Marfield[124] on the North Esk.

Renwick thinks this is correct, as local tradesman of the day would have been fully aware of their provenance. He goes on to say that it had been established that on at least one occasion a supply of stone had come from Dunsyre on the Medwyn which is about nine miles from Marfield. They both lie on the same side of the Pentland Hills and share a same rock strata, so that the type of stone would be similar.

In 1635 major repairs became necessary and the council agreed to make inquiries about a mason in Clydesdale who might carry out the work. The treasurer was instructed 'with all expedition', to buy lime, stones and all the other materials needed. The costs of the work and

---

121   Pillory
122   Pilfering
123   p 521
124   Lying between Peniciuk and West Linton

materials is set out in detail in the records, including things such as labour and transport. Some extracts give the flavour of what was involved:

Item, James Haddane gave in a compte of some works befor two baillies, beiring his calsaying (paving) of Peiblis water staine bridge, his repairing of the treye bridge and calsaying thereof, his going thryse to Dawikwood, his going one tyme to Dunsyre for frie staines, £25 6s 8d.

To James Nicoll, for 63 piece of frie staine to the bridge, £9 14s.

To Plora, for thrie great oak treyis to the bridge worke, £13 13s 4d. To the Plewes of the Eschellis, for carieing these tryis, ££6 6s 8d.

For yron leide (by and attour that whilk was bocht in Edinburgh), yron fyve quarteris wecht at 37s the staine, 56s 4d. A staine of leide, 37s 6d.

For four burding of hedder to melt the leid in the second worke of the bridge, 10s.

To fyve men, for laying the great treye to the bridge, and to thame upoun the morne thairefter for turning about the great stone and laying to the back thairof, 18s.

Payments are also made for providing the masons and their assistants with refreshments.

To Margaret Newtoun, for their morning and four hour drynkis, £6 13s 4d.

To James Haddane, and other fyve, waiding in Tueid watter and carieing stones to lay about the pillar of the bridge, their bread and drynk before and efter their said work, 21s 4d.

In total there was a very large outlay, which was a considerable burden on the revenue of the burgh and in 1636 an application was made to the Convention of Royal burghs for financial assistance. Although the records are unclear, it seems likely that the Convention did give at least some assistance in the form of a loan, which the burgh would repay in part and the balance would be covered by the payment of an annual rent.

As far as the ordinary maintenance of the bridge causeways and keeping them clean was concerned, there was an arrangement that those who carried out the repairs kept the refuse they gathered as payment for their efforts. This seems an odd arrangement and cannot have provided much incentive. Indeed in 1634, when this was the responsibility of

William Lowis, the council asked him if would maintain both the Tweed Bridge and the bridge over the Peebles Water (Cuddy) and be responsible 'for the sweiping and muck thairof, as his predecessouris was oblist to do befoir him.' Lowis declined and renounced his interest not only on his own behalf but also his successors, which suggests that it had been some kind of hereditary arrangement.

Lowis seems to have been a tiresome character. A few months earlier he had been held in the steeple for failing to pay certain of the town's dues and in addition, for disobedience to the magistrates and speaking out against them. One of the town's officers also had complained that he had heard him say, 'I compare the officeris of this toun to the hangman's men', a charge which he denied.

The management of the town's common grazing presented many problems not only in ensuring that the rules were adhered to, but also from time to time there was unauthorised cultivation and grazing of livestock and even on occasion unauthorised construction of buildings and in one instance the destruction of a building belonging to the town.

At the beginning of the seventeenth century the town was still in possession of quite extensive lands and grazings. Beyond the immediate bounds of the town and its lands of Skinnershaugh, the Foul Myre and the Kirklands, it had outright possession of Cademuir, Hamilton Hill and Venlaw and rights of grazing over Glentress, Shieldgreen and Easter Common. Some were quite some way beyond the bounds of the town, which made control difficult.

The main grazing area on which the townsfolk grazed its livestock was Cademuir. This was a large area and in order that livestock could be well distributed, it was divided into two parts, each allocated to a particular area of the town. The Innerhill and the Westerhill formed one part and the Dod and Borrowlees the other. In order to achieve a fair allocation, the town was also divided into two parts with equal numbers of inhabitants. The allocation to each of these was initially decided by drawing lots. The west half, including the Auld Toun was given the Inner and Westerhills, while the east was given the Dod and Borrowlees.

During the decade of the 1630s there are a number of entries in the records which give a picture of some of the problems which the council had to deal with. Those include not only administration of the lands themselves, but not infrequently encroachments by neighbours. For example, in December 1633, Thomas Tuedie was summoned before the council to answer for an alleged "spurring out"[125] by him onto town lands

---

[125] Encroachment

adjacent to his properties at Frankscroft and Dalatho. In May 1634 it ordered that the boundaries between Tuedie's land and the towns should be inspected and if it showed that Tuedie has strayed over what the town claimed was the boundary, he was to produce evidence of his father's title to it. Except for two sowmes[126] all his stock were also to be removed from Cademuir.

In May 1634 the council ordered that the balk or raised ridge and passage between the town's lands of Whitstonehill and the lands of Skinnerhaugh belonging to Thomas Young was to be inspected and removed. In June it ordered that the stock on Hamilton Hill, Venlaw and Cademuir were to be gathered and be brought to the Castlehill for inspection. The Castlehill was at that time an enclosure for livestock and effectively a public pound. In February 1635, anyone who had had stock on Cademuir and Venlaw for four years was to come before the provost and bailies and state on oath what stock they had grazing there and pay the appropriate rent charge. Failure to do so would make them liable to imprisonment. That same year, John Scott of Hundleshope and his accomplices, 'all bodin in feir of war'[127] had broken down a house on Cademuir which belonged to the town. According to the records of 22nd June, this had been done the previous night around midnight. The whole council was called on to convene at the clerk's chamber one hour after noon to dicuss this and take action.

Another typical entry is the one for 24th November 1636: 'Appointis the proveist and tua bailyeis, with tua of everie quarter, to visit Kaidmure hillis anent a new tilth thairof upon Thursday at morne nixt, being ane fair day, and falyeing thairof the nixt fair day thairefter.' On 9th April 1637: 'Ordanes the officeris with ane drummer, to go throu the toun commanding all these that hes nolt[128] or scheip to put the samyn to the common hirdis wthin 24 houris, under pane of £5, and skayth[129] done to owneris of cornes.'

On 23rd April, the shepherd of the common grazings, John Scheill, was ordered to appear before the council and asked to confirm if he would continue in the post for a further year. He replied that because John Young of Milton and his sons, tenants of the town, daily herded and disturbed the town's livestock, he would not continue as shepherd after the next

---

[126] Common grazings were divided into shares called "Sowmes", which was the amount of grazing for a cow or five or six sheep.
[127] As if prepared for war.
[128] Cattle
[129] Damage

Whitsunday, 15th of May which was the term day from which yearly tenancies and agreements ran. John Scott was in trouble shortly after, accused of killing sheep belonging to the town, the previous day which was the Sabbath. The town treasurer was instructed to pursue him and his wife for restitution.

Since the council had responsibility for supervising weights and measures, in the 1630s it continued to ensure that all kinds of produce were sold in strict accordance with the rules. In May 1633 it issued a regulation requiring weighing apparatus to be installed in every bakehouse to weigh all the bread baked on the premises. Not only that but the provost and bailies or someone appointed by them were to check the quality and quantity of the bread. Any contravention was to be punished by the magistrates. Quality control is nothing new!

Nor is price control: 31st August 1635, 'John Tuedie, merchant, being censurit upon his awin confession for selling of tua pennie candilles for four pennies, and being fund culpable of sindrie other puntis in wrangis selling of his merchandice be wechtis quhilkis ar unsufficient, the counsel hes contineuit his punischment till the nixt counsel day; and in the meanetyme the counsel ordanes him to bring hame sufficient wairis and sell the samyn at ane competent rait, and to haif ane half pound brasin (brass) wecht of brasin wechtis market with the *flue de lus,*[130] under the pane of ten pounds for each falt.'

15th October 1638, the council orders that, 'the hail aill to be proclamit to be sauld for sextene pennies the pynt. Ordanes the haill ait breid to be tryit and sauld for aucht pennies the loaf, and the loaf to be sextene uncis, and na loafis to be sold at ony uther pryce.'

Attendance at church on the Sabbath was obligatory. The whole council sat each Sunday in the Cross Kirk in the town's stall. All the members were required to wear a hat. Failure to comply attracted a fine of 40 shillings. In November 1637, a new pew for the magistrates had recently been completed and an inauguration service was held on the 6th of the month. For that occasion and as it was said, 'to enhance the dignity of the corporatio', every member of the council was to buy a new hat. A new pulpit also had been provided and the old one removed to the Chapel of St Mary in the High Gait (Street) for daily worship there.

Some years earlier, in May 1630, Robert Horsbruik, who was a burgess of Edinburgh and the son of Alexander Horsbruik of Horsburgh Castle, donated a mortcloth to the burgh and kirk session for the benefit of the

---

130   *fleur de lis,* the official stamp impressed on the standard one pound weight

poor of the parish. A mortcloth was a pall or covering for the body used at funerals, 'being of fyne blackclaith, lynit throw with blak buckasie[131]and compassit round about with ane blak silk frenzie in the bordouris thairof.'

The donor had stipulated that, 'the samyn micht be kepit be the kirk thesaurer, and he to geve furth the samyn for the decorment of all defunctis as he suld be requyrit' on payment of a fee fixed by the council and the kirk session. The proceeds were to be distributed among the poor. No other mortcloth was to be used by private individuals, whether they lived in the burgh or the landward area. The fee for those within the burgh borrowing it was 13s 4d, while for those outwith the burgh, but still in the parish it was 20s. It was widely available and borrowers within the parishes of Eddleston, Kailzie, Manor and Lyne paid 30s. Beyond that the fee was 5 merks and more according to the distance. For those feeling generous, they might give more, 'according to charitie and plesour'. It was clearly a valuable asset.

These then were some of the mundane affairs which occupied the authorities of the day. Meanwhile major storm clouds were gathering elsewhere in Scotland, which in time would engulf the kingdom and in time the whole of the British Isles. Peebles would not escape.

---

[131] From Old French "boquerant" - fine oriental cloth.

21.
King and Covenant

Following his coronation in 1633, with all its trappings of Episcopacy, against an increasing body of opposition, Charles I had continued to pursue his intention to establish Episcopacy as the state religious order in Scotland as well as England

In 1634, he established a new Court of High Commission with extended powers. The next year he appointed Archbishop Spottiswoode, Archbishop of St Andrews, as Chancellor of Scotland and in that same year, without consulting the Scottish parliament or the General Assembly (which had not met since it had met in Perth in 1618), using what he claimed as the Royal Prerogative, he ordered the introduction of a Book of Canons, which named him as Head of the Church and introduced a new form of liturgy based on the English Prayer Book. It has come to be known as *Laud's Liturgy*, after the Archbishop of Canterbury, although in practice it was largely the work of acquiescent Scottish bishops. Scottish Calvinist Presbyterianism saw it as an affront and a return to Papacy.

On the 23 July 1637 a service was held in the High Kirk of St Giles in Edinburgh. It was a packed affair, attended by Archbishop Spottiswoode, the Lords of Session, many of the bishops of Scotland, the magistrates of Edinburgh and a large and restless gathering of the ordinary citizens. The new liturgy was to be used for the first time at that service, which was conducted by the Dean It is a well known, if apocryphal story. It caused a riot. The ordinary members of the congregation normally stood at such services, but some brought stools with them. Services were long and tiring! It was not long before stools were hurled in rage at the officiating clergy, one propelled at the unfortunate Dean, as he attempted to read from the new Prayer Book, by the now famous Jenny Geddes, with the words, 'Traitor, dost thou say mass in my lug', or so it is alleged.

The service broke up in confusion and very soon the incident provoked a wave of protest which very quickly spread across southern Scotland. At the same time attempts were made to persuade Charles to change his mind, to little avail. In October 1637 a large number of lairds signed a "supplication" demanding that the Prayer book be withdrawn and that bishops should no longer be members of the Privy Council. The response of Charles to the supplication was entirely negative and in December 1637 a meeting was convened in Edinburgh by the leading supplicants to which the representatives of the nobles, lairds, the burghs and the clergy were invited. Each of these groups sat at a separate table and the combined group which had effectively become an opposition, came to be called "The Tables". As a result of the meeting a draft of what became the National Covenant was presented by Alexander Henderson, the minister of Leuchars in Fife and an Edinburgh lawyer, Archibald Johnston of Warriston.

Following that meeting a nationwide request was sent out for all parties to meet in Edinburgh. The letter sent to the burgh of Peebles is lengthy and is transcribed here in modern English. To make it clearer it has been been broken down into sections, preceded by a brief explanation. It begins with an invitation:

To our honourable and loving friends and neighbours, the provost and bailies of Peebles – The copy of the common advertisement sent from the commissioners unto all that are well affected, unto all parties of the kingdom, for coming to our meetings at Edinburgh the 22nd day of February 1638 – The noblemen, commissioners of shires and burghs, and others, convened upon for this common cause, which concerns the preservation of true religion, the laws and liberties of the kingdome,………

It goes on to explain how in the view of The Tables, Charles was misled by the bishops

…..understanding how the prelates, by misinformation of the king's majesty, had, after their accustomed manner, procured a proclamation to be made for establishing the service book and discharging all meetings under pain of treason,….

The next section is referring to the noblemen, commissioners etc.

………have (in God's providence) legally obviated the publication and ratification thereof by timeous protestation and declarator of the common adversaries, the prelates, at the cross of Stirling, Linlithgow and Edinburgh, and are resolved to do the like at all other places as need shall be, ………

The Proclamation referred to is one "procured" by the bishops.

where through, in the judgement of such as understand best, their proclamation and proceedings are made of no legal force to hinder the absolute meeting of all having interest in this common cause and extraordinary urgent need;

Next God's blessing of the action they propose to undertake is called for.

and seeing matters are now come to a height that either we must forsake the way of true religion, established by laws, and betray the lawful liberties of the kingdom, or else resolve upon such a solid course as may in a right manner prevent this imminent and irrevocable ruin of all whereto our sins and the bishops treachery are likely to draw us, except by timeous humbling of ourselves before God and craving God's blessing on our lawful consulations we prevent the same:

It is followed by a call to attend the meeting.

Let all these therefore whom this cause concerns, and who tenders God's glory, his majesty's honour, welfare of the kingdom, address themselves with all diligence to the solemn meeting now convened at Edinburgh, where their coming is attended for consultation how his majesty may yet be better informed and this present peril prevented, if so please the Lord.

The final section, at its end, contains a threat to expose any one invited who failed to attend

In the meantime let every one who shall hear hereof humble themselves before God for deprecating of his fearful wrath, whereunto our Lord Jesus now of long time, by disobedience of His word and despising of His glorious gospel and the ordinances of His kingdom, is provoked. At their coming here we are persuaded to make our loyalty and lawful proceedings clear to them as we have done to all such who we have acquainted thereof – From the commissioners of burghs, met at Edinburgh, the 22nd February 1638 – Let no man doubt for the not subscribing hereof, for the reasons shall be shown at meeting.

The meeting duly took place on the appointed day. The burgh of Peebles was represented by the Provost, James Williamson, who also attended as Commissioner for Peeblesshire. It approved the text of the document which Henderson and Johnston had prepared. It was to become one of the the most important documents in the long history of Scotland, known as the National Covenant.

It started with a denunciation of the Pope and the Church of Rome and a commitment to defend the reformed church. It repeated in full the King's

Covenant of James VI & I of 1582[132] and went on to show how the acts of Parliament which Charles had instigated were at variance with it and called on all to 'labour by all means lawful to recover the purity and liberty of the Gospel as it was professed before the foresaid inovations'.

On the 28th February, there was a great gathering in the kirkyard of Greyfriars Church in Edinburgh at which the whole population was called on to sign the document. Among the first to sign was Lord Yester, who had become an active supporter of the covenanting cause. Also signing on behalf of the the Royal Burgh of Peebles was James Williamson. A few days later copies of the Covenant were distributed throughout the country so that it could be signed by everyone who supported it. The evidence suggests that it was endorsed by the vast majority, although it is difficult to know how spontaneous that was. Certainly many were enthusiastic, but perhaps some persuasion was necessary. It is probable that a copy reached Peebles early in March and it seems to have been signed with only a few exceptions.

In response to the Covenanters, Charles issued a proclamation on 22nd September renewing the King's Covenant of 1581 and referring to 'the religion presently professed'. That was ambiguous, but the Covenanters took it to mean the acts which had been the very reason why they had introduced their own National Covenant.

While it is often difficult to establish just where Peebles and its citizens stood in relation to religious affairs, with the signing of the Covenant by the vast majority and the following extract from the record, it becomes clear that the town was fully behind the Covenanting cause;

> 1638-October 4 – Anent the missive letter sent from the commissioners of Edinburgh, and utheris burghis convenit at Edinburgh, to us, desyreing this burgh to protest aganes the proclamatioun of the general covenant, the counsel hes concludit that protestatioun sall be maid quhensoever the samyn salbe proclamit, and to that effect ordanes tua to attend the samyn daylie.

So, in Peebles at least, any attempt to make the king's proclamation, would be rebuffed. The requirement that two members of the council were to be available to protest against any attempt to issue the proclamation shows that it was something which was taken very seriously.

The pressures on the king were increasing and he was forced to call a meeting of the General Assembly which was to meet in Glasgow on 21st November. The town was to send a commissioner and on 15th October the

---

132   Also known as "The Negative Confession"

council agreed to appoint the provost, James Williamson. The vote in favour was by 'the maist part of the counsel', so was not unanimous, but it is not clear whether it was because of any disagreement on principal or because of the individual proposed. The provost duly attended the meeting of the Assembly which lasted from the 21st November until 20th December and on 24th December he reported back to the council on his attendance and the matters discussed.

Williamson was one of forty-seven burgh commissioners who met in Glasgow Cathedral with ministers and the representatives of sixty-three presbyteries and all the noblemen and lairds who had signed the Covenant. Each of the commissioners was also accompanied by between four and six lay "assessors" and it must be assumed that Williamson was supported by a number of others from the town, who would probably have been councillors. The gathering had not been authorised by the king and was in effect a rebel Assembly. Its first action was to confirm the right of lay members to attend and removed from office all bishops and those clergy who would not support the National Covenant. It then went on in the following days to reject the Five Articles of Perth, the Canons of 1636 and Prayer Book which had been introduced thereafter. It effectively abolished Episcopacy.

At the beginning of 1639 the king and the Covenanters were irreconcilable. In the spring of that year the king led an attempted attack on the Scottish forces, gathering a large but virtually untrained force at Berwick. The Scots Army, formidable and well trained under the command of the able and experienced Alexander Leslie, was encamped at Duns Law. The two armies faced each other. The Covenanters were still loyal to the Crown and anxious to avoid battle with their king. Charles recognised the weakness of his situation and agreed to almost all the demands of the Covenanters, including a free General Assembly and a free parliament, on condition that The Tables were disbanded, the army stood down and occupied castles returned to the king. The document confirming the agreement known as the Pacification of Berwick, was signed by both sides on 18th June 1639 and Charles departed south and did not attend the General Assembly. When it met later in the year, it endorsed everything that had been agreed in the Assembly of 1638 and in addition it instructed the Privy Council that acceptance of the Covenant should be a matter of obligation.

By that time, not all the inhabitants of Peebles had signed the Covenant and on 21st January 1639, the council issued an order that everyone who had not signed should come forward and do so. However, there still seems to have been back sliders and on 29th April the council ordered any remaining to sign that day. On the next day, the council ordered the officers of the council to instruct every person in the burgh who had still not signed, to come to the clerk's chamber within 24 hours to sign. They were warned that if they did not, they would be subject to penalties which the Tables had instructed the provost, bailies and council to impose on defaulters. So the process of signing was not entirely voluntary.

The stage had now been set for a confrontation with the king, which would lead to civil war throughout the British Isles and one of the bloodiest conflicts in British history. It would end with an entirely new form of government after centuries of monarchy. It started in Scotland and Peebles would soon have to play its part.

22.
Bishop's Wars

The General Assembly which met in Glasgow Cathedral in November 1638, had once more abolished Episcopacy, in spite of attempts by Charles to halt it.

On 1st of May 1639, the Burgh of Peebles and the local lairds received a letter from Lord Yester, written the previous day, telling them that 28 warships of the king's navy had sailed up the Forth to Leith. To defend against what was effectively an invading force, every fourth man in the Scottish kingdom would be required to take up arms. There had been a formal proclamation to that effect. So, one quarter of the men of the Royal Burgh was to set out for Leith that very day, fully armed and ready to join with his lordship and his colours.

Acting on that instruction, the magistrates and council decided that the first quarter of the men named on the burgh roll and one of the magistrates should be sent to Leith for a period of ten days and nights and at the end of that time, the men of the next quarter and another magistrate would replace them and that those of the third and fourth quarters would replace them in turn at the end of each ten day period, during the time of the emergency. The arms to be carried were to be muskets and pikes. Later in the year the cost of the armoury was to be raised from the inhabitants by the provost and bailies.

Further preparation for conflict was made by the burgh in the following year. It was decided that every fourth man going on service to the army should take his own weapons and armour with him. However, if any man was unable to provide the full complement, he was to be supplied by the other three members of his group of four. In August of that year, manpower was supplemented by two horses fully equipped at the town's expense with saddles and creels. Not only did the town provide manpower for the anti-royalist force, but soldiers from elsewhere were for a time billeted in the town, the provost and magistrates undertaking to pay for every soldier who was not paid for by the Commissary General.

Early in August, General Leslie led a sizeable army of 22,000 foot soldiers, 3000 cavalry and heavy artillery, from Edinburgh towards the Border. It was made up of regiments which each county was ordered to provide, together with provisions for thirty or forty days. As they had done previously, they camped first at Duns law. Some indication of the contribution of Peebles can be gauged from a number of contemporary entries in the records. The extracts which follow are in modern English, but based on the original Scots[133]:

1640 – March 16 - Orders the bailies to go through the town and seek payment from those who held onto pikes and muskets and their attachments between this date and eight days, under threat of warding.

April 20 – Orders the whole council to attend and be present with the provost and bailies at the meeting of the gentry here this day, each person under threat of five pounds (for not attending).

June 15 – Orders a colour (flag) with the town's arms to be bought.

On the 10th August, the provost and bailies were ordered to negotiate with James Dikeson for the purchase of his horse and gear and to send it to service with the army. On the same date they also met John Dikeson about the purchase of his horse which they thought was the same horse which had belonged to James Dikeson, but had been given to John in settlement of a debt. They said that the Council had decided to buy it for fifteen pounds and fifty shillings. They also met with William Wichtman to buy his horse for service in the army. He said it had cost him seventeen pounds and 'some oddes'. James Dikeson agreed to take both horses, together with their saddles and baskets to the army and to join the men who had already left the burgh. He agreed that he would 'serve the same men dutifully at all occasions required, upon this condition that if it please God the Army arise and the men of this burgh come home again within forty days next hereafter he shall come in the council's will for satisfaction; and if the said army dissolve not within forty days but that there be an encounter betwixt them and the English army, as God forbid, he bringing home both horses whole and sound he shall have half his choice of them.'

There are a number of entries which concern individual soldiers. In one case John Buchannan, who was a shoesmith in the town agreed to become a cautioner (a guarantor) for Robert Buchannan (probably his son), who was a soldier attached to the company of the laird of Keir, who was its

133   Renwick – *The Burgh of Peebles, Gleanings from its Records 1604 -1652* *p* 214 onwards

captain. Robert was to return immediately and John was to obtain a certificate confirming that Robert had first gone to the company of Captain William Lyle of Bassendean and that he had returned to his own company within eight days thereafter.

The accounts also provide evidence of the town raising troops for the army. On May 14th 1640 Patrik Trotter was given 'ane dolour, 54s', by the provost when he arranged for him to join Lieutenant Elphingstoun's troop as one of the town's soldiers. On 16th May Alexander Ewmond and Alexander Sunderland were each given half a dollar, 54s, when they joined Captain Home. On 28th August, John Robene received 16s 8d for providing five day's meat at the request of the provost.

In the case of Ewmond there is an amusing sidelight. It appears that he had been in prison at the time, 'being incarcerat and wairded for certaine criminall matteris lated to his chairg'. As the record says he was "borrowit" to go to the army. Presumably he would return to prison if he came back unscathed.

The army encamped at Duns did not remain there long and on 20th August, led by Leslie it marched south crossing the border at Coldstream and then heading for Newcastle, bypassing Berwick on the way. At Newburn on the Tweed just north of Newcastle they met and defeated a force sent against them by the king, led by Lord Conway. By the 30th they had reached and taken Newcastle itself. Not long thereafter, they had taken control and occupied the whole of Northumberland and with it control of the coal trade. The king could not resist and was forced to call a parliament in London and then to meet Scottish Commissioners at Ripon. There it was agreed that provided they made no further advance, the Scottish army would be paid a subsistence allowance of £850 per day. Well satisfied by that outcome, the Scottish army marched home, richer by £200,000.

On the return of the Peebles contingent, on the 1st November 1641 the council ordered the bailies to, 'tak tryell of the armour cum hame fra the camp.' An inventory was to be taken of the weapons provided by the inhabitants of the burgh in 1639 and now returned to them. It records 41 "musquettes" and 41 "pickes" (pikes), so it can be assumed that at least that number from the burgh had marched south with the Covenanter army and returned.

At this point, as he was to feature largely in what followed, the story turns to John Stuart, 1st Earl of Traquair, someone who does have a direct relevance to Peebles, not only because of the close proximity of his home and estates near Innerleithen, but because of his direct involvement with the affairs of the burgh from time to time. He has already been mentioned in connection with the ownership of the East Wark, which of itself would almost certainly have made him a burgess and his name appears from time to time in the burgh records.

Although John Stuart stood at the very epicentre of political life at the time, his name is one virtually forgotten today. None the less, his is a fascinating story of a rapid rise in the hierarchy of political power, followed by an even more rapid and catastrophic fall.

John Stuart was born around 1600, the son of a Border laird who was the proprietor of the lands and house of Traquair, not far from Peebles. He seems to have been well educated. His tutor was Thomas Sydserf, later to become Bishop of Galloway. He inherited the estate in 1606 on the death of his grandfather, and although far from wealthy,[134] he completed his education with extensive travels on the Continent, an early participant in the "Grand Tour".

Young as he was, he was clearly ambitious at a time when political power and influence, rather than industry or commerce, was the route to wealth. His political career started at the tender age of 21, shortly after his return from his continental travels, when he was elected Commissioner for Tweeddale to the Estates or Scottish parliament. Soon after he was granted a knighthood by James VI & I. He must have become a fairly regular visitor to London at the time, because he quickly became a favourite and confidant of Charles I after his accession in 1625. The new king created him Lord Stuart of Traquair in 1628. Then in 1630 he was appointed Treasurer Depute of Scotland and a Lord Extraordinary of Session. At last ambition had started to reap the benefits of political power and the wealth which went with it.

When Charles came to Scotland in 1633 for his belated coronation, he created John Stuart 1st Earl of Traquair and with that title came the Lordships of Linton and Caberston. During his visit to Edinburgh, the king was present at a meeting of the Estates.[135] In a single day 168 acts were passed. They included confirmation of the religious policies of James VI & I. There was considerable opposition and Charles noted the names of all those who voted against. They included John Elphinstone, 2nd Lord Balmerino, who was strongly opposed to all Charles' church policies. The dissidents did not let the matters rest and Balmerino, together with William Haig of Bemersyde, drew up a supplication setting out their

---

134 The estate then consisted mainly of poor upland farms and crofts in the Peeblesshire hills

135 The Scottish Parliament

grievances. Charles refused to accept it and declared it illegal and treasonable. A copy somehow found its way into the hands of John Spottiswoode, Archbishop of St Andrews and a strong supporter of Charles. The document was identified as Balmerino's as it had his notations on it. Spottiswoode duly informed the king who insisted that Balmerino be tried for treason. The trial followed in 1635 and in spite of public opinion being firmly behind Balmerino he was found guilty by the jury by 8 votes to 7. Traquair, as he was now called, was the foreman of the jury, which was largely selected by him, and his was the casting vote. In this he was no doubt influenced by the king who had written to him before the trial on 24 November, thanking him for his initial endeavours in the matter and pressing for a speedy prosecution. The unfortunate Balmerino was sentenced to death, but Traquair, conscious of local feeling[136] and perhaps exhibiting the ambivalence which would become his hall mark, persuaded the king that granting a pardon would be the wisest course. In this he was supported by Archbishop Laud and the king acceded.

Traquair had proved himself to be a loyal servant and more importantly a confidant to whom the king gave heed and in 1636 he was appointed Lord High Treasurer of Scotland. He had arrived and the huge improvement in his financial situation now made possible the enlargement of Traquair House, making it the residence worthy of someone of such high standing in the affairs of the nation, which it remains today. However his ambitions still do not seem to have been satisfied. He must have written to the king pleading for even greater rewards, because on the 20th November 1637, the King wrote:

> Traquaire I have taken this occasion to aseure you that I have not delayed your upcoming out of anie displeasure against you or the least distrust of your Councels; but to show you the contraire, I have commanded Roxburgh not onlie to show you the verie secrets of my thoughts, but also, to have your judgement, as well as your industrie, concur in my service: So referring you to Roxburgh I rest

> Your asseured frend
> Charles R

He had however, reached the summit of his power and the volatile political circumstances which now engulfed him were to prove beyond his control. 'Man cannot serve two masters' and neither could Traquair, in

---

[136]   He and some jurors had received death threats.

this case an obstinate and wayward king and a parliament bent on achieving independence in the government of the Kirk and curbing the power of the monarchy.

Traquair seems to have been able enough in his oversight of the financial affairs of the nation. Sir Edward Hyde, 1st Earl of Clarendon and later Chancellor to Charles II, is quoted as saying that 'he was not inferior to any in the Scottish Nation in wisdom and dexterity', although those attributes seem to have escaped him during the crisis which was to follow. The catalyst for the fall of both Traquair and later his royal master was the attempt by Charles to force the introduction to Scotland of a liturgy based on the English Prayer Book, and all its trappings of Episcopacy and echoes of Catholicism, so abhorrent to Calvinist Presbyterians.

Traquair was present as the king's representative at the notorious service in St Giles Cathedral when the attempt was made to read the new prayer book. In the aftermath, as a riot spread to the surrounding High Street, he was attacked and dragged from his carriage and had his staff of office broken, before gaining sanctuary in the nearby Council building.

Traquair, in common with the other members of the Privy Council was not present when the National Covenant was signed in Greyfriars kirkyard. Indeed it seems likely that he may have been in London at Court. Trouble had been brewing for some time, because in January Traquair, somewhat optimistically, had written to the king seeking permission to defer his going to court for a few days as 'business is nearly brought to a conclusion'. He did in fact go to the court in March with the Lord Privy Seal, the Earl of Haddington with a letter from the Privy Council giving its views as to 'the unhappy state of affairs'. By May he was back in Edinburgh, writing to the Marquis of Hamilton[137]informing him that he had:

> drawn up two commissions for repressing the disorders; the madness of the people is illimitable, especially of those in Edinburgh; their pulpits are filled with those ministers who have been put out of Ireland preaching false and seditious doctrine; ministers who refuse to sign the Covenant are deposed without warrant of the Bishop, and men of good quality are refused the benefit of the sacrament for their refusal; the "mischief" spreads rapidly in the north; the Earl of Montrose has not arrived in Edinburgh yet.[138]

---

[137]   Charles' principal Scottish advisor in London
[138]   A few years later, Montrose would feature briefly both in the life of Traquair, but also of Peebles.

The trouble for Traquair started in earnest when he was appointed Lord High Commissioner[139]to the General Assembly of 1639. It endorsed everything that had been agreed in the Assembly of 1638 and in addition instructed the Privy Council that acceptance of the Covenant should be a matter of obligation. The Privy Council gave its consent and Traquair as Lord High Commissioner, ratified all the acts which the Assembly had passed. He had little option, although he was under pressure from the king. He had been warned in a letter from the Marquis of Hamilton dated 16th August that 'the king conceives it to be to his prejudice to assent to the enacting that a yearly General Assembly be held' and Traquair was 'to have special care' how he proceeded on 'the Articles in his instructions which allows that the 1580 Covenant shall be subscribed - the bond be the same as that in the time of King James.' The king himself wrote to Traquair on 22 August regarding the proceedings of the Assembly and in particular about the draft of an Act which he had received 'the narrative of which we cannot pass by, without saying it is most damnable.' In a letter of 2nd September 1639 Hamilton wrote that he was commanded by the king to say that as the Parliament must have met before his letter could reach Traquair, 'he must be sure at the conclusion thereof to make a protestation in such terms as may give the King grounds for legally redressing what has not been done to the prejudice his service'. Traquair must be mindful, 'to make a right distinction between giving way and permitting to that Parliament and Assembly to proceed and consenting to their acts.' In terminating the Parliament, the more haste he makes the better, 'provided nothing be omitted that may prove advantageous to the King'.

Traquair must have replied because Hamilton writes once again on 1st October to say that the word 'unlawful' in his letter,[140]has greatly displeased the King and he would do well to think how to remedy it. At the conclusion of the Parliament 'it is necessary to make a protestation on the King's behalf' and he presumes that Traquair will understand that he must keep to his instructions, adding that he assures him that the King does not think his task is easy.

Further meetings of the Estates between August and November caused more problems. As there were now no bishops, Traquair had taken it upon himself to nominate those of the nobility who should sit on the Committee of the Articles, but when they approved all the Acts of the Assembly and recommended permanent exclusion of the clergy from their council as

---

[139]   The King's representative
[140]   presumably referring to those who would not support the Covenant

well as other changes of a constitutional nature, he declined to give the Royal Assent and, without consent of Parliament, prorogued that body until June 1640. Although doubtless his task of reconciliation (as Charles had recognised) was near impossible, his handling of the situation was seen as duplicitous and trust evaporated. He was in trouble with the king as well. When a quantity of ammunition, ostensibly under his control, was seized by the Covenanters at Dalkeith, the King held him to be responsible. On the other hand, his ambiguous actions as Lord High Commissioner made him the enemy of the king's opponents. He appealed to his Royal master. The king, now overlooking the lapse at Dalkeith, was sympathetic, and on the 1st of July wrote :

Traquair/ Since by your owen desire, & my permission ye are retired from my Court, to satisfie the needless suspitions of your Countrimen; I have thoughts, fitt by thease lynes, to asseure you, that I am so far, from having chased you away as a delingquent, that I esteem you to be as faithfull a Servant as anie I have, believing that the greatest cause of malice, that ye are vext with, is, for having served me as ye ought: Therefor I desire you to be confident, that I shall bothe fynde a fitt tyme, for you to wype away all these slanders, that are now against you; & lykewais, to recompense your past sufferings for my service: So, you shall trewly see, that I am

Your asseured frend
Charles R

Far from wiping away 'all these slanders', matters were coming to a head in Scotland and in 1641 he was impeached. The Act of Oblivion which implemented it declared "all bad counsillars quha, instead of giving his Majestie trew and effaul counsaill, has given or will give informatone and counsaill to the evident prejudice and ruine of the liberties of this kirk and kingdom, suld be exemplarlie judged and censured." He was found guilty, but saved from execution by the intervention of the king. However, he was deprived of his great office of state and Charles was compelled to promise not to give him any office of state or allow him to attend court in case he gave the king 'evil counsel'. It was the end, or nearly, although he did re-emerge briefly and disastrously in 1643.

23.
Great Britain at War with itself

After the return of the Scottish Covenanting Army early in 1641, Charles headed north again to Edinburgh, arriving there on 14 August in a belated attempt to persuade the Scottish Parliament to support him, which the English parliament had conspicuously failed to do. He probably hoped to take advantage of dissension which was appearing in the ranks of the Scottish nobility, principally between the Marquises of Argyll and Montrose, who had both been signatories of the National Covenant. Argyll would remain a steadfast supporter of the Covenanting cause, while in due course Montrose would turn away from it and transfer his support to the king. In the hope of bolstering his position, Charles said he would agree to the various Acts of the Scottish parliament which had abolished Episcopacy, but this failed to satisfy the Covenanters, who now demanded that all the principal State appointments should be made by the king, only if they had been approved by the Estates. Unable to make any progress to his satisfaction, Charles returned to London empty-handed.

In his absence in Scotland, there had been a massacre of Protestants in Ulster. Anger and antagonism had been simmering in the Province between the indigenous Catholic population and the largely Lowland Scottish Protestants who had settled there during the reign of James VI&I. The dominant Catholic leaders were the Macdonalds, descended from the Lords of the Isles, who at one time effectively ruled the north west of Ireland and the south west of Scotland for centuries before. The Jacobean settlers had been given substantial areas of land to the resentment of those native landholders who were deprived. It was an explosive mixture which had now been ignited. Charles, once again mis-judging the mood, assumed that the people of Scotland and England would support him in avenging what was seen to be an atrocity. He needed to raise an army to meet the threat, but the English parliament, now dominated by Puritans, refused to sanction the necessary funds unless he agreed to hand over the control of the army to Parliament. That was unacceptable to Charles. We need not go into the details of the mire of recrimination which followed on both sides, except to mention that on the 4th of January 1642, accompanied by 400 soldiers Charles entered the Houses of Parliament and arrested five of the leading members of the Commons. In this he failed, but it was the last straw and he headed north to York. Abortive negotiations continued between the King and the English Parliamentarians and on 22 August of that year he raised his standard at Nottingham. It was the start of the Civil War, a war which in time would lead on all sides to the greatest number of casualties of any conflict on the mainland of Britain throughout its history.

The Scottish Parliament, had to an extent, sat on the sidelines, but it now received approaches from its English counterpart, who at that time at least, recognised that it had insufficient strength to defeat Charles on its own. The re- assembled Scottish army would play a significant role in what followed. In the meantime there were negotiations between the representatives of the two parliaments, but the Scots were also being courted by the supporters of Charles. As a consequence they had a strong hand to play. The Covenanters had long had a vision of England, Wales and Scotland united, with Presbyterianism established as the national religion. The English Parliamentarians agreed to accept that as the price of Scottish support, although they would later renege. The Scottish Parliament supported by the General Assembly decided that the achievement of their religious objective trumped their loyalty to a king, in spite of the fact he was born a Scot and was King of Scots.

The outcome was a document known as the Solemn League and Covenant which was ratified by the Scottish Parliament on 17 August 1643. Immediately after, a proclamation was issued which was designed to enhance and strengthen the Scottish army. The whole country was to be put on a war footing. Every male between the age of sixteen and sixty was to arm himself, have provisions for forty days and be ready to mobilise on two days' notice. Committees of War were set up throughout the country. In Tweeddale it included most of the local lairds. Lord Yester was appointed as its commander.

The records of the Royal Burgh of Peebles are a testament to the concerns which this raised and there is a sense of real alarm and of preparation for conflict, which must have touched the lives of everyone. Every householder and every manservant in Peebles had to make a contribution towards the cost of fitting out every fourth man enlisted for the war, who would receive a payment of five dollars as pay and towards the cost of equipment. The town walls were to be repaired and the ports locked each night.

Once again a sizeable Scottish army, consisting of 18,000 foot soldiers and 3000 cavalry, was gathered together, led by Alexander Leslie, now the Earl of Leven. It was a well trained force on which Leven imposed rigid discipline. Every soldier had to swear allegiance to the Solemn League and Covenant and adhere to a strict code of morality. In January 1644 this formidable force crossed the border and swept south, destroying any Royalist opposition it met, before reaching York, where it joined up with the English Parliamentary army, led by Oliver Cromwell, which was besieging the city. A Royalist army led by the king's nephew, Prince Rupert had headed north to relieve York. It was met and defeated by the combined Scottish and Parliamentary force at Marston Moor. Cromwell claimed credit for the victory, although the contribution of the Scots had been a vital element. It was the start of military domination by Cromwell which would eventually engulf the whole of the British Isles. For the present, the Scots found that unacceptable and Leven marched his troops north, occupying Newcastle in October and remaining there over the following winter.

In spite of the differences which had arisen, the Parliamentarians tried to persuade the Scottish army to join them again in the south, but Leven was concerned by news he had received that the Marquis of Montrose, was now supporting the king and was commanding a Royalist force to oppose the Covenanters. He was also aware that while the Parliamentarians might welcome assistance, the Scots were not welcome in England by a large section of the population. The Scots did make a short-lived march south as far as Hereford. On their return north they besieged Newark. While they were there, Charles himself arrived at their camp unexpectedly. He managed to obtain the surrender of the town and although he refused to accept the Covenant, some sort of agreement was reached and he joined the Scots on their march back to Newcastle.

Not surprisingly that caused the Parliamentarians to doubt the sincerity of the Scots. The English were in any event, lukewarm in their support for the Solemne League and Covenant and the realistic prospect of Covenanted Presbyterianism being imposed as the national religious order, was remote, in spite of that being a central plank of the Solemn League as far as the Scots were concerned. The Scots still wanted to see an accommodation with the king, but the Puritan Independents, who dominated the Parliamentarians, were now determined to see the defeat and overthrow of the king. The two positions were irreconcilable and in May 1644 the Commons of the English parliament voted to have the Scottish army removed from English territory. The Scots, in response demanded a payment of two million pounds, to pay off its forces. The English offered £400,000 on condition that the king who was still with the Scots, was handed over to them. Reluctantly the Scots accepted. They knew that if they returned to Scotland with the king, this would be highly unpopular north of the border. They did try to ensure his safety, but shortly after they made their return to Scotland, he was arrested by the Parliamentary army in Northamptonshire.

As part of the discussions following the Solemn League, there had been a proposal for the Scottish and English parliaments to come together. At this point John Stuart, 1st Earl of Traquair re-appears, when he joined other Scottish nobility in signing a remonstrance against the suggested union. It was considered by the Scottish parliament to be a violation of the terms on which he had been freed and he was declared an enemy to the peace of the kingdom. His estates were sequestrated and his moveable goods were confiscated. He avoided total loss of his estates by making a payment of 40,000 merks and on condition that he accept the Covenant and remain within the counties of Roxburgh, Selkirk and Peebles and that he made no attempt to make contact with the king. So now discredited and impoverished, Traquair effectively retired to the calm of his Peeblesshire estate, but as will be seen, this is not quite the last that is heard of him

In 1645, James Graham, the Marquis of Montrose had decided that his loyalty to the House of Stuart took precedence over his Covenanting affiliations and had set out on a successful military campaign to win back Scotland for the king. He defeated the Covenanting forces in the north and west and then headed south, with further success at Kilsyth. He then headed south again with the intention of crossing the Border and joining with the remnants of the Royalist forces in the north of England.

Concerned by the prospect, the council issued a warning to the townsfolk, 'be oppin proclamation and twk of drum'. Under no circumstances was anyone, for whatever reason, to leave the town to go to any other place, 'bot to abyde constantlie within the burgh, and await upone the proveist and bailyeis thairof, for their counsel and advyse anent the preservatioun of this burgh during the time of their present trubles, and under pane of death and confiscatioun of their hail gudes and meanes.' This order was clearly meant to be taken seriously!

In the meantime the main Scottish Covenanter army now led by David Leslie, the nephew of Lord Leven, had marched north from a raid into England and was encamped near Selkirk. Hearing of the approach of Montrose, Traquair sent his son, Lord Linton with a troop of horse to join them. Linton, however, having sized up the situation, decided to withdraw without becoming involved. He returned to Traquair House. The next day Montrose was decisively beaten by the Covenanters at Philiphaugh. With a small retinue he left the field and to avoid pursuit, rode across the neighbouring hills towards Peebles, stopping at Traquair House where he demanded entry. No doubt now very conscious of the consequences of choosing the wrong side and no doubt encouraged by his son's thoughts about the strength of the Covenanter army, Traquair decided to refuse entry to Montrose.

The battle which ensued at Philiphaugh on 13th September, 1645, had been a bloody affair. Following their victory, to their considerable discredit, the Covenanters, massacred many of the Royalist troops as well as women and children, who were their camp followers. The Royalist army had included a number of Irish and Highland elements, who in the earlier battles in the the north had treated defeated Covenanters with the utmost savagery when Montrose had gained victories over them. This was no doubt their revenge.

The escaping Montrose and his party, must have been a sorry sight, as they headed for safety. After the rebuff at Traquair, they continued on their way to the west and in the evening they reached Peebles. The accounts of their arrival, such as they are, suggest that they came up the south side of the Tweed and crossed the Tweed Bridge. They may have hoped to find shelter in the town, but they were not welcome. All of the ports would have been closed and guarded and although they would likely have been observed, they must have gone on their way.

As if the threat of war and invasion of Peebles was not enough, the same year the plague returned. At the beginning of November members of the town council, the Kirk and others met in the kirkyard of the Cross Kirk and ordered a 'solemn fast and humiliation', which suggests that the arrival of the rightly dreaded disease was thought to be some form of Divine retribution, perhaps for heresy or opposition to royal authority.

In November payments were made for cutting timber in the grounds of the Cross Kirk which was to be used for building two lodges on the Green to house anyone who had lived and had survived in a house where a death from the disease had occurred. It was to allow the infected houses to be disinfected or possibly burned down. A kiln was built at Skinnerhaugh[141] to be used for burning the clothes of those deceased or infected. According to the records, in December two families, including both parents and children, were ordered to move out of their houses and move into the lodges, because their houses had been infected. They were to be provided with fuel and necessary furniture. In other cases the houses of two men were ordered to be boarded up, as there may have been deaths in them. The school also had to be disinfected and a load of peats was

---

[141]   Now the site of the bowling green and Gytes Leisure Centre.

bought for the purpose. In an age when the understanding of infectious diseases was limited, smoke was seen as means of combating the spread of infection. It may well have been at least partially effective.

Those who were sick were to be cared for by the elders and deacons, a rare example at that time of the religious authorities exercising pastoral care rather than the pursuit of sins, but orders were issued as with past outbreaks that anyone infected, 'sall keip their awin housis and places quhair they are commandit, and not to depairt thairfa under pane of death.' As before, in practical terms, remaining might also have ended in 'pane of death'.

Two cleaners came out from Edinburgh, hoping to find work in cleaning infected houses, but were sent back, presumably because there was sufficient local assistance available. Visitors who might bring further infection were rigorously discouraged. In any event the town paid 12s for the cost of their return.

Nothing further is heard of Traquair until 1647, when in a brief lull in the Civil War Charles appointed him to the Committee of Estates. By then the Covenanters were at variance with the English Parliamentarians. In Scotland itself they had lost control of the parliament to the "Engagers" who were those who, although seeking change, particularly in relation to religious observance, none the less opposed the removal of the king. They had made a secret agreement with him[142] and promised him the support of the Scottish armies provided that on his restoration he re-establish Presbyterianism for three years. That was endorsed by the Estates and an ultimatum was sent somewhat optimistically to the English parliament, demanding the release of the king, acceptance of the Covenant and that the Parliamentary army be disbanded. A Scottish Army, now led by Hamilton set off across the Border to achieve those ends. It was a disaster. The Scottish force which included a contingent raised by and including Traquair, was destroyed at Preston, by a force led by Oliver Cromwell. Traquair was amongst those captured. He was taken to Warwick Castle where he was to remain a prisoner for four years. Hamilton himself was less fortunate. Having fled south after the battle he was captured near Uttoxeter and seven months later he was beheaded in London by the order of the English parliament, despite his being a Scottish soldier, acting on the authority of the Scottish Government.

Following the defeat of the advance into England of the army then under the authority of a Scottish parliament controlled by Engagers, the

---

[142] The Engagement

pendulum swung almost immediately in favour of those who opposed the Engagement. As something of a side issue, a 6,000 strong force of Covenanters from the south west advanced to Edinburgh where they were welcomed by the anti-Engagers or Protesters, who were able to take control of the government. Cromwell came to Edinburgh in October and an agreement was reached that both sides would oppose the Royalist cause. In matters of religion there was a great deal of common ground. The Covenant was accepted and in January 1648 the Estates met and rescinded the Engagement. It also passed an "Act of Classes", which prohibited anyone holding office who did not accept the Covenant.

Charles I remained a captive of the English Parliamentarians. While on the one hand the Scots did not want to provoke their new allies, on the other they were opposed to any attempt to convict the king. The English Parliamentarians, led by Cromwell, secure in the knowledge that Scotland would not support the king by military action, brought Charles to trial and convicted him of the responsibility for the shedding of the blood of the very subjects, as monarch he ought to protect. In spite of Scottish protests he was sentenced to death and beheaded on 30 January 1649.

24.

Occupation and the Commonwealth

The news of the execution of Charles caused shock and anger in Scotland. A rebellious English parliament had executed the King of Scots and while Scotland led by the Lords of the Congregation and the Covenanters might have wished him to be brought to heel, they remained loyal to the monarchy and were outraged by this unilateral action. It resulted in an upsurge of support for royalty and immediately after the execution by 'that traitorous parliament and army', his son was proclaimed King Charles II at the Mercat Cross in Edinburgh on 5th February 1649.

Charles had been living in exile at Breda in the Netherlands and now sailed to Scotland, landing at Garmouth on the Moray Firth on 23rd June 1650. Before that, Montrose once again returned to the stage. In support of the new king he landed a small force in the north of Scotland, in the hope that he could raise support from the Highland Clans who had formed the backbone of his earlier campaign. It was a complete failure and after a heavy defeat at Carbisdale in Sutherland, he was captured, taken to Edinburgh and hanged at the Mercat Cross, to become an addition to the folklore of Scotland as one its "martyrs".

Before landing at Garmouth, Charles had signed the Covenants and after his arrival he set about raising an army with the support of the Covenanted Scottish parliament. The reaction in England by a government now called the Commonwealth, was to send a powerful force north. It was commanded by Cromwell, who was now styled the "Lord General".

The details of Cromwell's Scottish campaign need not concern us here. He brought with him a well trained and experienced force of what was now the New Model Army. Marching up the east into the Lothians and with support from shipping based at Dunbar,[143] he met a Covenanter force led by David Leslie who had taken up position on Doune Hill. Cromwell's army was actually in fairly poor condition after long marches and poor weather, which still persisted. The Scottish army had rather different problems. Although David Leslie was an able and experienced commander, he was under control of an extreme Covenanting element

---

[143]   part of the harbour there is still known as "Cromwell's Harbour"

who had removed all those commanders whom they considered did not conform to their religious views. In the event the Scots were heavily defeated and from there on Cromwell took control of the whole of the Lothians and Borders. He then made various attempts to engage the force led by Charles, but failed until the new king slipped south into England, where he eventually caught up with him at Worcester. The battle which followed resulted in defeat of the King's forces, Charles himself escaping and eventually returning to the Netherlands, where he remained until his restoration in 1660.

The burgh of Peebles had made its usual contribution to the Scots army, now sadly defeated. If the records are correct its contribution on that occasion was modest. On 18th July, 1650, a few weeks before the battle of Dunbar, the council ordered that nine men were to go on service to the army, equipped with six muskets, three pikes and nine swords. Each of them was to be paid twelve pounds. To meet the cost, a levy of 24s Scots was to be raised from every person in the town, except the magistrates.

The news of the defeat at Dunbar was not long in reaching Peebles. The records show that it raised alarms that the town might be attacked by "our auld enemies of England". Preparations for defence were needed once again. The town wall was once more in need of repair. The records show that it was the responsibility of burgesses owning property bounded by the wall, to repair the section which formed their "head dyke". An attack was anticipated at any time and arrangements were made for there to be a watch to be 'keipet ilk nicht' Another order was issued on 7 October 'to keep nichtlie a scout watche, sex at the North Port and the remanent to the uther portes proportionallie, with armes, to advetteis the toun of the enemies approach; ane of the town counsel nichtlie to be on the watche'.

On 24th October 1650, the provost, bailies and council and 'a great number of the burgessis and inhabitantis' of the burgh met. The meeting agreed that in addition to the night watch already established at the town's ports, two mounted scouts should be sent out, to check on any movements of the enemy. One was to ride to Gladhouse Mill to cover and report any approach from the north, while the other was to ride to 'David Heislope Hous', which was probably somewhere to the east of the town, to report any movement from that direction. The scouts were to be paid twenty shillings Scots for each night on duty. The cost was to be met by a levy paid by the inhabitants 'proportionallie'. Eight men were nominated to undertake the task and if any of them failed to take his turn they would not be paid and would be punished by the council as they thought appropriate.

Perhaps in anticipation of the arrival of the enemy, orders were given that nobody was to supply anything to them. Particularly mentioned is anything the occupying troops might have stolen from a neighbour or stolen goods they might have received. This 'consorting with the enemy' was viewed as serious and the penalty was to be banishment from the town and payment to the neighbour of the value of their loss. There was also an injunction that theft or looting during any time of conflict would be similarly punished.

Also at that meeting arrangements were put in place for quartering troops. It must be assumed that they were soldiers from outwith the town, probably from the landward areas of the county. Each of the four quarters of the town[144] together with the Old Town were allocated two soldiers and those who were to quarter them were selected by the council and the inhabitants. Those chosen would be required to meet the costs of providing accommodation from their own resources. All the arrangements were to be publicised 'throw the town be touk of drum'.[145]

The presence of Cromwell's army in Edinburgh, which he had occupied immediately after Dunbar, would have been well known and with it the knowledge that in all probability some part of the army at least, would make its way to the Borders, with Peebles a likely stopping point. Nearby Neidpath Castle was a target, as John, Lord Yester had made clear his intention to hold it against the invaders.

The expected "attack" duly took place towards the end of November. There is no evidence of there being any resistance and it seems to have been a peaceful affair, although its repercussions must have been considerable. 3000 mounted troops of the New Model Army had ridden out from Edinburgh, together with their usual accompaniment of armourers, farriers, grooms and cooks. At that time the whole population of Peebles probably numbered about 1,200, so the arrival of so many in the town must have had a huge effect, not only on the town itself, but also on the surrounding countryside.

The force which arrived in the town was commanded by Major-General Lambert with Colonel Francis Hacker as his deputy. Hacker is of particular interest, because he forms a direct link between Peebles and the execution of Charles I. It was Hacker who guarded the king before his execution and was responsible for its organisation. He read out the death

---

[144] East, south west, northwest and northgait.
[145] Public announcements were made by a town official, with the town drummer beating his drum to draw the attention of the inhabitants.

warrant on the scaffold. We know for certain that he was in Peebles at some point, because there is a letter written to him by Oliver Cromwell, which is addressed to him 'at Peebles or elsewhere'. Hacker had been one of those directly involved in the downfall, trial and conviction of Charles I. After the restoration of Charles II, he was identified as one of the "regicides", whom Charles pursued in revenge for the killing of his father. He was arrested, tried and convicted of treason and sentenced to death. He met his fate at Tyburn on 19th October 1660. Unlike most of the convicted regicides, he was not hung, drawn and quartered, but merely hung, as it was said 'by his majesty's great favour'. General Lambert avoided a similar fate because he had not been included with those who plotted and facilitated the death of the king.

Leaving behind a small garrison, Lambert led the remainder of his forces into Lanarkshire where he defeated a Scottish force led by Colonel Ker on 1st December, before returning to Peebles to besiege Neidpath Castle. It did not take long to persuade its garrison to capitulate. Lambert had drawn up cannon on the high ground on the bank of the River Tweed opposite the castle. It is not certain whether or not any shot was actually fired. It has been suggested that the tower at the south west corner shows the results of cannon ball impact, but it is just as likely to be the result of later decay of the stonework due to neglect when it ceased to be a residence after 1790. During the next few years of Commonwealth occupation of Peebles, it may have been used from time to time by the garrison. It was the last stronghold in the south of Scotland to hold out against the New Model Army and with its defeat the whole of the south of Scotland was under the control of Cromwell.

There is a curious piece of correspondence between General Lambert and Cromwell which has a reference to Peebles. It was written by Lambert while he was in Edinburgh. It read :

....their young King is gone to Aberdeen, where 'tis reported he sets up his standard: they will rise willingly, being very unanimous, yet the dumb man of Peebles makes signs that they will before long cut off the heads of the great ones. Truly I am confident that they have filled the measure of their iniquities, and that God will steadily judge them.

According to Buchan the letter was dated 8th January 1651. If that is correct, it is unlikely that 'their young King', presumably Charles II, had gone to Aberdeen. He had been crowned at Scone, near Perth on the 1st of January and then aware of the approach of Cromwell's troops who were in Fife, quickly departed south of the border. Perhaps Lambert's intelligence was wrong. The northeast did still hold out for the King and maybe there were fears that if he went north he would find support. What is totally unexplained is the reference to the 'dumb man of Peebles', which remains a mystery.

Peebles was now an occupied town and would remain so for the next nine years. The greater part of General Lambert's force may have departed soon after the capitulation of Neidpath, leaving a small garrison in the town. There have been unsubstantiated suggestions that during the time Lambert and his troops were present, they stabled their horses in what remained of St Andrew's Kirk. If so, it is unlikely that it could accommodate the horses of 3,000 cavalrymen, but is possible that it was used by the remaining garrison.

At this point the records come to a halt and were not resumed until 29th May 1651, by which time Peebles was occupied by those of Cromwell's troops who remained after the main body had departed. The reason for this may have been that for the time being at least the normal functions of the magistrates and council were suspended during the time when the town was occupied by the main body of the troops, when it would have been controlled by General Lambert or Colonel Hacker. It is also possible that the town records were moved or interfered with by the invaders, because there is a subsequent entry in the accounts for a payment of two shillings Scots 'for two candle to look at the writes in the steeple efter the Inglesmen had spoyled the same.' At that time the town's official documents and deeds would have been lodged in the steeple, which was effectively the town administrative centre, so it may be that this incursion by the English troops resulted in some of the current documents and records being destroyed or lost.

The presence of Puritan Cromwellian forces in the town, must have affected the daily lives of the townsfolk. It seems that the council co-operated with their visitors, although that did create problems, giving rise to disputes between the council and the government authorities. Not surprisingly, trouble between the townsfolk and the English soldiers erupted from time to time. There were a number of occasions when the town was forced to make payments to English soldiers injured in disturbances with some of the more energetic locals. Those fracas were not confined to the menfolk. There are records of some of the women folk such as Marjory Buchan also being involved. She is described as 'servitrix to Bessie Veitch' who was found guilty of an assault on 'a soldier in Captain Hatchman's company', for which she was fined twenty merks.

More seriously, some of the disturbances must have resulted in deaths, because on more than one occasion the council felt obliged to pay the cost of kists or coffins for the dead.

Those troops who did remain were billeted on householders in the town and once the records resume in May 1651 it is clear that they were a considerable burden on the community. In the years which immediately followed, there were a number of occasions when the council tried to recover the costs from the national authorities. They mainly concerned the cost of feeding and housing the troops billeted on them.

The cost of the occupation to the town, was particularly heavy in the autumn of 1651. The council decided to send a delegation to General Lambert, who was then based in Edinburgh, to ask for compensation. In August 1651 Provost James Williamson had died. He had played a leading role in defending the interests of Peebles at a national level for more than a quarter of a century, having served as provost on a number of occasions and also represented the Royal Burgh in parliament, conventions and the General Assembly. His place was taken for a brief period at least, by John Lowes, who was perhaps less forceful than his worthy predecessor, because in December, a further deputation had again to be sent to General Lambert to speak to him about the losses from which the town had suffered due to the activities of the English soldiery.

In time the occupiers and the occupied were able to reach some sort of reasonable understanding, but the costs of occupation were a continuing concern of the provost and council. It was also inevitable that there would be trouble from time to time between soldiers far from home and the native population. In spite of their religious background, there were some soldiers of the New Model Army who took advantage of their position. When a troop commanded by a Colonel Twistleton was stationed in the town there was theft of local property which the thieves attempted to dispose of to local folk. The council issued a public order that no one should purchase goods from the 'enemy' or reset them, but, if opportunity arose, the goods should be returned to their rightful owners.

Early in 1652 an event had occurred which was seen by many as a sign of Divine disapproval of their previous support for the Royalist cause. It was a total eclipse of the sun, seen throughout Britain, but it seems to have had a particular impact on Peebles. It was recorded by Thomas Smyth the town clerk at the time :

Mirk Monday 29th March 1652. The sun eclipsed from eight houres to haif hour to ellevine or thereby befor noon, the sun eclipsed 11 digittes, the darknes continwit 8 minutes or therabout : the people begane all to pray to

God ; a little therafter ther was seene upon the south side of the firmament ane clear perfyte star. Some affirmed they saw two, but I saw one onlie.

Et Quonian Hoc Fuit Rarum Prodigiosum
Idcirco Registari Dignum Existimavi..
(Since this was an unusual wonder
Therefore I thought it worth recording.)

That seemingly sinister event did nothing to alleviate the mood of sullen forbearance which had descended on the town and much of Scotland. Throughout the next seven years virtually the whole country remained occupied by Cromwell's forces under the control of their Puritan officers. It was a time of austerity which was not just confined to the conduct of worship. Fun and laughter, such a feature of burgh life, were replaced by solemn faces. Fairs which previously were held on a Sabbath Day or on a Monday were considered to be profane and the few that were permitted were now to be held on a Tuesday and were dismal affairs. Even fairs such as the St Andrews Fair 'thes mony aiges bygane been kept' held each year in November were severely restricted. The Beltane horse race and its accompanying games were strictly forbidden. "Peebles and the Play" became a distant memory!

   Soldiers billeted on burgh households remained a costly burden, not only to the burgh but also to householders saddled with the inconvenience of soldiers living in their households and needing to be fed and watered. Monthly assessments had to be levied on the townsfolk to meet the expense. Attempts were made by the council to recover the costs and once more deputations travelled to Edinburgh to the commander-in-chief in an attempt to obtain compensation. Typical was the deputation of two councillors who made their way to the Capital on 25th August 1653, but their journey seems to have been in vain because the following appears in the records dated 21st September :-

.....in respect ther is added monethlie to the tounes assessments twentie four punds more than was before; therfor, and for preventing of quartering, the counsel ordeanes the inhabitants to pay the same proportiones they payed in the month of Julij last, and the thesaurer to pay twelve pundes, which, with what is already collected for the inhabitants, will compleit the monethes assessment of Julij and August last by past, being monthlie thrie scoir pundes.'

The monthly sum was considerable but when a further attempt at recovery was made in November, the deputation was sent with the instruction to 'ryde in to Dalkeith upon Moonday nixt to present the tounes supplicatioun anent the assessment, and allowes him to give the secretarie tuo rex-dolleres'. Corruption is not new!

In some cases soldiers were quartered in houses whose occupiers were tenants. The council ordered that the payment received from the soldiers should be split between the landlord and tenant. The tenant was to be paid for providing food and lodging, but the landlord was to receive part of the payment as a contribution towards the rent of the property. In the event that the landlord and tenant were unable to reach agreement as to the apportionment of the payment received, one of the magistrates was to decide.

In November 1655 in view of the fact that what the town received in compensation for the cost of quartering troops did not cover the cost of 'fyre and candell',[146] the council agreed that anyone quartering troops should receive a payment to cover the cost and that it should be met by a weekly payment of five shillings Scots from everyone who did not have anyone quartered on them. It was further extended the next year in respect of householders who quartered horsemen. Presumably it included the cost of stabling as it was agreed that in those cases the householder should receive sixteen shillings, Scots monthlie. Once again the cost was to be met by a levy on those who did not have anyone quartered on them.

John Stuart, 1st earl of Traquair, had remained a prisoner in Warwick Castle since his capture at Preston in 1647. In October 1652 he was granted permission to go to Scotland for six months and on 2nd November he gave a written undertaking to the Council of the Commonwealth to return within six months, or whenever called upon to do so. It seems no call came and that he remained in Scotland until his death in 1659. The intervening years were, however far removed from the glory days as Lord Treasurer. During his captivity what remained of his estates had been sequestrated once more and he lived out his remaining years in abject poverty. One writer records that 'this once great noble and state officer would take alms though not publically ask for it. There are some still living in Peebles that have seen him dine upon a salt herring and an onion' Another records that 'he was a true emblem of the vanity of the world – a very meteor. He was in an antique garb, and a broad old hat, short cloak, and pannier breeches; and I contributed in my quarters in the Canon-gate towards his relief. We gave him a noble, he standing with his hat

---

146   heating and lighting.

off…..and he received the piece of money from my hand as humbly and thankfully as the poorest supplicant.'

Broken in spirit John Stuart died on 27th March 1659. It is said that 'there was no pall, but only a black apron over the coffin'. To add final insult to injury, his grave, on account of cost, was dug two feet too short.

*　*　*

The Commonwealth of England and Wales had been established following the capture of Charles I and the defeat of the Royalist forces. It was now extended to include Scotland, which was to become what in reality was a mere province, achieving what a succession of English monarchs had failed to do. Prompted by their own religious beliefs and with it their idea of equality under the law, it hoped to create a single state where everyone would enjoy equal rights. At the beginning of 1652 a meeting was held at Dalkeith, when commissioners from the English parliament met with the Estates, bringing with them a declaration which stated that England, Wales and Scotland were to be one unified Commonwealth. There was to be religious tolerance, but the Gospel was to be preached. In other words the Bible was to be at the centre of faith, but the rights and privileges already enjoyed by England would be enjoyed by Scots as well. Perhaps not so palatable was their demand that the cost of the English campaign north of the border should be met from the estates of the Duke of Hamilton in restitution for his invasion of English territory in 1647. It also proposed that representatives of the shires and burghs be appointed to meet for the purpose of formally agreeing to the union. In March 1652 the town council on behalf of the people of Peebles confirmed its agreement to those proposals. In common with the rest of Scotland and with the town occupied by soldiers of the New Model army, it had little alternative.

On 12th April 1654, Cromwell as Lord Protector issued what was called an "Ordinance of Union" with the approval of the Council of Commonwealth. It provided for a united parliament that was to have 460 members, but only 30 were to represent the former Kingdom of Scotland. Of those, 20 were to represent the shires and the remaining 10, the burghs. Edinburgh was allocated 2 members. The remaining 8 were to be divided into groups which would elect one member. Peebles was to be joined with Selkirk, Jedburgh, Lauder, North Berwick and Haddington. As might be expected, as a result the Scottish members would have little influence for all practical purposes. None the less on 21 July, Robert Thomsone, a former bailie was elected as commissioner for Peebles. He was to ride to Lauder to a meeting of the representatives of the burghs in the group to elect a commissioner to parliament.

In religious affairs, although there were great similarities between the Puritan form practised in England and the Scottish Kirk, the English form was more tolerant than Scottish Presbyterianism, which allowed for no other form. There were continuing disputes between the leading factions in Scotland. The Commonwealth government was inclined to support the Protesters, because of their opposition to royal authority. The General Assembly was a problem because it continued to be dominated by the Resolutioners, who supported monarchy, but when it met in July 1653 it was forcibly closed down by Commonwealth troops under the command of Colonel Cotterill. It did not meet again during Cromwell's lifetime. In practice kirk sessions, presbyteries and synods were left to their own devices, so that religious life carried on much as before, except that they were no longer permitted to impose civil penalties on anyone subject to their discipline.

Some indication of the place of religion in Cromwell's military philosophy can be gauged from the letter he wrote to Colonel Francis Hacker on 25th December 1650 which has already been mentioned. The letter concerned a discussion about the choice of an officer to be appointed to a particular commission. In the course of this letter Cromwell wrote the following:

Sir – I have the best consideration I can for the praesent in this businesse, and although I believe Capt Hubbert is a worthy man, and heere soe much, yett as the case stands, I cannott, with satisfaction to my selffe and some others, revoake the commission I had given to Capt. Empson, without offence to them, and reflection upon my owne judgment. I pray lett Capt. Hubbert knowe I shall not bee unmindful of him, and that noe disrespect is intended to him. But, indeed I was not satisfied with your last speech to mee about Empson, that he was a better praecher than a fighter or a souldier, or words to that effect. Truly I thinke Hee that prayes and praeches best will fight best. I know nothing will give like courage and confidence as the knowledge of God in Christ will, and I blesse God to see any in this armye able and willinge to impart knowledge they have for the good of others. And I expect itt bee encouraged by all Chiefe Officers in this Armye especially: and I hope you will doe soe. I pray receive Capt. Empson lovinglye. I dare assure you hee is a good man and a good officer. I would wee had noe worse. I rest your lovinge friend.

O.Cromwell

The minister of Peebles at that time was John Hay, who had been brought up in the Episcopal tradition. The religious order was decidedly complicated even within the Presbyterian fold. There were the Protesters who had opposed any sort of accommodation with Charles I and now were opposed to supporting Charles II, because they did not believe his support of the Covenant was genuine. Then there were the Resolutioners, who were prepared to support him, in spite of his lukewarm support for the Covenant. They thought he would not try to re-impose Episcopacy, mindful of the fate his father had suffered.

John Hay was born in 1613. He had studied at the University of Edinburgh, gaining the degree of Master of Arts in 1630 and later at Cambridge where he held a Fellowship and gained the degree of Bachelor of Divinity. His father Dr Theodore Hay had been appointed minister of Peebles in 1610. He was still in post in 1643, but was then already a great age and concerned about his age and poor health, the bailies and the majority of the councillors of the town, had sent a request to the presbytery, asking that John Hay be appointed as his assistant. His exact status was however, a matter of some controversy. The initial request had come from the kirk session and had been presented on its behalf by one Andrew Watson, asking that John Hay be appointed as "colleague". The council were of the view that the appointment should be limited to his assisting with preaching during the remainder of the lifetime of Dr Theodore. They went so far as to say that if presbytery went beyond what the council intended, they would dissent and require that dissent to be included in the presbytery record. Perhaps 33 years of one Hay ministry up until then had been enough for them!

Dr Theodore eventually retired in 1648 and died in 1651. Now in the midst of Cromwellian occupation John Hay must once again adjust to changing circumstances. He was probably a little uncomfortable with the idea of the officers of the New Model Army demanding the right to occupy his pulpit, where they were likely to harangue the parishioners about the evils and sins of the day, but at least they brought a new order and discipline to the worship of the Kirk. Many in the town might well have favoured those Puritan preachers. They supported the Protesters and their worship was centred on prayer and the exposition of the scriptures through extemporary preaching as opposed to formal and the repetitive prayers, scripture reading and sound of voices raised in song, with all their Episcopal and even Papist formality. One of the townsfolk by the name of

Nicol[147]recorded in his diary in October 1653 "There was no reading of the chapters nor singing of psalms on the Sabbath day".

With at least the tacit support of the occupying Puritans, whose ideals they broadly shared, it was the Protesters who held an increasing influence and for the next few years they were the dominating force in synod, presbytery and kirk session in spite of the suppression of the General Assembly by the Commonwealth government. As long as there was relative peace across the country, although they did not entirely approve of them, the Commonwealth government saw no point in antagonising those forces in the Kirk which had a broadly similar view of the place of the church in society and furthermore had the great merit of being anti-royalist.

The Commonwealth was at first welcomed by the more extreme elements in the Kirk, who, taking the lead from their strict Puritan masters, embarked on an orgy of disciplinary enforcement. In spite of the loss of right to impose civil penalties, the least minor demeanour did not escape the attention of the Kirk authorities. As Dr Gunn records :-

> The records of this time teem with cases of discipline. Punishments are inflicted for gossiping in the churchyard, ricking corn on a Sunday, flyting, drinking, keeping the mill going on Sunday, absenting from Church, hiring on Sunday, gathering nuts on Sunday, carrying meal on the same day, and for hounding a dog on sheep "mair thoroughly than orinar". These were indeed terrible days of Church discipline. Much attention was paid to evidence of a merely hearsay character; the result being that opportunity was afforded to the envious, to the malignant, to the slanderous and the revengeful, either to pay off old scores, or to destroy the reputation of a neighbour ....There was the fanatical massacre of the prisoners of Philiphaugh................There was the slavish worship of the Sabbath, with a literal attention to detail, rather than the God of the Sabbath..........There were the degrading humiliations of the cutty stool and of the jougs, which served merely to render the culprit callous and vindictive, rather than truly penitent.

The principal emphasis of the Kirk's philosophy towards the people was discipline and damnation rather than pastoral care and in that respect the Kirk in Peebles was no better or no worse than anywhere elsewhere in Scotland. Church affairs in the town had reached a state of calm equilibrium. Sabbath keeping was strictly enforced. The power of the kirk

---

[147]   this is very likely the same James Nicol who was to become known as "The Martyr of Peebles"

session was supreme. But perversely it did not produce a peaceful or law-abiding community. Theft, riots and disregard of council injunctions were commonplace and the enforcement of discipline was the paramount concern of both kirk session and council. A new Act was introduced by the Kirk's Committee on Discipline which required every kirk session to record all cases of discipline. These records give an insight into attitudes which prevailed at the time. Dr Gunn was critical of their legacy and comments[148]that, 'The tale of their brothers and sisters' weaknesses was chronicled with a simple straightforwardness that took no thought of the morrow or of those who might read and judge therin. Those honest folk forgot the future or despised it.' In other words they left an unfortunate impression, on the one hand of the failings of ordinary folk and on the other of an unsympathetic ruling class. He goes on to list some of the misdemeanours which exercised the Kirk authorities:

> Does A. come home late on a Saturday night – he is brought before the kirk-session, has to give the reason for this breach of elder's hours, and is exhorted to repent of the same. Does B. absent himself from worship for a time – he is cited to appear. Is C. heard swearing, or is said to have been heard swearing even – he must appear and be admonished to repent. D. is summoned for 'profanation' of the Sabbath by 'climbing at the old castell in time of sermon.' Even innocence will hardly save a man from rebuke. Thus, a certain E. being 'interrogat if he was guilty of mocking at the elders, answered "No."' But the elders, 'considereing that he is one brutishly ignorant, and suspecting that there was reality in the delation, determined that he should be sharply rebuked,' and 'upon his promise never to be guilty of the like again,' the said E. was dismissed, a less brutishly ignorant, at least, if not a better man.

What was deemed 'scandalous' behaviour had many forms. One case which lasted many months concerned a woman servant who left her employment before her due term ended. In time it involved not only the minister but also the Synod and even the General Assembly, who seemed to go to a considerable amount of trouble over what would now seem a trivial matter.

Another case exercised the kirk session as well as the presbytery over a period of more than six years. It concerned John Hay, the son of Sir John Hay of Smithsfield, one of the local lairds. In December 1651 he had married Jonnet Watsone in a ceremony conducted in Edinburgh by an English Minister. He had done so without a proclamation or the consent of

---

[148] *The Book of the Cross Kirk, Peebles A.D. 1560-1690* p 170

his parents. The presbytery declared the marriage to be 'scandalous'. Hay and his wife, or 'his woman' as she is referred to, were ordered to appear before the presbytery. Only Hay appeared and said that he was not convinced that they had committed any offence, but if he had, he was prepared to be censured. The case was further complicated when the minister of Peebles, another John Hay, reported that Hay and one of his cronies called John Pringle from Peebles, had been accused by the kirk session of blasphemy and drunkenness, which was observed by two witnesses, who said that they had uttered 'diverse hellish and devilish imprecations which escaped them amidst their cups.' The presbytery appointed two of their number to interview both men, with a view to persuading them to repent.   There follows a series of reports to the presbytery of failures by Hay, 'his woman' and Pringle to appear to answer the charges. The cases keep being adjourned or deferred. Quite apart from simply not appearing, Hay's absence is also reported on occasion to be because he was abroad or on two occasions because he was in prison in Edinburgh. In the meantime, Hay's woman had had a child.

Eventually in May 1656, Hay, who following the death of his father, was now Sir John Hay of Smithsfield, confessed to the various charges made against him 'after many blasphemies heard from him' and submitted himself to the will of the Presbytery. He was to appear to hear its verdict on 29th May, but failed once more to appear. That was considered along with all the other offences to be a gross offence, so much so that he was ordered to appear in the church in Peebles in a white sheet.[149].He eventually did appear on 3rd July and was duly berated from the pulpit and seemed to be 'weighed down with grief.' He was ordered to appear in public two Sundays later, to hear the minister verbally chastise him again and then he was to appear before the presbytery for a further dressing down, but once more he failed to appear. He wrote to say he was in Edinburgh and refused to obey the summonses in rather offensive terms.

All attempts to persuade him to comply failed but as nothing more is heard, it can only be assumed that at long last the matter was dropped. What it does show is that the church authorities were prepared to go to great lengths to pursue what were a series of moral rather than criminal offences, but that Sir John was impervious to their pursuit of him. He was clearly a strong character.

---

[149]   the symbol of repentance

25.
The Trade Guilds

Merchant guilds have existed in the burghs of Scotland since the thirteenth century. In 1593 the Scottish parliament introduced an Act which set out rules governing the activities of trade guilds and their place within a burgh, 'quhilk is to the great furtherance of justice to sovrane lords lieges in all actions maters concerning merchands, betwixt merchand and merchand and mariner.'[150]

Trade guilds may have been established in Peebles as early as 1450, but the first reference to them only occurs in the records in 1561. In February of that year the council instructed the websters or weavers to elect a deacon each year, in the same way that was already done in other burghs, particularly Dundee and Edinburgh. Although this is the earliest official reference, it is likely that the trade already had an organised collective membership by then. Other trades would in due course establish themselves as "guilds", but the websters would retain their pre-eminent position.

One of the duties of the deacon was to collect a penny each week from the members, which was then distributed to the poor under the supervision of the bailies, showing the close link which there was between council and the guild. The position of the Websters Guild within the town's hierarchy was further enhanced when as one of its privileges the guild became entitled to elect one of their number to membership of the town council.

After 1593, the Convention of Royal Burghs urged burghs to appoint a dean of guild who should be a merchant who was experienced in 'merchand billis and merchand caussis.' The name "merchand" in this context included trades. The charter granted to the burgh in 1621 by James VI&I, authorised the burgh to set up "guild courts" or councils. However, it appears that that was not followed up until 1647, although in 1640 the town council must have discussed the possibility of appointing a dean of guild, because the record of its meeting on 5th October says that among the matters discussed and 'thocht upone' and to be further discussed at the next meeting was the creation of the post of dean of guild. However, nothing further appears in the records until the annual town council

---

150   *The Guildry Corporation of Peebles* p 7.

election on 4th October 1647, when the council elected John Tuedy, Younger, to be dean of guild. He was selected from a leet of three chosen by the members of the Websters guild.

Shortly after on 11th October the council asked the dean to produce a copy of the dean of guild rules of Edinburgh at the next council meeting. Presumably they would form the basis for a similar set of rules for Peebles. On the 20th December, the council chose a dean of guild's council of six in addition to Dean of Guild Tuedy. In time it became the Guildry Corporation which still exists to this day.

At the same time the dean was instructed to "tak diligent tryall" of all weights and measures, including those of merchants, their weighing equipment, corn measures, Scots and English pint measures and all other types of measure and to report to the next Council meeting. One of those measures, a quart or "chopenis" measure, known as "the Peebles Measure",[151] is kept in the National Museum of Scotland. It is likely that it was kept by the dean of guild, as the words "Dean of Guild" are inscribed on the inside.

The powers of the dean of guild took some time to be defined and on Christmas Day 1648 (at this time the observance of Christmas or "Yule" Day as a holiday was effectively banned by an Act of 1640, 'the kirke within this kingdome is now purged of all superstitious observatione of dayes... thairfor the saidis estatis have dischairged and simply dischairges the foirsaid Yule vacance and all observation thairof in tymecomeing,...'. It was partly repealed in 1686) when the council instructed John Tuedy to produce his dean of guild laws or regulations for consideration by the council or one of its committees. Whether personally or on account of his position, John Tuedy was clearly not popular in the execution of his duties, because he was instructed by the council to pursue anyone of those who fell foul of the rules and in particular anyone who 'raillit upone' (abused) him or his associates.

There seems to have been a continuing debate about the powers of the dean. In February 1649, the council asked one of its members, William Lowis (he would later become provost) to look into the whole matter. He was to compare the regulations of the burgh of Linlithgow with those which John Tuedy had produced. Tuedy himself was instructed to ride to Linlithgow and buy a copy of its regulations.

The dean of guild was an annual appointment, as was the appointment of the members of the dean of guild council, who were each required to swear the following oath of allegiance *(de fideli administratione):*

---

[151] It can be seen in the National Museum of Scotland

I do protest before God that I shall be a faithful Gild brother: I shall not clock nor colour any unfreeman's goods under pretence of my owne, I shall not pack nor peill with ony unfreeman. I shall not pass ony unsufficient goods, nor fyne at my own hands without discovering the same to the judge ordinary, and so oft as I shall break ony part of this my oath, I shall be liable to pay to the Guildry of Peebles the sum of 40 pounds Scots money.

This oath is still taken to this day by anyone becoming a member of the Guildry Corporation of Peebles.

The dean of guild was effectively the town's officer with the responsibility for the control of all trade within the burgh, including not only weights and measures and the quality of foodstuffs, but also the level of profit which a trader could earn. For example in October 1651, merchants, bakers and butchers were ordered to appear before the magistrates and the dean of guild in the tollbooth, between seven and eight in the morning. There they were lectured to 'keepe conscience' in selling their merchandise and to take only a reasonable profit. The butchers were not to 'blow' meat[152] while the bakers were to bake bread costing twelve pennies at the approved weight. The price was to be adjusted according to the price of wheat at the time. The sellers of wine and 'strong waters' were also warned that they should only take a reasonable profit. If anyone in those trades failed to comply, they would be punished as laid down in accordance with the Acts of parliament and former laws of the council, which suggests that by then national rather than local government regulation was now predominant. Perhaps it was the result of centralisation by the Commonwealth.

In 1669, the cordiners or shoemakers guild received formal recognition by the council. It included both the makers and sellers of shoes. At that time it had been the common practice in other burghs throughout Scotland, for members of the trade, to maintain a fund collected from the guild members, which was used to support old, infirm, weak and indigent members of the trade, surely an early example of Social Security. It was also to be used as a subsidy towards the cost of young members becoming burgesses. The money collected was kept in a "common box" by a member elected by the guild. For added security, a second member was elected to hold the key to the box. The council stipulated that anyone

---

152   in an attempt to make the carcases of slaughtered animals appear fatter and more attractive than they really were, unscrupulous butchers would blow air into the stomach of the animal or bird to inflate it,

within the burgh selling shoes should contribute twelve pennies Scots every quarter, while shoemakers from outside the burgh selling their products in the town were to pay twelve pennies Scots for every market or fair day at which they sold their wares.

A few years later the guild again made representations to the council, asking that it should make a legally binding rule that when apprentices or journeymen were to be taken on by any guild member, this and the amount of any payment for indenture should be approved by the council.

There is an amusing entry in the record of 12th March 1683 relating to the cordiners. At that time there was a fixed time for the start of trading in the shoemarket. It was marked by the ringing of the town bell, but there was no time fixed for closure. The guild complained to the council that as a result they 'and uther strangers ar greatly prejuged (prejudiced) by being forced to stand ther till night, the buyers still expecting the best pennie worth last'. Sale reductions are not new! The council duly considered the appeal and agreed that the shoemarket should begin on every market day at one o'clock in the afternoon and continue until three o'clock.

In 1680, it was the turn of the tailors who asked the council permission to raise subscriptions and keep a "box", which like the cordiners was to be used for members of the trade who were 'fallen off, seik and infirm, and has nothing to intertaine themselves upon.' The council gave its approval and again stipulated the amounts to be collected. Every burgess or freeman in the trade was to pay two shillings Scots, once a quarter. In addition, anyone entering into an apprenticeship was to pay thirteen shillings and four pence and if he then became a freeman to the trade a further thirty shillings and four pence. Any journeyman coming to work in the trade who had not served an apprenticeship within the burgh was required to pay twenty shillings and when he became a freeman he would have to pay four merks. The council were once again also to have the responsibility of appointing a trade member as keeper of "the box" and another as keeper of the key.

In March 1698, the dean of guild was authorised to install a seat in the kirk for himself and the members of his council. Today there is a seat still officially reserved for the Guildry Corporation in Peebles Old Parish Church.

26.
A Kenspeckle Character

The previously acknowledged histories of the burgh, record a great deal of detail about events and yet it is rare to find substantive information about the personal lives and character of individuals who lived in the town. One exception is Andrew Watson, (who has already been mentioned). He was something of a kenspeckle figure. He appears over a period of 30 years as schoolmaster, surgeon, vicar and clerk.

He is first mentioned in May 1624. At that time he held the post of schoolmaster, but it seems that his performance had not been very satisfactory. Appearing before the council, acknowledging that he had been properly paid, he promised to attend to his duties better than he had done in the past. In the following year there is the first reference to his activities as a surgeon. He had treated Thomas Dewar for a sore arm during 1623, but his fees had been disputed. The bill was to be paid by Thomas's brother John, who had instructed the treatment. The dispute about payment must have been brought to the council, because some time later, in March of 1625, the bailies ordered John to pay a modified fee to Watson for his services. Gunn says the amount was to be £18 to include the cost of the ingredients used in the cure, all in accordance with the account which Watson had produced. He was also required to pay an additional £12 for further ingredients and 'for fomenting Thomas's arm at sundry times' and £6 'for his pains.' It must be assumed that those payments were in pounds Scots. That would not be the last time that Watson was in dispute about his medical services.

We next hear of him in 1629. In April of that year he was admitted as vicar of Peebles in a ceremony in the Cross Kirk before a large company. He is specifically referred to as "Mr" Andrew Watson. The use of this title denotes that he held a degree in arts. In his ecclesiastical role he was the intermediary between the town and the Bishop of Glasgow and in April of 1634 finds him riding to Glasgow with some of the council. He is paid expenses for wine, ale and bread when he returns. Shortly after he is paid expenses of £8 for a five day visit to the bishop in Edinburgh with James Williamson, the provost. In the years from 1633 to 1636 there seem to have been many transactions between the archbishop of Glasgow and the burgh and a great deal of time and money was spent on the officials and deputations which travelled to Glasgow. In his role as vicar Watson played an important part in the transactions. As Dr Gunn comments ; 'In fact this official appears to have had a finger in most of the ecclesiastical and scholastic business of the parish, from prosecuting witches to interviewing my lord the bishop.'

Part of Watson's duty as vicar was to conduct daily and weekly services, but in 1639 there was dispute about the way in which he carried out those duties. The matter was referred in the first instance to the Presbytery of Peebles on 27th February 1640. According to the record of the meeting, it had issued an Act in favour of the town and parish of Peebles against Watson on 18th July 1639, ordering him to provide weekly and daily services in the form prescribed by the presbytery in the Act. Watson declined to accept the presbytery's ruling and appealed to the General Assembly which had been called by the king for 12 August 1639. The town called for all the relevant documents to be lodged and cited Watson to appear personally before the Assembly, which he did on 22 August. The Assembly in its wisdom merely referred the matter back to the presbytery[153] as being the appropriate body to deal with it.

Presumably because the complaint against Watson had been brought by the town council, the presbytery pointed out that the documents sent to the Assembly were unclear and that part of the complaint related to civil law and part to ecclesiastic law. The presbytery could only deal with the latter. They ordered Watson to conduct daily services, including evening and morning prayers and Bible reading. The decision was accepted on behalf of the town council by the provost, James Williamson. An amusing side light on the proceedings is a note in the council records that a payment was made to Catherine Stewart, who was the town clerk's servant, 'for wyne that was druken that day Mr Andro Watsone was injoyned to make morning and evening prayers'.

Andrew Watson made many enemies and there were a number of incidents when his property and even his life were put at risk. On one occasion in 1640, he complained to the council that he had been subject to the crime of "hamesucken" or personal assault. He reported that while he had been on the front stair of his house (this would have been an outside stair) the previous night, there had been a shot at the north side and then another fired at the east gable. There is no suggestion of any injury, so whoever fired the shots was probably intending to threaten the vicar.

---

153   Renwick *The Burgh of Peebles* Gleanings from its Records p 188

Another incident involved James Williamson, the Younger, possibly the son of the provost, who had often vowed to strip the roof above his head. It seems that he was true to his word, because in February 1642, Watson complained to the Privy Council, no less, that during the previous year his house had been damaged on several occasions by Williamson. On one occasion he had come to his house before daylight one morning while he was away from home, and had climbed to the top of the roof and removed part of the thatch.

On another occasion while Watson was again away at St Andrews, he claimed that Williamson returned with John Mure. This time they must have actually holed the roof, because when Watson returned he found that the contents had been soaked by a deluge of rain and the house was uninhabitable. That was not the end of what must have been a campaign of hate. In October that same year Watson claimed that the two culprits came during the night, entered by the back door and having gone upstairs removed floor boards from an upper floor. On his return as he said 'but for the providence of God' he might have fallen down the stairway with fatal consequences!

His complaint came before the Privy Council and was heard on 3rd February 1642. Strangely Watson could not produce any evidence against the two accused. Williamson denied everything on oath and he and Mure were acquitted and Watson was made to pay each of them ten merks for time they had spent in prison.

In December 1643, he is complaining to the town council once again about unpaid bills. This time it was against John Holden, described as a dryster[154] and James Holden, a miller, who had acted as cautioner for John. The complaint was, 'that where about a year since the said John and James employed me in curing the said John of diverse wounds and dislocations, which had then befallen him through a fall, and promised me satisfaction for my pains and disbursements; and true it is that for the space of many weeks I attended the said John at all such diets, both night and day, and debursed great charges in his cure until he was whole and sound. Nevertheless they refuse to give me their promised satisfaction, which extend to a hundred merks.' No doubt, once again the vicar would have had to compromise and accept a smaller amount!

In 1644 Watson was involved in another dispute. It arose again from his medical services. In May there had been a disturbance at the market cross in which one of the night watchmen was injured. William Burnett, who is described in the records as 'treasurer clerk of Scotland' and was

---

154   someone whose job it was to dry grain in a kiln

probably the same William Burnett who was laird of Cringletie. Burnett, for whatever reason, had come to the market cross during the night and when accosted by William Hislop, one of the night watchmen, he launched into a diatribe against the town with 'divers and sundry oaths and imprecations, and wishing that the whole town of Peebles were all burnt in a fire.' The row disturbed the watch and everyone round about 'out of their beds at that time.' Not only that but he then drew his sword and wounded Hislop, 'in the left hand...... thereby mutilating him to the effusion of blood in great quantity, and dismembering him of his left hand.' Into the scene of carnage stepped Andrew Watson to employ his medical skills to repair and heal the damage to Hislop's hand.

Burnett was duly accused of his actions. He admitted everything except that he denied 'mutilating' Hislop. He agreed to enter into ward for his actions, but sadly Watson had to raise an action before the council for the payment of his fee. The case was heard by the provost and bailies on 7th August. Watson claimed £240 Scots from Hislop for curing his left hand and 'restoring the two foremost fingers thereof, which were cut and mutilated by Mr William Burnett', which Hislop had 'promised him thankful payment.' Having heard the evidence the provost and bailies ordered that the defendant should pay Watson a reduced sum of 200 merks. The value a "merk" against £1 Scots was approximately two thirds, so this was a substantially reduced amount. Given the earlier case where again Watson had to accept a modified fee, he was clearly not averse to overcharging,

Much earlier in this book the story of the finding of 'a stately and venerable cross' in 1261 as narrated by John of Fordoun has been told. The story is a little more complicated than that and involves the finding of documents in the University of Cambridge. What is of interest here is that it was Andrew Watson who brought what was believed to be an extract from a document called *Erection of the Cross Kirk of Peebles* back to Peebles.

In December 1640 Watson made a journey to Cambridge. A description of the finding of the document by him appears in Dr Alexander Pennecuik's *Description of Tweeddale*, originally published in 1715. He describes it as follows :

At and within the Library of St John's College, in Cambridge, the seventeenth day of December, the year of God One Thousand Six Hundred and Forty years, Mr Andrew Watson vicar of Peebles, having made search of the records of North Britain, found extant therein the *Erection of the Cross Kirk of Peebles*, in manner as is after described, and thereafter did extract the

275

same under his own hand, in presence of an good number of the masters and fellows of several colledges in the University, to evidence unto present and future ages, that the said *Cross-Kirk* with enduements thereof, was erected by the King of Scots, for the special benefit and good of the incorporation and burgh of Peebles, which in the original manuscripts and records, is to that end called Plebes, that is the common or lay people of that place.

At that time John Hay, who was the son of Dr Theodore Hay and would succeed him in later years as minister of Peebles, was a student of theology at Cambridge, so he would have personally known Watson.

It may be that it was he who had actually found the document in the university library, although Dr Pennicuik implies that it was found following researches by Watson. However, it does appear that it was Hay, together with other fellows of St John's College who authenticated it.

A man of many parts was Andrew Watson. Unfortunately it is the negative side of his character which emerges again in later years. His pursuit of clients for unpaid bills seems to have been common, so much so that in July 1644 the council agreed to financially support any inhabitants of the town who were pursued by Watson.

When next we hear of him it is in 1651, when he is once again appointed as schoolmaster. His annual stipend was to be 200 merks. He was to be provided with a schoolroom and also receive payment from children both in the town and the landward area. As he had done previously he was to teach them 'divinity and humanity and all other liberal sciences.' The chapel bell was to be rung every morning at six to call children to school. This appointment was in addition to his role as vicar.

In December 1652 the presbytery of Peebles was asked by the provost to arrange a visit to the Grammar School. It is interesting here to note that while the provision of education was the responsibility of the town council, the presbytery was the higher authority.

A delegation from the presbytery duly visited in January following and reported that they found the school well attended by Mr Watson and that there was 'great proficiency' in the scholars as a result of his efforts. 'Whereupon the said Mr Andrew was encouraged and exhorted to go on in his duty.' None the less only two months later Watson resigned as he did not feel up to the post although he still remained vicar.

Meanwhile, in July 1652 he received a payment of £3 Scots as a part payment of 100 merks due to him by the presbytery, for his part in organising the burning of witches. It is likely that in his role as clerk he was responsible for the official documentation of those terrible events.

Trouble was never very far away for Andrew. Later in 1653 John Hay, the son of Dr Theodore, who was by then the minister of Peebles complained that Watson was not attending to his charge as vicar. He also had a serious complaint about Watson's behaviour during the time he was absent from his charge, which was reported to be 'scandalous'. He had been instructed by the presbytery to investigate and to report to the Kirk session of Peebles. He reported that, 'the truth of the scandal, I found that at Elibank there was one night a juggling man called Lawson in company with my Lord Lynton,[155] with whom also Mr Andro was, and after supper or dinner, the juggling man committed impropriety. Mr Andro was in the house (as I heard), but whether he was present in the room or not I could not learn, only this I have for a truth that Lawson could not get anyone to join him in his debauched act.'

The presbytery asked that further information be obtained from Lord Elibank, but it was reported that he had no servants in his employ who were there at the time of Watson's alleged scandalous behaviour and that 'my lord himself solemnly declared that he did neither hear nor see any such thing as was alleged to have taken place.' It was none the less decided to pursue the matter further and to trace other possible witnesses. None was found. In March 1655, the kirk session of Peebles reported that they had no knowledge of the alleged scandal, or indeed any other charge against him, but the case remained unresolved.

Although he had resigned in March 1653, at this time Watson was schoolmaster again and possibly because of the alleged scandal, the town's magistrates appeared before the Presbytery with a request that they appoint a delegation to visit the school in Peebles, to see if the pupils were benefiting from Watson's teaching. The members of Presbytery appointed to visit the school subsequently reported that, 'they found pains taken in teaching the grammar and rhetoric in respect of grammatical and rhetorical questions, but found deficiencies in making of congruous[156]themes. The magistrates and schoolmaster being called in, the moderator, in the presence of the magistrates, did exhort the schoolmaster to amend what was amiss in themes and turning of verse, and to make conscience of his charge by giving more attendance.' So, once again Watson is found wanting in performance of his duties.

He was in further trouble in July of 1656. It involved the case already mentioned, which was being pursued by the presbytery against John Hay,

---

155   The son of the 1st Earl of Traquair
156   Meaning harmonious

Younger of Smithfield and John Pringle. It was claimed that Watson had used 'disrespectful language' about the kirk session, presumably about the way in which it had dealt with the matter. He was cited to appear before it to explain himself.

In the meantime the matter of his alleged scandalous behaviour was still ongoing. The case was finally settled early in 1657. After trial by both the kirk session and the presbytery, Watson was acquitted. The complaint of scandal against him, originally brought by William Lowes, was found to have been 'a mere forgery for his (Watson's) defamation'.

During the lengthy investigation Watson had been suspended from his duties as clerk to the kirk session, yet another of his many activities. Now that the affair had been brought to a conclusion, he was asked if he would return to this post. On 25 February, at a meeting of the kirk session he said that he was satisfied with the way the whole matter had been hhandled andagreed to take up his duties again.

This then, is the last we hear of this colourful character. In 1624 when his name first appears, it is as schoolmaster. Assuming he was probably at that time in his early twenties by the time of his final appearance, he would probably have been approaching 60, for the time a considerable age. In all the references to him, there is nothing said about any family and it may be that he was a solitary figure. He was certainly controversial.

An odd footnote appears in December 1662. James Byres, who had been a servant of a former provost, John Plenderleith, was charged with theft. He confessed that having found a key lying on the causeway of the Northgate, which he must have recognised, he had used it to open the door of his master's wine cellar. He was accosted by Plenderleith and his wife, whereupon he took the key and threw it into the Tweed. For that offence he had his goods, including his chest, sequestered by the magistrates. When the chest was opened it was found to contain things which belonged to a several people, among them some clothes and other items which had belonged to Andrew Watson, who is described as 'deceased'. Byres duly confessed to stealing those things. As punishment he was ordered to stand for an hour in the public pillory on a market day, with a paper on his head, detailing his crime. Thereafter he was to be banished from the burgh, on pain of death if he was found within its bounds.

27.
The end of the Commonwealth

The Cromwellian occupation lasted for the best part of ten years from 1650. English troops came and went. The records say very little about their movements, but there are a few references which show that there was still military activity in the latter years of the decade:

8 Sept. 1657. That a pairt of Captain Blisset's troops came to Peebles: removed 17 Oct. 1657.

22 Oct. 1657. That pairt of Captain Tounours troope; in Lilburnes Regiment[157] came to this burgh: removed Weddensday 19 May 1658.

24 Sept. 1658. The forsaid pairtie entered into their winter quarter; removed May 1659.

Remarkably for a time which must have greatly affected the whole community, not only in religious affairs, but in ordinary living, the records give every appearance of life continuing largely as normal. Markets are supervised; trades are regulated; assaults, disturbances and felonies are punished; the common lands are strictly managed; disputes about rights of occupation; ownership and pasturage are settled; middens are a continuing hazard; pigs and poultry roam the streets and vennels in spite of rules which are meant to control them; causeways are cleaned; bridges are mended; and town walls are repaired.

What was no longer normal was the attitude of moral rectitude which then prevailed. Those committing moral misdemeanours suffer the pain and embarrassment of the "cutty stool" or the "jougs" and throughout it all the town council and the kirk session reign supreme. It remained a time of moral and spiritual austerity dominated by English Puritan authority aided and abetted by Scottish Covenanting Presbyterianism. Absent from the records is any reference to public or private fun and amusement, other than to condemn them as sinful. Women and men dancing together was regarded as promiscuous and marked out for condemnation, particularly at

---

[157]   Colonel Robert Lilburne for a time commander-in-chief of Scotland, imprisoned after the Restoration

weddings. There was a long established tradition of chatting and gossiping in the churchyard on Sundays, before and after the service. It was an opportunity for families, friends to exchange news, but in the narrow minded world of religious bigotry of the time, it was deemed to be an affront to the purity of thought which should attend Sabbath devotion and its aftermath. The kirk session made strenuous efforts to discourage the practice, issuing dire warnings about the punishments which would follow what is considered to be a serious offence.

Notably absent is any reference to the Beltane horse race. Up until that time the horse race had been a major feature of the Beltane festival, but this indicates that in all likelihood it was now banned. Originally the race had been run on a course from Nether Horsburgh, some way out of the town, ending at the East Port of the burgh, but in 1644 it seems to have been moved to Whitehaugh, just east of the town. In advance of the festival there was a public proclamation, which ordered the council and the 'hail remenant honest men' of the town to accompany the provost and bailies on the morning following Beltane day, with a sword in their belt and a staff in hand, during the whole time of the horse races. Failure to attend would result in a fine of forty shillings. No doubt it was a reflection of the violent disputes which have previously been referred to, which on one occasion resulted in the race being banned by the Privy Council.

The winner of the race received a trophy which was called the Beltane Bell, which the winner held for one year, provided an undertaking was given to return it before the next year's event. In 1641 the bell was won by Robert Vaitche of Dawyck. The bell is described as weighing one pound, 'wanting nyne droppe, guid and sufficient silver', with three bells and five appendicles.[158] As surety for the redelivery of the trophy before the 4th of May in the following year, William Vaitche, described as a burgess of Peebles (presumably a relative), provided a caution of 500 merks (about £28 sterling).[159] The trophy was of significant value, but for the moment at least, the race was a thing of the past.

The authorities viewed the holding of fairs on a Saturday or a Monday as a 'prophanatioun of the Sabbath', presumably because Saturday should be a day of preparation and Monday a day of reflection. In 1656, the Beltane fair day fell on a Saturday and the council decided that it must be moved to the first Wednesday of May and that this should remain the case in subsequent years. The fair itself was a shadow of former years, reflecting the moral austerity of the time.

[158]   Hanging jewels
[159]   Approximately £4,000 in today's money

The conduct of worship and civil life in Peebles, probably in common with burghs and communities throughout Scotland, had descended into a state of barren and colourless uniformity, which only a major political and ecclesiastical upheaval could reverse. That upheaval was about to happen. On 3rd September 1658 Oliver Cromwell died.

As a footnote to the middle decades of the seventeenth century, it was during the time of the Cromwellian occupation that the earliest description of the Tweeddale countryside appears. In 1654 the Dutch cartographer Johannes Blaew, recorded that :

> The country is very [scenic?], the air is serene and pleasant. There are many hilly places, of which those which are near Tweed and the other rivers are always green, pleasant and useful for pasture. There are still more valleys and plains on each side of the Tweed and the other rivers some abound in "Fruicts" (fruit?) and other in hay. So well indeed that this country has enough [food?] and pasture for itself so that most of the inhabitants are self sufficient from their beasts, a goodly quality of milk, cheese and butter. In the lower parts of the area particularly around Selkirk, sheep find the grass so good and healthier for them than anywhere else that they live up to 15 years old unless they die of disease.[160]

The death of Cromwell did not immediately result in any great change, certainly as far as the ordinary people were concerned. Scotland remained occupied by the troops of the New Model Army. Although Cromwell had been offered the Crown, he had not accepted it, but in practice he had ruled as a virtual dictator. It was perhaps ironic that a man who had set out to destroy a dynasty, should have created his own. He was succeeded by his son, Richard, but someone less like his father is difficult to imagine. He had been living as a country squire and probably would have preferred to continue to do so. He was weak and ineffective, derided as "Queen Dick". Within a year he was removed by the army and left to return to his former life as country gentleman.

The Protectorate which the army itself had created was abolished. In May 1659 the revived Rump Parliament,[161] in a remarkable and speedy "u turn", declared all the legislation of the previous six years invalid. The union collapsed. Scotland remained under the grip of the New Model Army. This well-trained and disciplined force was now commanded by General George Monk, who was to play a significant role in what was to

---

160   Translated from original French by Ann Goodburn
161   So called because all the Royalist members had been removed.

follow. Known as "Honest George", General Monk was autocratic, but an able military commander, highly respected for his fair mindedness and common sense. He was well aware that the military government was becoming increasingly unpopular. It was now composed of a group of fundamentalist Puritan officers, who showed every sign of being more intolerant of opposition than Cromwell had been. News had reached Monk of English Presbyterians and Royalists joining together to demand a new parliament to curb the powers of the military. This was accompanied by growing support for the restoration of the monarchy.

Support for the return of monarchy was gaining strength in Scotland also. In response, Monk called a convention in Edinburgh, which elected the royalist Earl of Glencairn as one of its presidents. Satisfied that the government in Scotland was by then in safe hands, Monk led his formidable army south, leaving Scotland free of its less-than-welcome occupying force at long last. As had happened a number of times in the past decades, the arrival of an army from north of the border was to have a significant effect on the history of Britain, although on that occasion it was a returning English one. A parliament which did meet in London failed to make any progress, but the arrival of Monk in London brought matters to a head. The leading commander of the Puritan faction was General Lambert, who had earlier been the scourge of Scotland, but his power and influence was now waning. Cromwell's other great military commander, Sir Thomas Fairfax now supported Monk who was able to take control of the political agenda in February 1660. In March a convention held at Westminster, eventually decided that there should be a return to the former constitutional arrangements. The Commonwealth Union was at an end and Charles was accepted as the rightful King of England. He had remained in exile in the Netherlands, but in May he sent an envoy to London with a document which became known as the Declaration of Breda. In it Charles promised a general amnesty, but also to recognise the liberty of the individual and religious tolerance. He promised :

A liberty to tender consciences and that no man shall be disquieted or called upon for differences of opinion in the matter of religion which do not disturb the peace of the Kingdom, and that we are ready to consent to such an act of parliament as upon mature deliberation shall be offered to us for the full granting of indulgence.

Although it was sufficient to pave the way for his restoration, they were promises he would not keep. Soon after his return he started a campaign against all those who had been implicated in the death of his father. The

Regicides as they were called were pursued relentlessly and most suffered bloody and painful deaths. While they were all English, in Scotland, his promise of religious toleration would evaporate in a few years, as he sought to impose Episcopacy north of the border once again. He was proclaimed King of England in London on the 8th of May and King of Scots at the Mercat Cross in Edinburgh a few days later.

The restoration of the monarchy brought a collective sigh of relief, not least to the Scottish kingdom. The English occupation had at best been an embarrassment to national pride and at worst a sore burden of heavy taxation to support the occupying forces and much else. There was wild celebration throughout the country. In douce Edinburgh there were fireworks and even a banquet in the High Street. Fountains flowed with claret and bells rang.

Bells also rang in Peebles. The Royal Burgh, which for a time past had lost its loyalty to the Stuart dynasty, regained its fervour for the Scottish Crown. There was a bonfire and on the 19th June a Thanksgiving Day for the king's restoration, both provided for at the town's expense. Fun and laughter returned and after an absence of some years, the Beltane Fair and its horse race were revived in 1661. It was a happy and carefree event. Ale and wine flowed. Four gallons of ale were provided at the Cross for the townsfolk by command of the magistrates as a prelude to the race, some days in advance on 22nd April. Probably it was for the refreshment of the competitors or possibly the officials, as that quantity would hardly have quenched the thirst of the general public. Whoever was involved, it must have been a jolly and boisterous affair, because the town treasurer carefully notes that three ale cups were broken at a cost to the town of 6s. However, that was minor compared with the Edinburgh celebration at which it was estimated that 'three hundred dozen of glasses' were broken in 'loyal toasts to the king'. There was further celebration on 1st May when the Beltane Cup, gaily decorated with red ribbons was displayed at the Cross, while on the day of the race itself the council expended the substantial sum of £27.12s for 'wyn and uther furnitor when the King was crownd, and at Beltan fair when the earl of Tuedell came to the toun'. There was an additional item of 16s for 'four stowps (of ale) to the mure wher the race hors did run.'

Released from the shackles, restrictions and stifling moral rectitude of Puritan interlopers and extreme Presbyterianism, which were never a characteristic of the town, Peebles returned to "the Play" once more.

*   *   *

If the first six decades of the century had been a time of political upheaval, including a period of nationwide bloodletting, the remaining four would culminate in a final political and constitutional settlement, which provided the basis for the modern era. In Scotland it would also provide the final settlement of the religious order, with the establishment of a Presbyterian Church of Scotland, which subsists to the present day. The political settlement would largely be achieved without major bloodshed. The religious settlement would not and would lead to what became known as the "Killing Times".

The story of both merits wider consideration. Peebles has a small but significant part to play, but the national story dominates and will be dealt with in the final part of this section of the book. Before turning to that, there is none the less good reason to pause and reflect on the perhaps more parochial issues which affected the Royal Burgh in the latter part of the seventeenth century. The days of royal visitation were long since gone and with the departure of the occupying forces of the former Commonwealth, Peebles no longer attracted the attention of the major players on the Scottish stage. It is fair to say that it was becoming something of a backwater.

A review of the records for this period may suggest that not much had progressed since the sixteenth century. The same problems seem to recur. In the realm of law and order it is the same crimes and disturbances which are repeated. The town council remains the principal source of justice and retribution. The dignity of its members continues to be reaffirmed. Every member is to wear a hat when attending council meetings. The magistrates continue to suffer abuse from the more forthright citizens, sometimes even from within their own ranks. Punishment generally takes the form of public humiliation at the pillory or incarceration in the steeple until the fault is acknowledged or a fine is paid.

There are disputes between neighbours, sometimes resulting in violence. "Flyting"[162]is common and many cases come before the council. The "stair heed" brawl is nothing new, although in Peebles it was more likely to be a "close heed" brawl. Again the humiliation of the pillory was the frequent punishment.

From time to time there are cases of what are described as "riot". In most cases they are nothing more than the sort of disturbance already referred to, but one notable occasion is worth recording. In March 1682

---

[162]   Abuse of others.

there was a major riot in the town. Although the disturbance was the result of a purely local dispute, in due course it did involve the Privy Council.

It followed a decision by the magistrates to let a small area of the town's common grazings by public roup or auction. Traditionally burgesses had the right to graze their livestock on the common at no cost and although magistrates claimed the rent they received would be used to defray public costs and also to add to the Common Good fund, as, strictly they were entitled to do, the good citizens thought otherwise and on 1st March an irate mob gathered and invaded the tolbooth where the magistrates were sitting. They threatened violence, not least to the provost who, their leaders said, 'would be lyke proveist Dickisone who was sticted'.[163] Two of the ring leaders were promptly arrested and imprisoned, but later in the day the mob returned and invaded the prison, releasing both men. No sooner had they done so when they were re-arrested along with their rescuers. The following day, a group of women 'did in a most tumultuary and irregular way' manage to free the two ringleaders and their rescuers and the whole party proceeded to the town cross where about three hundred townsfolk were gathered. There was considerable disorder and much to the consternation of the magistrates, the health of the rioters was drunk, as 'protectors of the liberties of the poor'. Some of the company even went so far as to gather stones at the cross, threatening to stone to death anyone who opposed them. The council appealed to the Privy Council and the principal rioters were taken to Edinburgh to appear before the Privy Council who imprisoned them in the tolbooth of Edinburgh for an indefinite period. They also had their burgess rights removed. The magistrates were authorised to call 'the haill rest of the inhabitants that were accessory to the tumult and ryot libelled and to proceed against them therefore in fyning, imprisonment and ryveing their burgess-tickets as they shall find cause'. The "hot heads" were immediately dealt with, but the ringleaders petitioned the Privy Council for their freedom, pleading that 'they were poore ignorant men, who did not think they could have given offence to the magistrates of Peebles, and are willing to undergo any censure.' They were freed on 31st March on giving caution for good behaviour and ordered to appear before the magistrates to 'acknowledge their fault and crave pardon'. As a result of the riot some fifty-nine people including a number of women were fined for their part in what had clearly been a serious breach of public order.

---

163   Dickisone, a provost of an earlier era had been beaten up and murdered in the High Street in 1572

Less dramatic were the actions of the council in controlling the general administration of the town and its facilities. Much that occurs repeats earlier actions and orders. As before, markets and fairs were regulated. In 1667, the council ordered that the market on St Peter's day (29th June) should begin at four o'clock in the morning. Fair days falling on a Saturday or Monday were instead to be held on week days except Beltane day, which was to be held on the first Wednesday of May, while Trinity Monday was to be celebrated on the following Tuesday.

As so frequently in former years, there are still problems with straying poultry and once again in 1674 the rules which require them to have a clog tied to their foot or for their wings to be clipped are re-stated. Street cleaning remains an ongoing issue. The Tweed bridge causeway needs to be cleaned. Middens still obstruct and contaminate the High Street. The council considers this to be a 'great abuse' and in January 1680 order all middens to be removed by the 22nd February. Anyone dumping any refuse on the High Street beyond the line of their own gutter after that date will be fined half a crown by the town officials.

There are apparently a number of inhabitants who have allowed their boundary walls to fall into disrepair to the detriment of their neighbours. They are to immediately build up any slaps (gaps) and if they fail they are to be fined half a crown and also be liable to compensate their neighbours for any damage which may have been caused to their property.

In 1674 the magistrates and council were exercised about complaints concerning the quality of woollen yarn being sold on public markets and fair days, which reflected badly on the reputation of the town. Buyers were also suffering because of shortages of yarn, which presumably had the effect of increasing prices. It was caused by wool being sold loose rather than in measured lengths. In future wool sold at the markets had to be in proper rolled hanks.

Arrangements for the running of the Beltane horse races were regularly reviewed. In March 1684. The prize for the race to be run on Tuesday, 8th of May was to be a plate valued at eight pounds sterling, while the prize for the second race, run on the following Friday, was to be a saddle costing thirty shillings sterling. Both races were to be run on Whithaugh Muir, but only if there were three or more competitors. In the event that there were only three entries for the race for the plate, each would be required to pay five dollars and four pounds for the race for the saddle. Only those entries for the plate race lodged with the town clerk four days before the race would be accepted and for the second race it was two days.

An unusual entry which shows some spirit of community care, involved a payment of compensation to Thomas King, who was a merchant burgess of the burgh and whose house, stable and all their contents had been destroyed by an accidental fire in 1668. The council, 'out of their bowelles of compassione' instructed the treasurer to make him a grant of forty pounds Scots.

An Act of parliament had placed a limit on the number of people who could attend baptisms and marriages. That may well have been a consequence of laws which had been introduced because of the problems which faced the government in trying to control and prevent large gatherings of people for religious services outwith recognised church buildings. They were called conventicles and were held to hear the preaching of Covenanting clergy. They were illegal, as were any gatherings of more than five people in addition to family members. In January 1688 the town council felt obliged to summon 84 town's folk accused of attending baptisms since the previous October and 39 who were accused of having more at their weddings than allowed by law. All were found guilty and fined.

So, at a local level at least, life continued much as it had done before and during the time of Cromwell's Commonwealth, but further afield matters were far from stable. There was about to be a dramatic change in the religious order. Episcopacy was to be restored and with it the authority of the king as the head of the church.

28.
Politics and the Church

In spite of having promised to respect the liberty of the individual and religious tolerance, it did not take Charles II long to renege on those undertakings. As a young and inexperienced monarch he would have been influenced by his close confidants and advisors, many of whom were committed Episcopalians. However, the reluctance with which he was persuaded to accept the Covenant should not be forgotten. What was by then at issue was the re-introduction of Episcopacy to the governance of the Scottish Kirk. The political significance was that it placed the monarch at the Head of the Kirk. From that flowed the power to appoint bishops and through them to control not only the Kirk, but exercise influence over civil government as well.

Because supporters of the Covenant had played a significant part in the downfall of his father, Charles was determined that Covenanting Presbyterianism should never again have control in Scotland. Early in 1661 he appointed a Committee of Estates, made up of a group of men on whom he could rely to carry out his will. A parliament was called which met for the first time on 1ˢᵗ January 1661. It sat for six months during which time it passed no less than 393 Acts including, an Act which gave the king sole authority to appoint the principal Officers of State, Privy Councillors and Lords of Session. The Lords of the Articles, who were effectively the government, were restored. More significantly for the general wellbeing of the nation, an Act was passed which required every holder of a public office, both at local as well as national level, to take an oath of allegiance to the king, acknowledging him as the "Supreme Governor" of the Kingdom, with authority over 'all persons and all causes'. It gave the king sole authority to call Parliament and restored the monarch to absolute power. A further Act annulled every Act of Parliament passed by the Estates after 1633, so returning statute law to what it had been prior in that year. Included, was the form of government of the Scottish Church, which once again became Episcopalian. The powers of kirk sessions, presbyteries and synods were to be retained, but for all practical purposes the governance of the Kirk reverted to what it had been during the reign of James VI&I – and bishops were back.

The oath of allegiance, which all in public office were required to take, also included a declaration acknowledging that the Covenants and any form of armed insurrection were unlawful. The oath was to be taken by all magistrates (provost and bailies) as well as council members. The council records of Peebles first refer to it in 1661, when the entry for 30th September notes that it had been informed that there 'is ane act proclaimed in Edinburgh, bearing the qualifications of magistrattes and council'. A copy had not reached them, so further discussion was postponed, but the treasurer was instructed to send for a copy.

At the subsequent council meeting on 14th October, which included the annual election of magistrates and councillors, Alexander Williamson, the past provost, reported that at the last session of parliament which he had attended, all the commissioners of burghs who were present, were authorised to present the oath of allegiance to the magistrates and councillors of their own burgh. He asked that the oath be administered to all those who were now elected. They, 'all in ane voice, declared they ar most willing to take the said oath of alleadgeance' as soon as a public order came from the king and parliament to have it administered. The practical result was that in Peebles, if not universally throughout Scotland, the new order was accepted. With it came Episcopacy and for the next 38 years it remained the established order of worship in the parish kirk.

In its determination to meet the demands of the king, the Estates when it met in June 1662, decided that all ministers who had been admitted to the Kirk since 1649, should be suspended. They could however, seek reinstatement as Episcopalians, provided that they were supported by a patron (usually a local laird) and were properly consecrated by their bishop. Not only did those who failed to conform lose their livings, but they and their families were turned out of their homes.

The Rev John Hay retained his position as minister of Peebles and no doubt, if the evidence of his past leanings is anything to go by, he would not have been unhappy about this outcome. In any event he must have conformed and met the requirements of the new order, because he had been invited to preach to the parliament in Edinburgh in April of that year, which shows that not only had he conformed, but that he was also acceptable to the government hierarchy. He would remain the minister of Peebles until his death in 1666.

This is not the place to set out the history of the national events which were to follow, which can be found in the present author's book *The*

Bloody Covenant,[164]but an outline is necessary if the events of the next few years, both nationally and as they affected Peebles, are to be understood.

Elsewhere in Scotland there were stirrings of revolt, particularly in the southwest, in Galloway and Ayrshire, where Protestor clergy who continued to support the Covenant held sway. In time that movement would spread and lead to a punitive crack down and persecution by the government, which became known as "the Killing Times". Those whom they pursued are known as "the Covenanters" and their stories are part of Scottish legend. Unwilling to accept Episcopacy as now decreed and practised in parish churches, they conducted their own services, which might include Holy Communion and baptism. Those services, known as "conventicles" were usually held in the open air and could attract huge crowds. Not far from Peebles several were held at Talla Linn, reportedly attended by upwards of 5000 people. There were also gatherings at Broughton and elsewhere just beyond the county boundary of Peeblesshire and Edinburgh.

In 1666, a rebellion had broken out in Ayrshire, when a gathering of about 700 Covenanters at Brig O'Doon, encouraged by fanatical preachers set out with the intention of attacking Glasgow. Their way was barred by a government force led by Sir Tam Dalziel. They decided to head for Edinburgh instead, marching by way of Lanark, their number had grown to about 1,200, but on reaching Colinton, on the outskirts of Edinburgh they found the capital heavily guarded. Dalziel had followed them and confronted them on the south side of the Pentland Hills, at Rullion Green. The battle, such as it was, ended in a rout. Fifty Covenanters were killed and fifty more were captured, the remainder fled. Rullion Green is little more than twelve miles from Peebles.

In the aftermath, of those taken prisoner, thirty three were hanged and the so-called "Pentland Rebellion" sparked a campaign of repression mainly centred in the south west. The man appointed to lead it was James Graham of Claverhouse, known in the mythology of Scotland as "Bonnie Dundee". To those who suffered under his repression he is better known as "Bloody Clavers".

His campaign in the south west was to reach its climax in two battles in June 1679. The first was a fairly minor affair at Drumclog in Ayrshire, where Covenanters attending an open air meeting met and defeated a small force led by Claverhouse himself. Three weeks later a much larger force of Covenanters was met at Bothwell Brig by a government army,

---

164   *The Bloody Covenant, Crown and Kirk in Conflict.* History Press 2010

commanded by the Duke of Monmouth, bastard son of King Charles II. The Covenanters were heavily defeated and the majority, but not all of the survivors were rounded up and marched to Edinburgh where they were imprisoned in appalling conditions for several months.

None of those activities is likely to have escaped the knowledge of those living in Peebles or the surrounding area. Indeed as will be seen at least one of its citizens was involved at Bothwell Brig. Following the battle at Rullion Green a militia was formed in the town and in October 1668 the town council instructed the treasurer to buy weapons. The cost was to be met by a levy on the townsfolk. It also seems likely that at least a small contingent from the town was present at Bothwell Brig in support of the government forces.

In 1680 the Presbytery of Peebles was seriously concerned about covenanting activity as the following minute of 7th April confirms :-

This day, the Presbytery taking into consideration the frequent and rebellious meetings there are amongst them, where persons who have been intercommoned since the rebellion in the year 1665, now go publicly to other persons' houses, and take upon them to preach in the doors and entries of the houses where they are reset, at all which meetings there are several hundreds out of doors, who either have been at Bothwell Bridge themselves, or frequent the company of such; and their meetings being new-kindled fire in this place of the kingdom, where never any rebellious meeting of this nature formerly was, they humbly crave advice from the archbishop and Synod what to do in such cases.'

It has been suggested that Peebles was not a covenanting town. Certainly all the indications are that it adhered to Episcopacy right up until 1690. In August 1684, perhaps as a demonstration of loyalty to the Episcopal order, four communion cups were presented to the parish kirk, one of them donated by the town council. Two were presented as a result of bequests by two natives of Peebles, who had gone on to achieve high office in the capital city of Edinburgh. One, Alexander Williamson, as Provost of the City and the second, John Govan as Treasurer. Alexander Williamson was almost certainly a descendant of those Williamsons who had been provosts of Peebles and had played a prominent role during the period both before and after the Commonwealth. The fourth cup was presented by Mr John Hay, who had succeeded his predecessor, also John Hay, in 1666 as the Rector of Peebles and Manor. Mr Hay was of course a firm Episcopalian. Those gifts show that whatever the ripples and rumbling which may have touched Peebles, the powers that be in the Royal Burgh were in no doubt where they stood, even if some of their citizens might not agree. All four cups survive in the possession of the Old Parish Church and are still used from time to time.

However, that is not the whole story! The concerns of the presbytery have already been noted, but there is a far more personal story. The Scottish government of the day regarded anyone who refused to deny the Covenants and those who took part in any insurrection in support of the Covenants, as guilty of treason. Many of the leading figures died for their beliefs. Some 149 suffered death on the gallows in the Grassmarket of Edinburgh. Today a memorial to those who died can be found at the upper end of the Grassmarket, marking the spot where the gallows stood. The memorial records the names of all those who died, among them is the name of James Nicol, who is described as a 'merchant burgess of Peebles'.

Not a lot is known about James Nicol. He was probably born in 1633, the son of Walter Nicol and Mergat Watson. Marriage to Jennet Vaitche is recorded on 10th May 1654. There were a number of children of the marriage and in the records of the Kirk Session of Peebles on 5th October 1665 he was summoned to appear before it to explain why he had been absent from the Kirk and his attendance at conventicles. It was also recorded that he had a child 'long unbaptised'. His support of the Covenant is clearly evident in this.

His father Walter, had been a burgess of the Royal Burgh and no doubt James had inherited that status. The Grassmarket memorial describes him a "merchant" burgess, so it is probable that he traded in the woollen-based products of the town, travelling round the country selling those goods and no doubt that would have brought him into contact with other supporters of the Covenant. What is known is that he was at Bothwell Bridge and took part in the battle, but he must have been among those few who escaped capture. What took him there is not known, although as subsequent events would show he was a proud supporter of the Covenanting cause and quite prepared to die for it.

In May 1684 a royal proclamation was issued which denounced those who had fled, charging them with rebellion. The proclamation included a long list of fugitives among whom were twelve from Peeblesshire. It included the name of James Nicol, who is described as 'vagabond in the said shire.' This hardly equates with his status as a "merchant burgess", but perhaps he was keeping out of the way and not in Peebles where he could be arrested. However, he must have continued his trading, because what is also known is that on an August day in 1684 he was in Edinburgh on the same day that three Covenanters were hanged in the Grassmarket.

His return to Peebles had been delayed because some repairs were needed to his horse's harness. He witnessed their final end and in a fit of anger and disgust he shouted out 'A cow of Bashan has pushed three men to death at one push, contrary to their own base laws and in an inhumane way'. He was immediately arrested and a few days later on 18th August he was brought before the Privy Council to answer the charge of treason. Although so little is known about him, the fact that he appeared before what was effectively the highest authority in the land shows that he must have been known and of some significance.

In 1871 a book was published called *A CLOUD OF WITNESSES*.[165] It includes the Testimony of James Nicol and gives an account of his trial, which was conducted in the main by Sir George Mackenzie, known because of his brutal justice and treatment of those Covenanters who came before him as, "bluidy Mackenzie".

In it Nicol makes no secret of his religious beliefs or where his loyalties lay. He was asked if he had been at Bothwell Brig, he replied that he had. In answer to the question 'Do ye own the King's authority?' he replied 'I own all things that the precious Word of God owns less or more, and all faithful magistrates'. His interrogators then asked, 'But do you own King Charles also?' to which he replied, 'I dare not for a world; because it is perjury; for he has unkinged himself in a high degree, and that in doing all things contrary to the Word of God, and Confession of Faith, and Catechism Larger and shorter.' Those answers alone would have been sufficient to condemn him, but throughout a lengthy interrogation lasting two days, he held his ground, challenged their assumptions and conceded nothing. A brave man James Nicol! The outcome was inevitable. He was condemned to death and on the 27th of August 1684 he met his fate on the Grassmarket gallows, an unrepentant Covenanted Presbyterian to the end.

By a strange coincidence it was in the same month that the four communion cups, proclaiming loyalty to the king and his Episcopacy were dedicated in the parish kirk of Peebles. One of those cups bears the inscription, "In this conquer", but it was not to be Episcopacy which survived as the religious order in the parish kirk of Peebles

---

[165] Full title *A CLOUD OF WITNESSES for the ROYAL PREROGATIVES of JESUS CHRIST being the LAST SPEECHES AND TESTIMONIES of those WHO HAVE SUFFERED FOR THE TRUTH SINCE THE YEAR 1680*. The essential extracts are set out in full in the author's previous book *The Bloody Covenant*

29.
A Glorious Revolution

During the last years of the reign of Charles II and James II&VII, who succeeded him, the whole struggle between the supporters of the Covenant and the government centred on the campaign of religious persecution, but it also involved the question of loyalty to the Crown.

In August 1681 the Scots parliament met. The new High Commissioner, the king's representative, was his brother James, Duke of York.[166] He was a professed Catholic and in England attempts to exclude him from the succession had failed. At his behest the Estates passed an Act in which the right of succession to the crown of Scotland by lineal descent could not be barred on religious grounds. Later in the month an Act was passed which required every holder of a public office to once again, take an oath of loyalty to the king and Kirk and to declare the Covenants to be unlawful. That was the infamous Test Act. There had of course been an earlier law in similar terms, but this time it was to be applied much more universally. It caused a wave of protest, not least because it required acceptance of royal supremacy in all civil and church affairs, in addition to acceptance of the Reformation Confession of 1560 and that taking up arms against the government was unlawful. The issue of royal supremacy was equally unacceptable to Episcopalians and Presbyterians alike. Several of the high officers of state, including the Lord President, Sir James Dalrymple, refused to take the oath. Even some of the leaders of the Kirk sent a formal protest. Some eighty Episcopalian ministers resigned their charges, rather than take the oath. All shades of Presbyterians, both moderate and Whig,[167] objected, as of course did the Catholics. It is probable that no Act of Parliament in the history of Scotland has been so universally disliked.

Not only did the Test Act cause protest, it also caused confusion. The wording of the Act seemed to contain many inconsistencies. It is doubtful if there were many who knew the Reformation Confession which had been unused for many years and was forgotten even by the scholars of the Church. Nowhere was confusion more evident than in Peebles. The

---

[166] later James VII&II
[167] The name given to the extreme Covenanters, particularly those from the south west of Scotland

provost and magistrates could not understand it and felt obliged to present a petition to the Privy Council. It stated that the petitioners were anxious to take the Test, but as Peebles was a small and in their words 'remote place' and the petitioners were 'ignorant and illiterate', they could find no one who could advise them about the difference between the Act of Parliament and the Act of Council and as they did not possess a copy of the Act of Parliament or the Confession of Faith which was referred to, they 'humbly' requested time to take advice. Because they could not be without magistrates, they had gone ahead in October with the annual election in the normal way and hoped that it would be time enough to take the Test in January following. However, as soon as they were in a position to understand the Act of Parliament, they said they were perfectly willing to take the Test, when and wherever the Privy Council might agree. They went on to affirm that they had always been very loyal and ready to serve the king on all occasions and among other instances their 'care and diligence in the late rebellion'.[168]had been noted by the Privy Council 'who did the petitioners the honour to return them their particular thanks therefor'. They asked if the provost and magistrates could take the Test in the presence of a member of the Privy Council in Edinburgh and then be authorised in turn, to administer it to the remaining magistrates and councillors before a date to be set. The Privy Council heard the petition and did appoint one of its members to administer the Test to the provost, bailies and the treasurer and agreed that the magistrates could administer it to the remainder of the council. They were to report back to the Privy Council before the third Thursday in December.

The Test was duly administered to the provost, one of the bailies and the treasurer and they then returned to Peebles to administer it in turn to the remainder of the town council, who met for the purpose in the tolbooth of Peebles on 28th November 1681. Out of the seventeen members of the council four refused to take it. They were William Scott, who was then Dean of Guild, Alexander Jonkinson, James Grieve and Archibald Sheill. Strangely this does not seem to have affected their position, as all four appear on the list of councillors in office in October 1682 and of those four, Scott, Jonkinson and Grieve were all re-elected at that time, which is curious, given that failure to take the Test was a bar to office. It could of course be that an initial act of courage crumbled under the pressure of threat and coercion or that a moral standpoint was easily corrupted by the advantages and privileges of office!

---

168   The Battle of Bothwell Brig

Where now did Peebles stand as a loyal Royal Burgh? In response to the second Covenanter rebellion a detachment of the local militia, equipped with arms supplied by the town, had responded to the government's call and had been present at Bothwell Brig, something for which they had received recognition and thanks. The petition to the Privy Council had been at pains to explain the collective willingness of the town council to take the Test (if they could understand it!) and its loyalty to the king and wish to serve him. Yet when it came to the point, that was clearly not a universally held view. Peebles was probably not very different from many communities in Scotland at the time, especially those influenced to a degree by rebellious activity not very far away and the knowledge of the government's response which amounted to little more than atrocities committed in Edinburgh.

Charles II died on 5th February 1685. He was succeeded by his brother James, Duke of York as James II&VII. He had proved himself to be an able administrator and naval commander and his time spent in Scotland as his brother's Commissioner must have made him aware of the ever-strengthening tide of opposition to Episcopacy and the concept of royal supremacy, but he was politically inept, obstinate and above all an avowed Roman Catholic.

One of his early actions on succeeding to the throne was to try to control and to extend his influence at a more parochial level and in September 1686 he ordered the suspension of the annual election of town councils. The experience of Peebles may well have been typical. The provost received a letter from the Privy Council which he produced to a meeting of the council on 27th September which authorised it to 'continow and exerce as magistrates and counsel until his Majesties all signify his further pleasur.' That was the first occasion that the Crown had attempted to interfere directly with the workings of local government. Never before had the council received such an instruction! Elections to the council were often influenced or manipulated by the local gentry,[169] but never before had the central authority attempted to interfere with the age old privileges of the Royal Burgh.

The following year matters were taken a stage further. The Earl of Traquair, the son of the 1st earl, who was a Catholic and a firm supporter of the king, attended a meeting of the town council on 5th February and submitted a list of magistrates and councillors the king wished to

---

169   The influence of the Hays had been a regular feature since the fifteenth century,

nominate. In Peebles at least, the council for its part seems to have accepted the situation in spite of that clear interference with their ancient rights. It was apparently content and 'accordingly entered upon the execution of their lawful offices.' However, that was the last time that the king's legislation would affect Peebles.

James was determined to follow a policy of Catholic emancipation, which of course was strongly opposed by Presbyterian Scots. In order to placate them, he issued what were called "letters of Indulgence". Similar letters had been issued by his late brother, which effectively allowed clergy who had been put out of their livings on account of their failure to accept Episcopacy, to return provided they accepted the Test. The letters of Indulgence which James issued were to grant toleration to all faiths to worship as they wished, provided that they did not promote disloyalty to the Crown. Although clearly intended to aid Catholics, what the Indulgence did do, was to legitimise the great body of moderate Presbyterians who had for so long lived and worshipped in a kind of "no man's land" between legitimacy and illegality.

The leader of the Covenanters was now a man called James Renwick. He was born in the Dumfriesshire village of Moniaive in 1662, the son of a weaver. He had attended Edinburgh University and he had had a great interest in the Bible from an early age, so much so that he was able to debate its content and meaning. However, University life and particularly its social life, were almost his undoing and he began to question his youthful religious beliefs. What changed all that was the execution of one of the leading Covenanters which Renwick witnessed in the Grassmarket. His name was Donald Cargill and he had been one of the great preachers. His execution changed everything for Renwick and he determined to follow the Covenanting movement and become a preacher himself. He was accepted at a conventicle at Talla Linn in October 1682 and was ordained as a minister in Holland where he had gone to study at the University of Groningen.

He returned to Scotland in October 1684 and published a manifesto, *An Apologetical Declaration and Admonitory Vindication*, which endorsed all the previous declarations by the Covenanters. It was widely distributed and he immediately became a national figure. It proclaimed that all who opposed them were enemies of God, who should be punished as such. That of course included the king and government and their officers and soldiers, but also 'all viperous and malicious bishops and curates'.

As a result of the government's suppression, the Covenanting cause had faltered. So many of their leaders had died or had been forced to flee abroad. Renwick reignited the cause. In the face of changing public opinion, he became the last bastion of the Covenanting extremists. He still commanded large congregations at field conventicles held throughout southern Scotland, but he was a hunted man and his days were numbered and the net was closing! On 29th December 1687 he was in Peebles from where he wrote to Robert Hamilton :

> I have been at Peebles this week, and, through our Lord's providence, wonderfully escaped; our intended meeting near to the town, about nine of the clock at night, in the time of our gathering, being by strange providence discovered. It is a place I had not been before, and we had no armed men; there were four taken and imprisoned.

He reports the incident in rather more detail in a letter to Alexander Shields dated 12th January 1688 :

> I came forward to Peebles, where our meeting in the time of the gathering was discovered by a wonderful providence, namely, as I am informed, the pursuing of some for theft when people were observed to crowd out of the town; which made the clerk to enquire what they were, and whither they were going; the report whereof came unto me, being lodged in a most suspected house, I went forth and passed on towards the place of meeting until I came within speaking and hearing of the clerk and some with him, who were without all the town challenging people, and being in no capacity to resist, I turned again into the town, where there was some little uproar, and went forth of it another way, where I waited a considerable space for my horse, which was at length got into me with some difficulty; and finding that the meeting could not be kept I came away; but there were four persons taken. And since I came to this place I have lodged with Thomas and John, and lest I should trouble mine own spirit, I have not denied any to keep silent anent my being here, nor reproved any for coming into my quarters, whatever the hazard might be; but left that to the providence of God, and people to their own discretion, and I find not the worse way.

It is a matter of speculation as to where the 'most suspected house' may have been or to whom it belonged. Clearly the risks of harbouring a wanted man, must indicate that there were some at least in the town who were strongly in support of the Covenanting cause.

Shortly after, he preached for the last time not far from Peebles, at Riskenhope in Yarrow. According to James Hogg, the "Ettrick Shepherd", 'When he prayed that day, few of his hearers cheeks were dry'. The following month he was captured in Edinburgh during a secret visit there.

He was brought before the Privy Council and freely admitted to disowning the King's authority and encouraging his followers to attend conventicles and to carry arms. The inevitable execution took place on 17th February 1688. He was the last Covenanting martyr.

South of the border things were going from bad to worse for the king. In April 1688 he issued a new Indulgence, granting further freedom to Catholics. English bishops protested. Then in June a son was born to his second wife, Mary of Modena, a Catholic. Their son James would also be a Catholic. It was the final straw and in December, James his wife and baby son fled to France in clandestine circumstances, never to return.

No sooner had news of the king's flight become known, than the remnants of the Covenanters in the west began a campaign against the sitting curates. On Christmas Day 1688, just days after the king's ignominious departure from London, they had gathered sufficient strength to be able to evict about 200 ministers and their households, who were ejected from their manses, without consideration for the effects of mid-winter weather. A wider campaign was also directed against known Catholics

There was support for the Covenanters in Peebles and Tweeddale as the following extract from an Edinburgh publication of 1727 by one Patrick Walker seems to confirm:

> In the end of 1688, at the happy Revolution, when..............the crown was vacant, in which time we had no King nor judicatories in the kingdom, the United Societies[170] (as the extreme Covenanters were called) in their general correspondence, considering the surprising, unexpected, merciful step of the Lord's dispensation, thought it some way belonged to us in the interregnum to go to all popish houses and destroy their monuments of idolatry, with their priests' robes, and to apprehend and put to prison themselves; which was done at the cross of Dumfries and Peebles and other places. That honourable and worthy gentleman, Donald Ker of Kersland, having a considerable number of us with him, went to the House of Traquair in frost and snow, and found a great deal of popish wares there, but wanted the cradle, Mary and the Babe, and the priest.

The earl and his priest having fled, what they found were two locked trunks, which they broke open to reveal, in one a golden cradle, with Mary and the Babe and in the other the priest's robes. These items were taken to

---

[170] The name given to extreme Covenanters

the cross of Peebles, 'with a great deal of popish books and many other things of great value, all Romish wares, and burned them there.'

At the same time they decided to approach 'all prelatic intruding curates' and warn them to remove with all their belongings 'that we should call for the Church's goods, cups and basons, and also for the kirk-box, wherein was nothing but a few doits; likewise for the session book and kirk-door keys; and that we should deliver all to men of credit.'

What had effectively been the collapse of the Stuart dynasty left the country in a state of limbo, but as early as March 1688, some time before this, it is clear that there were stirrings of a new order. That was certainly the case in Tweeddale. There is every indication that with the execution of James Renwick in February of that year, the Covenanting cause, at least in its extreme form, was a spent force. At long last the government's campaign of repression and terror seems to have been at an end. Though as yet there had been no changes in the Law, the more moderate Presbyterians were beginning to re-emerge and assert themselves. There is ample evidence that Presbyterian congregations were already being formed, presided over by Presbyterian ministers, some of whom had been supporters of the Covenant. In Tweeddale, on 22nd March 1688 a group of ministers met in a farmhouse at Stobo, which lies about 6 miles west of Peebles. Their leader was James Feithie, who is described as 'minister at Peebles'. The official (that is Episcopal) incumbent was of course, still the Rev John Hay. Feithie had studied at Edinburgh University and had been a supporter of the Covenant. He was imprisoned for a time for holding conventicles, part of that time on the Bass Rock, which was a common, if unpleasant location for religious dissidents. He was released in July 1679. It must be assumed that he was one of those ministers who benefited from the Indulgence of 1687 which had more or less permitted freedom of worship and by November that year he had been admitted as "minister" of Peebles.

The established church remained Episcopalian with an Episcopalian minister still in place. In 1667, John Hay had died and was succeeded by yet another Hay, a second John, who appears to have been his son-in-law. Thus there were two congregations in the town, one Episcopalian still worshipping in the parish kirk and the other Presbyterian. The conclusion can only be that the support for Covenanted Presbyterianism in Peebles as elsewhere, was stronger than might otherwise be supposed.

James Feithie died in 1689 and John Hay followed him shortly after in 1690. Hay's assistant Robert Knox was nominated by the Duke of Queensberry. Knox of course was an Episcopalian and the nomination was rejected on behalf of the town by the town council, which must by then have moved firmly into the Presbyterian camp.

In 1690, patronage[171] he had been abolished and in July of that year the magistrates complained that Mr Knox continued to occupy the kirk and resisted attempts to remove him, in spite of the presbytery issuing an order prohibiting him from continuing. Things must have been moving fast, given that the presbytery itself must now have been firmly opposed to Episcopacy. In August, a number of people in the parish of Peebles signified their intention of issuing a "call"[172] to Mr William Veitch. In September the call was issued, but under protest from those who still supported Episcopacy. The Presbyterians prevailed and the Presbytery went ahead and ordained him as minister of Peebles and Manor. In spite of what might have been thought as a final decision, there seems to have been a continuing dispute, because in January 1692 the council and magistrates appointed the former provost, John Mure and Archibald Sheill, who was a bailie, to attend the General Assembly in Edinburgh, to ask it to support the call to Mr Veitch by the council and the heritors of Peebles and to do everything required and necessary for this purpose, as if they themselves were making the appointment. Mr Veitch became the minister of Peebles and Manor, so it must be assumed that the Assembly endorsed the call.

William Veitch had had a colourful career. He was a long standing Covenanter. He had taken part in the battle of Rullion Green and had strong connections with the Covenanters of the south west. He had been imprisoned, like James Feithie, spending some time on the Bass Rock and following release from there, had been banished from Scotland. He avoided further capture and continued to preach at conventicles. He went through a series of adventures to retain his liberty, eventually escaping to Holland. Following the Act of Indemnity introduced by James VII&II, which allowed freedom to preach, he returned to Scotland where he was able to preach openly. He had been extremely fortunate in his earlier years to avoid the ultimate penalty suffered by so many of his brethren. This remarkable man was the first minister of Peebles to take his place as a minister of the Kirk of Scotland as it is still constituted to this day. He remained as minister until 1694, when he became the minister of St Michael's, Dumfries.

---

[171] The right of a landowner to nominate clergy.
[172] The formal method by which someone is invited to become the minister of a parish in Scotland.

The minister who followed him was James Thomson, who had been minister at Tweedsmuir, which in the past had had strong Covenanting affiliations. He had been minister there since 1688. Perhaps because of this his appointment as minister of Peebles did not finally take effect until 25th November 1696. The reason for the delay was that the Duke of Queensberry and some of the heritors had given a call to a Mr Orrock, who was the minister of Hawick, but he was not acceptable to the majority of the people of Peebles. The dispute was referred to the General Assembly and the provost and one of the bailies went to Edinburgh to oppose the call to Mr Orrock. In September 1696, Lord William Douglas, together with the heritors and the magistrates of Peebles issued a formal call to Mr Thomson and the presbytery duly admitted him as minister, a position he held until his death in 1712.

Following the flight to France of James VII&II in 1688, the 'lords and gentlemen of the kingdome of Scotland' met in London at Whitehall in January 1689 at the invitation of William of Orange, now installed with his wife, Mary as joint monarchs of England. Having heard his assurances that he would preserve the Protestant religion, they invited him to 'take upon him the administratione of public affaires both civill and military' of Scotland as joint monarch with his wife. So began the reign of King William and Queen Mary, the first and only joint monarchy of the Kingdom of Scotland.

William's first act in relation to Scotland was to call a meeting of the Estates or parliament which was to be held in Edinburgh on the 14th March. A letter was sent by the king to the town clerk of Peebles on 17th February, requiring that public intimation should be made on the following market day and also intimating the date when the burgesses should meet to choose a commissioner to represent them at the Convention of Estates. The meeting was held on 27th February attended by the members of the town council and burgesses and elected John Mure, a merchant of the burgh as their representative. He was described as a 'protestant fearing God.'

Town councils had effectively been suspended by James VII&II in 1686, but in April the Estates, meeting in Edinburgh, decided that their powers should be restored and that new elections should now take place. The new councils were to be chosen by a poll of the burgesses and those elected were to continue until Michaelmas of that year when annual elections would take place as they had done before 1686. In Peebles, the election was fixed for 27th April and the Act of the Estates was immediately made public by the usual means of being proclaimed throughout the burgh 'by tuck of drum.' The election was held in the tolbooth between 10 am. and midday on the appointed day. The Act of the Estates had stated that the laird of Cardrona should be present as adjudicator. The new council was duly appointed and James Williamson, laird of Cardrona, signed the roll, certifying that he had been present and that all was in order.[173]

At its April meeting, the Estates passed an edict which required all ministers of the Kirk to pray publicly for the new king and queen and to read a proclamation dethroning James. Penalties were to be imposed for failure. The minister of Peebles was John Hay who had a son Henry, who had been appointed as schoolmaster in 1688. He must have had a religious role also, perhaps as his father's assistant and it seems that the task was given to him, a task he failed to perform, because on 9th September 1689 they were both summoned to appear before the Privy Council to explain their failure to comply with the strict injunction of the Estates. John Hay was of course a committed Episcopalian, so perhaps his failure to comply is understandable, if imprudent. The outcome is not recorded but he was probably by then a spent force, there now being a Presbyterian minister of Peebles. In any event he died in following year. However, it is significant that the council discharged Henry Hay from his post as schoolmaster at the end of October and no more is heard of him after that.

The religious order might now have been settled and the power of the kirk session reinforced, but the power and influence of the town council in matters of public morality remained. On the 18th September 1693, the council confirmed rules for public order which were designed to control what it deemed to be 'profanation of the Sabbath'. It reminded the townsfolk that there had been many Acts of parliament introduced in the past which related to excessive drinking, drunkenness, cursing and swearing and 'other immoralities'. An Act of James VI&I had ordered that there be no markets held or labouring on the Sabbath. Nor were taverns and ale houses to be visited, or any meat or drink sold. It was also an

---

[173] Those appointed were, John Muir (or Mure) provost; John Tueddy, elder and Patrick Brotherstones, bailies; Robert Forrester, Dean of Guild; Archibald Sheill, treasurer; Thomas Bell, William Wood, Alexander Law, William Ker, Thomas Wallace, John Freir, John Tueddy, younger; Adam Robiesone, William Brotherstones, elder, James Brotherstones, younger, John Murray, wright and Thomas Fotheringhame, weaver, as ordinary councillors.

offence to wilfully avoid attendance at the parish church. An Act of Charles I had restated those rules and expressly introduced a minimum fine of ten pounds for any offence. If the guilty party was unable to pay, he or she would be 'punished on his body according to the merits of his offence.' An Act of James VI &I had also provided that anyone convicted of drunkenness and visiting taverns after ten o'clock at night, or at any time of day except when travelling or for refreshment (what else would it be for?) would be fined three pounds Scots for the first offence, or be put in the jougs (stocks) or jail for six hours. For the second offence the fine was six pounds or twelve hours in the jougs or jail and for the third it was a fine of ten pounds or twenty-four hours in the jougs or jail. If the offences continued beyond that the offender would be jailed indefinitely until such time as he was able to find sufficient caution for his (or her) future good behaviour.

The council Act goes on to relate that the former statutes had subsequently been ratified by Charles II and they now set out their own penalties for the offence of drinking to excess. A nobleman was to pay twenty pounds; a baron twenty merks; a gentleman, heritor or burgess, ten merks; a yeoman forty shillings and a servant twenty shillings. These penalties were to apply on each occasion the offence occurred. Those unable to pay would be physically punished. It adds that if the minister was the offender he would be fined an amount equal to one fifth of his stipend. It is certainly an example of universal justice and it is quite modern in its introduction of the concept of 'ability to pay'.

It does not end there. Quoting statutes as far back as Mary Queen of Scots, again ratified by later monarchs, it notes that 'profane swearing of abominable oaths, and detestable execrations' is forbidden, as is blasphemy. The penalties are to be similar to those to be imposed for drink related offences, but adds that offences repeated regularly will ultimately result in banishment from the town or imprisonment for a year and a day. The minister is once again not exempt.

To implement these rules of behaviour the council appointed "censors" who were to attend public markets and fairs and were given powers to arrest offenders and extract the appropriate penalty. Householders were required to report any offenders in their house. Failure could result in they themselves being penalised.

The close relationship with the religious order of the day is made clear in the final part of this lengthy council record when it declares that in spite of all these many Acts introduced and ratified by a succession of monarchs and 'the most holy and express law of God' it was clear and much regretted that 'the forsaid transgressions and excess doe every wher abound to the dishonour of God and the reproach of the Protestant religion'. The provost, bailies and council undertake to ensure that all these acts of parliament are strictly adhered to within the bounds of the burgh. They will ensure in addition that no work of any kind is allowed on 'the Lord's day', nor will anyone be allowed to stand or walk idly in the streets or go in company or go to fields or yards at any time on that day. No one was allowed to frequent taverns and alehouses, to drink or eat at the time of the preaching of the Word or at any time after on that day, unless it be necessary. The tavern owners were in any case also prohibited from selling food or drink at any time on that day. Householders were even limited to carrying one pint of water to their house. Naturally children were to be restrained. A payment of ten pounds was the penalty for any or these contraventions. The Scottish Presbyterian Sabbath had arrived in Peebles.

The final establishment of the Church of Scotland and the restoration of the town council in Peebles brought to a conclusion what has become known as the "Glorious Revolution". A new monarchy was firmly established which would bring to a close the seventeenth century, although Queen Mary would not live to see the opening of the next century. She died in December 1694. At its meeting on 9th January 1695, the town council of Peebles in the tolbooth 'fenced in his majestie King William his name her majestie Queen Mary being deceist, conform to a proclamation of council.' William had been proclaimed as king in his own right and the Royal Burgh of Peebles confirmed its approval.

So the "long" seventeenth century drew to a close. "Long", not because it was any longer than any other century, how could it be? "Long" because it was the century which was perhaps the most significant and dramatic in the history of the British Isles.

How had life in Peebles changed? At the start of the century it was still visited quite regularly by the monarchs of Scotland. By its end it had become something of a backwater, more concerned with its own affairs and survival, than national events. In between, it had shared in the turmoil which had enveloped Scotland from the third decade onwards. It had suffered the indignity of occupation by what was at that time effectively a foreign power. It had witnessed the struggle between Episcopacy and Covenanted Presbyterianism. It had suffered the further indignity of having its town council proscribed for a period, yet life had gone on in many ways much as before. Markets were held; merchants continued to trade; petty quarrels and public disorder disturbed the peace from time to time; livestock still roamed the streets and vennels; the town council did its best to control trade and maintain law and order, protect the town from unwanted intrusion and control any unseemly and unhealthy accumulations of rubbish and ordure, often exacerbated by uncontrolled livestock. Peebles remained the administrative centre of the county and the official centre for the collection of taxes due to the Crown.

Towards the close of the century something occurred which was to have a devastating impact on the fragile economy of Scotland. That was the Darien Scheme. There was a considerable interest on the part of Scottish entrepreneurs in setting up companies to trade overseas and in 1693 an Act of Parliament authorised the establishment of companies to trade with any country with which the king was not at war. A scheme was devised to set up a trading colony on the Isthmus of Darien. The necessary capital amounting to £400,000, representing almost half the value of the Scottish coinage was duly subscribed, but the scheme was a disaster and virtually bankrupted Scotland and plunged it into a period of economic decline.

There is no evidence that it had any direct effect on any citizen of Peebles, but the town was to suffer a long period of steady decline. In January 1699, the provost attended a Commission for the Communication of Trade. Pleading that 'all trade being decayed in the town' he argued that the burden of taxation on royal burghs was unfair and that burghs of regality and barony should be made to carry a greater liability for tax. As further evidence of austerity, in 1703, the magistates and the treasuer were prohibited from contributing to the cost of the burial of the poor.

In the century which followed, Peebles, in the words of Lord Cockburn would become "Quiet as the grave",[174] only disturbed by events such as a visitation by Jacobite Highlanders.

---

[174]   Henry Cockburn – *Memorials of his time*. The actual quotation is, *"quiet as the grave, or Peebles"* and is thought to refer to Edinburgh in the first half of the 19th century)

Part V
1700 – 1850

30.
The Age of Enlightenment

After the turmoil of the 17th century, the new century which dawned in A.D. 1700 opened in a period of relative calm. It was to be very different from the one before, which had been characterised by 60 years of political and religious strife and bloodshed. Although the dark days of civil war and religious martyrdom were a fading memory, matters were still far from settled and the political order in particular was about to see a dramatic change, while the religious order would go through a period of dissention and fragmentation. Happily, those changes would be achieved without bloodshed, although personal egos of politicians and clergy might be bruised and long held views and prejudices suffer defeat.

King William III remained alone on the throne following the death of his wife and joint monarch Mary Stuart six years earlier. He died in 1702 and was succeeded by his sister-in-law Anne, the last of the long line of Stuart monarchs of Scotland and in 1707 the parliaments of Scotland and England were joined in union. On her death in 1714, Queen Anne would be succeeded as monarch of the United Kingdom by the German, Elector of Hanover, who took the throne as George I.

In 1715 and again in 1745, the peace of Scotland was to be disturbed by Jacobite rebellions, seeking the restoration of the Stuart monarchy. Both would fail.

On a brighter note, as the century progressed, there was a blossoming of literature, the arts and sciences and it saw the start of the industrial revolution, with all its associated infrastructure. It was the century of the poet Robert Burns, James Watt and his improved steam engine, the civil engineer Thomas Telford, the architects William and Robert Adam, the portrait painter Allan Ramsay and many others who left their mark not only on Scotland, but on the whole of the United Kingdom as it was now called. With the union of the parliaments, Edinburgh, deprived of its place as the centre of government, none the less became the centre of intellectual activity which become known as The Enlightenment.

Towards the end of the eighteenth century, revolution in France would disturb the whole of Europe and lead to a major war which would in time involve most of its major nations and spill over into the first two decades of the following century. As part of the United Kingdom, Scotland would play its part.

It was to be a century in which the Royal Burgh of Peebles, became something of a backwater. Some national events touched it and shaped its life, some passed it by. It remained the centre of Tweeddale, but no longer of any great national significance. From being a place favoured by the monarchs of Scotland and one of an exclusive number of royal burghs of ancient origin, it became much like many another Scottish market town.

*   *   *

In the year 1700, the life of the Royal Burgh and that of its citizens was not markedly different from what had gone before. It was still the focus of its immediate surroundings, but more and more parochial, with little influence beyond the bounds of the county it served. Like many another burgh in Scotland at that time the economic circumstances were dire and would continue to be so for most of the century. There was little trade and an ever increasing number of poor to be supported. In February 1700 the council noted that there were 'stranger beggars' in the town, 'quhich occasiones the touns poor to be much straitened in ther provisiones.' An entry on 25 January, 1703 refers to the 'mean condition of the toun'.

One of the earliest first hand descriptions of the town and the surrounding countryside comes from Daniel Defoe. He is of course best known as the author of *Robinson Crusoe*. He was also the agent of the government and spent some time in Scotland in the early part of the century. Following the Union of the Parliaments, he travelled the length and breadth of the country and recorded these journeys in *A Tour Through the Whole Island of Great Britain*, published in three volumes between 1724 and 1726. The third volume concerns southern Scotland, including Tweeddale.

From Lanerk we left the wild place called Crawford Muir on the right, the business that brought us round the way being finished, and went away west into the shire of Peebles, and so into Tweedale[sic]; the first town we came into of any note upon the Tweed, is the town of Peebles, capital of the country. The town is small, and but indifferently built or inhabited, yet the High Street has some good houses on it. There is a handsome stone-bridge over the Tweed, which is not a great river here, though the current is sometimes very violent.

The country is hilly, as is the rest of Tweedale, and those hills cover'd with sheep, which is, indeed, a principal part of the estates of the gentlemen; and the overplus quantity of the sheep, as also their wool, is mostly sent to England, to the irreparable damage of the poor; who, were they employ'd to manufacture their own wool, would live much better than they do, and find benefit of the Union in a different manner, from what they have yet done.

The records, echoing Defoe's description, paint a picture of a general decline in the condition of the principal buildings and facilities within the town. Many were in an advanced state of disrepair and before the end of the 18th century some of the buildings that graced the town for centuries would no longer exist. After seven centuries at the centre of religious life, the Cross Kirk was abandoned and left to decline into no more than a ruinous memory, to be replaced by a new church built on the Castlehill, which in earlier centuries had been the focus of royal authority.

As the eighteenth century opened, there was undoubtedly a crisis in the lives of many of the population, but the public purse was also under strain. It was austerity and not unlike the actions of modern governments in times of financial stringency, the council took the serious step of selling off some of the town's assets in the shape of ten roods of land, known as Walker's Land, by public roup or auction. The rules of the roup are interesting. The minimum opening bid was to be five hundred pounds Scots and subsequent bids were to be at least five pounds. This raised £860 Scots, which was considered to be a good sum, bearing in mind that the land previously attracted an annual rent of only twenty nine pounds. The land in question was re-purchased by the town in in 1727, when the town's finances must have improved, but it cost 1350 merks (£900 Scots), 1200 of which was borrowed.

Not only was the economic state of the burgh in great decline, but the moral fabric was a matter of concern in spite of the power of the kirk session, its sabbatarian discipline and its threat of the stool of repentance. In October 1701, the council noted 'the abounding immoralityes' including drunkenness, swearing, blaspheming and frequenting ale houses at unreasonable times. It was decided to appoint constables to patrol the town and to take action against anyone behaving badly. If they heard anyone swearing, cursing or blaspheming 'aither horridly or mincedly', they were given powers to extract a fine of 14 shillings Scots on the spot. Failure to pay would result in prison. Anyone found drunk in the street was to be subject to the same penalty. Half of the fine went to the constable himself, so there was every incentive for him to be assiduous in

311

his duties. The constables were given the same powers as magistrates to ask for assistance in the exercise of their responsibilities.

It seems that there was a constable assigned to each quarter and it was his duty to go through his area each night at ten o'clock. If he heard any noise coming from a house or a light still on, he could search the premises in question.[175] If anyone was found drunk or anyone was found there who could not give a reasonable explanation why he was there, he was to be fined 14 shillings, while the landlord was to be fined twice that amount.

Not only were ale houses and the like subject to entry and inspection, after November 1701, the constables were given the power of entry to any house from which came a 'confused noise'. Refusal of entry made the landlord or owner subject to a fine and imprisonment. In spite of those seemingly stringent rules, they do not appear to have achieved much, because in November 1703, the council was once again discussing 'the abounding of immoralities'. As has been related earlier, a council Act of 1693 had set out rules for the conduct of citizens on Sunday, the Sabbath Day, but now the constables were specifically instructed to, 'take a turn through the streits every Sabbath day, both before and after sermons, and tak notice of all persones carrying any sort of burdens, or standing idley upon the streits, or below staires, or vaging in any place of the fields, except in summar they be with ther beasts, or winter bringing them hame.' The rules about drinking on the Sabbath were also amended, permitting the sale of drink only to country folk, 'between the sermons'. The religious observation of the Sabbath was a lengthy affair and no doubt refreshment was welcome, although quite why this should have been restricted to country folk is not clear. Perhaps the townsfolk could slip back home and refresh themselves in private?

Following the death of King William in March of 1702, the council and its officials took an oath of allegiance to the new monarch, Queen Anne. They also took an oath which confirmed that she was the only true sovereign of the realm and undertook to defend her rights and government against any attempt by the late King James VII&II and his supporters or indeed anyone else, to challenge her right, either publicly or secretly. In September the council appointed the provost, Archibald Sheill to be its commissioner to the next parliament. So, Peebles was now firmly in the mainstream of the political life and any lingering support there might have been for the former king was clearly at an end.

---

175   Presumably ale houses of which there seems to have been many in the town.

Although Scotland as a whole suffered a general decline, the debacle of the Darien Scheme had not impacted directly on the Royal Burgh. It had had a devastating effect on the national economy to the extent that the country was to all intents and purposes bankrupt. There is no doubt that this had a significant bearing on the great political change which resulted in the Union of the parliaments of Scotland and England. While the prospect was not universally approved, many of the great and the good of Scotland saw that as an opportunity to retrieve their fortunes and build a better future which might well have been impossible for the nation of Scotland on its own.

The final outcome was controversial and on the signing of the Treaty of Union, the Edinburgh mob made its opposition known in no uncertain terms. The situation in Peebles was somewhat calmer. As the discussions on a possible treaty started, on the 24th October, 1706, the provost, now John Tueiddy, was appointed to attend a meeting of the Convention of Royal Burghs to be held on 29th October. The meeting had been called by the provost of Edinburgh, 'in case the great concerne of the Union with England should happen to be laid and considered by the parliament.' It would appear that the Royal Burghs were understandably anxious to have their say in advance of an agreement.

The Treaty of Union was in due course approved by the Scottish parliament. There have been many theories as to how that came about, with widespread accusations of personal gain by supporters. Whether those supporters were as Robert Burns would later claim, 'bought and sold for English gold' and 'such a parcel of rogues in a nation', is open to question. Doubtless there were those whose allegiance could be bought, something which was not unusual at the time.

One man who was not 'bought by English gold', was Archibald Sheill. When the parliament met for the final time as an independent body, he represented the Royal Burgh. Throughout the proceedings he consistently voted against all the articles of the treaty as they were debated and at the end against the final version of the treaty which parliament adopted. It must be assumed that he acted in accordance with instructions from the council and in turn that would suggest that it also reflected majority opinion in the burgh itself. However, the commissioner representing the county of Peeblesshire voted in favour and this division of opinion probably reflects the division in Scotland as a whole. In spite of its declared opposition, none the less Peebles seems ultimately to have accepted the situation without comment, as there is no further reference to the parliamentary proceedings or their outcome in the immediate aftermath.

Prior to the Union, Peebles, as a royal burgh, had been entitled to send a commissioner to the Scottish parliament. As a consequence of the arrangements agreed under the Union, the number of representatives to the united parliament at Westminster was considerably smaller than had been the case with the former Scottish parliament. Peebles now became part of a group of four burghs and joined with Selkirk, Lanark and Linlithgow, which was entitled to appoint one representative to the House of Commons. At the first election to the new parliament, the presiding burgh was Linlithgow and a meeting was held there on 26th May 1708 to choose the representative for the combined burghs. Peebles was represented by the provost, Robert Forrester, who was instructed to vote for Colonel George Douglas, a brother of the Earl of Morton, 'so far as their vote can make him'.

Another writer to give a first-hand description of Peebles and Tweeddale was Dr Alexander Pennecuik of Newhall. Writing in 1715 he describes the topography, fauna and flora, as well as its people and the economic activity of the time. Although he does not have much to say about the condition of the Royal Burgh, he has a lengthy description of the valley of the Tweed descending from its source.[176]

> In the course of the Tweed we come next to the strong castle of Neidpath, called of old the Castle of Peebles, situate a little above the river, upon a descent of a steep and green hill.

Dr Pennecuik was something of a poet and adds this verse:

> *The noble Neidpath, Peebles over looks,*
> *With its fair bridge, and Tweeds' meandereing crooks:*
> *Upon a Rock it proud and stately stands*
> *And to the fields about gives forth commands.*

After describing the vegetation around the castle he goes on:

> Furder down the path, about three furlongs, stands the *Ancient Burgh of Peebles*, in a large and fertile plain upon the river *Tweed*; through which

---

[176]   *The Works in Prose and Verse of Alexander Pennecuik, Esq of Newhall, including the DESCRIPTION OF TWEEDDALE.*

Town runs *Athelstoun*, or *Peebles Water*, and divides the Old Town from the new. Of which pretty burgh, notice the following ornaments,

Peebles, the Metropolis of the Shire,
Six times *three* praises do from me require,
Three streets; *three* ports; *three* bridges it adorn;
And three old steeples, by *three* churches born.
Three mills do serve their town in time of need,
On Peebles water and the river Tweed.
Their armes are proper, and point forth their meaning;
Three salmond fishes nimbly counter swimming. The motto of their armes is,
Contra nando incrementum.

He then adds some further comments.

I have here observed, that about this town, both fruit and forest tree have a smoother skin than elsewhere, and are seldom seen either to fog or be bark bound, the soil is so clean and good, and supplied with the scent of water sufficiently. And here, upon the *fourth of May*, is yearly run a famous *horse race*, for a large silver cup. Upon the river, on the south side of Peebles, is a pretty bridge of five arches. Its antiquity is not known.

He describes of the produce of the county in some detail.

TWEEDDALE, in regard of its high and steep situation, having little plain and champaigne, is more fit for Pasturage than the production of Corn and Grain, to answer the toyls of the husbandman: and is stored with such number of sheep, that in Lintoun Mercats, which are kept every Wednesday during the months of June and July, there are frequently 9000 in the customer's roll, and most of these sold and vented in one day. The sheep of this country, are but small, yet very sweet and delicious, and live to a greater age than elsewhere, by reason of the salubrity of the air, and wholesome dry feeding: and are indeed the greatest merchant commodity that brings money to the place, with their product of lambs, wool, skins, butter and cheese. There are but few pease, and less wheat sown in Tweeddale; but of barley, rough Bear especially, and Oats, greater plenty than is sufficeient for the inhabitants..............Lint prospers well in the country; Hemp and Rye too; but little of the last they put to trial

He says that the 'air of Tweeddale is pure and well perflat'. As a result the inhabitants are 'lively, and put off to a greater age than elsewhere........

Few cripples or crook backs are to be seen in this country; but the inhabitants for the most part are strong, nimble, and well-proportioned, both sexes promiscuously[177]being conspicuous for as comely features as any other country in the kingdom, would but the meaner sort take a little more pains to keep their bodies and dwellings clean, which is too much neglected among them, and pity it is to see a clear complexion and lovely countenance appear with so much disadvantage through foul disguise of smoke and dirt.

They are an industrious careful, people, yet something wilful, stubborn, and tenacious of old customs.

musick is so great a stranger to their temper, that you shall hardly light upon one amongst six, that can distinguish one tune from another; yet those of them that hit upon the vein, may match the skilfullest.

They are more sober in their diet and drinking than many of the neighbouring shires, and when they fall into a fit of good fellowship, they use it as a cement and bond of society, and not to foment, or revenge quarrels and murders, which is too ordinary in other places.

This last comment is somewhat at variance with the impression given in the town records as noted previously, which certainly does not paint a picture of sobriety.

---

[177]   Without distinction

31.
Civic Life

Although the composition and membership of the council remained as it had done for years gone by, there had been one difference over the past thirty years or so. The Weavers Guild had had a long standing right to nominate a leet of their members from whom the one was chosen as deacon and become a member of the council. This right had lapsed some thirty years earlier, when the deacon of the day had been removed from the council because of his unacceptable behaviour. In September 1703, William Chambers, who was then the deacon of the Weavers Guild, lodged a petition on behalf of himself and his guild brothers, asking that the privilege of nominating their deacon as a permanent member of the council be reinstated. He pointed out that it was the ancient custom in all other burghs for this privilege to be granted. He went on to say that it was 'mighty hard to punish a whole trade for ones fault who is now long since decest.' After due consideration the magistrates and council agreed to the request and allowed the deacon of the weavers to be a councillor 'in all time coming'. The procedure for choosing the deacon was to be as it had always been in the past, with a list of six nominees submitted to the provost and magistrates before the annual council election. They then reduced that to three from whom the guild chose one.

The weavers and tailors trade guilds had been given formal status by incorporation, in 1561 and 1680 respectively. Then it was the turn of the masons, wrights, glaziers and smiths, who collectively formed the building trades in the town. On 29 April 1713 they lodged a petition to the council asking for formal recognition as a guild. They pointed out that other trades were already incorporated, which had given them an advantage over their trades and that had been very prejudicial to the petitioners. They were not able to maintain a "box" (fund) for the benefit of poor members of their trades and there were tradesmen coming into the town who were unregulated and made no contribution to public burdens and taxation.

The petition was accepted and incorporation approved, subject to a number of conditions. All members who were freemen would have to pay four shillings Scots to the guild's box. Those who were journeymen were to contribute two shillings Scots. Anyone not paying his quarterly dues was to be charged double. All apprentices were to pay ten shillings Scots to the box at the start of their apprenticeship and any member who took his own son as an apprentice was to give him a binding indenture and also pay ten shillings to the box. Guild members were entitled to a seat in the kirk and on their death that right was passed on to his son, but only if he was married.

The maintenance of law and order remained a primary responsibility of the town council. Inevitably there were those who broke the law and ended up with a spell in the town's jail within the Tolbooth. A problem arose in 1707 when the then keeper, William Rankine refused to continue to hold the keys. No doubt there were frequent prisoners who required to be supervised. His complaint was that he had had to supervise a prisoner without any other officer being present and this he was not prepared to do. That was in spite of the fact that John Hunter who was one of the town's officers had looked after the same prisoner for eight or ten days previously, without any help or assistance. There seems to have been words between himself and the provost and Rankine deposited the keys on the council table in front of the whole council. This was considered to be a 'great, slight, affront and contempt' of the provost and Rankine was immediately relieved of his post and a temporary replacement was arranged.

John Hunter, (who has already been mentioned), was himself in trouble shortly after. The provost reported to the council on 3rd November, 1708, that on the previous Saturday, Hunter was 'notoriously drunk', at midnight. At the time there were a number of thieves locked up in the jail. He had left a lamp burning, which the prisoners used to burn down the doors, the resulting fire posing a danger to the whole town. Hunter was immediately suspended from office and was ordered to repair the doors at his own expense as an example to others. The council further ordered that in future any officer responsible for a prisoner must be in the prison all the time the prisoner was held. A failure to comply would result in a fine of a £100 Scots. As a result of that episode the treasurer was instructed to take the iron chain from the bridge and use it together with any other iron needed to make an iron door for the prison cell.

The severe economic state of the country naturally had widespread effects on what was a large proportion of the populace already suffering poverty. People moved about seeking work and better living conditions. Beggars and other vagrants were numerous and that posed particular problems for the town. It had always been one of the responsibilities of the town council to control access to the town and incomers could only take up residence with the permission of the council. In June 1717, the council noted 'the great abuse and evill consequences that attend several persons coming into the burgh' without the necessary permission, particularly those who brought horses with them, without fodder for them. Under cover of darkness they grazed their animals on grass which the townsfolk had cut for their animals. As a consequence, the council passed an act which prohibited anyone keeping horses in the burgh who did not have sufficient pasturage to maintain them. It went further, prohibiting the letting of a house to anyone without permission from the council.

The problem of regulating unwanted strangers continued. Any who came to the town had to demonstrate that they were worthy citizens and there seem to have been a number of cases where the new arrivals presented what turned out to be fake documents. A regulation of January 1728 mentions, 'cripples, sturdy beggars and other vagrant persons who can give no account of themselves, some of which have taken upon themselves to make use of counterfeit testimonials from ministers and elders of the parish'. Later in January 1733, the council in another regulation, prohibited burgesses from letting their property to anyone who might become a burden on the town.

Cut backs in public expenditure are not new! It was a time of financial austerity and in October 1717 the council looked for ways in which it might reduce its expenses. In the immediate past it had incurred a vast amount of expenditure in defence of lawsuits which involved disputes about the ownership of Hamilton Hill. In an effort to control ongoing costs the provost and his successors were not to spend more than £12 Scots, in addition to the two sheep which were traditionally provided by the tenant of Shieldgreen, on the annual dinner which followed the council election each October, the treasurer was instructed to be more diligent in collecting burgh revenue. It had been usual to hold a public dinner each year, following the letting of mills and customs, but this too was abandoned for reasons of cost in 1722. Another expense was saved when the practice of supplying morning drinks to workmen employed by the council was stopped, 'in respect the same are very expensive to the toun.'

On a more positive note, an attempt was made to improve trade in the town by organising a horse race in the following August. Dr Pennecuik, writing in 1715, says that, 'here, upon *the fourth of May*, is yearly run a famous *Horse Race*,' for a large silver cup, so this race held in August 1723 seems be an additional event. The council minute explains that the Earl of March had offered to give plate worth £20 sterling to the winner and the council thought this would be an opportunity to improve things, 'trade being very dead here.' They themselves decided to provide a plate valued at about £6 sterling. The object was to raise money from entrance fees and they would provide the plate, 'for the encouragement of gentlemen subscribing for the plate, and the benefit of the community.' As a further encouragement to potential entrants in August 1721, the treasurer was instructed to provide another plate valued at £7 sterling. The race did take place for several years, but in spite of those inducements, it was not a great success and soon lapsed.

Borrowing as a means of maintaining public services is also something which is not new, although perhaps not carrying the political implications which it does today. The council was incurring considerable expense in fighting further court battles to preserve the burgh's ancient common rights and largely as a consequence, income derived from the mills, customs dues and other property was insufficient to meet the ordinary expenditure of the burgh. On a number of occasions the council resorted to borrowing, using the value of common good as collateral.

The state of the poor was made worse by severe weather conditions. It was a time of very cold weather known as the "Little Ice Age" which, following the Medieval Warm Period, persisted from about 1300 AD until 1850 AD. The eighteenth century had a number of particularly cold winters and January 1740 saw a very severe frost covering most of northern Europe. There was a serious failure of crops in the following summer and great scarcity resulted, hitting the poor particularly. There was a 'clamant case of the poor ones for help and relief.' The council saw it as part of its civic duty to make some provision for those most in need and in February 1742 it decided to buy supplies of food to be distributed to the townsfolk and parcelled out according to their needs. It came at a price and the burgh had to borrow a 1000 merks to meet it, increasing an already large debt. Later that same year a further sum of 1000 merks was borrowed to buy more supplies, as the treasurer reported that it could not be found from the town's tenants 'in regard of the calamity these two years'.

The extent of decay is clear from the number of buildings and infrastructure for which repairs were instructed in the first three decades of the century. The town's mills and cauld were in a bad state, having suffered damage from constant intrusion by townsfolk. In February 1702 the council decided to take them back into its own hands until such time as they were repaired and the cauld rebuilt. They instructed a deputation to meet with Andrew Thomson from Galashiels, who was 'a myln wright and capable to doe that work'. They were to arrange terms, either on the basis that he carried out the work and supplied materials or that he did the work only with materials supplied by the council. Later in May of that year the treasurer was instructed to borrow five hundred merks to defray the costs of the work.

In 1718 the town wall needed repair. It was necessary not so much as a protection against warring enemies, but to enable the inflow of unwanted vagrants, beggars and other undesirable strangers to be controlled. Quite apart from economic migrants, the aftermath of the 1715 Jacobite Rebellion was still causing alarm throughout the country. In March of that year the council ordered every heritor and burgess to properly build up the section of the wall bounding their property. They were to use stone and lime. The ports were also put into order to ensure control of ingress.

The steeple was dilapidated and required major repair in February 1720. It was by then very old and would not survive the century. The adjacent former Chapel of St Mary is described as being 'ruinous', but was repaired in 1723. Although it was no longer a place of worship, it must have served some useful purpose to justify the expenditure of the then not inconsiderable sum of £223. 7s Scots. As noted earlier, together with the steeple, it did form part of a complex of buildings which were the centre of municipal administration and may even have been used for council meetings and part of it possibly as a school.

The great bell was no longer working. It was 'riven' and 'useless' and could no longer strike when required by the clock. The provost had negotiated a price of £3 sterling per hundred weight for a new bell to be supplied by Robert Maxwell, a founder in Edinburgh. The council agreed that the old bell should immediately be taken down and delivered to Maxwell in Edinburgh, after it had been weighed at the burgh weigh house. The weigh house clerk was to provide written confirmation of the weight to ensure that the town received a new bell of the same weight.

The kirkyard wall was yet another cause of expenditure and had to be rebuilt in 1725. Part of the cost was met from contributions from the council, but the remainder came from the parishioners after a plea from the pulpit.

Even the prison in the tolbooth seems to have been in a bad state, so much so that it was no longer secure. As a result two of the town's officers had to be on duty to watch over the prisoners. Unfortunately it did not always happen. On one occasion in 1728 two of the officers were sacked because, 'they owned that they had not seen the prisoners after seven of the clock at night Sunday last, whereby the prisoners had time to break prison and make their escape, whereas if the officers had visit the prisoners at eight or nine at night, they had been catched.'

In spite of it being a time of economic stringency, the council added to the town's property by buying six acres of land on the south side of the Tweed, now known as Frankscroft. Far from indicating an improvement in the town's finances, more borrowing was required. The land which was rented by the town, was good grazing and was being offered for sale on the open market. The council was concerned that someone might buy it and fence it off, with the loss of good grazing to the town. The magistrates were authorised to negotiate the purchase from the owner Robert Stewart at as 'easy a rate as possible'. The bargain was agreed at 2500 merks, all of which had to be borrowed. While that was thought to be a reasonable price, it seems that Stewart's wife used her influence with her husband to accept the town's offer if an entry in the records dated 8th August 1726 is correct. It says :

> his wife having prevailed with her husband to let the lands fall in the town's hands cheaper than they would have given it to any other, the magistrates provide her with a compliment, and the council this day allows the treasurer at his convenience to give 30s, let her dispose of it as she pleases.

There were problems with the cauld on the Eddleston Water. Following an inspection by the council in January 1709, it was reported that there was a "great breach" in it which could not be repaired at that time of the year. Never the less they agreed that workmen should be employed in an attempt to keep the water flowing to the mills so that they could continue operating. Whether the tenant or the town should pay would have to be further considered. Those steps do not seem to have been successful, because only two weeks later a second breach was reported. As a result there was no water supply to the mill, so that grain could no longer be milled. The council decided that until repairs were carried out, all grain and malt was to be taken to the mill at Haystoun. The council normally benefited from the multures or dues paid for the grinding of grain at the town's mill, so that it would have been a significant loss of revenue to the town. As a consequence, the council ordered everyone using the Haystoun mill to make a payment to the town of £10 Scots and also that the multures which would have been due had the grain been milled at the town's mill should be paid in addition, so that there would be no loss to the town's revenue. It was to be publicly intimated in the usual way by 'tuck of drum', so that no one could 'pretend ignorance' of this instruction. This was in spite of the fact that payment of multures would also have to be made to the owners for the use of the Haystoun mill. Not surprisingly that arrangement was not popular and it is questionable if it was strictly observed.

The Tweed cauld was also in a bad state. In its straitened financial situation, the council appealed to the Convention of Burghs and a deputation including the Lord Provost of Edinburgh came to the town to assess the situation, but instead of repairing the Tweed cauld, in August 1726 it was decided to construct a new cauld near the bottom of the Eddleston Water which could be used for driving the mill on Tweedside. As a result of the visit, the Convention granted £30 towards the cost of this work. The lord provost and his delegation were thanked for their help and assured by the council that 'there shall be nothing wanting on their part to serve his lordship in particular, and the good town of Edinburgh in general, for the singular and great favour conferred upon them.'

The following year the council heard that the treasurer had taken it upon himself to have four slaps or breaches made in the Tweed cauld, without the council's consent. It was considered to be a possible public danger and he was immediately instructed to have the slaps rebuilt and was warned that he should not instruct any public works without special permission from the council. The treasurer however, had other ideas. He delayed any action, with the result that in January 1728 a protest was made to the council that no work had taken place, but no further action seems to have followed as the cauld was allowed to gradually decay completely. It was not rebuilt until 1829.

The tanning of hides and skins had been carried out in the town for centuries, as it had in most rural towns. It was a thoroughly smelly and unpleasant process, involving the use of urine and animal excrement. At that time the tanneries were situated immediately outside the town on the Eddleston Water, but close to the Tree Bridge. The process was carried out in vats or holes, some filled with lime and others, referred understandably as 'stink' holes, by urine and excrement. On 17 December 1705 because of complaints of 'the great abuse sustained by the inhabitants, by the tanners' as a result of these stink and lime holes, the council ordered that they should be removed before the following Whitsunday (15 May). They were to be prohibited from washing or steeping hides in the Eddleston Water and were to remove the holes to new a location approved by the magistrates. The new holes were be fitted with tight lids. If they failed to do so they would be fined £40 Scots.

The tanners must have complied because in November 1706 the council received a petition from one of the shoemakers who did his own tanning. His problem was that while he had removed his 'holes' from the Eddleston Water and installed them on Tweed Green, where the council in their wisdom had directed him, he found that the new holes were useless and he asked that he be allowed to return to his old holes on the Eddleston Water. He undertook to ensure that he did not wash or dispose of anything which might pollute the water. Somewhat surprisingly his request was granted and others must also have been allowed to return, because in November 1722 a number of tanners were taken to task for causing pollution in the Eddleston Water. One of them was actually a bailie of the burgh. He and the other tanners and skinners were prohibited from washing or throwing out 'stink water' or doing anything which might cause pollution to the Eddleston Water.

At the beginning of the eighteenth century Peebles had no public water supply. The only sources of drinking water were wells or the River Tweed and Eddleston Water. In view of what has just gone before, it is not difficult to imagine that this was less than satisfactory and an ever present source of disease. However, things were changing as the problems of water pollution were clearly now understood and in 1728, a supply was brought to the town from a spring on Venlaw called St Mungo's Well. John Murray of Philihaugh, the member of parliament for the joint burghs, offered the council £100 towards the cost. That was accepted and in June of the following year a contract was entered into with John Scott, an Edinburgh plumber. The supply was to run in earthen pipes from the well for 200 yards and then in lead pipes with a bore of one and a quarter inches. The council was to provide the earthen pipes and Scott the lead pipes for which he was to be paid 9s per yard. In September 1729 a site in the High Street was chosen for a well in the town. The site chosen was to be 'at or about the Dean's gutter, being the centre betwixt the east and the west port.' It was thought to be the best site as it would allow any surplus water to flow into a channel which already existed and ran down to the Eddleston Water. The actual site was opposite the Dean's Wynd where the Chambers institution stands today. In the event the cost was more than the Gift of £100 and the treasurer had to borrow 1000 merks, once again increasing the town's already burgeoning debt.

32.

Jacobites

Queen Anne died on 1ˢᵗ August, 1714. In spite of having given birth to a number of children, none had survived. In order to ensure the continuation of a Protestant monarchy, the Treaty of Union had included a provision that on her death she should be succeeded by the granddaughter of James VI&I, Sophia, Electress of the German state of Hanover. She had died before Anne and it was her son who succeeded as George I. He spoke no English, let alone Scots and never learned to do so. Nevertheless, he was a Protestant and descended from the royal House of Stuart and this was acceptable to the majority of Scots.

His succession to the throne seems to have been little remarked upon in Peebles. The only reference is an entry on 29ᵗʰ September 1714 which records that the clerk took an oath of allegiance to the new king and in turn a few days later, administered the same oath to the whole council. As so often happened in the past, in spite of possible reservations, Peebles once again seems to have accepted the national situation and continued on its way, with little change in its quiet and parochial existence.

Although the accession of George I was grudgeingly accepted across Scotland, there remained supporters of James Stuart, the son of James VII & II,[178]whose birth had precipitated the "Glorious Revolution" of 1688. They had hoped that perhaps the settled rule that only a Protestant could succeed to the throne might be reversed. James was of course a Roman Catholic. They were duly disappointed and it did not take long for stirrings of revolt to emerge. However it was mainly in the north where the Earl of Mar did his best to raise support for the Jacobite cause. On 6ᵗʰ September 1715 he raised the royal standard at Braemar. With an army which at its peak numbered 12,000 men, he succeeded in occupying Perth and Inverness and controlled much of the land north of the Tay, but further south remained largely loyal to the government. Attempts to gain support in south west Scotland and northern England failed. The only major battle took place at Sheriffmuir, close to Dunblane on 13ᵗʰ November, where he was opposed by a much smaller government force led by the Duke of Argyll. Although the battle was inconclusive, Mar withdrew to Perth and from there on his support began to dwindle and even the arrival from

---

178   The Old Pretender

France of the Pretender himself in December failed to salvage what had become a lost cause. Recognising their failure both the Prince and Mar escaped to France from Montrose in February 1716.

The Jacobite rebellion of 1715 passed Peebles by although there do seem to have been some who supported the Old Pretender. The long established family of the Burnets of Barns, who at the time owned property in Manor Valley and in Peebles itself, have been identified as having Jacobite sympathies.

The rebellion of 1745 was an altogether different affair. It was personally led by Charles Edward Stuart, son of the Old Pretender of 1715 and known as the "Young Pretender". The story, although much romanticised, is well known; how he sailed from France and landed at Moidart in the north west of Scotland; raised his standard among the Highland clans on 9th August 1745 at Glenfinnan; marched south to Edinburgh, where he held court at Holyrood after an enthusiastic reception by a large body of the citizens of Edinburgh; defeated a government army led by General John Cope at Prestonpans; marched south to capture Carlisle; then marched on further south towards London, failing to raise significant support south of the border and stopping at Derby, as members of his mainly Highland army started to desert and make their way homewards; how he reluctantly retraced his steps following his depleted army back to Scotland; then pursued by the government army commanded by the Duke of Cumberland, he and his army retreated northwards; meeting the government army and suffering a drastic defeat on 16th April 1746 at Culloden in Morayshire; how he fled the field and spent the next five months as a fugitive, aided at one stage by Flora Macdonald and finally escaped back to France from Moidart from where his adventure had started.

During its march south into England the prince's army split into two. The main body made its way south by way of Kelso, Jedburgh and on down through Liddesdale to Carlisle, while a large detachment led by Lord George Murray, the son of the Duke of Atholl and one of the prince's principal advisors, marched from Dalkeith to join with the main force at Carlisle. Its route took it into the Tweed Valley and on to Moffat. On the way it stopped at Peebles. They were mainly Atholl men and were in charge of the cannon and most of the baggage. The arrival on 2nd November 1745 in Peebles of these 'wild' Highlanders must have caused considerable alarm. They camped in what is now Hay Lodge Park. Robert Chambers describes the scene :

The sun was setting as the first lines devolved from the hills which environ the place on every side, and throwing back a thousand threatening glances from the arms of the moving band, caused alarm among the peaceful townsmen, who had only heard about the insurrection and its agents to make them fear the worst from their visit. Contrary to expectation, the mountaineers neither attempted to cut the throats nor violate the property of the inhabitants. The leader demanded payment of cess[179] (a local tax) on pain of return of military execution and little parties calling on various householders, within and without the town, requested such supplies of provisions as could properly be spared, with the alternative of having their houses given up to plunder; but scarcely any incivility was shown at the outset.[180]

The following Sunday the Highlanders had the town's mills set to work to grind sufficient meal to keep them going on the next stage of their march south through Stobo and on to Biggar, Elvanfoot and Moffat. They left the following day, no doubt to the great relief of the town, but shortly after in January 1746 the council attempted to raise a volunteer defence force for the town. An appeal was issued and publicly announced to all the inhabitants in the usual way 'by tuik of drum', asking them to take up arms and to join an Association of Volunteers. Anyone they thought was unable to meet the costs involved would be paid 'eighteen pence per day from their mustering and whatever have arms to bring them with them. And what arms shall be wanting, the Council Recommend to the Magistrats to provide them in the best manner they can.' In the event, their services were never required, as none of the Jacobite army on its retreat northwards came back by way of Peebles.

---

[179]   A local tax.
[180]   Robert Chambers – *History of the Rebellion of 1745-46* -W & R Chambers 1869

33.
Church Affairs

Throughout its long history the Church had played a central role in Peebles. From the earliest days after the Synod of Whitby established the Church of Rome as the sole Christian authority, it remained a major influence in the town until the Reformation of 1560. Its religious relics had made the Cross Kirk a place of pilgrimage for three centuries and the friars and priests dominated much of its civil life as well.

The changes and challenges with which Protestantism in its various forms filled the years after 1560 have already been told. Although Presbyterianism finally prevailed by the end of the seventeenth century and has broadly remained the settled order since then, it too was to undergo change and division. At the start of the eighteenth century things were calm for a time at least, although beneath the surface there may have been personal differences and the early years of the new century were not without their problems.

The Rev James Thomson had become the minister of Peebles in 1696, in somewhat controversial circumstances. Although the Duke of Queensberry and some heritors had proposed someone else, Mr Thomson had been supported by Lord William Douglas, the remainder of the heritors and the magistrates of the town. Lord William, who by then was the first Earl of March must have been well enough satisfied with his choice, because in 1702 he presented a solid silver baptismal basin and laver to the Church of Peebles. It is still in regular use today in the Old Parish Church. The earl died in 1705 and was interred in the burial vault on the north side of the Cross Kirk.

Although James Thomson seems to have been the popular choice, and his subsequent performance approved by Lord William, by 1711, the town council was unhappy about his ministry. It clearly did not think he was 'efficient', judging by the fact that in June of that year it commissioned the ex-provost John Tweeddale and the treasurer, Robert Forrester to attend the next meeting of presbytery, asking it to visit the parish of Peebles at an early date, because in the council's view it was being neglected. The next month it appointed John Henderson, the Dean of Guild and Robert Forrester to attend the presbytery again to present 'the grievances against Mr Thomsone minister here, in their name, and as representing the community of the burgh.' They were to try to have the matter fully discussed and if necessary to have it appealed to the next synod or the General Assembly. Just what the problem was is not clear and in any event Mr Thomson died in September of the following year. Whatever his failings, he must have had some feeling at least for the poor of the town, because he left 200 merks for their relief.

The appointment of Mr Thomson's successor once again produced a conflict. This time it was between the magistrates and William, the 2nd Earl of March, who, exercising his "patronage", had presented John Hay, the third of that name and nephew of the last John Hay, who died in1690. Patronage, which was the right of the principal landowner to nominate or "present" their personal choice of minister had been abolished in 1690 when it became the right of heritors and elders. Had patronage still been in place in 1696, the people of Peebles would have had to accept the Earl of March's nomination, like it or not. patronage was restored once again by an Act of 1712.

John Hay had been born in 1680 and so was 33 years old at the time of his presentation, but the magistrates and the community thought he was too young and opposed the appointment. The matter came before the presbytery and Alexander Williamson, who was the Sheriff Clerk appeared on behalf of Lord March. However, the presbytery supported the town. It had done so after it had appointed several presbytery members to visit the parish to listen to the views of the parishioners. They found that most of them were against Mr Hay's appointment.

The case then went to the synod which directed the presbytery to settle Mr Hay in Peebles, but some of the presbytery members objected and the magistrates continued their opposition. The whole matter dragged on with each side protesting against the other. In the meantime Mr Hay had undergone his "trials for ordination" before the presbytery in January 1717. He failed in Greek and Hebrew, but in April at long last he had his trials approved. The presbytery still declined to proceed and the matter was appealed to the General Assembly, which decided that Mr Hay should be ordained as minister. Because of the attitude of the Presbytery of Peebles, it appointed seven ministers from the Presbytery of Edinburgh to act as assessors. They, together with the few members of the presbytery who supported Hay were able to reach an agreement and at long last on 26th June 1717, John Hay was finally ordained as minister of Peebles. He would remain minister until 1760.

During his ministry, the plight of the poor was a matter for the church as well as the civil authority. In 1725 it was noted that there were thirty three people within the parish who were classified as 'poor', although there is no indication as to the criteria which defined that status. Of those identified, eighteen were receiving a pension every two weeks from the 'poor's box' maintained by the church. Sadly the remaining fifteen were not provided for at all out of the church's resources.

There was a number of individual cases where help was given. One in particular is of special interest. It concerned Duncan More who was apparently held as a slave in Algiers. A collection was taken in April 1725 to raise money for his redemption. Sufficient funds were raised by September for him to be released. He returned to Peebles and appeared in the kirk to thank all who had helped in gaining his freedom. This has echoes of an earlier time when the Red Friars of the Cross Kirk had raised funds for the relief of captives held by anti-Christian forces in the Holy Land.

A contribution to the poor funds of the parish was made from a bequest by James Williamson of Cardrona at about that time. With accrued interest for the previous five years, it amounted to over £400 Scots, a substantial sum. Other contributors to funds for the poor included a sum of £10 sterling given in perpetuity for the poor of the parish by Thomas Tweeddale, who was a tailor based in London. He clearly wished his charity to be highlighted, because his gift was conditional on its being recorded on a public notice board in 'gilded letters'.

Although after his disputed appointment Mr Hay appears to have been accepted in his ministry by the community, in August 1731, he became involved with the town council over his use of the kirkyard as grazing for his horses. Some of the tombstones and monuments had been knocked over or damaged. The council took him to task, but the minister replied that he would use the grass as he wished. In response, the council had the gate locked, but that did not seem to be effective and in September the council made an order forbidding him from grazing any of the kirkyard with his cows, sheep or horses. He was, however, permitted to cut the grass as fodder.

The kirk session continued to be the judge of public morality, with the minister and elders dispensing arbitrary punishment on those they judged to be in error. The kirk session might be respected, but it was also feared and the traditional picture of its members as dour, cheerless and unsmiling men of little humour, wrapped up in their own sense of righteousness, is probably not far wide of the mark. Perhaps not all were the "Holy Willies" of Burns' well known poem and no doubt many were solid citizens, as they saw it, doing their best for society.

The cases of human failure that came before them were varied, ranging from minor offences such as failing to contribute to funds for relief of the poor, to adultery and fornication. There was a case in 1747 which related to a somewhat tangled set of marriage relationships and lengthy repercussions which eventually spread beyond the kirk session.

It concerned John Neilson, the son of a lawyer in Peebles and Margaret Russell, the daughter of Alexander Russell, a surgeon and a former provost of the town. They had said that they were married, but that was being called into question. Margaret Russell had previously appeared before the kirk session in April 1744. It had come to the notice of the kirk session that she had given birth to a child in Edinburgh some time previously. She admitted that it was the case and claimed that the father was Charles Naesmyth and that she had married him in April 1742, some time before the child was born. She claimed that she had a document confirming that in Naesmyth's own handwriting.

Nothing further is then heard about the matter until August 1747, when John Neilson and Margaret Russell were called before the kirk session to answer the charge that they were not legally married on account of the earlier declaration by Margaret. Not only that, but Neilson had recently returned from the West Indies and had told a number of people that he was married to an Irish woman whom he had met in America and that he had brought her back to Ireland and left her there. In the circumstances it is not surprising that questions should have been asked.

They both appeared before the kirk session on 7th September and produced a certificate of marriage. Neilson was asked if he had married an Irish woman in America. He denied that that was the case and said that he had lied about it so that he could inherit a legacy left to him by his late uncle. It was presumably a condition that he received it only if he was married. Margaret Russell was asked if she was married to a Mr Charles Naesmyth. She replied she had claimed to be married to him in order to protect her own character, but it was a lie. She now denied that she was ever married to him. The session no doubt somewhat perplexed thought that it was either bigamy or adultery or both and decided that the matter should be referred to a higher authority, the Presbytery.

The two accused appeared before the presbytery and again claimed that they were married. In a bizarre twist to the story, Margaret then said that in the document written by Charles Naesmyth, what he had actually written was that he was married to *Margaret Nonsuch* and she had altered this to *Russell*. In order to confirm the story, Neilson produced an extract from the Court Books of Peebles which showed that Naesmyth and

Margaret had previously been called on to answer a charge that their marriage was illegal. The magistrates had found that the hand written document was flawed and could not be accepted as proof of marriage. Margaret had therefore been free to marry him. It was very troubling and the moderator of the presbytery accused them both of lying and prevarication, all of which was grossly sinful. They now confessed that neither of them had in fact been married before.

Not only was the unhappy couple found wanting, but the affair also proved to be an embarrassment to the kirk session of Peebles. The minister, the clerk and one of the elders had examined Naesmyth's document, but admitted that they had not done so very carefully. Somewhat belatedly they recalled that they had noticed that the word *Russell* had been altered. One of the Presbytery members also remembered that he had noticed that.

After long deliberation the presbytery found Neilson guilty of lying and lack of transparency. It found Margaret Russell guilty of lying and prevarication, altering Naesmyth's document attempting to claim marriage to Naesmyth knowing that to be false and having a child to him out of wedlock. Both parties deserved to be severely censured. At a meeting of the presbytery in January 1748 it was decided that the moderator should 'judicially rebuke' both of them, which he duly did. For her confessed sin of fornication, Margaret Russell had to make a confession before the congregation, as it was said for "public satisfaction." No doubt there would have been many in the congregation who wagged their heads and muttered condemnation at such immoral behaviour. Others might have said nothing but thought their own thoughts!

John Hay died on 1st June 1760. In spite of ups and downs he had been the minister of Peebles for 43 years. The minister who followed him was the Rev Dr William Dalgleish D.D.

Dr Dalgleish was an altogether different character from his predecessor. He was born in Galloway and had studied at Edinburgh University. He was licensed by the Presbytery of Edinburgh in 1760 and was "presented" to the church and parish of Peebles by the Earl of Wemyss and March in 1761. Strangely, in view of the problems which had arisen when John Hay was presented, the fact that he had little experience before coming to Peebles and was only 28 years old[181] seems not to have caused a problem in his case. From accounts that exist, there is every reason to think that he was an attractive and possibly charismatic

---

[181]   John Hay had been 33, but was thought to be too young.

character. When writing his *Glimpses of Peebles* in 1894, the Rev Alex Williamson describes him as 'of good appearance, with an open, frank countenance and kindly manner, combined with considerable dignity.' At the time Williamson was writing there could have been no one alive who had seen or met Mr Dalgleish, but there would have been those who had first-hand accounts of him from their immediately preceding generation. Hearing from them, Williamson is able to write the following about him:

> Although no one now living saw Mr Dalgliesh, many in their youth may have heard of him from old people who remembered him well – with his cocked hat, knee breeches, silver buckles, powdered hair, and gold topped cane. He was regarded with great respect, as on Sunday mornings he walked with slow and stately steps from the manse to the Cross Kirk, along the path between the high hedgerows; and when he appeared at the head of the High Street, or was coming down the Old Town, the "wives claivering at the close heads" suddenly stopped their animated conversation and swiftly disappeared. Yet no man had a kinder heart or did more good in the town.[182]

He was clearly highly thought of and by all accounts his ministry in Peebles until his death in September 1807 at the age of 74 was very successful.

He arrived in Peebles as a bachelor and remained so until 1773 when he married Miss Jean Gibson. When he first came to Peebles, the manse, like many other properties in the town, was in poor condition. After an inspection, it was reported that the manse was repairable, but the barn was so far gone that it would have to be rebuilt. By 1770 the manse had deteriorated further and in that year a new manse was built. It was situated on the east side of Hay Lodge, where Riverside House stands today.

The one contentious matter was the issue of the grazing rights of the minister. Once again it involved the churchyard. It was alleged that Dr Dalgleish, like his predecessor, had grazed the churchyard with his cattle and horses and the council in a letter to him claimed that as a result, several tombstones had been broken down. The letter added that in the council's opinion it was 'a very indecent practice to have cattle trampling upon the graves of their dearest friends.' Dr Dalgleish responded that he had no other grass for grazing and that grazing the churchyard was the normal practice of ministers in Scotland. He said that his cow was never in the churchyard and that his mare only grazed what was left after the grass

---

[182] Rev Alex Williamson - *Glimpses of Peebles or Forgotten Chapters in its History*, PP 58,61/62

was cut and only because he had no other grass to feed her on. He denied that his stock had caused any damage to the tombstones. None the less the council instructed the treasurer to put a lock on the church yard gate as they had done previously in their dispute with Mr Hay. Probably as a result of that problem, Dr Dalgleish raised the whole matter of the minister's grazing rights with the presbytery, who ruled in April 1771 that he was entitled to grazing for one cow and two horses. They appointed a delegation to discuss it with the heritors. Long delays followed and the matter was still under discussion in April 1781 when the Procurator of the Church[183] advised that as the minister of Peebles had a landward parish as well as the burgh, he was entitled to have an arable and a grass glebe and that the lands which the church still owned lying next to the present glebe could be used for that purpose. There was a problem because the land was occupied by tenants, but after much argument the presbytery finally agreed that an area of two and one half acres at Kirkmyre and Glencraig[184] was suitable for grazing a horse and two cows and that the minister could take possession immediately. The present occupiers were to seek compensation from the heritors.

Later in his ministry, as will be seen, Dr Dalgleish was instrumental in having a new church built on the Castlelhill. He also gained some notoriety by publishing a book called *The True Sonship of Christ Investigated* in 1776. It raised something of a storm in certain ecclesiastical quarters, but none the less, two years later he was awarded a doctorate by the University of Edinburgh, which in those days was regarded as a very significant honour. Towards the end of the century he also contributed the section on the Parish of Peebles to the first *Statistical Account of Scotland* of 1794.

---

183   Its legal advisor
184   Where Kingsland School now stands

34.
Out with the Old – In with the New

A visitor to Peebles in 1750 would not have been impressed by what he or she found! The royal and ancient burgh was in a state of decay. The town walls were crumbling; the Tweed cauld serving the mills of the town hardly existed; the Tweed Bridge was in need of repair; the West Port was a ruin: the steeple and tolbooth were falling apart; even the adjacent building of the former Chapel of St Mary, which in recent times had been used as the meeting place of the town council, was dilapidated; the Cross Kirk, the town's parish church was in a perilous condition and all this in spite of many attempts and much expense incurred during the first three decades of the century to stem the tide of decline.

The town was deeply in debt and a significant part of the population was in poverty and many in dire distress. In all its long history over many centuries, 1750 probably marks the nadir of its life. Whether of necessity or in attempt to improve the image of the town, the council none the less decided in 1749 to build a new "town house" which would become the centre of municipal affairs. They were following what had become the practice in many other royal burghs. At its meeting on 19th July it was decided to go ahead with the project. Finding a suitable site proved to be a problem. First it tried to buy a property in the High Street, belonging to James Veitch, who was later to become Lord Elliock. It was on the north side of the street and a ruin. That fell through and eventually an old property on the south side of the street was bought for £29. The property lay between the High Street and the town wall on Tweed Green, or what of it that remained. It had belonged to James Brotherstains, who at that time was the town clerk.

It was not until 1752 that work on constructing the building started. In March of that year the burgh treasurer was instructed to employ "Masons and Wrights" resident in the burgh to undertake the work, which then proceeded over the next four years. Its designer is unknown, but the building, which stands to this day, suggests that whoever created it had considerable skills, as the frontage in particular, is a handsome piece of architecture. It originally consisted of the council chamber on the first floor, with two archways at ground level, creating two pends giving access to the ground beyond.[185]

The first meeting of the town council, in the new and vastly improved building, took place on 25th June 1756. The cost must have been substantial and it is unlikely that in straightened times, the burgh had sufficient resources of its own to meet it. As had been the frequent practice since the beginning of the century, the council may have resorted to borrowing once again.

At that time the west end of the High Street, where it met the West Port was much higher than it is today. The Port Brae leading to Tweed Green and the Tweed Bridge and the lane leading north to the bridge over the Eddleston Water, were so steep that the access to the High Street through what remained of the West Port was awkward and dangerous for horse drawn carriages and mounted horses. In June 1758 a decision was taken by the council to demolish what remained of the West Port and to reduce the levels.

Steps were also taken to further improve the water supply which relied on the system installed some thirty years before from St Mungo's Well. Although that had been a great improvement, domestic usage was limited. The brewers in the town were major users to the extent that they were using so much that householders were being deprived. In December 1759 the council made an order prohibiting brewers from using water from the well itself, although they could use anything flowing from the overflow. In 1766 the situation had reached a point where action was needed. The council sought advice on the possibility of creating a reservoir fed from the well, with pipes running from it to supply other parts of the town. A reservoir was constructed in the Eastgate shortly thereafter. The Old Town remained without a supply until 1780 when a well was sunk at the Ludgate.[186] It remained in use until the end of the next century. Even that proved to be inadequate and a further well was sunk at the foot of the Old Town in 1793.

---

[185]   The interior was been somewhat altered in later years and a further building was added at the rear in 1860 as a Corn exchange. In 1925 the ground floor of the combined building became the headquarters of the local fire brigade and then from 1964 until the present, part of the ground floor, including one of the pends, became a shop, while the former Corn Exchange has become a recreation area for youth activities.

[186]   Now Young Street.

In April 1760, the Tweed bridge had to be closed to cart traffic because of its poor state. It remained closed to all but foot and ridden horses for some years. The provost was instructed to consult with 'some knowing, skilful mason' about necessary repairs as the bridge had suffered recent storm damage. Drovers were also complaining that the parapet was too low, with the result that they often lost sheep and lambs which were able to jump over it. Towards the end of the century it was decided that not only repair was needed but also that the bridge should be improved by the addition of one or two arches or a mound at the south end. Estimates were obtained in 1794, but the work was not done until 1799, when three arches were to be added. The work was carried out by John Hislop, a local mason. Sadly he died, when one of the arches collapsed during the course of construction.[187]Charles Blyth's painting of the Tweed Green in 1848 shows the bridge with its completed extension. The south end would be altered again when the railway line from the Caledonian Station was built in 1863.

To further add to the picture of decay and dilapidation, a report to the council in December 1766, described the streets as being in very bad repair. The magistrates were instructed to obtain estimates for the cost of remedial work. In May 1769, an estimate from an Edinburgh pavior was accepted. The town would supply the materials and he would be paid 7s 6d per rood (quarter of an acre). Work must still have been ongoing in April 1774 when repairs to the High Street between the well and St Mary's Chapel is mentioned.

There still remained the problem of what to do with the old tolbooth, the steeple and the former Chapel of St Mary which were all by now little more than ruins, although part of the tolbooth still functioned as the town jail. In 1770 a decision had been made to demolish all of those buildings and estimates were obtained for the work from a mason from outwith the town. Local masons had declined to offer for the work as they thought it to be 'dark and difficult'. The council then sought advice from an Edinburgh architect who advised that the steeple should be taken down immediately. He further advised that people living in the vicinity should move out of their houses, in case of accidents, which is a clear indication that it was by then unsafe. The architect gave very specific instructions as to how the work should proceed. It should be undertaken by skilled masons; the stonework should be taken down course by course and the stones should not be thrown down, but lowered to the ground in boxes by ropes and

187   RCAHMS *Peeblesshire 2* – p 341

pulleys. In days long before the modern obsession with health and safety all those measures indicate a common sense approach.

All the recommendations were agreed to, but it was not until 1776 that the work was finally undertaken. All the stone removed was taken to the Castle Hill and the remaining rubbish was piled in heaps and then sold by public auction. The cleared site remained vacant until partly built on in the late nineteenth century. No trace remains of the former buildings, with the possible exception of what is thought to be part of the foundation of the Chapel of St Mary which is visible in a cellar beneath one of the Victorian buildings.

Prior to the final work of demolition, part of the steeple continued to be used as the town jail, but that became untenable as the building deteriorated. In January 1774, the council was forced to find an alternative. The provost was authorised to negotiate the purchase of a cellar on the north side of the High Street, opposite the new Town House. It belonged to Lord Elliock and at the beginning of 1775 he agreed to sell it for £20 sterling. It was not ideal. The cells were separated from the High Street by a grating and through it friends of prisoners were able to pass drink and 'other things not necessary'. To prevent that, an inner grating was installed in 1776, but even so the temporary jail was far from satisfactory. It was small and difficult to manage.

A general Act of Parliament had required all Scottish burghs to provide adequate jail facilities and in 1789 the council decided to build a completely new jail. It was built at the foot of the Castle Hill. It stands to this day and forms the rear portion of the building known as the Peebles Sheriff Courthouse. The original jail building is still quite clearly identifiable as the rear whinstone block of the present building. When it stood on its own there was an extension on the frontage enclosing a stairway which gave access to the three levels of cells.[188]

*　*　*

The Cross Kirk had been the Parish Church since the Reformation of 1560, but by 1770 it was also in a sorry state, in spite of attempts to repair it. The roof leaked; its seats were bare unpainted wood and far from comfortable, although that might have seemed to be appropriate in an era

---

[188]　Some of the former windows have been filled in, but their outline is still visible.

338

of penitential discomfort; the stalls of the provost, magistrates and council were crumbling.

The minister, Dr Dalgleish proposed that a new church should be built, a major project at a time of economic depression. He had discussed the possibility with several of the heritors and some of the townsfolk , as well as the presbytery, all of whom were in agreement. He presented his proposal to a meeting of the town council on 13th July 1776. As well as the poor condition of the Cross Kirk, Dr Dalgleish pointed out that it was badly situated, especially in winter, when often the roads leading to it were blocked with snow for several weeks. Consequently many people were unable to attend worship, with the result that the poor of the parish, who benefited from the collections, suffered because they were much reduced.

A lengthy debate followed and a number of meetings were held between the heritors, the council and the presbytery. While the council was willing to pay its fair share, it was agreed that the cost of putting the Cross Kirk into good order must first be established. An Edinburgh architect by the name of Brown was commissioned to prepare a report, which he submitted in 1778. The conclusion was clear. The cost would exceed what it would cost to build a new church. The heritors were sceptical and argued that Brown's report was not sufficiently detailed. He was asked to reconsider it, but in the meantime Provost Ker, who was clearly a supporter of the new church proposal, pointed out that the Cross Kirk was not convenient for the elderly and infirm, because of its position outside the town. He said he knew of a suitable site which could be bought for a new building. Provost Ker was highly respected in the burgh and his influence carried a lot of weight. At a further meeting it was decided that Mr Brown's report would be reconsidered along with Provost Ker's proposal. In the event Mr Brown failed to give any clearer explanation, so the provost's proposal was the only realistic one which could be considered. A decision was delayed and in the meantime Provost Ker had been succeeded by Provost Reid. He was a physician and surgeon, with a large practice and considerable influence and had bought the property called Queensberry Lodging in the High Street.[189] He was a supporter of a new church proposal and at the next meeting with the heritors, which Mr Ker attended, he strongly supported the former provost and at last it was finally agreed that a new church should be built on ground on the Castle Hill which would be given by the council who also agreed to contribute towards its cost, 'provided that their Steeple for their clock and bells shall be carried up with the building of the church.'

---

[189]   In the next century it would become the basis of the Chambers Institution.

In December 1778 agreement was finally reached. The heritors were to contribute £300 sterling and be entitled to one third of the seats, for which they would be able to charge a rent and the council seats from the Cross Kirk would be renovated and installed in the new church and would remain the property of the town. A further condition was that the steeple should be built at the east end and, along with the bells, remain the property of the town in all time coming.[190] Plans were prepared by Mr Brown, who it seems was appointed, in spite of reservations about his earlier report. His plans were approved in May 1779 and work started immediately

The new steeple was completed in September 1782, the town's arms having been added in 1780. Initially the council were apparently happy with the completed work and went so far as to create all the masons burgesses in recognition of their efforts. However, a year later a dispute arose about the design of the steeple. Here Williamson and Buchan differ in what ensued. Williamson says that the spire was considered to be 'stunted and inelegant', while Buchan says that it was 'by mistake… carried seven feet higher than it ought to have been, beside an improper Taper in the finishing.' According to Williamson, when Brown was approached his response was that 'his plans had been shamefully departed from.' He suggests that, in spite of the difficulty of regularly travelling from Edinburgh, Brown might have taken the trouble to come to see the progress of the work.

For his part Buchan says that the dispute was with the masons. Their request for final payment was refused, 'unless they agreed to take down the spire and finish it in a neat and tidy manner.' The masons declined, although the council minute indicates that any additional cost would have been met by public donations. The dispute continued until finally the council decided to appoint an independent mason to give his opinion. He was James Henry from Kersewell and he advised that the cost of alteration would make it impractical. So, whatever the detail of the dispute, the spire remained and was as it later appeared in early photographs and in the well-known etching of the parish church and corn mill of circa 1790.

When completed the church had seating for 439 of which 242 were on the ground floor and 197 in the gallery. In addition, there was a pew at the front of the gallery reserved for the magistrates and council. All the seats were subject to an annual rent Those in the area were let at 1s. 4d. and those in the gallery at 1s. 5d., the higher rent perhaps because they were

---

[190]   The condition was repeated when the church was replaced in 1884 by the building which stands on the site today.

nearer to God, or perhaps more pragmatically because their occupants were separated from lesser mortals. Householders were allowed to buy pews and the seats in the gallery were offered to the various trade and craft guilds at a cost of twenty times the annual letting value. The whole business of seat letting was highly lucrative and raised the sum of £24 sterling annually, a sizeable sum at the time.

Some years after the new church was completed, there were problems with the ventilation. There were many complaints particularly in summer. One can well imagine that in the confined space, with a full congregation, as was normally the case, the atmosphere would have been oppressive and unhealthy. It was said that even the minister, Dr Dalgleish suffered as a consequence. The council was asked to find a remedy. It was quite simple. All that was needed was for the uppermost panes of the middle window in the west gable to be made to open!

The Cross Kirk closed as a place of worship in December 1783 and the new church came into use at the beginning of 1784. The town council took steps over the next 4 years to sell off the roof and masonry of the Cross Kirk. In 1789 there was a public protest about the destruction of the ancient building which had been part of the heritage of Peebles for over 400 years. A petition signed by a number of burgesses as well as Dr Dalgleish was submitted to the council on18th July 1789. It read;

> Since the new Church and Steeple of Peebles were erected and the roof taken off the old church, the remaining walls of it display a most agreeable prospect in ruins from every part of the town and neighbouring fields as the eye ever beheld or the mind could wish for; besides to those who know anything of the history of that Church its antiquity must add an additional Lustre to what yet still remains. To erase then a place built by a King, occupied as a monastery, and thereafter an established church would at once bury in oblivion a Building the remains of which are the greatest ornament of the Borough. But a word to the wise is enough – the Petitioners being convinced their honours would grasp at the least hint of this kind and give orders for preserving the walls of the Cross Church of Peebles for ages yet to come.

This must be one of the earliest examples of an attempt at preserving a building and its heritage. The council saw the error of its ways and in July 1789 when it was by then a wreck, decided that it should remain in its present state "in all time coming". What remained of the building was restored to its present state in the first half of the twentieth century.

Although the road from Peebles to Edinburgh had been established for centuries, it was little more than a track, making it difficult for wheeled traffic, which frequently needed four horses to pull a carriage. As a consequence. Speeds were no more than three miles per hour, making the journey to Edinburgh upwards of seven hours. In 1770, the Lord Advocate, Mr James Montgomery, who used the route regularly, wrote to the provost proposing that a new road should be built to provide an adequate link from the Royal Burgh to the border of Midlothian and on towards Edinburgh, with the cost met by a public subscription, mainly raised from the landed gentry of the county, so that a Turnpike Act could be promoted. It was an Act made under national legislation. The proposal was strongly supported by the town council and a meeting of landowners and other interested parties was held. On the 10th October it was agreed to promote a Turnpike Bill. The council for its part, agreed to contribute £10 towards the cost.

It is not entirely clear what route the existing road (or track) followed. It seems to have twisted and turned and risen and fallen to avoid boggy areas along the valley of the Eddleston Water. According to Chambers, initially on leaving the town it climbed steeply to Venlaw and then continued along the hill tops to Windylaws, before dropping down again to the valley floor, just south of Eddleston and then climbed again towards Portmore.

Armstong's *Map of the County of Peebles,* published in 1775 appears to show the route of the new road, at least in part and to confirm that it was a Turnpike, as he shows tolls just south of Eddleston and at Nether Falla. Nearer Peebles at Redscarhead, there is a house close to the current road which is known to be a former toll house. His map shows the route running north from Peebles, following the Eddleston Water to Eddleston Village, much as it does today, avoiding the climbs to Venlaw and Windylaws.

At Eddleston village, one branch bears right and passing round Portmore Loch before heading towards Dalkeith and that may have been the original route to Edinburgh. The other, continues north to Nether Falla, but then runs on the west side of the Eddleston Water, rather than to the east as it does today. It continues by Shiphorns to Nether Falla and then broadly follows the modern route to Leadburn, joining the road from Leadburn to Howgate at Mosshouses. The last section of the route from Upper Falla is shown on Armstrong's map as dotted lines, which may well indicate that it was still under construction in 1775.

Street lighting with oil lamps had been introduced in Edinburgh, possibly as early as 1684. The city's first official lamp lighter was appointed in 1701, but it was not until 1771 that public lighting was first introduced to Peebles. In November of that year, fifteen lamps were bought and erected in the streets. James Ewart was appointed to light them and keep them clean. By 1773 the number had increased to eighteen and task of lamplighter was put out to tender. Private sector provision of public services is not new! The contract conditions were that the lamps should be lit from mid October until the first of April. The contractor was to provide the wicks and oil and 'regularly to light, trim and clean them so as to make them burn from twilight until eleven o'clock each night, except from the tenth day of every moon till the eighteenth.' It would have been the period of the full moon. Such reliance on natural lighting must have been problematical. Even in the eighteenth century weather conditions cannot have been so reliable! The bidding started at £9 and ultimately an offer of £8.7s was accepted from William Oram, who at that time was a town councillor. In those days such a conflict of interest was not considered a problem.

The initial scheme does not seem to have been very successful, because street lighting was stopped for a number of years and only seems to have been revived again in 1787. At that time six new lamps were bought and a public subscription was raised to buy thirty gallons of oil. One of the burgh officers, David Henderson was sent to Edinburgh to find out how the city arranged the lighting and cleaning of lamps. He was to come back to Peebles and to light and clean the lamps, with the knowledge he had gained during his Edinburgh excursion. The council would decide how much he should be paid more or less on a "take it, or leave basis". Evidently, he was not happy with the arrangement, because in 1789 the work was again put out to tender. The following year the contract was awarded again to Henderson, but for a fixed amount of two guineas. If he was not satisfied he would lose the job. Probably that is what happened, because by 1791 the work was being done by a certain John Tait. In September, 1792, he was invited to continue. One of the bailies was to provide the oil, while the town treasurer was instructed to pay for the replacement of any broken lamps. The public lighting of the town remained in that somewhat crude state until the introduction of gas lighting in 1828.

As will already be clear, the economic condition of the town in every respect throughout most of the eighteenth century was a matter of serious concern. Early in the century the long established, but faltering trade of weaving woollen cloth was supplemented by the production of linen. Towards the end of the century cotton also started to be produced in the town. According to Joe Brown,[191] William Chambers, the grandfather of William and Robert Chambers of later literary fame, introduced cotton manufacturing in 1703 and that at its peak, he had upwards of 100 looms working for him. However, that seems unlikely, given that manufacture of cotton goods on any scale did not start until the second half of the century. In 1778 a small scale mill was set up in Rothesay and a second in Penicuik a year later, which were the first two of their kind in Scotland. Perhaps more accurate is his grandson, Robert's account:

> My father growing up at the time when cotton manufacture was introduced into Glasgow, studied it, and now conducted it on an extensive scale in Peebles, having sometimes as many as a hundred hand-looms in his employment.

Robert was born in 1802 and this extract appears in his memoirs of his earliest youth, when his father acted as agent in selling the cloth produced by the weavers.

The council did its best to try to establish new sources of employment. In 1735, there was a proposal to set up a factory to manufacture yarn. At that time as Daniel Defoe had recorded, virtually all the wool which was produced in the area was sent to England for processing there and it was probably a sensible attempt to establish an industry adding value locally and providing material for local weavers.

The proposal came from Alexander Sheriff, acting on behalf of Charles Cockburn, who was an advocate. The council minute of 25th August sets out some detail of what he had in mind:

> The yarn is to be very round and course…. Mr Sheriff is content for a trial to give good careful diligent spinsters[192] 4s Scots per day from 6 of the morning till 8 at night, and he is content to give spinners who are not so able (now when harvest is approaching and woman will be scarce) what the council shall think fit to conform to their work…..After trial Mr Sheriff is content when it shall be sufficiently known what a stone of the wool may be spun for, to give out stones of wool to their own houses both to strong and weak, and to take sufficient time for it, but no time to be lost.

---

191   *History of Peebles 1850 -1990*
192   Meaning those who spun, not single ladies.

344

What was clearly envisaged here was a scheme to establish if such a venture could be economically viable. Sheriff had already confirmed that he was satisfied that Peebles was a suitable location and that he preferred it to any other place. The council was very supportive of the idea and instructed the quartermasters to find out those who would be suitable to employ as spinners. Sadly it appears that for whatever reason, the scheme failed, because nothing more is heard of it, in spite of the fact that the weaving of woollen cloth was carried out in the town and had been for centuries, presumably using yarn from wool re-exported from England.

The weaving of cloth was very much a "cottage industry". In the previous year the council had received a letter from the trustees appointed to oversee the woollen manufacturing industries in Scotland. In it the trustees intent on seeing the continuation of woollen manufacture, appointed Charles Nassmyth, the brother of Sir James Nassmyth of Posso, to establish a central location with the necessary equipment. The council decided that as it did not have a suitable building, a new building should be constructed, 'at the foot of the high green next Tweed'. It was to be 300 feet long and 16 feet wide. Unfortunately that scheme also failed. There had been many complaints that Nassmyth who had had the site for five or six years had done nothing to carry out the proposal 'for building a house on the green for the woollen manufacture of coarse wool settled by the government.' The provost was instructed to find someone suitable to carry it out, but as nothing more is heard about it, the attempt must have failed. One of the factors which must have made the development of viable industries difficult was communication. Roads were still poor and often impassable in adverse weather conditions, making it difficult to distribute finished cloth at least until the advent of turnpike roads later in the century.

Another venture which failed was an attempt to find a source of coal close to Peebles. Coal was increasingly becoming the preferred fuel. The nearest source was from mines in the neighbouring county of Midlothian, where it had been mined since at least the sixteenth century, by the monks of Newbattle Abbey. The problem was transport, not only the distance but the conditions of roads such as they were, made it expensive. Although the science of geology was in its infancy, in 1755 the council were told by Dr George Grieve, who was a physician in the town, that there was a possibility of finding a workable seam of coal on the town's common lands near Winkston. The council were excited by the prospect and immediately agreed to lease the land to Dr Grieve and James Kerr a former Dean of Guild, for a period of nineteen years and also contributed

£5 towards the costs of exploration, provided that the lessees themselves spent £30. It was also a condition that if coal was found, the maximum cost to inhabitants of Peebles should not exceed 3 pence per cart load. Exploration went on for several years. In December 1759 William Malcolm, who had been searching for coal on the common near the Windylaws burnfoot, presumably on behalf of the leaseholders, reported that he was still confident of finding coal, 'there being all good appearances and sign thereof.' Encouraged by that assessment, the council agreed to supply timber to support the excavations which had already taken place and to supply labour to help him in the work. It also agreed to financially support Malcolm until such time as money which had been raised by public subscription ran out. Sadly it was all in vain. No coal was found.

Yet another project which did not materialise was a proposal to build a snuff mill in the town. In August 1789, an Edinburgh tobacco manufacturer called Adam Peacock, suggested that it could be added to the Waulk Mill which at that time was being repaired. Plans were prepared and submitted to the council in March 1790, but seem to have come to nothing as no more is heard of it.

All of those failures must have been frustrating and disheartening, but they indicate a clear purpose of trying to improve the life of the town and its people and a commendable attempt to tackle an economic situation which must have been the cause of much hardship to many. It would be several decades before there would be a noticeable improvement, but by the end of the century there were signs that better days lay ahead. In a report of 1776, David Loch, General Inspector of Fisheries in Scotland, noted that there were forty looms in Peebles for the weaving of coarse woollen cloth. That was rather more than found in Galashiels at that time, but it was not until 1856 that the first "modern" woollen mill was established in the town.[193]

---

[193]   *History of Peebles 1850-1990*, p25

35.
Social and Civic Life in the 2nd half of the Eighteenth Century

The composition of the town council was unchanged as it had been since time immemorial. The magistrates were the provost and two bailies and in addition there was the dean of guild, twelve councillors and the deacon of the weavers who sat on the council as an *ex officio* member, making seventeen in all. Elections were still held annually on the first Monday after Michaelmas (29th September) and since 1469 it had been the practice for the old council to elect the new. The process was somewhat complicated. The method of election was enshrined in the "sett" or constitution of the burgh. To start with, the provost and the elder of the two bailies went out of the room and the remaining fifteen members then voted in favour or against each of them. Those two then returned and two more went out of the room and the same procedure followed and so on two by two until every one had been voted on by the other members of the old council. The system was designed to ensure that no one could vote for himself.

At the election of 1775 there was a major problem which resulted in a petition being made to the Court of Session asking for the election be declared null and void. It all started because of an allegation that the new council intended to sell off part of the town's common land. That may have been Heathpool. Party politics are not new and at that time the council was divided into two groups who were strongly opposed to each other. James Ballantyne, a member of the old council had died before the election and one of the bailies had declined to accept office, so that the total number was reduced to fifteen. One group was led by the provost William Ker and included one of the bailies and four councillors. The remaining seven councillors led by William Oram formed the second group.

It seems likely that the second group was intent in engineering a change of government and was using the alleged sale as a pretext. In the Memorial[194] to the Court of Session, the provost's "party" claimed that its opponents :

---

194   Statement of Case

devised and propagated cunning lies to the prejudice of the magistrates and council, who were not of their party, with a design to inflame the minds of the Inhabitants against them, and to alarm them with the apprehension that a particular Common the property of the burgh would be disposed of if it were not removed, and turned totally out of the administration at the ensuing election.

To modern ears these "political" tactics may sound all too familiar. The opposition alleged that it was supported by the Earl of March. That was probably not true and it was more likely that it had been in touch with some of his local employees. It does seem that unknown to his Lordship they had held meetings in Queensberry Lodging, his house in the High Street.

Before the election took place, the provost's party numbered eight, while the opposition numbered seven, so there was a strong likelihood of a close contest. The election fell on a Monday and on the preceding Sunday 'malicious and inflammatory' pamphlets were distributed throughout the town. In response the magistrates called a meeting of the Head Court of the burgh. It was a public meeting of the burgesses. There was nothing unusual about that as it was the normal practice to call such a meeting before each election to give an opportunity to a wider representation of the community to air its grievances and to comment on candidates for the election. No doubt the meeting would have been somewhat fractious. The political divisions would probably have been a reflection of the views of the community as a whole.

The election followed but the fact that the total number of old councillors entitled to vote for the new was reduced by two presented a problem. Under the rules the first to withdraw were to be the provost and the one remaining bailie. It meant that only six of their party remained to vote, while the opposition could muster seven. The constitution however, provided that where a vacancy had arisen caused by the death of a councillor, it should be filled before the main election began. The provost moved a motion that the vacancy due to the death of Ballantyne should be filled and with his majority it was approved. Not surprisingly the new councillor was a supporter of Provost Ker. The election proceeded with the provost and bailie withdrawing, leaving the remainder equally balanced. In the event of a tie, the rules prescribed that the casting vote be given by the oldest member, who was the dean of guild and a member of the provost's party. The election continued and none of the opposition was elected except for the deacon of the weavers, who in any case earned his place as of right.

In the petition lodged with the Court of Session, the petitioners argued that the constitution of the burgh had been infringed on the grounds that the vacancy should not have been filled until after the new council had been elected. In the sett, the words, 'first of all' are used in connection with the filling of a vacancy, but the petitioners argued that those words implied that it was the first thing the new council should do after the election and before the election of the office bearers. However, if the old council elected the new member as its last act before electing the new council, that could mean that the new councillor might not be elected to the new and only be a councillor for the short period between the two events in the election meeting. That was clearly an anomaly, but the Court of Session rejected the petition. In the event it seems that the case never went ahead, although the petitioners had incurred some £15 with the agent who was to pursue their case.

In order to avoid a similar problem arising again, the rules were revised in advance of the following year's election. The solution was fairly simple. Instead of candidates withdrawing two by two, which could result in a minority winning, it was agreed that in future each member of the old council standing for re-election should withdraw individually, starting with the provost, followed by the remainder in order of precedence.

Dissatisfaction with the role of the council was not new. The council elected itself and many of its deliberations were conducted in secret, something that is not unheard of in modern times. One of the matters of concern to the public, was that the magistrates could serve for an indefinite period and be elected again and again. To its credit the council in Peebles was sensitive to public opinion and in 1771 a committee was appointed to look into the matter. It failed to come up with a solution at that time, but a few years later in 1779, just before the annual election, recognising the need to satisfy the concerns of the townsfolk, the council decided that there should be some limitation on the length of service. The provost should not serve for more than five years and in order to ensure that "new blood" was regularly admitted, no longer than two years should elapse without at least one of the councillors being replaced. That was enlightened thinking and very much to the improvement of democracy in the town.

The ownership of the various lands and properties owned by the town, the "Common Good", has been a concern to the people of Peebles throughout its long history. It remains so to this day. In 1769 the council granted a feu of two areas of ground forming part of Tweed Green. They were granted to Bailie Kerr, seemingly ignoring a possible conflict of interest. The feus were probably situated at the east end of the Green. It provoked a sizeable protest by 34 burgesses, traders and merchants, who presented a petition to the council. One of the feus was for a distillery, to which there was no objection, provided that was its sole purpose. The other was for a pig stye and that was totally unacceptable. The petition asked the council to confirm that after due consideration and taking proper legal advice, the Green could not be given away or feued to any individual member of the community, as it had been held for the benefit of 'the Good of the Whole Community in General'. The council responded with a lengthy and reasoned document which rejected the petition.

The petitioners had argued that the Green had always been used for drying and bleaching clothes and also for penning cattle and sheep at the time of public fairs. They also noted that 'a certain noble Lord' who owned property in the High Street with a garden bordering the Green, had been refused a feu of a small piece of ground as an addition to his garden. It was likely to have been Lord March who at that time owned a house which is now part of the Chambers Institution. They also mentioned that another adjacent householder had been refused permission to make a doorway opening on to the Green. In response the council replied that 'the noble lord' had actually wanted most of the Green and not just a small part. It also pointed out that at the time the feus had been granted, some of the petitioners were members of the council and questioned why they raised their complaint now. It added that the first to sign the petition had himself a door at the bottom of his garden for which he had never been given permission. There was clearly a degree of hypocrisy in the air!

The council further defended its decision by saying that the land feued to Bailie Kerr was part of the green that had never been used for bleaching clothes and also that he had paid a price which was greatly above the current value of land. They concluded by accusing the petitioners of using the case to disturb the spirit of 'concord and friendship' that prevailed in the burgh, 'which all good men must behold with abhorrence'. Strong words, but Buchan concludes that in fact the council had acted illegally. In later times up to the present there has been a number of settled cases which confirm that Common Good land cannot be disposed of unless for a purpose that benefits the community.

Not all of the actions of the council provoked a negative response. There is ample evidence that it was sensitive to the problems of the townsfolk, particularly those in poverty. One of the effects of trade remaining in the doldrums and of continuing austerity was the high price of grain and throughout the country food riots had become common.

Peebles did not escape. A large part of the population was in poverty and in 1793 the council decided that it should compile a register of all those in distress, so that money collected for their relief could be fairly distributed. The finances of the burgh were at a low ebb, while the price of meal was high.

In 1796 there was a notable riot in the town. One of the leaders was May Ingram. She was a lady of some spirit and was the cause of a major disturbance, so much so that the Guildry Corporation made it known to the council that its members were scandalised by the behaviour of May and her followers and that they would use their authority to prevent any of their members or their families from joining the rioters. May was the wife of a weaver called John Donald, although in the fashion of the time she went by her maiden name. She lived on the top floor of a building in the High Street, one of those with an outside stair, opposite where the Tontine Hotel stands today. She was therefore very much at the centre of things.

At a time when meal was both expensive and in short supply, it was alleged that some farmers were hoarding large supplies, so that they could sell when the market price rose to its peak. May Ingram emerged as the champion of the poor and their challenger. The Rev Alex Williamson tells the story:

> She appeared one day in the High Street with a girdle in the left hand and a porridge stick in the right, and by loud and not very refined exhortations gathered a mob, at the head of which she marched to Chapelhill, where, however, nothing was to be found: next to Edston, which was searched in vain also, till an incident occurred that crowned her efforts with success. A servant maid had compassion on two hungry looking boys, to whom she gave bread and milk. As they were coming out, one of the party, John Salton, pushed open a door to see what was inside. A large "ark" or meal chest was revealed, the crowd was at once summoned, and the contents distributed. Sacks were filled with meal, the horse was unyoked from the harrows in a field where it was working, and the "booty" was brought to Peebles, where it was offered to the Sheriff at 3s 9d a peck; the farmer wanted, it seems, 4s. The Sheriff would not give him the sum, and was threatened with prosecution by the farmer (Mr Somerville) who vented his displeasure on the people of Peebles. The sacks, it is said, lay and rotted in the meal market.

May remained a colourful figure. Williamson says that in her old age she wore a white mutch[195] with black edges. She had strong arms and a sharp

---

195   Traditional head wear of a country woman.

tongue with a temper to match. It was said that 'she was not easily pacified when the spirit was in her'.

As the story of May Ingram demonstrates, the situation was serious. Among the "mob" who supported her would be many cottars and their families from the surrounding countryside, who could no longer support themselves and were coming into the town in the hope of better things. Naturally it was the cause of considerable anger and discontent among the townsfolk. Farmers were being blamed for making the situation worse. Many preferred to sell their meal to dealers in the Lothians who would pay a higher price, rather than to the townsfolk.

At last in March 1796, the council decided to act. It thought that the best solution would be for the town to buy the meal from the farmers and then sell it on to the townsfolk. It would be sold on at cost price, but those who were on the poor register, would pay a reduced price. The provost called a meeting with the farmers who were agreeable. However, they were concerned that there was public hostility to them and they asked that every effort be made to 'ensure their safety and a proper behaviour towards them when bringing meal into the town.'

The provost called a meeting with the dean of guild and the Boxmasters[196] (treasurers) of the guilds. He read out a letter from the council in which it regretted that the farmers were being threatened with fire and robbery by 'a number of thoughtless and idle people'. The letter was quite explicit. It read:

> That prices are at a most unheard of height is a melancholy truth, and felt all over the country, but do you expect farmers will supply you at one fourth less price than they can get at their own door with thanks? Do you go and offer to work at less wages than you can get, or sell your own articles at five shillings when offered seven without any trouble or risk?.......Without concurrence of our inhabitants you cannot expect magistrates will exert themselves either for your safety or protection. So, seriously weigh the consequences.

That very reasonable approach by the council seems to have been effective. The meal was bought and duly distributed. Old people were given a fixed amount of meal free, while the remaining poor were supplied at a price which was one fifth below cost price. Even May Ingram would have been satisfied.

Education then as now was a matter of concern to the whole community. In the last decade of the eighteenth century, Scotland could

---

196   Treasurers

boast of one of the best systems and quality in Europe. In Peebles, there were both public and private schools. In 1794 there were at least 250 pupils being educated in the town, some from far outside Peebles, which would seem to indicate that the town had a significant reputation as a place of learning. It was said that those external pupils contributed more than £2000 a year to the local economy in school fees and the purchase of food and clothing.

There were three private schools, one run exclusively for girls. Dr Williamson describes all of them as "adventure schools"[197] and says that they were well attended and that they paid particular attention to deportment and to the 'more ornamental parts of education.' It is perhaps an indication that "a polite society" was now evolving in the town as it clawed its way back from the depression of the earlier years of the century, just as it was in other parts of Scotland, especially in the capital city of Edinburgh, where the world of the genteel people of an ever more enlightened and literary society was taking centre stage in the drawing rooms of the New Town.

In July 1796, Miss Marion Watson, who ran one of the schools, asked for an increase in salary as she had, 'keept a school for teaching girls sewing and other parts of education' and had done so for two years. She was however concerned that it would have an effect on poorer children who could ill afford increased fees. As she said they would be deprived of 'that education they so much stand in need of.' Clearly a lady of good social conscience!

An advertisement which appeared around that time for a schoolmistress for the town, gives an insight into what was expected of them. The applicants were to be properly qualified to teach 'sewing, white seam, coloured work and the other branches of female education.' The salary was to be £10 per annum and the advertisement added that, 'a well qualified and diligent teacher might depend on good encouragement.'

There was a number of applicants. One of them, promised to send 'her moral character and abilities by Respectable Persons.' Another, who had friends in Peebles, wrote that she noted 'in Mondye's papers' that the applicant was to be 'wel qualified to thatch white seme and corlad worck.' Standard spelling, even of the time, was not her strong point! Yet another was keen to gain the appointment and hoped by 'constant application and

---

[197]   These were unregulated and often set up by parents. The teachers were unlicensed. In some towns the kirk session might try to have them closed, because they drew pupils away from the parish schools but in Peebles they seem to have been accepted as part of the education system.

attention,' to have the approval of 'her friends'. She added that she would be happy to teach writing and reading, adding, 'as it gives an opportunity of improving the mind.' The successful applicant was a Miss Dove who had worked as a governess for families 'of high respectability'.

In 1796 Mr James Gray, then the English School master asked for his salary to be increased. He said that he had taught reading, writing and arithmetic from the beginning of his appointment in 1776 and for twenty years thereafter. He seems to have been paid at a rate per head of the pupils, starting at one shilling per quarter and rising in 1782 to one shilling and sixpence. The council agreed to raise the fees by a further six pence.

In 1804, another James Gray was appointed as master of the English School. Although he hailed from Dundee he may have been a relative of the previous James Gray. In his letter accepting the appointment he mentions his 'attachment to the good town of Peebles for various reasons.' He seems to have been particularly skilled in arithmetic and had written a book on the subject, which was in general use for many years. However, whatever his merits as a student of arithmetic, he seems to have been less able in controlling the large number of pupils who attended his classes. William Chambers suggests that he had a liking for alcohol and that far too often as a consequence he amused his pupils rather than teaching them.

Schooling was not confined to literacy, numeracy and the 'more ornamental parts' of education. At about this time a Mr James Turnbull came to the town to teach dancing. It is not known where he initially held his classes. Wherever it was, it was not very satisfactory. Parents complained, children complained and ultimately, Mr Turnbull himself had had enough and asked the council to provide him with suitable accommodation. It was agreed to the let "the Ballroom" to him for 5s per month. The holding of balls was becoming quite common. There had been a "ballroom" in the Northgate and that may have been where Mr Turnbull originally held his classes. By 1807, a ballroom had been established in the new building which formed an extension to the rear of the Town House, which subsequently became the Corn Exchange in 1860. There is a report of a ball being held there by the Yeomanry Cavalry in December that year. It is probable that Mr Turnbull now held his classes in this new ballroom. It also seems that a ball was held by the farmers each year in October, as there is a reference to it being cancelled in 1803, 'on account of the imminent danger of invasion', as it was the time of the Napoleonic Wars with France.

The wearing of wigs and powdering of hair by the more affluent members of society had become common by the end of the eighteenth century. Although an expensive luxury and a mark of one's position in society, it did give employment to hairdressers and barbers, who often plied their trade in the houses of their clients. As early as 1712, the council authorised John Law to undertake wig making in the town. Samuel Thomson already held that privilege and no doubt the council acted to avoid a monopoly situation.

Taken together, schooling, dancing and the attention to personal appearance confirmed by portraits of the time, demonstrate that by the turn of the century there was in Scotland an emerging social stratum, below the level of the nobility, which now had sufficient disposable income to allow them a greater choice in the education of their children and their personal appearance and dress. On all the evidence there was at least a minority of the citizens of Peebles who were part of that social improvement.

The church remained very much at the centre of social life. During Dr Dalgleish's time, the Sabbath Day remained the most important of the week with attendance at church by the whole community, a matter, not of choice, but of obligation. The Rev Alex Williamson paints a picture of those days, when the 'jowin' of the auld kirk bell' summoned the faithful and indeed the less faithful to worship:

> People pore out of houses and from the closes of the High Street, Northgate, Old Town, and Briggait. Some of the principal burgesses, "men of light and leading", wear pigtails hanging over the collars of their blue coats, top boots, knee-breeches, buckles, vest of bright colours, frilled shirt fronts, and cuffs. Others are in coarser garments – men with flat round bonnets; elderly women with squinny mutches, carrying their bibles with a sprig of southernwood or wild thyme laid out on a folded pocket handkerchief white as the driven snow. The country contingent arrive, some on foot, others on horseback, with their female folk, wives or daughters sitting on pillions behind them, unable to dismount till the "loupin'-on stane" is reached; others again in strange, lumbering vehicles, which are left at the Cross Keys till the service is over. All wend their way across the high arched Cuddy Bridge.....or across the "Tree Brig" at the end of the Briggait, or, by Biggies Knowe from the Old Town foot, or by the narrow lane from the head of the Old Town. The provost and Magistrates in state proceed to their "loft" – recently repaired – and Mr Oman's and Mr Brown's scholars march two and two in solemn silence to their proper places under the eagle eyes of the teachers.

The history of the Protestant religion from its very beginnings in 1517 has been a catalogue of disputation and dissension. Its guiding light from the beginning has been the Bible, the Word of God, but how that word has been interpreted and by whom, over the centuries has resulted in a multitude of branches, sects and cults. There have been fanatics and martyrs, each and all of them claiming to be preaching the one and only true message of the Bible.

It might be thought that after the establishment of the Church of Scotland, as a unified and Presbyterian national church, all was settled, but it was far from being the case. Setting aside fundamental differences with Roman Catholicism and Episcopalianism, there was division within Presbyterianism.

Within the Church of Scotland, quite apart from differences on theological and liturgical grounds, there were also disputes concerning the government of the Kirk. At the same time as murmurings of discontent were stirring, the General Assembly supported the right of patrons to present their choices of ministers. In 1732 it passed an Act which prohibited the election of ministers by congregations. That produced an immediate reaction. The Rev Ebenezer Erskine, minister of Stirling, preached a sermon against the Act. The following year, together with three other ministers, he was thrown out of the Church of Scotland. They became known as the "Secession Fathers" and formed themselves into a separate Presbytery. In 1744, by which time they had a large following, they formed themselves into "the Associate Synod", which was entirely outwith the national church.[198]

In the coming years their numbers increased considerably with congregations spread throughout the country. In 1755 a Secession congregation was established in Peebles and in 1797 a building called the Gytes Meeting House was erected. It was a plain and simple building situated at the east end of Tweed Green, built in the austere style favoured by non-conformists. The first minister was Thomas Leckie, who remained as minister until his death in 1821. He was a popular preacher and soon had built up a reasonable congregation. In 1794 the Statistical Account of the Parish of Peebles gives the number of members as 61. Small as it was, the congregation must have gathered sufficient resources to build a manse on the slope facing the Tweed Green, close to the site of today's Leckie St Andrew's Church

---

[198]   This became known as the "First Secession"

Thomas Leckie had a large family, 13 in all and no doubt on account of the small size of his congregation, his stipend was small and life would have been austere. None the less, when they grew up many of his family prospered. In 1871, his son Charles Leckie died after a successful business career in India. At that time the old meeting house was in a poor state. At his funeral his remaining brothers came up with the idea of a church being built in memory of their father. They agreed to donate the area of ground on which St Andrews Leckie Church stands today and in addition they agreed to jointly contribute towards the cost of the new building which was to be called the Leckie Memorial Church.

36.
The First Statistical Account of Scotland

Although the history of Scotland and its people had been recorded in a multitude of documents, papers and publications, there had been no attempt to draw an accurate picture of the country, but in 1794 a major exercise was carried out to document the state of the land, its soil and usage; the numbers and types of animal; population, its age and employment and industry and commerce in each parish. It was called the *Statistical Account of Scotland* and was drawn up by the ministers of each parish throughout the country. *The Statistical Account of the Parish of Peebles* was written by Dr Dalgleish.

Dr Gunn and others have been somewhat disparaging of Dr Dalgleish's skills as a historian and the Peebles Parish Account is a fairly thin record, although it does contain a number of important, interesting facts and observations. Unfortunately the following statistics may be far from accurate and are probably a considerable underestimate.

According to Dr Dalgleish, the total number of people of all ages living within the parish in 1791 was 1920, with the following distribution :

In the Old Town	350
In the New Town	1130
Landward area of parish	440
	1920

The age distribution was:

Under 5 years of age,	263		
From 5 to 10	284	From 50 to 60	158
10 to 20	365	60 to 70	164
20 to 30	258	70 to 80	50
30 to 40	192	80 to 90	8
40 to 50	176	90 to 100	2
			1920

Other statistics of note were that there were 61 members of Seceeder and Free Church congregations, looked after by one minister, while there was one minister of the established church. The average number of marriages over the previous 12 years was only 12 per annum, while in the same period average annual births were 56 and burials 52.

What is perhaps remarkable to modern eyes is that at that time there were as many as 60 people aged more than 70 years and 2 more than 90. Dr Dalgleish's narrative goes on to say, 'The inhabitants of the parish, in town and country, are generally healthy, and live many of them to very advanced age. Lately there were 6 men living at the same time within fifty yards of one another, in the Old Town of Peebles, whose ages together amounted to 518 years, and who, several of them died near 100 years.'

In an age when the treatment of disease and the virtual elimination of some is taken for granted, it may come as a surprise to find that inoculation against smallpox was common place. Dr Dalgleish records that:

Inoculation has been practised for many years in this county by able surgeons, with great success, and becomes more and more general. Above a thousand have been inoculated, without one dying. Nay, some parents have even inoculated their children themselves, and have perfectly succeeded.[199]

Agriculture played a prominent part in the economy of the parish. According to Dr Dalgleish, commenting on modern improvements in housing and trade and industry he records that:

Formerly Peebles was supported by the houses and burgh acres belonging to the burgesses, by their merchandise and their trade and by valuable commonties granted by the kings of Scotland to the burgh for its loyalty and good services. Now, improvements begin to be carried on upon a larger scale. Of late years, about fifty houses have been built or thoroughly repaired. Woollen, linen, and cottar weavers are making greater exertions, and larger houses are built for them.

---

[199] The first recognised use of a vaccine against smallpox was attributed to Edward Jenner, an English doctor, in 1796. However, before that time a crude form of vaccination was already being practised. Dairymaids often contracted cowpox, but thereafter appeared to be immune to the much more serious and frequently fatal disease of smallpox. It had been discovered that immunity could transferred by scraping a cowpox scab and transferring the scrapings and so infecting the recipient with cowpox, which in turn gave that person immunity. It is likely that this is the process to which Dr Dalgleish referred.

Excellent mills for flour, barley and corn had been provided for a long time by the town council, who had also provided a fulling mill for the town's growing textile industries.

Dr James Hay, the laird of Haystoun had built a lint mill[200]for the use of the whole county, while Mr William Ker of Kerfield had built a brewery and distillery, which represented a great improvement in the art of brewing, 'Perceiving a part of the fine effluvia of the hop to fly off during the boiling of the worts, he contrived a most ingenious and effectual method of preserving it.' What he did was to cover the top of his "copper", the vessel used for the liquid with a close-fitting lid, fitted with a copper pipe leading down from it, which passed through cold water. The steam emerging was then condensed and led into to a collecting vessel, where any oil from the hops was skimmed off and returned to the worts once boiling was completed. A third of the hops was saved by this process and the moist, aromatic part of it was retained, which gave the beer a finer flavour. It also prevented it from becoming sour, so that it could be kept longer, while retaining flavour. Mr Ker had also produced a plan for a woollen factory of modern design which was for general use.

As a result of the significant 'increases of trade and opulence', the wages of all kinds of labourers had increased by a third over the previous twenty years. Dr Dalgleish adds that:

All classes are better educated, better lodged, better clothed and fed than in former years. It is also happy for those in the lower classes, that though Peebles is the thoroughfare for oatmeal, carried from the richer corn country on the east, to the mining and manufacturing country on the west, yet the average price of this meal for twenty years past, has not exceeded 9d or at most 10d the peck;[201]and it is a received maxim, that while a labourer can earn a peck of oatmeal in a day, he will, in common cases be able to support his family.

So it becomes clear that as the eighteenth century drew to a close, the economic circumstances were at last improving and that the worst of times were a thing of the past. There were however events on the wider stage of Great Britain and Europe, which would for a time arrest further progress.

The eighteenth century saw perhaps the greatest progress that has taken place in the development of agricultural practice, until the modern era. In

---

200   Lint is a soft fleecy material used for poultices and dressings for wounds and made from linen usually by scraping.
201   A dry measure equivalent to 2 imperial gallons or 8 dry quarts.

England improvement in cultivation and in the quality of livestock had been on the march since the middle of the previous century, but in Scotland farming practice had remained virtually unchanged for centuries. Holdings were small and cultivated land consisted of little more than narrow strips known as run-rigs. Pasture was generally poor quality, dependant on natural herbage. Outwith the burghs, land was in the hands of large landowners and lairds, whose lands were farmed by small tenants and cottars.

Following the Union of 1707, there was a significant increase in communication with the southern partner. Lords and lairds travelled south to attend parliament in London and to engage in commerce. The contrast between the management of agricultural land in the two former kingdoms was stark and travellers to London passing through prosperous farming lands would have noted enclosed acres of abundant cereal and fodder crops, compared to the meagre rigs of oats and bere found in Scotland. They would also have noted cattle and sheep far bigger than those they left behind. They would have seen that whereas in Scotland, cultivation still involved the use of a primitive wooden plough pulled by a team of oxen, in England new iron ploughs pulled by two horses were in use and a system of crop rotation which maintained soil fertility was being practised. It was those landowners and lairds who returned to Scotland and who together with their more enlightened tenants, set in motion a revolution in farming methods. It included enclosure of land and the introduction of new crops such as turnips and cabbages and the sowing of rye grass to provide improved grazing. Potatoes had been established for some time, but improved methods of cultivation and fertilisation gave much better yields. By the end of the century, much of the Lothians, Angus and parts of Ayrshire, as noted by Professor Tom Devine, had become 'a byeword across Europe for "state of the art" arable agricultur'[202]

The Royal Burgh of Peebles was of course the centre for the marketing of agricultural produce from the whole county, but the town also had a direct interest in agriculture. Its common lands were extensive and in addition to grazings extending into the neighbouring hills, much of the land bordering the town was cultivated by burgesses. Those working as labourers and weavers supplemented their meagre earnings by grazing a cow on the common grazings. On a daily basis cows were released from their byres and driven out to the common grazings by the town herd, who announced the time of departure by blowing an ox horn. The majority of

---

[202] T.M.Devine – *The Scottish Clearances* P 143.

the inhabitants were dependant on agriculture and urban pursuits in almost equal proportion. In the wider parish there were cottars who depended entirely for their livelihood on agriculture. The *Statistical Account* of 1794 provides clear evidence that by that time modern developments in agriculture were beginning to take effect in the parish:

> Improvements of late years made a rapid progress in the parish of Peebles:1500 acres are already enclosed. There are 700 acres more of infield ground, a great part of which will be enclosed in a short time. Of outfield ground, which is sometimes in tillage, but more commonly in natural grass, for pasturing cows and horses, there are 800 acres. The other land, being hilly, afford excellent pasture for sheep, and are employed for this purpose.

On account of the quality of the soil, the Peebles grey pea grown in the parish, 'has long been in high estimation all over the country for feed.' Because of the warm soil, oats are also highly regarded and make 'excellent feed for lands that are higher and colder.'

Potatoes had by then been an established crop since the middle of the seventeenth century. As the *Statistical Account* says it is, 'the most useful root ever imported into this, or any other country' and that, 'they are nowhere cultivated with more care, and raised in greater excellence than at Peebles.' The planting of the crop seems to have been a shared activity. The owner or occupier of the ground would divide it up into parcels of 110 to 120 square yards.[203] It would be rented out, but the proprietor himself would plough, manure the ground and plant the potatoes. He would benefit from the cleaning and fertilisation of the ground in addition to receiving rent in exchange for his labour. In a system which also provided an important social benefit, he would be assisted by cottars or small tenants, who would provide the dung and feed, help with cleaning the ground and planting the potatoes and would hoe them and dig them after their regular working hours, 'which contributes to their health, and have their potatoes for half of the price at which they could otherwise purchase them, and which, to many families, furnish a third part of their subsistence at a very cheap rate.'

Improvement was not confined to land and crops. Selective breeding had also begun to produce livestock of much better quality. In the parish as a whole, there were 200 horses, 500 cows and about 8000 sheep. Both horses and cows were, 'both much better than in former times.'

---

203   About two and a half acres.

The sheep were still generally the traditional Border type and new breeds had not yet been introduced, but 'by their being kept fewer in number, and being better fed, they are much improved in quality.' As a result of all those improvements, the rental value of the parish had doubled in the previous twenty years and was now seven times what it had been in 1681.

Possibly as a consequence of improved economic conditions in agriculture and particularly the improvement in the quality and value of livestock, sheep stealing was becoming a problem. The theft of cattle and sheep, "reiving", had up until the start of the seventeenth century, been almost endemic in parts of the Borders, although it never seems to have been a problem that affected Tweeddale to any extent. However, Robert Chambers tells of a curious case in 1772 within the county, which involved a remarkable sheep dog. The story was that a farmer called Murdison had been stealing sheep from his neighbours for several years, but had remained undetected. A ewe which had gone missing from the farm of Newby, after a time reappeared on the farm, but it now had a second brand on its face. The actual circumstances of its re-appearance were unusual. It seems that the ewe had been separated from her lamb and returned in search of her offspring. That she did so was quite strange, because it subsequently turned out that not only had she travelled a distance, but she had also managed to cross the Tweed. James Hislop, the Newby shepherd, immediately reported the re-appearance to his master, Mr Gibson, who was soon able to establish that the second brand belonged to a Mr Murdison. Newby had lost quite a number of sheep and Hislop was sent to Murdison's farm to investigate. There he discovered a large number of sheep all bearing Mr Gibson's brand, over which Murdison's had been added. Murdison and his shepherd, Miller were arrested, tried and hanged in the Grassmarket in Edinburgh. There was a further twist to the story. The success of the crime turned out to be due to the exceptional senses of Miller's dog Yarrow. Miller made a habit of paying social calls on his neighbours farms. It was claimed that all he needed to do was point to a particular sheep or sheep and the dog would return at night, round up the animals which had been pointed out and drive them back to Murdison's farm, even when necessary driving them across the Tweed. According to Chambers, who in fact doubted the story, it was rumoured that the dog was also hanged as a dangerous predator.

37.
Characters

By the end of the eighteenth century, we begin to see first hand pen portraits of some of the more interesting characters who lived through that time. Several are mentioned by Dr Alex Williamson, in his *Glimpses of Peebles*. He had been born in Peebles in 1833 and when writing his book in 1895, he would have known many people whose first hand memories might have easily stretched back into the previous two or three decades of the previous century, so the picture he paints of those characters is clearly authentic. One mentioned by him and also by William Chambers, was Robert Brown, who was known as "Beni Minori". He was a travelling showman, who carried about a "raree show". It was a sort of peep show, contained in a wooden box with one or more holes through which people could look (after a suitable payment). They usually contained pictures set up to resemble theatrical scenes, which the operator could manipulate, while giving a recitation telling the story illustrated.

Beni claimed to have been born in London in 1737. In his early years he had been a post boy and then for a time a sailor, spending some time in a French prison and then as an adventurer in the West Indies, before becoming an entertainer, travelling throughout England and Scotland. His visits to Peebles, particularly at the time of fairs, were very popular and apparently attracted large crowds of both young and old. He died in the Edinburgh Charity Workhouse in 1840, at the ripe old age of 103.

Another was Andrew Gemmell, who was a licensed beggar who travelled around Peeblesshire and the neighbouring counties of Selkirk and Roxburgh. Licensed beggars or "king's bedesmen" as they were called, had existed in Scotland since the fifteenth century. They carried a badge which allowed them to move freely throughout the country and also qualified them to receive alms. They generally moved from farm to farm, usually staying overnight in the barn. Those who were better known were often made welcome in the farm house or cottage. Their visits were especially appreciated because they brought with them news of the happenings in the wider world and were often the only source of such information.

As was the usual practice, Andrew Gemmell wore a blue gown, with his badge attached and carried a staff and a meal "pock" or bag carried in his hand in which to collect meal and other food offered to him. He seems to have been very welcome at the farm of Newby just outside Peebles. He was an accomplished player of the game of draughts and taught Mrs Gibson, "the guid wife" how to play. She however, became an able pupil and on one occasion another visitor backed her to defeat Gemmell for a guinea. When it seemed that she would beat him, he was not pleased and in a fit of anger picked up the board and threw the draughts into the ash pit. Sir Walter Scott based his character of Edie Ochiltree on him in his novel *The Antiquary*.

Two more of the characters who appear in novels by Scott are based on real people living in or about Peebles. Those are David Ritchie (Bow'd Davie of Wudhus) who was the origin of his character "Elshender the Recluse" in *The Black Dwarf* and Marion Ritchie who appears as Meg Dods, the proprietress of the Cleikum Inn in *St Ronan's Wells*.

David Ritchie was born at the farm of Easter Happrew in 1741. He was deformed and misshapen from birth. In adulthood, he had immense strength. In his introduction to *The Black Dwarf*, Sir Walter Scott, who met him on at least one occasion, describes how he built the cottage at Woodhouse in Manor valley, known as the "Black Dwarf's Cottage", which still stands to this day:

> The cottage which he built was extremely small, but the walls, as well as those of the little garden that surrounded it, were constructed with an ambitious degree of solidarity, being composed of layers of large stones and turf; and some of the corner stones were so weighty as to puzzle the spectators how such a person as the architect could have possibly raised them

There is a very large stone built into the roadside wall about quarter of a mile from Manor Village which is said to have been carried there by him. It is known as the "Black Dwarf's stone." It is however, questionable whether Ritchie, strong as he was, could have carried such a large stone and placed it there. It is more likely that is a monolith from a much earlier era, although the fact that it forms part of a stone wall adjacent to the public road, seems coincidental!

Sadly Ritchie does not seem to have been a pleasant character. Robert Chambers, who would have had personal knowledge of him, says that, 'A jealous, misanthropical, and irritable temper was his most prominent characteristic.' He had a very large head with long hair. His feet were twisted, while his legs were very short and his body was large and fat. His face was sour and angry. He did not wear any shoes and his toes were exposed. Rumour also had it that he had mystical powers. In fairness to the poor man, it seems that he was the butt of insults and ridicule on account of his ugly appearance, from his earliest days working in Edinburgh as a brush maker, which caused him to leave the city and take refuge in Manor Valley. Unfortunately, although in his cottage and garden he may have found some peace, when he came into Peebles as he often did to buy provisions and made his way across the Tweed Bridge and along the High Street, according to Williamson, he was 'followed and hooted by a band of boys, who kept well out of the reach of his long heavy stick, for his temper was fierce and his arm was powerful.' On one occasion when he was in Peebles for his fortnightly shave, the barber shaved only one side of his face. When he returned to the street the usual band of tormentors saw this and told him of his ridiculous appearance. As soon as he realised what had happened he ran back in a fury with every intention of killing the practical joker, who fortunately made his escape through the back door. He died in December 1811 and is buried in Manor churchyard. A statue of him stands in the grounds of Hallyards House.

One other "character" of a completely different kind was William Douglas, 3rd Earl of March and 4th Duke of Queensberry. He has a place in the story of Peebles because he was born in the Royal Burgh at Queensberry Lodging on 16th December 1725, the son of William Douglas 2nd Earl of March and Lady Anne Hamilton. He succeeded his father to the earldom of March in 1731 making him the principal landowner and heritor of the parish. He became Duke of Queensberry in 1778 on the death of his cousin. He was known as "Old Q", and was clearly a colourful, if somewhat disreputable character. He never married but has been described as a disgusting old lecher, with a liking for young girls. Dr Williamson has this description of him :

> He was long one of the leaders of fashion and he acquired an unenviable notoriety by the unblushing manner in which he practised his vices. His long life was a career of selfishness and profligacy. Thackeray mentions him by name in *The Virginians* as a lover of gambling, horse-racing, and as a roué.

He does not seem to have paid much attention to Peebles after his early years, although when the new church was completed in 1784, there was a dispute because he had not been given a pew. One was eventually provided in spite of the likelihood that it would rarely if ever, be used by his Grace.

In 1795, in order to prevent his successor from enjoying the ancient yews at Neidpath, he had them and other trees cut down. Robert Chambers commented that, 'The wholesale stripping of his lands of centuries of growth was neither more nor less than greedy vandalism.' It was certainly something which infuriated the poet William Wordsworth when he visited the castle in 1803. It prompted the following verses from him:

> *Degenerate Douglas! Oh, the unworthy lord!*
> *When mere despite of heart could so far please,*
> *And love of havoc (for with such disease*
> *Fame taxes him) that he could send forth word*
> *To level with the dust a noble horde,*
> *A brotherhood of venerable trees,*
> *Leaving an ancient Dome and Towers like these*
> *Beggar'd and outraged! Many hearts deplored*
> *The fate of those old trees, and oft with pain*
> *The traveller at this day will stop and gaze.*[204]

When asked by the provost to subscribe to the fund which was set up in 1800 to buy meal for the destitute, he failed to respond. He died on 23rd December 1810, presumably not much lamented by the town of his birth.

---

[204]   Extract from Dorothy Wordsworth - *Recollection of a Tour Made in Scotland A.D. 1803*

38.
War and Peace

As the eighteenth century was drawing to a close there was turmoil in Europe. In 1789 France had been plunged into a revolution which destroyed the monarchy and replaced with it with a republic. Ten years earlier the United States had gained independence and had also established a republic. In Britain too, reform of the political system was being debated. Even before the start of the French Revolution, there was a climate of unrest in Scotland. Poverty and a general dissatisfaction with parliamentary rule raised hopes that reform could make a better life for the "common weal". Slavery and its abolition was also a matter of concern.

It is evident that those issues touched Peebles. On 21st March 1792 a letter was sent by the council to the parliamentary representative asking him to support the movement to abolish the African slave trade. In its letter the council noted that it seemed 'to be the general wish of the Inhabitants of Britain, and as that Traffic is so contrary to humanity.'

That same year, an organisation called the "Society of the Freedom of the People" was set up. It had many branches and gave a platform to some of the wilder elements who advocated constitutional reform. According to Williamson it had its adherents in Peebles:

> It is well known that the wild opinions which were floated about found favour in the quiet burgh town, and that certain politicians embraced them as, in their belief, favourable to what they styled "liberty". There were those persons who casting off religion altogether, burned the Bible: and it is said that several on a Communion Sabbath sacrificed a calf in a sequestered spot about Venlaw. But these people formed a small minority, and were regarded with horror by the rest of the community.

Minority or not, the council were clearly concerned by the current state of affairs. At its meeting on 15th December 1792, it discussed the 'Seditions, writings and open efforts of turbulent and designing men for subversion of our present in favour of republican government by holding out as bait for idle and thoughtless people the very extraordinary idea of equality in rank and property.' To further emphasise its views it was agreed to minute the following:

That they venerate and support the British Constitution because it equally secures the life and property of every individual, and by it the Country has arrived at an envied state of opulence and manufacture.

These are fine words and perhaps overlook the fact that in practice a "state of opulence" was not necessarily enjoyed by all the citizens of Peebles at a time when the local economy was still suffering from the decline of earlier decades.

The minute continued :

That when real grievances are sensibly felt they trust to the cautious hand of a prudent legislature – and not the Levelling hand of mock patriots: That they give every aid for the support of good order, countenancing the sober, peaceable and industrious of all occupations, but marking with distinguished neglect and suspicious observance the idle, disorderly and seditious.

Following this the council called a general meeting of the burgesses and sent out a letter to the various crafts and trades in the town setting out its views broadly as recorded in the minute. It emphasised the dangers of heeding political activists who advocated anarchy and revolution. Those were people they described as 'designing rogues and political blunderers'. The letter concluded by saying that:

We as a Magistracy wish the countenance and concurrence of every prudent member of the community for preserving the liberty and property of all, and submit it whether you should not publicly declare and subscribe your opinion against all violent innovations, tumultuous meetings and seditious publications.

They were views which were presumably endorsed by the majority of the inhabitants. In adopting those sentiments the town and its council were following precedents which had governed it for centuries, namely adhering to the general rule of the nation and its government of whatever complexion.

The French Revolution which, following shortly thereafter, did have its consequences for the town. The new republic had embarked on a war with Great Britain and the Netherlands in February 1793. As it progressed, the possibility of invasion caused alarm throughout the country. In response, the government introduced a Militia Act in 1796, which called for volunteers and the council duly played its part. In November of that year it offered twenty guineas to the first three able-bodied men to volunteer. Unfortunately it did not have the intended effect and a year later there is evidence that there was a great deal of opposition to the legislation not only in Peebles, but throughout the country and a public fund was set up to offer further incentives. As will be seen, a few years later things had changed and as the Revolutionary Wars evolved into the Napoleonic Wars, with their very real threat of invasion, significant numbers took up duties in the Volunteer Yeomanry Cavalry and the Volunteer Infantry.

While the possibility of a French invasion remained a concern, the recent influx of large numbers of immigrants from Ireland, where the economic circumstances were even worse than in Scotland, was also a problem. The newcomers were generally not popular and Peebles in common with other Scottish burghs, disliked them. Rightly or wrongly, their standards and mode of living were seen as being a corrupting influence. The rules regarding who might come to live in the town were already strict, but in 1798 in response to the threat, the council gave instructions to the town's officers to 'prevent suspicious persons' from staying in the burgh.

The years that followed would see a general improvement in all aspects in the life of the Royal Burgh and its people. The worst days were over and a new era was dawning which would ultimately transform the whole country.

39.
Into the Modern Era - 1800 - 1850

At the beginning of the nineteenth century, Britain remained at war with France, a conflict renewed more vigorously in 1803 with the advent of Napoleon as its leader and Emperor of France. It would continue until his final defeat at the battle of Waterloo.

During the next fifty years four monarchs would occupy the throne of Great Britain and Ireland. By 1800 George III had already reigned for forty years. He died in 1820, the longest reigning monarch in British history up until that time. He was succeeded by his son George IV who had been Regent when his father was mentally incapacitated. He died in 1830 and was succeeded by his brother, William IV, who in turn died in 1837, to be succeeded by his niece Victoria. Her reign would come to symbolise a new age of industrial, technical, literary, artistic and social development.

The next fifty years would see the careers of some of the great names in British history reach their zenith. To name but a few, in engineering Thomas Telford, George Stephenson and Isambard Kingdom Brunel; in technology Michael Faraday and James Clerk Maxwell; in literature, a host of names including Sir Walter Scott, the Bronte Sisters and Charles Dickens: in architecture, Alexander "Greek" Thomson and David Bryce; in social development William Wilberforce, championing the abolition of slavery and John Howard in prison reform; in military affairs, the Duke of Wellington and in politics, Lord Melbourne and Robert Peel.

None the less, while the future would be one of promise largely fulfilled, the immediate present was far from a happy state. In Scotland as in most of the United Kingdom, poverty was a universal problem as was exploitation of workers. The mass of the people still lived in little more than hovels with little or no sanitation. There were exceptions. In New Lanark, towards the end of the previous century David Dale had established cotton manufacturing on an industrial scale and had coupled it with providing, by the standards of the day, modern working facilities for his workers, a project further developed by his son-in-law Robert Owen in the provision of housing which became a model for progressive employers.

During the first fifty years of the new century, the mass production of iron and steel would transform engineering. There would be great developments in the provision of public services. Street lighting in towns and cities, initially by gas, would become common place as would domestic water supply. In central Scotland the construction of canals made possible the movement of coal and goods on a large scale. Following an investigation and report by Thomas Telford in 1803, nearly 1000 miles of new road and over 1100 bridges had been constructed in the Highland area by 1820, but above all, the advent of railways would revolutionise communication. The first line to operate commercially was from Stockton to Darlington in the north of England, opened by George Stephenson in 1821. During the 1840s, there was to be a huge expansion of routes. In 1842 a line between Glasgow and Edinburgh was opened and quite soon lines were opened connecting most of the main centres in Scotland as well as links south of the Border. Taken together with the expansion of heavy industry, those developments created an industrial revolution which transformed Scotland and its neighbours.

*   *   *

The story of Peebles for the years covered by this book is drawing to a close. The first fifty years of the century began to see a gradual return to modest prosperity, although it would be the second half which would see the greatest progress.

After eighteen centuries as an established community, where did Peebles stand in the year 1800? Its population had increased little over the past three centuries. The built environment remained largely defined by the wall which had enclosed it since 1575, although what now remained of it was little more than a reminder of its past. Much of its stone had become a source of building material for the more substantial houses which were now appearing.

The Old Town was occupied mainly by weavers and labourers. Their houses were thatched cottages, with a byre attached for the cow which grazed on the town's common lands and provided a supplement to their meagre earnings. In the new town there remained many thatched houses, although as the *Statistical Account* noted, a significant number had been improved and there had been some new building. Those were the houses of a more affluent class which was emerging and were built of stone and mortar, with slated roofs.

Robert Chambers, who was born in the town 1802, has left extensive first hand descriptions of it in the early years of the century. Here he describes the New Town and its shops.

The New Town was a smarter place than the Old; yet it contained many homely old thatched houses and few of any elegance. The shops were for the most part confined and choky places, with what were called half doors, a bell being generally struck or shaken when this door was opened by a customer, so as to summon the worthy trader from an equally stifling back parlour, or quite likely from some place in the street thirty yards off, where he had been holding conference with a group of neighbours on some gossip of the day. No attempt was made to keep up appearances of business. The grocer laid no empty sugar cask at his door, for everybody would have known that the boys had picked the last particle of the sweet contents out of the chinks of wood many weeks ago. The draper never thought of busying himself with the packaging of imaginary parcels of female fineries, to induce women to come in for their new gowns and shawls. All was quiet and sombre by day; and in the evenings, a dim candle on the counter made the only difference. A favourite position of the shopkeeper was to lean on his arms over the half-door, gazing abroad into the vacant street or chatting to a casual bystander.[205]

William Wordsworth and his sister Dorothy visited Peebles in 1803 during an extensive tour of Scotland.   They seem to have gained a gentler impression of the town and its surroundings as her diary[206] published that same year shows She wrote :

Sunday, September 8th – The town of Peebles is on the banks of the Tweed. After breakfast walked up the river to Neidpath Castle, about a mile and a half from the town. The castle stands upon a green hill, overlooking the Tweed, a strong square-towered edifice, neglected and desolate, though not a ruin, the garden overgrown with grass, and the high walls that fenced it broken down. The Tweed winds between green steeps, upon which, and close to the riverside, large flocks of sheep pasturing; higher still are the grey mountains; but I need not describe the scene, for William has done it better than I could do in a sonnet which he wrote the same day; the five last lines, at least, of his poem will impart to you more of the feeling of the place than would be possible for me to do.

---

[205]   *Memoir of Robert Chambers with Autobiographic Reminiscences of William Chambers* Fifth Edition (W & R Chambers) 1872)
[206]   *Recollections of a Tour made in Scotland, A.D. 1803*

Here she is referring to the poem already quoted which Wordsworth wrote in response to the damage done by "Old Q" by felling trees at Neidpath. The last five lines are:-

> *The Traveller at this day will stop and gaze*
> *On wrongs which nature scarcely seems to heed;*
> *For shelter'd places, bosoms, nook, and bays*
> *And the pure mountains, and the gentle Tweed,*
> *And the green silent pastures yet remain.*

Dorothy continues:

> I was spared any regret for fallen woods when we were there, not knowing the history of them. The soft low mountains, the castle, and the decayed pleasure-grounds, the scattered trees which have been left in different parts, and the road carried in a very beautiful line along the side of the hill, with the Tweed murmuring through the unfenced green pastures spotted with sheep, together composed a harmonious scene, and I wished for nothing that was not there.

She and her brother continued their walk to Peebles.

> The town of Peebles looks very pretty from the road in returning: it is an old town, built of grey stone, the same as the castle. Well dressed people were going to church. Sent the car before, and walked ourselves, and while going along the main street William was called aside in a mysterious manner by a person who gravely examined him – whether he was an Irishman or a foreigner, or who he was; I suppose our car was the occasion of suspicion at a time when every one was talking of threatened invasion.

The incident of William's interrogation, although certainly caused by pure curiosity, is perhaps an indication of how insular Peebles had become.

At that time there was still no bank in the town. The first was not established until 1825. Employers of labour paying wages had to have cash sent from Edinburgh by carrier, which could often be delayed by bad weather, particularly in winter. There was no local newspaper as there was no printer in the town. *The Edinburgh Star* did come twice a week. Newspapers then were costly and a number of people in the town would club together to buy a copy which was then circulated to the members under a strict time table. Robert Chambers' father was a member of such a club as Robert recounts:

My father could not afford to subscribe for the Star. All he could do was to be a member of a club to take in the paper, which was handed about to one after another, each member being allowed to have it in turn for a certain number of hours. Such, in the days of taxed and dear newspapers, was almost universal practice, and in our community it was no way singular.

Local affairs were still publicised by the long standing means of "tuck of drum". Another somewhat strange way of receiving news from the wider world was by wandering beggars, who were generally welcomed to the town, because on their travels they collected news from across the country.

There had been a national postal system of sorts since the seventeenth century throughout the country. An Act of William III in 1695 had established a General Post Office in Edinburgh:

from whence all letters and pacquets whatsoever may with speed and expedition be sent into any part of the kingdom, or any other of his Majesty's dominions, or into any kingdom or country beyond seas, by the pacquets sealed to London. It is also enacted, that a Postmaster-General shall be appointed by letters patent under the Privy Seal,

but there was no regular system for local delivery of letters or packets which would have arrived in Peebles from Edinburgh. Charges were variable and expensive. Dr Williamson, referring to "the note book"[207] notes that in 1807 an express delivery from Peebles to Macbiehill near West Linton, cost three shillings, an express letter to Edinburgh, seven shillings and four pence and that William Thomson was paid three shillings and six pence for "burial" letters to Traquair and Pirn.[208] That contrasts with universal postage introduced by Rowland Hill in 1840, of one or two pence, depending on the size, which covered delivery anywhere in the country.

There was no police force as such. The only official appointed to maintain law and order and apprehend wrong doers, was an official with the somewhat awesome title of "public hangman or deputy executor of the law". In practice, his role as "executioner" was no longer a reality, but the title remained. Had there been anyone who committed a capital crime, that

---

[207] Williamson, on several occasions, makes reference to "the note book", but does not indicate whose it is. It would appear to be a prominent Peebles citizen.
[208] Innerleithen

would have been dealt with in Edinburgh. The role did however, include the administration of corporal punishment or placing delinquents in the stocks and that of town crier, when official proclamations were publicised by "tuck of drum." He was also responsible for arresting law breakers. At that time the administration of justice was somewhat informal. On occasions, when a particular misdemeanour had been brought to the attention of the provost, he instructed the hangman to arrest the culprit, without any formal court appearance. It was not unknown for the provost of the day to dispense justice informally, while serving customers in his shop and for no formal record to be kept. It was not until 1840 that a proper police force was set up.

In spite of the lack of many of the facilities such as a bank and availability of regular newspaper coverage, the town did boast a bookseller. As Robert Chambers recalls,

> There was a bookseller in Peebles: a great fact. There had not always been one; but some years before my entrance upon existence, a decent man named Alexander Elder had come to the town and established himself as a dealer in intellectual wares. He was a careful and sober man, and in the end, as was fitting, became rich in comparison with many of his neighbours. The shop was somewhat unusual in that books were shared with a cow. It seems a curious reminiscence of my first bookseller's shop, that on entering it, one always got a peep of a cow, which quietly chewed her cud behind the bookshelves, such being one of Sandy's means of providing for his family.

As yet water was not provided to individual houses. It still came from Venlaw to a public well in front of Queensberry Lodging[209] and there the womenfolk of the town would arrive to fill their pitchers, pausing to exchange gossip as they waited for them to be filled. However, it was quite inadequate to meet the needs of the whole town. An attempt was made at some improvement and the council explored the possibility of finding additional springs on Venlaw which might be tapped, but none was found. An additional cistern for storage was built in the Eastgate, but that still was not enough. In 1813 a scheme was proposed to bring an additional supply from Jedderfield and the Kirklands, but although the necessary approvals were obtained, nothing seems to have been done. Yet another scheme to increase the supply from Venlaw by tapping springs on Soonhope seems to have been abortive as well.

---

[209] Now the Chambers Institution

Such lighting of the streets as there was, was still by oil lamps. The introduction of gas lighting would be a transformation, but it did not arrive until 1828.

Prior to the improvement of the road system which followed the establishment of turnpikes in the 1770s, the roads north to Edinburgh and to the east and west, had been little more than cart tracks. Most who used them travelled on horseback or walked. Wheeled public transport able to carry passengers, consisted of little more than an unsprung box on wheels. The first regular service to Edinburgh was in being at the turn of the century and was provided by William Wilson's "Caravan" which was a two wheeled vehicle, pulled by a single horse. It left Peebles at 8 o'clock in the morning and was scheduled to arrive at the Grassmarket in Edinburgh at 6 o'clock in the evening. The price of a seat for the 10 hour journey, which included a stop at Howgate for a bowl of soup, was 2s 6d. In 1806 a new service was started with a much better vehicle called "the Fly", which was able to complete the journey in six to seven hours in considerable more comfort than the Caravan. It could carry three people inside and one on the outside "dickey" seat at the back. It was pulled by two horses and also stopped at Howgate, where passengers had time to dine on something a little more lavish than a mere bowl of soup. It provided a return service three days each week for the next twenty years. The fare was 10s 6d, considerably more than the "Caravan" it now replaced, but it was evidently highly popular and seats had to be booked in advance to avoid disappointment. There were alternatives including what was a private hire service. Dr Williamson quotes a letter from an Edinburgh lawyer, Mr James Little W.S., which gives a flavour of the times, relating to the modern equivalent of a local taxi service and the journey to Edinburgh:

Edinburgh, 30th May, 1816

My Dear Sir – I am to be at Eddleston Manse on Saturday forenoon, where I shall remain until Monday morning. Please send a chaise to Eddleston on that day by ten o'clock, to carry me to Peebles, and if you are alone at dinner, I shall take my chance with you. I shall require the chaise in the evening to bring me back to Eddleston, which will save the change of a bed. You will oblige me by taking a seat in the Tuesday's Fly, to be taken up at Dr Robertson's. As I take a post chaise on Saturday, and Mrs Murray goes with me and returns in the evening. If any of your friends wish for a conveyance to Edinburgh, let them be at the Manse by six o'clock in the evening, when Mrs Murray will be glad to see them and travel with them to Edinburgh.

A post chaise was a four wheeled covered carriage, which could carry two to four people. It was usually pulled by two horses, but sometimes by four, which made it much faster than the Fly, which is no doubt why the prospective journey referred to at the end of the letter, could start at six in the evening and on a summer's evening reach Edinburgh before dark. It also had the advantage that when shared by a number of people, the cost was less than the Fly.

In 1825, the public transport system was further improved by the introduction of a stage coach service. Initially there were two Edinburgh based firms. One was run by a Mr Campbell and the other by Croall & Co. The latter would in time become John Croall & Sons, the well known firm of Edinburgh garage owners and coachbuilders.

Croall had established a major enterprise running stage coaches from Edinburgh to major centres in Scotland, which would have given him a considerable advantage over Campbell who could not compete on price and his service was not well used, with the result that in a short time he gave up, leaving Croall in a monopoly position. His coach could carry six on the inside and up to sixteen on the outside. The fare was five shillings and with a journey time of just three hours, it was possible to make the return journey the same day, starting from Durward's Crown Inn in the High Street (now the Crown Hotel) and arriving in Princes Street in Edinburgh.

Initially while both services operated, it resulted in the two coaches racing to Edinburgh, sometimes with unfortunate results and often to the considerable alarm of the passengers. Accidents inevitably happened. On one occasion, Campbell's coach, perhaps all too aptly named "the Surprise", racing down Liberton Brae on the outskirts of Edinburgh far too fast overturned and the coach driver, Andrew Kinross was thrown into a ditch and badly injured. On another occasion Croall's coach, driven by its regular driver Willie Hogg, had an accident at Winkston. When the coach did not appear in Peebles at the normal time as expected, it caused considerable alarm. In the event several passengers were injured, but none fatally.

Mention has already been made of people in the town, on whom Sir Walter Scott based characters. By the beginning of the nineteenth century, Marion Ritchie, the proprietor of the Cross Keys, in the Northgate[210] was at the height of her powers. Robert Chambers describes her as, 'a clever sprightly woman of irreproachable character, who, so far from the obsequiousness of her profession, required to be treated by her guests with

---

210   Meg Dodds and the Cleikum Inn of *St Ronan's Wells* by Sir Walter Scott.

no small amount of deference, and in special, would never allow them to have liquor after a decent hour.'

William Chambers says that the Cross Keys was, ' a favourite *howff* '. It was highly respectable and even the members of the Presbytery dined there regularly. With ordinary customers she would not allow any excess and had no qualms in refusing to serve anyone whom she deemed to have had sufficient. She was well known to say to younger men who had in her view reached their limit, 'Ye have just got plenty now: gae away hame tae yer mither.'

In 1807 a rival establishment was set up, much to Miss Ritchie's annoyance. That was the Tontine Hotel, but she continued to run the Cross Keys until her death one afternoon in 1841 while the members of the presbytery were dining. It is said that almost her last words were, 'are the ministers a' richt.'

Someone who also left his mark on Peebles, but in addition became nationally known, was Mungo Park. Nationally he is known as a pioneer of African exploration. He was not a native of Peebles having been born in 1771 as one of thirteen children of a farmer at Foulshiels, Yarrow. He was educated initially at Selkirk Grammar School. He was very bright and that enabled him complete his education at Edinburgh University, where he qualified as a doctor.

In 1792 he was appointed as a surgeon in the East India Company and sailed to the East Indies. On his return, he joined the African Association which had been founded in 1788 to promote interest in African exploration, particularly in its possibilities for commercial exploitation. In 1795 on its behalf he undertook an expedition to the interior of East Africa, exploring the route of the River Niger. He undertook it virtually alone, accompanied by only six natives who very soon either died or left him. After a year of incredible hardship he did reach the Niger, the first European to do so and followed its course for nearly 500 kilometres. During the journey he came in contact with the native tribes, often at considerable risk to his own safety. On his return he wrote a book about his journey. It was called *Travels in the Interior of Africa.* It was the first reliable account of African tribal people and their way of life and brought him widespread public recognition.

Following his marriage, he came to Peebles in 1801. He rented a house in the Northgate, which still stands today and set up a surgery and a chemist's shop in the High Street. It was a good medical practice, but his African experience had whetted his appetite for travel and adventure and in 1803 he returned to London and set out once again for Africa, but the expedition was aborted and he returned to Peebles for a few months in 1804, bringing with him an African native called Sidi Omback Bombi, who taught him Arabic. It was the first time a black man had been seen in Peebles, which caused something of a stir. His sojourn did not last long. He was by then a well known national figure and later that year he was asked by the government to lead a new expedition to what at that time was known as the "Dark Continent". In September, he parted from his wife Ailie in Peebles and set off south. She never saw him again.

In the following months, he set out from the East African coast with a much larger team of 45 Europeans, which included a number of boatbuilders and soldiers. They reached the Niger in three months, but by then thirty four of the Europeans had died of fever. None the less the remaining team managed to build a boat and set sail down the river Niger. By then they were reduced to five, including Park himself, a lieutenant and three soldiers, one of whom had gone mad and before long died. They still managed to cover nearly 1300 kilometres, suffering attacks from hostile natives and encountering many dangerous rapids on the way before they were finally attacked going through more rapids during which time their boat was wrecked and the whole party drowned. Their fate was not discovered until long afterwards and it was many years before any further attempt was made to explore the area again.

40.
Napoleonic Wars

Britain had been at war with France as part of a coalition with Austria, Prussia and Spain since 1794. A war-weary Britain had agreed a peace treaty at Amiens in 1802, but it was short lived. France, now led by Napoleon Bonaparte, refused to remove its troops from the Netherlands, which posed a potentially serious threat to Britain. In return Britain refused to give up Malta which she had agreed to do in the treaty and by 1803 Britain and France were once again at war. The following year Napoleon would make himself Emperor of France.

Once again there was fear of invasion. The response from the people of Peeblesshire was impressive. *The New Statistical Account of Peeblesshire 1841*, recording the civil history of the parish to that date has the following:

> When the war broke out after treaty of Amiens, and the country was threatened with foreign invasion, an additional levy of volunteers and yeomanry was ordered, and the loyal inhabitants of Peebles, considering the exigencies of the times, mustered no less than 682 effective officers and men as infantry corps, and two troops of cavalry, making a total of 820 soldiers, - besides furnishing their *quota* to the militia. This force, out of a population of 8800, exceeded the muster made by any other county in Scotland, according to the number of inhabitants; and in that spirit-stirring period, a finer body of men could not be found in Britain, nor one more prepared to repel foreign invasion, or "nobly die the second glorious part," than the hardy and patriotic sons of Tweeddale.[211]

There was a review of those troops in Peebles in January 1804 when the infantry was commanded by Lord Elibank and the yeomanry by Sir James Montgomery. In June 1805 they took part in a general muster at Kelso. Regular musters took place including one in May 1809 when they were required to assemble for twenty eight days' duty in Peebles on the orders of the government. The order included the following threat. 'If any local militiaman (not labouring under any infirmity incapacitating him) shall not

---

[211]   *The Statistical Account of Peebles-Shire* – page 6. Willam Blackwood and Sons, Edinburgh 1841

appear at the time and place appointed for the annual exercise, he shall be deemed a deserter; and if not taken until after the time of such exercise, shall forfeit and pay ten pounds; and if not immediately paid, is liable to be committed to the house of correction, to hard labour, there to remain, without bail or mainprize, for the space of six months, or until he shall have paid the penalty.'[212]

Apart from two who were drilling elsewhere, there was a full turnout and it seems that the whole town had been fully supportive, particularly in accommodating those of the county who came from outwith the town. Musters continued on an annual basis until 1816, by which time the French wars were finally at an end.

The wars did have another particular significance for Peebles. Shortly after hostilities restarted in 1803, the town was chosen by the government as a suitable place to send prisoners of war. Shortly after the war started again, between twenty and thirty prisoners came to the town. They were prisoners "on parole", which meant that they had a fair amount of freedom to live in the community, but were honour bound not to escape. Initially they were mainly Dutch and Walloons from what is now part of modern Belgium. Later there were a few Danes also. The majority were sailors. It seems that they were quite content to find themselves confined to a pleasant Scottish town. They were free to live much as they wished and within reasonable limits to move about the immediate countryside. Most of them took up handicrafts of one sort or another as a means of supplementing their income allowance.[213] It appears that they were readily accepted into the community by the townsfolk and none of them ever attempted to escape.

One later addition to their number in about 1806, was the captain of a ship from the West Indies, who brought his wife with him and also his servant boy who was a native West Indian, called Jack. To quote William Chambers, 'Black Jack, as we called him, was sent to the school, where he played with the other boys on the town green, and at length read and spoke like a native. He was a good-natured creature, and became a general favourite. Jack was the first pure native whom the boys at that time had ever seen.'

In 1810, a much larger group of one hundred and eleven prisoners were sent to Peebles. This time French, captured in the Peninsular War. News

---

212   From *PEEBLES during the NAPOLEONIC WARS* by Sheila Scott 1980
213   In the Tweeddale Museum there are two ships carved from bone, with rigging made from human hair, which are fine examples of their work.

of their impending arrival, expected in two or three days time, spread quickly through the town. William takes up the story again:

> There was speedily a vast sensation in the place. The local militia had been disbanded. Lodgings of all sorts were vacant. The new arrivals would on all hands be heartily welcomed. On Tuesday, the expected French prisoners in an unceremonious way began to drop in. As one of several boys, I went out to meet these new prisoners of war on the road from Edinburgh. They came walking in twos and threes – a few of them lame. Their appearance was startling, for they were in military garb, in which they had been captured in Spain. Some were in light blue hussar dresses, braided, with marks of sabre wounds. Others in dark-blue uniform. Several wore large cocked-hats, but the greater number had undress caps. All had a gentlemanly air, notwithstanding their general dishevelled attire, their soiled boots, and their visible marks of fatigue. Before night, they had all arrived; and through the activity of the agent appointed by the Transport Board, they had been provided with lodgings suitable to their slender allowance.

Many of the prisoners in the new group were naval or military officers and had had considerable experience in actual combat and were quite senior commanders. They included several doctors and about a dozen midshipmen. As William discovered, after talking to them: 'Though spoken of as French, there was in the party a mixture of Italians, Swiss, Poles.' He adds, 'Whatever their origin, they were warm adherents of Napoleon, whose glory at this time was at its height. Lively in manner, their minds were full of the recent struggles in the Peninsula.'

The prisoners soon settled into the life in Peebles. As well as walking in the countryside and fishing for trout and eels in the Tweed, they played billiards on a table which had been given to them by one of the local grocers. Their living conditions were far from lavish and on the small allowance they received from the government, they struggled to feed and clothe themselves adequately. Some of the more fortunate had been able to bring gold coins with them concealed in their clothing, with which they were able to buy more food, but many were half starved. There seems to have been a system of communal eating which helped, with the more affluent, gold coin holders subsidising those who would otherwise subsist on a minimum diet. William Chambers recalls that the communal meals were held in a house which they hired and where food was cooked by one of the prisoners, 'who, as is not unusual with Frenchmen, was skilled in cuisine.' Even in the first decade of the nineteenth century the reputation of French "haute cuisine" was clearly already well known! Showing some of the commercial enterprise which was to stand William and his brother

Robert in such good stead in years to come, the two brothers, kept rabbits in a hutch which they had built in the back garden of their home and sold them to the French as a welcome addition to their menu. The money they received was used to buy books.

Some of the prisoners, tired of what must have been a fairly tedious life, with little more than fishing, walking and billiards to amuse them, decided to set up a theatre, not only for their own entertainment, but also for those of the townsfolk whom they had come to know and create some measure of friendship. They persuaded the council to let them use the old ballroom. They built a stage at one end and enough benches to seat up to one hundred and twenty in addition to a number in the former musicians' gallery. They painted scenery, some of it by a young Pole called Raguliski, who had some artistic talent. All the productions were free to prisoners and complimentary tickets were given to those of the locals whom they had befriended. Among them was William and Robert's father, who became a favourite of the Frenchmen. Sadly however, it would eventually be the cause of his financial ruin.

It is said that, 'the Devil finds work for idle hands'. While many of the prisoners were able occupy the long hours of the day in activities such theatricals and country pursuits, there were others who passed the long hours in craft work. One group in particular, demonstrated far from "idle hands", employing great skill in the creation of a number of model ships of war. These were made mainly out of bone, with animal hair used for rigging. Some of the results of their efforts can still be seen today in the Tweeddale Museum. The quality of their work, with an attention to the finest detail, is remarkable.

The prisoners remained in the town until 1814, when they were repatriated during the pause in the conflict with France, before the final defeat of Waterloo. Dr Williamson had a first-hand account from John Stirling, who was the provost of the burgh between 1855 and 1864, but still young enough to remember the event. On a warm June afternoon in 1815, John Stirling had been bathing in the Eddleston Water, when he saw the "Fly" coming along the Edinburgh Road covered in flags. As it passed along the Northgate people started to come out of their houses to see what it was about. In the High Street a large crowd gathered and there was cheering and wild celebration when the news of the final victory was heard. It was the end of a long, weary campaign which had cast a long shadow over the whole nation. While Peebles had been little affected by battles taking place far away on the continent of Europe, it had none the less touched the lives of many in different ways in the Royal and Ancient burgh, either as participants in a militia set up to defend it or in playing host to some of those who were its losers, although they might have been fortunate indeed to find themselves in a place which was not hostile and was far from the fields of battle where they might have fared less well.

41.
Brotherhood of Books

No history of Peebles would be complete without telling the story of two brothers born in the town, who would make their mark, not only on the national stage but also become world renowned. They were William and Robert Chambers.

William was born in 1800 and his brother in 1802. Their early years were spent in the house in the Biggiesknowe which still stands today. They were the eldest of a family of five. Their father James, was an important and initially successful figure in the local textile trade, but all that would change over the following few years, but in the first decade of the nineteenth century, the Chambers were clearly a middle class family. Robert recalls the house and life in it:

> ..our family dwelt...... in a modern-slated house, which my father had had built for him by his father when about to be married...................My earliest recollections bring before me a neat small mansion, fronting Eddleston water: a tastefully furnished sitting room, containing a concealed bed, one or two other little rooms, and a kitchen; a ground floor full of looms, and a garret full of webs and weft. Games at marbles played with my elder brother on the figures of the parlour carpet, when recovering from illness come back upon me as among the pleasantest things I have experienced in life; or wandering into the workshop below, it was great entertainment to sit beside one of the weavers, and watch the movements of the heddles and treddles, and hear the songs and the gossip of the man.

Their father James Chambers was involved in the textile trade, mainly as an agent, selling the produce of a large number of the cottage-based weavers in the town as well as those who were directly employed by him, including those who worked in the house at Biggiesknowe. As well as selling woollen cloth, James had introduced the weaving of cotton to the town and was agent for the sale of all the cotton cloth produced. He was a man who took a keen interest in current affairs and also had a great interest in science and generally learning about the world and its workings. He was a regular reader of the *Edinburgh Review*, a newspaper which appeared three times a week and which he read as a member of the club earlier referred to. He had bought a copy of the fourth edition

Encyclopedia Britannica, which from its first publication in 1771 had expanded from the original three volumes to twenty. He instilled in his sons an interest in and love of books, in particular those which were a source of knowledge, which would stand both of them in good stead in future.

Sadly the somewhat idyllic picture painted by Robert did not last. As the Napoleonic Wars progressed, trade declined and in addition, innovations were rapidly taking place which would transform the linen trade in particular. The introduction of powered looms and other machinery was having a profound effect and the old style hand looms and their weavers were no longer financially viable. In an attempt to meet the challenge and loss of commission from sales, James set up as a draper in another part of the town. Although he had no training for that, he might have succeeded but for circumstances partly out of his control but partly of his own making. It involved the prisoners of war. James had come to know many of them and had even entertained them in his house. After some years in exile from their home country, many of them were in need of new clothing. James took pity on a number of them and gave them clothing on credit having been given assurances that repayment would be made in due time. In 1812 an order came for all the prisoners to leave Peebles, most of them going to Dumfriesshire. They left behind them a number of problems including two pregnant Peebles girls and debts due to James unpaid. It ruined him. He might have survived, but having declared himself insolvent, it should have been still possible for him to resolve that as he had sufficient assets to cover his debts. However, his main creditor was an uncle of his wife, who was an Edinburgh merchant and a successful businessman who now became James' advisor, making himself trustee in the process of sequestration which followed. All the stock was offered for sale and bought by an agent at a low price virtually unopposed, as others interested had been led to believe that he was acting on behalf of Mrs Chambers, whereas he had been acting on behalf of the uncle. As Robert Chambers writes:

> The result was that the sage advisor, as trustee, managed everything so adroitly for his own benefit, that the creditors received but a small dividend, and the family lost almost everything.

He continues:

By various shifts, the family continued to struggle on for a year or two in Peebles after this catastrophe. The penury which was endured was less painful than the acute sense of social degradation.

With the exception of Robert, who remained in Peebles to complete his schooling, the family moved to Edinburgh in 1813. In a state of abject poverty they could only afford accommodation in the south side slums. James, who by then had a drink problem had difficulty in finding work. To support the family, his wife undertook menial tasks and moved the family for a time to Musselburgh. It was at that time that the two brothers set out on a career path which would transform their lives.

In 1814, Robert left Peebles to join them. Edinburgh was becoming one of the great centres of books and publishing. William became apprenticed to a book seller and later Robert set up as a bookseller on his own account in 1818, as did William in 1819.

Writing in 1904, James Thin who was to become one of the most prominent booksellers in Edinburgh and would personally have known the brothers, recalled his experiences as an apprentice bookseller. In 1836 at the age of twelve he describes his working day which often consisted of collecting books from various publishers throughout the city :

> Turning east to Waterloo Place the collecting boy reaches 19 Waterloo Place, where William and Robert Chambers had 4 years before this opened the publishing office of their well-known and world renowned "Edinburgh Journal". The two brothers had risen from the very humblest ranks of the trade, that is bookstall keepers on Leith Walk. Robert commencing in 1818 in a wooden ruckle nearly opposite Pilrig St. with a stock of books which he valued at £2, and covering the small space of 13 feet in his frail stall. This was his whole capital. Robert had no previous training in bookselling, so that he now set his feet on the very lowest rung of the business, up which he, with his brother were destined to ascend to the very summit. His brother William had been apprenticed to John Sutherland, 12 Calton Street, and was with him from 1814 to 1819. At the expiry of his apprenticeship he resolved to do as his younger brother had done, and began life as a bookstall keeper, which he did in similar premises a few yards farther up the Walk. William's capital was less than Robert's, all he had being 5s of last week's wages, with which he bought a few deals at a woodyard and with these he made the stall. He had however the advantage over Robert of being known in the trade, and was soon offered stock to the value of £10, which he disposed of, and with the

proceeds thereof buying more books and paying also for what he had sold laid the foundation of that great firm of William and Robert Chambers.[214]

In 1822 the brothers joined together to publish a literary journal called the *Kaleidoscope*. Although it was a failure, it provided valuable experience. Robert had begun to develop a career as a writer and William persuaded him to join with him in publishing a new journal which would sell cheaply to a mass audience and aim to entertain as well as educate and instruct. It was launched in 1832 with the title *Chambers Edinburgh Journal*. It became an instant success. By 1844 its circulation had reached 84,000 and the firm of W & R Chambers was by then, one of the largest publishers in the World.

William concentrated on the management of the publishing business, but this was combined with philanthropy and eventually a spell as Lord Provost of Edinburgh, which still left him time to write a number of books including *A History of Peeblesshire* in 1864. He collected and edited *Charters and Documents and Extracts from the Records of the Burgh A.D. 1165 -1710(1872)*. His gift to the town and County of Peebles of the Chambers Institution in 1859 remains a memorial to his establishment of a source of learning and cultural enlightenment for all its people, in the form of a museum and public library.

Robert became a prolific writer, publishing more than 60 works over a period of 46 years covering a huge range of subjects as diverse as literature, philosophy, arts and science. Although originally published anonymously, one of his best known works is *Vestiges of the Natural History of Creation*. It introduced a version of the theory of evolution some fifteen years before Charles Darwin published *On the Origin of Species*. He did not neglect his native burgh and countryside, which featured in his *Picture of Scotland*, published in 1837 and also in his *Domestic Annals of Scotland*, published 1859-61 With additions by his brother he wrote the *Memoir*, covering his early years in Peebles and in Edinburgh, which provides a "window" into the life of Peebles and its peoples in the first 14 years of the nineteenth century and from which several extracts now appear in this book.

---

[214]   *James Thin, 1824 – 1915*, extract from his hand written diary, 1904.

42.
A Changing World

Throughout its long history, the river Tweed and its tributary, the Eddleston Water have been a central feature of the town. They have been a source of water and of food; a source of power for the mills; a physical divide, necessitating the construction of bridges; a source of recreation and even a means of execution. They have been the cause of turmoil and destruction in times of flood, which have been frequent. Possibly one of the most serious ever to afflict the town occurred in 1807.

On 5th September of that year there was an exceptionally severe storm. Rain started to fall around 2 o'clock in the afternoon and was accompanied by a strong wind which continued unabated until late in the evening. The Eddleston Water rose so high that it covered the Tree Bridge and part of the parapet wall was destroyed. By seven o'clock the Tweed had risen above the piers of the Tweed Bridge, more than two metres above the normal height of the river. The water continued to rise throughout the evening and after dark. When morning came it was seen that the whole of the area still known as Dukehaugh was inundated, almost as far as the road to Manor (now Caledonian Road). Dr Williamson says that it was, 'the highest flood known in the history of man.' Kerfield was also inundated. The Soonhope Burn which runs through it was blocked by stones and gravel. Bridges at Eddleston, Innerleithen and Galashiels were all destroyed.

The year 1807 saw a number of significant events. After a long ministry of 47 years, Dr Dalgleish died at the age of 74, during the same month as the flood and was buried in the churchyard. His death, even at what then was an advanced age, was a sad loss to the town, where he was greatly respected as a part of the inscription on his tombstone shows :

His fervent piety, his persuasive eloquence, the sweetness of his Christian temper, and his unwearied diligence in the service of the great Master, rendered him admired and beloved while he lived, and at his death deeply lamented.

The minister who followed him was Dr John Lee, who became minister of Peebles in April 1808. He was presented by the Duke of Queensberry and unlike many of his predecessors his appointment was unopposed. He had been born at Torwoodlee, near Galashiels in 1779 and initially educated at Caddonfoot, before attending Edinburgh University where he followed an academic career for several years, as well as at the university of St Andrews and elsewhere, before briefly becoming the minister of the Scots Church in London. Academia was clearly his primary interest and in 1812 he left Peebles to become Professor of Ecclesiastical History at St Andrews. The one notable legacy that he left, was that he introduced the practice of interviewing and reprimanding sinners in private rather than in church in front of the congregation. This approach, compassionate as it was, doubtless represented a loss of entertainment for the "unco guid"!

1807 also saw the election of Thomas Smibert as provost. He succeeded Provost Ker who had been instrumental in the building of the new church on the castlehill. Provost Smibert evidently did not have a great sense of history. Shortly after his appointment he proposed that the ruined Cross Kirk should become a coal yard. The idea was initially supported by the council, in spite of a decision which had been made less than twenty years before, that the Kirk was to be kept in all time coming as a historic monument. It caused consternation and was quickly rejected. Happily, an alternative site was found and a few years later, in 1817, Mr John Hay of Smithfield and Haystoun, asked permission to conserve the building at his own expense. It was granted and the building remained in the custody of the Hay family until 1917, when the council bought some of the surrounding ground from the Earl of Wemyss. Subsequently it became a Scheduled Ancient Monument and in 1925 became the responsibility of the Ministry of Works who undertook substantial repairs and conservation. Today it is administered by its successor, Historic Environment Scotland.

Provost Smibert caused further consternation shortly after when he wanted to remove the Cross which still stood as it had done for centuries at the end of the High Street. He proposed to sell it describing it as 'useless rubbish'. Arrangements were actually put in hand to demolish it, but at the last moment Sir John Hay bought it and took it to Kingsmeadows. Years later his son Sir Adam Hay had it erected in the courtyard of what had become the Chambers Institution. Later still it was removed to the site at the junction of the High Street and the Eastgate where it stands today. Had Provost Smibert succeeded, this ancient and lasting link with the past of the Royal Burgh would have been lost for ever.

At that time the town's best known inn was the Cross Keys in the Northgate, run by the indomitable Miss Ritchie, but times and tastes were changing. A more affluent society was looking for something more sophisticated than the homely, but basic accommodation which Miss Ritchie offered. In October 1806, a group of the more prosperous members of the community met together and decided that a new hotel should be built. The cost was to be financed on the "Tontine" principal. Under that arrangement 158 shares of £25 were issued, raising £3,950. It included the cost of the site for the new hotel on the south side of the High Street, where it still stands today. Several old houses were bought and demolished.

Under a "Tontine" arrangement, the last surviving original shareholder became the sole owner. However, shares could be taken in the name of a nominee who could be any age, which made it possible to extend the time over which the interest of a shareholder continued and would increase the chance of that shareholder or a family member becoming the ultimate "winner". At the outset there was a total of 144 shareholders or their nominees, so there must have been a number who bought more than one share. By 1855 there were 74 still alive and by 1864 it had reduced to 53. The last survivor was Sir John Adam Hay, who became sole owner in 1888. He sold the property for £2,750 and while it was considerably less than the original cost, it represented a considerable profit on the cost of his original shares.

Construction was completed in 1808. It included a ballroom which still exists as the dining room of the present-day hotel. Originally it was decorated at a cost of £150 paid for by the ladies of polite society in the town and district, which says much about the rising affluence of middle-class society in the town by then.

While the construction of the new hotel and its ballroom were indicative of an increasing level of wealth in the town and county, at the other end of the scale there remained a very real problem of poverty amongst the lower classes. It was made worse by soldiers returning after the French wars ended. In addition to natives of the town, there were large numbers of licensed beggars or blue gowned "king's bedesdmen" roaming the country, as well as homeless beggars always on the outlook for a meal. The town could afford little by way of support as its resources were stretched to the limit, largely because the town's mills were one of its main sources of income and were producing little in the adverse trading conditions which continued for two or more decades. Sir John Hay, who clearly had sympathy for the poor, supplied a boiler for a soup kitchen which opened in 1817. In a letter to the council of 14th January 1817, he gave instructions as to how the soup was to be made and calculated that the boiler could hold 300 chopins (150 pints) costing £1.5s and that a plate of soup could be produced for one penny. Samples were given to the council who approved it as 'wholesome and nutritious'.

Unemployment was very high among the weavers who constituted the main working population in the town. Many could not afford to buy yarn, but in 1826, with the recession still at its height, a fund was set up to allow yarn to be bought. The council subscribed £200 and together with what was given by members of the public, the scheme gave employment to 100 weavers for the next two years.

Following on the disruption and distress caused by the war with France, there had been a period of unrest throughout Scotland and England. Unemployment was rife, not only as a result of the loss of trade which the war had created, but also because of the introduction of machinery as the industrial revolution progressed. Wages were depressed. In 1819, laws were introduced to prohibit what were regarded as inflammatory and seditious publications and public protest meetings. 1820 saw signs of active revolt in the west of Scotland and in Glasgow in particular, where vast numbers of workers went on strike, resulting in clashes between the assembled mobs and the local militia.

In 1820 King George III died, after the longest reign of any monarch up to that time. The minute of the meeting of the town council of 12th February of that year, records that it formally recognised the accession of his son, the Prince Regent as George IV.

The economy of Peebles was still in the doldrums and the council was alarmed by those developments. It made its attitude very clear, when it presented an Address to the new king in December, which included the following :

...with equal detestation and horror the daring and unwearied efforts of the impious and disaffected to erase from the minds of the people of this country all veneration for the Christian religion, loyalty to their Sovereign and obedience to the law....It is incumbent on us to express our determination to use every exertion in our power to frustrate the designs of the disaffected, and to oppose the progress of their principles, which, if generally prevalent, must end in subversion of our present happy form of Government, and in involving the nation in confusion, misery and ruin.

These are lofty, if somewhat pompous words, but once again they reflect something which, with few exceptions, has been a continuous thread throughout the history of the Royal and Ancient burgh; loyalty to the crown and government and the status quo. None the less, change was coming and within the next decade the first steps in the broadening of electoral franchise and reform of local government would be achieved.

In 1822, the people of Scotland, at least in the lowlands had an opportunity to publicly demonstrate its loyalty to the crown. On the 12th August of that year King George IV made a visit to Scotland which lasted until the 29th. Sir Walter Scott was the prime mover and set about presenting the king with days of spectacle and pageantry which showcased his romantic view of Scotland and its people, merging the culture of the Highlands, so long suppressed, with that of the Lowlands. It was the first official visit by a monarch since Charles I in 1633. Tartan flourished, the king himself appearing in a flamboyant mix of a Stuart tartan kilt and flesh coloured tights to cover his ample form, setting in train the Scottish love affair with kilts and "Highland" dress which had been for years outlawed after the 1745 rebellion, but which continues to this day. Edinburgh and all Scotland, or most of it, revelled in this theatrical display. Such costly and ostentation at a time of austerity, must have caused many eyebrows to be raised, but it was a demonstration of what was becoming a confident nation with a positive view of the future.

There is no mention of the king's visit in any of the extant records or histories of Peebles, but it is unlikely that such a major event could have passed the Royal Burgh by. With an improving transport system the journey to Edinburgh was a matter of only a few hours. The town's officials and councillors almost certainly would have attended the jamboree and no doubt many of the townsfolk who could afford it would also have joined in.

At a rather more parochial level, perhaps inspired by the jewelled symbols of office and power which would have been on display in Edinburgh, during the king's visit, it was decided that the time had come for the Royal Burgh to have its own symbol of office. In July 1823, it was decided that a gold medal and chain, to be used on formal occasions should be made available to the provost. The provost at that time was James Kerr, who had held the office for many years, first from 1803 until 1807 and then for an unbroken term from 1811.[215] It was largely because of his long service and in recognition of it that this time was chosen,

---

215   He continued in office for a further three years.

because he 'had so long filled the situation with honour to himself, and complete satisfaction to the Magistrates, Council and community.' The medal and chain were duly purchased and presented to Provost Kerr on 3rd October and remained as the symbols of office from that time until the final demise of the town council in 1975.

One of the darker issues of the time was the threat posed by "Resurrectionists". The story of Burke and Hare, the two Irishmen who caused terror in Edinburgh is well known; how they started their criminal career by raiding churchyards at dead of night and removing freshly buried corpses which they then sold to Dr Knox, the famous teacher of anatomy at the capital's university. Not content with raiding graves, the pair soon expanded their trade by befriending beggars and other vulnerable people, plying them with alcohol or drugs and murdering them. They were not alone in the practice of grave raiding, which was quite widespread throughout Britain. Those who practised it were known as "Resurrectionists".

Peebles did not escape. In January 1820, the provost reported the 'extensive depredations which had been committed in the churchyard, and that many bodies had been carried off.' Action was needed and the council instructed one of the town's officers to go through the town to find volunteers who would be prepared to keep watch on the churchyard. There was a large response. A shelter was put up in the churchyard for the comfort of watchers and coal and candles were provided at public expense. A watch was kept on a nightly basis for the next three or four years. The last recorded entry for coal and candles was on 22 September 1823.

Rev Dr Williamson tells the story of something which happened in the Peebles churchyard at that time. A chemistry lecturer who was a stranger to the town, arrived on a day when there was a funeral. That night as usual there were three tradesmen on duty as watchers. One of them, looking out at dead of night, thought he had seen movement and called out to warn his companions. One of them, Robert Brydon, a shoemaker from the Old Town, had a loaded gun and ran out to where the noise had come from. As he approached, the intruders ran off towards the north. He pursued them, calling to them to halt, but they continued. He fired in their direction, but they escaped. Next day, blood was found on the metal railing of one of the graves and on the adjacent wall. The shot had been heard by one of the neighbours who lived at Hay Lodge and he ran out wearing only his nightshirt, with a pitchfork in his hand. His appearance in the blackness of the night naturally alarmed the already nervous watchers only recognising him when finally he spoke. Who was the stranger who had watched the funeral? He was never again seen in Peebles.

The criminal career of Burke and Hare was actually several years later, reaching its peak in 1827 and 1828, but Burke does have a particular connection with Peebles. He was well known in the town having worked as a labourer on the roads in Manor parish and also as a farm labourer at Nether Horsburgh, a short distance down river from the town. When ill on one occasion he is known to have consulted with Dr Craig, one of the local doctors. In 1827, he and his wife Helen McDougall moved to Penicuik to work at harvest time. It is likely that Burke's time in Tweeddale preceded this as it was at Penicuik they met Hare, who was also an itinerant labourer at that time. They moved with him to Edinburgh and began their grizzly trade. In November 1828, the trio were arrested and charged with 16 murders. Hare turned "king's evidence" and escaped punishment, but Burke was found guilty and sentenced to death. The case against McDougall was not proven and she was released. Burke was hanged on the morning of 28th January 1829. It was said that his execution was watched by a crowd of 25,000.

It was a few years after, first in 1832 and then in 1848, that there were outbreaks of cholera in England, raising fears of an epidemic not seen since the days long past of the plague. There were at least four doctors in the town. They recommended to the council that as a precaution, everyone 'should pay every attention to temperance, and cleanliness in their houses; that the streets and byelanes and particularly the closes be cleaned of every nuisance, and of animal impurities as the best means of preventing the approach of malignant diseases.'

It was a time when medical science had begun to make real progress. In England in particular the causes of disease were beginning to be understood. In London, John Snow had observed the way in which cholera developed and spread during the outbreaks of 1848 and 1832 and became convinced that it was a water borne disease, caused by contamination of water sources. The Peebles doctors do seem to have been advanced in their thinking. Their advice to the council clearly shows that they understood the link between contamination and the transmission of the disease. It was accepted and steps were taken to put their advice into action. A committee, formed of members of the public, was set up to implement it. The following year, the disease was once again spreading and in February, shortly before the start of the period of Lent, the provost was instructed to set up a meeting with "County Gentlemen", in other words the landowners throughout Tweeddale. Its purpose was to persuade them to monitor those coming into the county and establish where they had come from as the best way of preventing the disease from entering the county. In the event there is no record of any outbreak in the town or county.

The practice of religion thrived in the nineteenth century, at least in its various Protestant Presbyterian forms. After he returned to the life of an academic in 1812, the Rev Dr John Lee was succeeded by Rev Robert Buchanan, a tutor to the family of Francis, Earl of Wemyss and March, who not surprisingly presented him as his choice for the Peebles vacancy. He was duly admitted in 1813. His ministry in Peebles seems to have been unremarkable, although he was a popular preacher and he appears to have been well regarded by his parishioners. He remained minister until October 1824 when he resigned, like his predecessor, to take up an academic post at the University of Glasgow, in his case as Professor of Logic and Rhetoric.

In turn he was succeeded by the Rev John Elliot. His principal claim to fame was his description of the Parish of Peebles, which was his contribution to the *New Statistical Account of Scotland* of 1841. He was not altogether approved of by some of the congregation, who felt that he did not come up to the standard of his predecessor. A number of the members transferred their allegiance to the Secession Church at the Gytes. Perhaps they had a premonition about the length of Mr Elliot's services. They may well have been correct. Until relatively recent times, one of the characteristics of a Scottish Presbyterian service was its length, if not always its quality. Mr Elliot's communion services in particular seem to have been something of a marathon. He remained minister for twenty two years until his death in 1847.

Following his death, the appointment of his successor was somewhat unusual, in so far as the Earl of Wemyss and March allowed the choice to be made by the congregation. In time that would become the normal practice, but in 1847, the earl as the major landowner of the parish still had the right to "present" his choice. Although there were a number of possible candidates, one or two of whom preached in the Parish Church, the congregation appointed a delegation to go to Tulliallan in Fife to hear the Rev George Hope Monilaws of whom they had heard good reports. They returned with a very favourable report and following a vote by the congregation he was duly appointed. He wrote a number of pamphlets, including one on "Islamism". He was a popular preacher and according to the Rev Alex Williamson, who would have known him, 'his manner in the pulpit was often singularly animated and energetic'. He remained minister of Peebles until 1870.

He had studied at Edinburgh University and had shared lodgings with Thomas Chalmers, who as the Rev Thomas Chalmers was to become the champion of the poor in Scotland and perhaps more significantly, the leader of the almost 450 ministers who left the established Church of Scotland in 1843 to form the Free Church of Scotland. The "Disruption" as it is known does not seem to have had any direct effect in Peebles, at least for some time, as none of the recognised historians of the town, including Williamson has anything to say about it. Dr Gunn does record that a branch of the Free Church was opened in Peebles in 1844, having used temporary accommodation in the Northgate after the Disruption.

The Relief and Secession churches were still active and in 1836 the Scottish Episcopal Church was built, although its membership was small. Thus all the various recognised denominations of Protestantism were by now represented in the town. Missing was the Roman Catholic Church, but in July 1850 a Mass was held in a flat above a carpenter's shop in the High Street, the first to be held in the Royal Burgh since the Reformation. It was attended by some 200 people, many from the surrounding district. A permanent building known as St Joseph's, which still stands today, was opened in 1858.

* * *

In the second decade of the century, progress in industrialisation and public works was gathering momentum at a rapid rate. Mechanisation was replacing traditional craft industries; new sources of power and energy were being developed and a revolution in transport, with the construction of railways was about to create an explosion of development across the whole country. Trade was beginning to expand and the opportunities for wealth creation were everywhere to be seen. Financial services were being set up to cater for a more sophisticated economy. There were great construction projects. In the previous century the construction of canals and bridges designed and engineered by Thomas Telford and others had been a major source of employment which continued with the construction of an expanding rail network, although it had not yet reached Peebles. There had been major immigration, mainly from Ireland, which had contributed to a steady increase in the population of Scotland.

For the time being at least, the impact on Peebles appears to have been relatively modest, although that would change. The *Statistical Account* of 1841 records that an 1830 survey by elders of the church, estimated the total population of the parish to be 2817 of which 2100 were resident in the town and 717 in the landward area. It also notes that a government survey of 1831 records a total for the parish of 2750. In the *Statistical Account* of 1794, Dr Dalgleish recorded the total population of the parish as 1920 inclusive of all ages. He also gives a breakdown of age groups from birth. He records inhabitants of the town as 1480 and 440 in the landward area. Later statistics for the town give a total of 1,982 in 1851 and 2,045 in 1861, which although lower than the 1830 figure are reasonably consistent with it. Although the town would show considerable growth after 1861, it seems very unlikely that the population had been as low as 1480 in 1795. There is nothing to suggest that there were circumstances or events which would have given rise to an increase of 670, which is more than 45%. The only reasonable conclusion is that Dr Dalgleish's figures are wrong, which is unfortunate, given the detail he provided in relation to age structure and other details.

What is clear is that in many areas of civic life in Peebles as elsewhere, change was taking place. In 1825, a branch of the British Linen Bank was opened in the town, at long last making it unnecessary to rely on a system of couriers between the town and Edinburgh, which had been unreliable, particularly in adverse weather.

There was progress of a much more significant nature in 1828 when a gas company was established in the Royal Burgh. The use of coal gas was pioneered by a Scottish engineer called William Murdoch, who was born in Old Cumnock in Ayrshire in 1754 and moved to Cornwall in 1779. It was there that he experimented with the use of coal gas as a source of energy for lighting his own house. By the early part of the nineteenth century, his technology had been developed to the stage where it could be used for street lighting, first in London in 1807 and then in Edinburgh in 1819.

In December 1828, the Peebles council agreed to allow the newly formed company to open up and lay pipes in the streets. If it proved to be successful, they would then have the street lamps lit by gas. Initially a site for a gasworks on the Old Town Green (now Greenside) was chosen, but it proved to be unsuitable. A site was found on the area of ground lying to the west of the Parish Church. Today the site is still visible and forms part of the parkland and walkways close to the modern swimming pool. It remained in operation there until 1905, when a new site was developed outside the town. One of the factors which made the development of a gasworks feasible was the great improvement in major roads serving the town following the Turnpike Acts. That allowed coking coal to be brought to the town from the coalfields of Lanarkshire and Midlothian. To begin with, gas was produced for only ten months of the year and the street lights were lit for only about a third of the year, during the darkest winter months.

The cauld on the Tweed had been abandoned in 1726. Since that time the town's corn mill had used water from the Eddleston Water as its source of power. By 1829 that was no longer satisfactory and in April of that year a decision was made to build a new cauld across the Tweed once more. The council no longer had rights of ownership and any scheme was dependent on the owners of land immediately upstream giving consent. They were the two owners of Hay Lodge, a Mr Campbell and the Earl of Wemyss. They agreed so long as any damage to their property was made good.

The construction was put out to tender and the contract was awarded to the Galashiels firm of Adam Brown who had tendered the lowest cost of £466. The height which had been specified was 18 inches (65 centimetres), but the finished height exceeded that, with the result that both Mr Campbell and Lord Wemyss complained that their lands were being flooded. In the dispute which followed, an engineer was instructed to look into the matter and report. He recommended that the cauld should be reduced in height. A lengthy dispute followed with the contractor which was only resolved by arbitration. As a result the council agreed to lower it by 1 foot (35 centimetres). That was not the end of the matter and in 1835 Lord Wemyss insisted that there be an undertaking that the height of the cauld should never be increased and that his lands should not be damaged in any way. Lord Wemyss was still not satisfied and in 1842 he raised a legal action against the council, who took advice from Mr Andrew Rutherford, a leading advocate of the day. His advice was that Lord Wemyss would likely succeed in his action in so far as it sought to protect his land from flooding. A settlement was finally reached in 1848, when there was an agreement which specified the height of the cauld. At the same time the burn which flowed down from Edderston was altered so that it discharged into the Tweed below the cauld. The banking was also strengthened to give additional protection to Lord Wemyss land, all at the expense of the council.

While the principal roads had been vastly improved over the previous five decades, the ancient Tweed Bridge remained a problem. It was narrow and rough and was already subject to restrictions in use. There was now a committee which operated under the Road Trustees, who had statutory powers under the Turnpike Acts. The committee had a responsibility to improve the town's highways, but its funds were limited and relied mainly on public subscription. In 1834 plans were made to widen the bridge to provide a carriageway 20 feet (6 metres) wide. The cost was estimated to be £1000. Sufficient funds were raised, with the council agreeing to contribute up to £500 after lengthy negotiations. On 15th August, there was a ceremony to mark the keying of the last arch, followed by a procession through the town and a celebratory dinner in the Tontine Hotel.

43.
Electoral Reform

Largely as a result of the unrest which had followed the end of the wars with France, parliamentary reform was being actively discussed throughout the country, even in quiet and peaceable Peebles. In 1830 a Reform Bill for England and Wales and a separate Bill for Scotland, were presented to Parliament. They aroused widespread interest throughout the United Kingdom and seem to have made a particular impact on the people of Peebles. In December of that year, a number of the townsfolk submitted a request to the council, calling on it to arrange a public meeting to discuss and draw up a petition in favour of reform to both Houses of Parliament. The council, aware that it was a controversial subject which split opinion, responded that it was not in favour of a public meeting, but would draft a petition and would give citizens the opportunity of supporting it.

Progress of the Reform Bills through Parliament was keenly followed. The Member of Parliament, who represented the town jointly with Selkirk, Lanark and Linlithgow, was Mr W D Gillon. He was a supporter of the proposed reforms, but in October, 1831, the Bills were rejected by the House of Lords. Mr Gillon wrote to the council to report that and that supporters of the Bills in the House of Commons had set down a motion confirming that they would continue to support the moves for reform. He suggested to the council that it should draw up a motion addressed to the king, expressing confidence in his ministers and its continuing hope for the successful achievement of reform and, 'praying his Majesty to use his undoubled prerogative to ensure that success'.

The council took his advice and drafted the following "Address" to his Majesty:

It is with the utmost regret and astonishment we have seen the Bill rejected by the House of Lords. We most earnestly and humbly pray your Majesty (on whose paternal regard we place the most implicit reliance) to take such measures as in your wisdom may seem best calculated to insure the passing into law the most salutary Reform in the Representation; that your Majesty will be pleased to continue in office your present Ministers who so justly possess the confidence of the Country..... as the only means of preserving the peace and safety of the Kingdom, which in any change at this time would not only greatly endanger but might so shake all the Institutions of the Country as to end in the subversion of all Law and Order; which may God prevent, and may your Majesty be the happy instrument in his hands.

In April, 1832, the council sent another "Address", this time to the House of Lords in support of the Bill and said that they were alarmed and regretted the exclusion of the middle classes from the democratic process. How much weight the views of the council of a small burgh in rural Scotland was noticed is questionable. In any event, the Lords once again threw the Bill out. Responding to this, Mr Gillon wrote to the council on 10th May, reporting that a new government had not been formed, but that he was confident that the reformers would win. He went on to report that the City of London had petitioned the House of Commons to stop approval of a budget. He thought that was something which the whole country should adopt, adding, 'this will bring the insane Lords to their senses, and if followed will much strengthen our hands'.

The very strong feeling of support for reform throughout the country ultimately brought success and in June 1832 the Third Reading of the Bill was passed and on 19th July it received the royal assent and passed into law. As a result, the number of electors in Scotland rose from 4,240 in 1820 to 65,000. In the burghs those now eligible to vote, were the householders and occupiers of property worth more than £10. In the counties, occupiers of property who were worth more than £50 were also eligible.

One consequence of the Reform Act, as it then became, was that Peebles lost its previous electoral privileges as a burgh and was joined with the whole of Peeblesshire. However, that did mean that its future parliamentary representative would be more closely associated with the locality rather being shared with a group other of burghs, which were not even contiguous. It must be assumed, in view of the town's enthusiasm for reform that that change was acceptable.

Although the 1832 Reform Act takes its place as a milestone in the nation's history and is often referred to as the "Great Reform Act", it was a very modest step towards universal franchise, which would not be achieved until almost 100 years later. None the less it opened the door to a new democracy and removed the government of the country from a tiny elite, who had dominated it almost from the beginnings of time. Reform of local government now entered the frame. As with national government, local government had been controlled by what was essentially a self-appointed elite. For three centuries, although paying lip service to public opinion, as earlier explained, at each annual "election", the members of the existing council decided who the members of the next council should be. It was a system which was open to abuse.

Peebles Town Council had shown earlier that it had some understanding that that was questionable, by introducing limits on the length of time any magistrate or councillor could serve. They were probably not alone and similar steps might have been adopted nationally, but had been opposed by Henry Dundas, 1st Viscount Melville, who was effectively the First Minister of Scotland.

Following the 1832 parliamentary reform Act, a Burgh Reform Bill was introduced to Parliament at Westminster. A copy of the Bill was considered by the town council, in March, 1833, who called a public meeting. By then it had actually been passed by the House of Commons. The conclusion of the meeting was that the Bill did not go far enough and in July a petition was drafted by the council who sent it to the Earl of Haddington to present to the House of Lords, which was then considering it. It was concerned that by limiting the voting rights to the owners and occupiers of property valued at more than £10:

> …the object of the Bill will be rendered quite nugatory,[216]the constituency being so circumscribed that the right of Election will be confined to such a small portion, a mere junto of its inhabitants, so as in fact to give them a control and power approximating in no small degree to the long complained of close system of elections, while those proprietors and occupants of subjects of from five to ten pounds in Burghs of this class, who form the major number, are in point of responsibility equal to those upon whom the present Bill devolves the right of election.

In spite of that protestation, probably shared by most of the burghs of Scotland, the Bill was passed. The first election to the council under the new arrangements took place in November 1833. The number of councillors remained the same. The Statistical Account of 1841, records that there were 94 eligible voters in the burgh out of an adult population of about 1300.

The first parliamentary election under the new arrangements was held in 1837. It was not the secret ballot of later times. On the contrary it was a very public affair. The secret ballot was not introduced until 1872. A raised platform called the "hustings"[217] was erected in front of the Town

---

216   Futile

217   A name that has remained associated with parliamentary elections ever since.

House in the High Street. On election day a large crowd gathered and each candidate in turn mounted the platform and gave a speech setting out why he (no woman candidates then) should be elected. They were generally rowdy affairs and the crowd made its support or otherwise very evident. There were questions and interruptions, cheers for those they supported and jeers and cat calls for those they opposed. Each voter indicated which candidate he supported. Polling continued throughout the day and the running totals of votes were announced every hour until polling closed. If the contest was a close one, the cheers or jeers would be enormous and if the leading candidate was not to the liking of the people, as opposed to the voters, it was quite usual for the whole proceedings to descend into violence. The first member for the town and county after the reform Act was Mr Forbes Mackenzie of Portmore who served from 1837 until 1852.

44.
Into the Victorian Age

George IV died, without a legitimate heir on 26 June 1830 and was succeeded by his brother, William IV, who in turn died without a legitimate heir on 20 June 1837. He was succeeded by his niece, Alexandra Victoria, the daughter of his brother, the Duke of Kent. Although her reign as Queen Victoria is one of the best known and documented of any monarch in British history, it seems that her accession at least was passed without comment by the Peebles council and no Address was sent to her as had been the case with George IV. It did however, send addresses of support to her

The success of political reform, limited as it was, does seem to have raised the awareness of councillors as to the reality of party politics. Nationally, parliament now had two well-defined parties, Whigs and Tories. Up until the early nineteenth century those names had been loosely applied to the factions in parliament. Whigs were the supporters of constitutional monarchy and full parliamentary democracy as representing the will of the people. Their supporters were religious non- conformists and the emerging industrialists. Tories stood for the old order and were supported by the aristocracy and country gentry, as well as the merchant classes. After the Reform Act of 1832 their political philosophies became more clearly defined, with the Whigs evolving under Lord John Russell and later William Ewart Gladstone as the Liberal party, while the Tories under Sir Robert Peel and then Benjamin Disraeli, became the Conservative Party.

It appears that the town council of Peebles was becoming directly interested in national politics, so much so that it felt able to comment on national political events. When Queen Victoria ascended the throne, her first Prime Minister was Lord Melbourne, a Whig, who remained a great favourite on whom she relied, at least in the early years of her reign, but in May 1839 he announced that he wanted to resign and recommended that the Queen ask Sir Robert Peel to form a new government. He was a Tory. The Queen's closest courtiers were all Whigs and Peel made it clear that that would have to change. Victoria refused and Peel declined to accept the premiership, with the result that Melbourne was persuaded to return. The town council made its support of the Whigs clear when it announced approval of, 'the determined resistance of our Gracious Sovereign in resisting the very unreasonable request made to her on the part of Sir Robert Peel for the dismissal of the Ladies of her Household.' They approved of her appointing Melbourne as Prime Minister once again and agreed to present her with 'an humble address' expressing the council's approval of 'her majesty's conduct.' How far her Majesty was impressed or comforted by this expression of support from a small Scottish burgh, even a "Royal and Ancient" one, is not recorded.

On 10th February 1840, Queen Victoria married Prince Albert of Saxe-Coburg and Gotha. In June of that year, once again showing their support of the Queen, the council agreed to present an address of loyalty to the newly married couple following the attempt by Edward Oxford on the 10th of the month to shoot the royal couple as they were driven along The Mall in London, a 'foul, diabolical and villainous attempt', which the council viewed with 'horror'. The council's address was to be presented to their Majesties on their, 'miraculous and providential prevention from assassination, two pistols having been discharged at the Royal pair when taking an airing that afternoon by a young man of the name of Oxford.' Once again, the Queen was no doubt gratified. Oxford later was found not guilty on grounds of insanity.

The Victorian era is synonymous with progress in technology and industrial development. Weaving of woollen cloth had long been a cottage industry in Peebles but trade was still struggling and it was becoming evident that if weaving was to survive, changes would need to be made if it was to compete with cloth produced by the industrial processes which were beginning to appear throughout the country. *The New Statistical Account of Scotland* of 1841, refers to the high price of coal as one obstacle and questions whether sufficient water for power could be provided in addition to what was already used to power the corn and waulk mills.

As well as its civic duties, the town council had long been conscious of its role in supporting and promoting local industry and employment. In 1835, in an attempt to establish woollen manufacturing in the town, it advertised a site in the part of the town still known as Ninianshaugh where water power could be provided from a lade running from the rebuilt cauld. There was a problem however, as the route of the proposed lade ran through land owned by Sir John Hay, who was reluctant to grant the necessary wayleave. As a result, no progress could be made at that time. Trading conditions did not improve in the following years, indeed they seem to have worsened.

In 1839, a public meeting was called at which it was decided that steps should be taken to establish factories with modern machinery. In response, the council set up a committee to look into the practicalities of using water power to drive machinery, employing a qualified civil engineer to carry out a survey and prepare a report. It must be assumed that it was received and that its recommendations were positive, as it was decided to publicly advertise the availability of water power. The advertisement which followed was specifically addressed 'To manufacturers, Capitalists and others'. It pointed out that the town was geographically well-suited as a centre of the woollen industry, as it was within an area of predominantly sheep farming and associated wool production and was only 22 miles from the City of Edinburgh. It also pointed out that there were many skilled weavers in the town and that there was a large number of unemployed who could provide labour. In a quite modern touch, the council offered financial inducements to anyone willing to enter into negotiations with them. Sadly that worthwhile initiative produced no response, as did another attempt at industrialisation a few years later in 1853, although on that occasion it also tried to promote paper manufacturing. It would be another three years before its efforts finally succeeded when the old mill on Tweedside was rebuilt as a factory to produce tweed.

Not all the council's attempts to modernise the town were in vain. In the 1840s, a number of major building and infrastructure projects were completed. First in 1841, it was decided to build a new courthouse adjacent to the jail. The architect chosen was Thomas Brown, who had been appointed to the Scottish Prison Board in 1837. The Peebles Sheriff Courthouse was one of his earliest designs. He was also responsible for the design of jails at Ayr, Wigtown, Jedburgh and Inverness as well as the Debtors Prison on Calton Hill Edinburgh and the courthouses at Berwick and Dingwall.

His first design for a courthouse at Peebles sat directly in front of the earlier jail. In addition to the court facilities it provided fourteen cells and a fumigating room, as well as a large open exercise or "airing" yard at the rear, which had a caged enclosure within it. In 1843 he revised the scheme, moving the entire new block southwards, which created a symmetrical juxtaposition with the original jail. By then the citizens of Peebles must have become more law abiding as the number of cells was reduced to thirteen. It was that amended scheme which was built and although the use of the building would change somewhat in later years, the external appearance has remained virtually unchanged since then.

The state of the streets was becoming a major concern. They had remained virtually unchanged and unimproved for centuries. In 1844 the council set up a committee to look at the whole matter, to make recommendations for improvement and to provide costings showing how it could be financed. The committee recommended that the High Street should be lowered, proper drains built and that pavements should be laid. It also recommended that all outside stairs should be removed and that a public subscription should be opened to meet the cost. Following the report, in 1846 the provost, John Stirling and John Bathgate, the town clerk, opened a subscription list. After considerable efforts almost £1000 was collected and later that year work started. The High Street was lowered between two and three feet (60-90 cm); the old causeway was replaced by a pavement; the centre of the street was "macadamised"[218] and all but one of the outside stairs and various projections were removed. After years of neglect, the High Street of Peebles had now reached the standard of what was by then expected of a royal burgh in the mid-nineteenth century.

The water supply also received attention at about that time. In 1846 a company was set up which was given the right by the council to use the springs on Venlaw and also the right to lay pipes through the town, provided that the company supplied water to seven wells, three in the High Street, two in the Northgate and one in the Old Town. The council reserved the right, on giving three months prior notice, to acquire the shares of the company at the original issue price or less by agreement. The council had a direct interest in the company as the magistrates and dean of guild were *ex officio* members of the board of management. Dividends to shareholders were not to exceed five percent, and any surplus was to be used to buy shares on behalf of the community. In order to further augment the supplies, the council also granted permission for water to be taken from springs at Shielgreen, which was part of the town's common lands lying to the north east of the town.

The council bought 20 shares at the outset, but in spite of what at this distance seems a perfectly reasonable scheme, things did not work out well and there was soon conflict between the council and the board of management. It seems that there were complaints from consumers who complained to the council rather than the company and that caused resentment. The council claimed the right to have the supply to the reservoir shut off in times of drought and the apparent division of

---

[218]   A process in which layers of single sized crushed stone are laid and compacted by rolling and a layer of dust then rolled in to bind them together.

responsibilities for what was by then an essential public service, could not be made to work satisfactorily. In 1856, the original capital of the company was no longer sufficient. At that time it had accumulated a debt of £250. The constitution of the company made no provision for borrowing. Consequently it offered the whole assets to the council. The council declined, but after some haggling, it agreed to advance the £250 at 5% interest. Eventually in 1862 the council did acquire the assets of the company, so that the supply of water to the town became a public service, owned and maintained by the council.

The first printing press in the town had been started in 1810 by Alexander Elder, described as a man of "considerable ingenuity and enterprise", but in 1845 the town's first local newspaper called the *Peeblesshire Monthly Advertiser and Tweedside Journal* was set up. The publisher was Alexander Scott, who was a printer in the town. In 1853 its name was changed to the *Peeblesshire Advertiser* and it became a weekly, published each Friday.

In 1833, the artist Charles Blyth painted a *View of Peebles from Tweed Green*. It shows the Tweed Green more or less as it is today, only the present trees lining its edges and central pathway are missing. It shows a number of figures, some in groups. Several versions of the picture exist. A number of families were offered the opportunity to purchase a version of the picture with themselves appearing in it. Each version is virtually identical, except that the main figure groups are different with the purchaser's family represented.

What the picture shows, apart from this personal interest, is that the Tweed Green was now a single level area whereas previously the surface had not been level but had been broken up by mounds and hollows. The eastern side had been the playground of the Grammar School, while the western side was the playground of the Burgh School and there had been a "high green" and a "low green". The work of levelling and creating the paths along the bank of the river Tweed was carried out early in the century.

Dr Williamson mentions that 'from time immemorial', "shows" were allowed to be held on the Green. He describes one in particular:

a ring was made by Mr Ord and his equestrian company, when they came to display their wonderful feats of horsemanship. Ord was a highly respected man, the son of a parish minister in one of the border counties, and his advent was always hailed with enthusiasm in Peebles. His feats were considered unrivalled, and the constantly repeated jokes of the "fool," generally

410

conveyed in questions addressed to "Mister Master," never failed to excite universal and uproarious hilarity.

Tweed Green had become what it remains today, a pleasant area of parkland for public recreation, where townsfolk and visitors alike can walk, play or simply sit to admire the passing river and the hills beyond and is a fitting complement to an ancient town.

In 1841 a *New Statistical Account of Scotland* was published. As with all parts of Scotland, the Account for Peeblesshire was written by the minister of the Parish Church, the Rev. John Elliot, A.M. It adds little to our knowledge of the built environment from what Dr Dalgleish recorded 47 years earlier, which itself was limited, other than to say that, 'The town is not extending its limits, and when a house is built, it is generally a handsome structure raised on the site of one that has fallen to decay, adding to the beauty of the town without increasing its inhabitants.'

There were six inns and seven taverns and quite remarkably, seventeen grocers shops where spirits were sold. There had been a reduction in the duty on whisky in an attempt by the government to stop smuggling and the production of illicit liquor. The consequence as the Account notes:

> …many districts, formerly strangers to the small still, and distinguished for the order and sobriety of the inhabitants, now suffer from its baneful effects. Private vices have, in the fullest sense of the word, been made for the time to produce, not public benefits, but an increased revenue, as if any state could be benefited by the corruption and moral degradation of its inhabitants. The consumption of whisky by the drunkard, may for a while swell the returns of the excise, but eventually, the prosperity and the welfare of the country must suffer from his unproductive labour.

It has to be assumed that the writer, the Rev Mr Elliot, was here reflecting that Peebles was no different from any other community in this regard, as he makes no attempt to suggest otherwise!

Mr Elliot suggests that in former times the population may have been greater. As already noted he records the population of the whole parish in 1830 as 2817, of which 2100 were resident within the royal burgh. There were 850 adults who attended the parish church and 681 who attended the three "dissenting" congregations and a mere 7 who attended the Episcopal meeting house.

The town was still well provided with educational facilities, including two public schools and three private schools. Unfortunately the numbers of pupils recorded by Mr Elliot simply do not add up. According to him the Grammar School had 66 and the three private schools 'taught by females', had 87. In a footnote the number attending the English School was 81, which makes a total of 234, but he then goes on to say, 'making in all 491,' which cannot be correct. The earlier record of Dr Dalgleish gave the total number of pupils in 1791 as 'no fewer than 250'. Dr Dalgleish also recorded that in 1791 the number of children in the parish of Peebles between the ages of 5 and 10 was 284. In the circumstances it would be best to regard all these figures with some scepticism, although it does seem probable that the number in education in 1841 remained around 250.

In relation to manufacturing Mr Elliot records that:

A manufactory for carding, spinning, and making cloth and flannel, and plaiding to a very considerable extent, for several years existed. In the same establishment waulking and dying are carried on. Stocking making is also a branch of manufacture here, but of limited extent. Cotton webs are sent from Glasgow, but afford a very poor remuneration to weavers, few of whom can with the utmost diligence earn more than six shillings a week.

What is referred to here as "A manufactory", is the traditional cottage industries, rather than "factories" on an industrial scale which were not established until more than a decade later.

By 1850, Peebles had made major strides on the road to being a modern market town. The economic circumstances, although improved, still had a long way to go. Much was yet to be done, but it had come a very long way from its birth, probably as much as eighteen centuries before, through the aftermath of Roman occupation and the Dark Ages which followed their departure and through the early medieval years, until finally established as a place of importance and real significance, a "Royal Burgh". It was a role which retained its importance, as a place of regular royal visitation for the next four hundred years and throughout those years as a centre of trade and commerce. It played its part in the years of Civil War in the seventeenth century and during the time of the Commonwealth and occupation by the forces of Oliver Cromwell. In religious affairs it had been a centre of pilgrimage and monastic life from the thirteenth century until the reformation of 1560 and thereafter embraced Protestantism, first Presbyterian, then Episcopal and then Presbyterian again. Some of its citizens, one in particular, had supported the Covenanting cause of the latter part of the seventeenth century. The eighteenth century saw it support conventional Presbyterianism, while the middle of the nineteenth saw the rise of a more fragmented Scottish Presbyterian church with a number of the new groupings represented in the town as well as a re-establishment of a small Episcopal adherence. Through all those many centuries there runs a thread, rarely broken, of loyalty to the crown and government

By 1850, it had transformed itself from the impermanence of the Roman era and dwellings of wood and hide, to the stone and slate and the architecture of the Victorian. It had a settled if less significant place as a county market town with hopes of a better future in a changing world of trade and commerce. Its citizens were beginning to reflect a class structure which remained largely unchanged into the twentieth century, with an emerging middle and professional class, artisans, and labourers, but still a sizeable number of unemployed. Perhaps above all, it retained as it had done since the middle ages, a sense of civic pride and independence.

That is of course not the end of the story, but it signals the end of a long history of an independent community, largely living on its own resources, somewhat detached economically from the wider nation. The year 1850 can be seen as a catalyst in the life of Peebles. From the beginning of the seventeenth century and up until then it had taken on the attitudes of a quiet country town of little consequence, following a more auspicious past. In spite of efforts by its rulers, it had failed to generate a viable economy sufficient to sustain the majority of its population. Attempts to introduce "modern" manufacturing into a traditional textile trade which was largely a cottage industry, had made no progress. Although some modest expansion of commerce and professional services had created a small middle class with improving material wealth and social standing, the great majority of the Royal Burgh's citizens were poor and short of the means to provide for their families through honest labour. That was about to change and the next fifty years would see a dramatic improvement in the fortunes of the town and its people.

Postscript

The transformation of a quiet and rather sleepy market town, albeit with a long and distinguished past, to a modern commercial centre, was made possible by perhaps two of the most important developments in the history of the whole nation of Great Britain: first the age of steel and then the coming of railways, the second dependent on the first.

The first commercial railway using a steam powered locomotive was the Middleton railway near Leeds which started in 1812, primarily for the haulage of coal. It was followed in 1825 by the first public railway built from Stockton to Darlington. The huge potential of the railway was immediately recognised as a far superior means of transport of goods to that by horse and cart and personal travel by stage coach. In the following three decades a system of railways spread rapidly throughout Britain.

Numerous companies sprang up, usually to establish relatively short rail connections, mainly providing commercial transport for basic commodities such as coal. Fortunes were made and lost, but by 1845 many local routes had been established. Edinburgh had been connected to Glasgow and the race was on to connect Scotland to its southern neighbour.

The history of the development of the railway has been well documented elsewhere and the detail need not concern us here. Two companies, the North British Railway Company and the Caledonian Railway Company, had become the dominant players, the former by 1846 linking Edinburgh with Berwick and the south and the latter, Glasgow with Carlisle and beyond. In 1847 the North British created a route from Edinburgh to Hawick by way of Galashiels. In the subsequent years a number schemes were proposed, linking communities to those two main operators.

In 1851 a group of local interests, amongst the most prominent of whom was William Chambers, set up the Peebles Railway Company and planned a single line to connect to the Edinburgh to Hawick line at Eskbank in Midlothian. Statutory powers were granted in 1853 and construction started that same year and the line opened on 2nd April, 1855 for both goods and passenger traffic.

In 1858 another small independent company the Symington, Biggar and Broughton Railway linked to the Caledonian Railway, was established. The Caledonian saw the advantage of creating a link into the

Borders by way of Peebles and gave its backing to an extension from Broughton to Peebles. This was opened on 1st February 1864. It was a challenge to North British and the Peebles Railway and the former now took control and set about building a new station and an extension to link Peebles to Innerleithen and Galashiels, which was completed in October 1866. In the meantime both the major operators had reached a compromise deal which linked the two systems together with a line from the Caledonian Station at Dukehaugh to a new station where the Edinburgh Road car park is today. After years of effective isolation from a rapidly developing industrial economy, Peebles now had direct links with Glasgow, Edinburgh and on into England. Those communication links transformed Peebles. The story of the developments which followed is told in much greater detail in *History of Peebles 1850-1990* by J L Brown and I C Lawson, but a broader narrative is appropriate here as a bridge between the historic past and the modern era.

Many attempts had been made in the past to try to develop a modern textile industry. Those had largely failed as a result of poor transport communications. It had not been for lack of ideas or initiative, but now the major stumbling block had been removed.

Within a few years major textile manufacturing factories were built at Tweedside and Damdale on the Eddleston Water and by 1883 a further mill was built in March Street. By then the population had increased to nearly 3,500, almost entirely driven by the need for labour which these new factories required. They would continue to dominate the town and its people for the next 80 years, producing knitwear and Tweed cloth of the highest quality.

Peebles had been an established market town from time immemorial, although its importance as such had waxed and waned over the centuries, but now the town could once again develop as an agricultural centre with major livestock markets serving the county and further afield. An auction mart was established in the present Edinburgh Road car park and a second at Clark Place. Those were both subsequently replaced by a large facility at South Parks, which continued until 1998.

Growing affluence in the latter part of the nineteenth century brought with it an expanding interest in country pursuits, which until then had largely been the preserve of the upper classes. Affordable rail travel made it possible for many city dwellers to enjoy all that the countryside had to offer. Set in a landscape of rivers and hills, Peebles soon became a mecca for visitors from Glasgow, Edinburgh and far beyond. Tourism had arrived. New facilities appeared. Principal among them was the building of the somewhat ponderously named Peebles Hydropathic Establishment. It opened in 1880. Originally it was linked to a nearby spring at neighbouring Innerleithen which had therapeutic properties, so that it could provide facilities for visitors and patients alike. It became the leading centre for visitors to the Borders. It has been described as "palatial" which photographs confirm. Fire destroyed the original building in 1905, but it was rebuilt and re-opened in 1907. It remains today as the Peebles Hotel Hydro.

Two world wars left their mark on the town, no less than it did throughout the length and breadth of Great Britain. Initially at the start of the Great War, following the government's policy of "business as usual", most mill workers remained at their looms and did not take up the call to arms. None the less theirs was an important contribution to the conflict as the mills changed from the production of cloth for the domestic market to producing khaki cloth for uniforms. That was to change following Lord Kitchener's appeal. By the end of 1915, 1,764 men had enlisted from Peeblesshire and with the advent of national conscription, a further 1,000 from Peebles had joined up. The town itself became a major military training centre. By 1915 it played host to some 7,000 men in training.

The effect on the town was much wider and involved many of the woman folk, as hospital nurses and voluntary aid workers. Working parties from the town's churches provided surgical dressings and hospital garments for the wounded. It was total war and total commitment. Peebles Hotel Hydro and one of the local mansion houses became hospitals for naval personnel, while the Peebles Poor House became a military hospital.

As had happened in the Napoleonic Wars, Peebles received its complement of foreign visitors, this time not as prisoners, but as refugees. Those were Belgians, displaced by the battles on the Western Front. Eventually some 40 were settled in the town.

In common with almost every community in the country, many of those who went to war did not return. One in ten of the male population of Peebles did not. The names of all those from the county of Peebles who died, are commemorated at the spectacular war memorial situated in the courtyard of the Chambers Institution, dedicated in 1922. The names and personal details of those from Peebles are also recorded in the two volumes of *The Book of Remembrance for Tweeddale- Burgh and Parish of Peebles* by Dr Clement Gunn.

Peebles was to pay its part in the war of 1939-45 too. Once again Peebles Hotel Hydro was requisitioned as a hospital, this time as a Military General Hospital. It provided training for medical personnel who then went on to serve in field hospitals in war zones. As before many of the town's people were called upon to serve in every capacity and once again the town became a military centre, with the Tontine and Crown hotels becoming regimental headquarters. Although there were casualties, they were nothing like those of the First World War, no doubt due to advances in medical practice. None the less 70 died in the conflict.

Once again foreign visitors from abroad came to the town. In 1941 members of a Polish armoured division were encamped in Victoria Park and became a common sight. A number who had lost their homeland to Soviet Russia returned to settle in the town after the war. There are a number of Polish war graves to be found in Peebles cemetery and the strong Polish connection is commemorated in a memorial in the grounds of Peebles Hotel Hydro.

Other visitors during war, although not of their own choosing, were Italian prisoners of war who arrived in 1942. These were men who were brought to the area as farm workers and a camp was built for them in Caledonian Road. They left in 1944/5. On their departure, in common with many communities in south and central Scotland, they were replaced by what were known as "Displaced Persons". They were people who had fled the advance of the Russian army at the end of the war and came from as far afield as Ukraine and Lithuania.

At the end of the conflict, there was a slow return to the normality of pre-war years and by the early 1950's much was as it had been in those former years, but with austerity which only slowly declined. As it had done following the doldrums of the 1840s and earlier, Peebles once again rose to be a thriving community, which it remains today, although major economic circumstances have transformed it once again. Challenges from the emerging economies of the far East gradually eroded the competitive edge of the textile industries. A major fire in 1965 destroyed the Tweedside Mill. It was not rebuilt. The Damdale Mill closed in 1967 and the March Street Mill in 2015. For the first time in perhaps 500 years there is now no form of textile production in the town. From a time when at its peak as many as 400 families in the town and district relied on the textile mills for their livelihood, none now do so.

Fortunately those changes which might otherwise have been cataclysmic, have been spread over an extended period and other forms of economic activity have emerged. Where previously there were three sources of mass employment now there are many small businesses, collectively giving employment to several hundred and there has been huge expansion in housing, attracting not only those who have found employment in the town, but many who have made it their base and home for employment further afield in the Borders and the capital city of Edinburgh.

In recent years it has gained a significant place in the realm of cycling. With its many varied trails, nearby Glentress Forest is now recognised as one of the premier locations for mountain biking in Scotland. Peebles itself has become the starting point for a number of major cycling events, all of which has been a great boost to the local economy.

In the years since the 1960s the population has grown from just under 5000 to almost 10,000 in 2021 and yet it remains a special place, with a lively community and as a centre for recreation and access to a countryside of beautiful hills and valleys, which surround it.

Linking the present to its historic past, there is a fragment of the encircling wall of 1579 to be seen in the Station car park and the base of a tower on the descent of the Post Office Brae, while the remnants of the 17th century slaughter house, the oldest surviving structure in the town, can be glimpsed through a gate in the Deans Wynd which descends northwards from the High Street. The ancient ruins of St Andrews Church are still visible in the town's cemetery, although the tower is a Victorian restoration. The remains of the Cross Kirk and monastery are preserved in the care of Historic Environment Scotland. Beneath the High Street there are cellars that bear witness to a long gone era. Apart from those, little tangible evidence remains of its ancient past. It is a past which remains preserved, none the less, in its story of two thousand years as part of the story of Scotland.

Although today Peebles is far removed from the burgh of medieval times. Where once it stood as centre of commerce and industry, today it offers the visitor and citizen alike a pleasant and lively environment in which to work and to indulge in the beauty of the countryside on its doorstep and its sporting activities, but at its heart it retains its traditions. Still it is, "Peebles to the play". Its long and eventful history, "Royal and Ancient", is celebrated annually in its Beltane Festival, recalling the celebrations and fairs of centuries ago. As an old Peebles worthy at the end of the nineteenth century declared after making a visit to Paris, 'Aye, Paris is fine, but it's Peebles for Pleasure.' Long may it continue to be so!

Appendix I
Writers who have contributed to the history of Peebles

Robert Renwick was born in Peeblesshire in 1841. He embarked on a legal career, starting with one of the Peebles law firms and in 1865 he obtained an appointment as assistant to Sir James Marwick, at that time Town Clerk of Edinburgh. Sir James had a major involvement with the Scottish Records Society and did valuable work in researching the records of the burghs of Scotland and Renwick became associated with him in that work, as well as becoming assistant Town Clerk of Glasgow.

Towards the end of the nineteenth century and into the early years of the twentieth, Renwick undertook the considerable task of researching the Burgh records of Peebles and other local records. As anyone who has attempted to read and understand the written records and documents of centuries gone by will appreciate, this was a Herculean task, which resulted in a number of volumes including, *The Burgh of Peebles: Gleanings from its Records, 1604-1652 (1892), Peebles: Burgh and Parish in Early History (1903), Peebles during the Reign of Queen Mary (1903),* and *Extracts from the Records of the Burgh of Peebles 1652-1714. (1910)*

The Rev Alex Williamson was born in Peebles in 1833. He was educated at Peebles Grammar School and the University of Edinburgh. From 1859 until 1875 he was the parish minister of Innerleithen and thereafter until his death in 1911, he was the minister of West St Giles in Edinburgh. He was a Fellow of the Society of Antiquaries of Scotland. In 1896 he was awarded the degree of Doctor of Divinity from Edinburgh University. He published a number of books, including in 1895, *Glimpses of Peebles or Forgotten Chapters in its History.* It largely relates to the years after 1760, but touches on some of the material appearing in Chambers and Renwick about the years before then and adds some additional anecdotes.

Dr Clement Gunn came to Peebles in 1885 when he set up as a medical practitioner and remained in the burgh until his death in 1935. He developed a deep interest and affection for the town and its surrounding countryside. In spite of the claims of his medical practice on his time, he became a prolific writer. In 1908, he published *The Church and Monastery of the Holy Cross of Peebles 1261-1560* and *The Book of Peebles Parish Church of St Andrew's Collegiate Church, 1195-1560,* followed in 1912 by *The Book of the Cross Kirk, Peebles, AD 1560 -1690.* These shared some of the sources explored by Renwick, but with his own added researches of the Kirk records. The two men became close friends and together they provide an immense source of information and anecdotes, which when brought together with the earlier work of the Chambers Brothers and Williamson provide a picture of the Royal and Ancient Burgh of Peebles and its long, fascinating and distinguished history.

Walter Buchan was a member of a well known Peeblesshire family. His brother John, is rather better known as the author of many books and as a politician and latterly as Lord Tweedsmuir, Governor of Canada. Walter was a lawyer and until his retirement in 1947 a partner in the firm of J & W Buchan, based in Peebles and Town Clerk to the Burgh. In spite of his business responsibilities, he found time to edit three volumns of *A History of Peeblesshire* published in 1925. He himself was a major contributor, especially to those sections covering the burgh and parish of Peebles. Much of the material is based on the earlier sources already mentioned, but was expanded and brought up to date by him in the language of his age.

Appendix II
Scottish Currency[219]

1373 4d Scots = 3d English
1390 2d Scots = 1d English
1451 2d Scots = 1d English
1456 3d Scots = 1d English
1467 3½ Scots = 1d English
1483 3½ Scots = 1d English
1560 5d Scots = 1d English
1565 6d Scots = 1d English
1579 8d Scots = 1d English
1597 10d Scots = 1d English
1601 12d Scots = 1d English

Between 1603 and 1707 £12 Scots = £1 English.

As well as the pound Scots, there were silver coins denominated in merk, which was a unit of value, worth 13 shillings 4 pence (two-thirds of a pound Scots).

Following the Union of Parliaments in 1707, the pound Scots was officially phased

---

[219]   J D Mackie - A History of Scotland p10

List of Sources

- Armstrong, Mostyn J – *Map of the County of Peebles*, 1775
- Borman, Tracy - *Witches – A Tale of Sorcery and Seduction* (Vintage Books) 2013
- Brown, J.L & Lawson, L.C. (Editors) – *History of Peebles, 1850 – 1990* (Mainstream Publishing Company (Edinburgh)Ltd) 1990
- Buchan, J Walter (Editor) *A HISTORY OF PEEBLESSHIRE VOLUME II – 1925*
- Chambers, Robert – *Domestic Annals of Scotland from the Reformation to the Revolution* (W & R Chambers, Edinburgh and London) 1874
- Chambers, Robert – *History of the Rebellion of 1745-46* – (W & R Chambers, Edinburgh & London) 1869
- Chambers, Robert - *Memoir of Robert Chambers with Autobiographic Reminiscences of William Chambers Fifth Edition* (W & R Chambers, Edinburgh & London) 1872
- Chambers, Robert – *Picture of Scotland, Volume First, Second Edition* 1828
- Chambers, Robert (editor) *The Book of Days. A Miscellany of Popular Antiquities* (W & R Chambers: London & Edinburgh) 1886
- Chambers, William – *History of Peeblesshire* – (W & R Chambers, Edinburgh & London) 1864
- Chambers, William (Editor)- *Charters and Documents relating to The Burgh of Peebles with Extracts from the Records of the Burgh A.D. 1165-1710* – (Scottish Burgh Records Society) 1872
- Craig, Mary W. – *Borders Witch Hunt – The Story of the 17th Century Witchcraft Trials in the Scottish Borders* (Luath Press) 2020
- Cruft, Kitty, Dunbar, John and Fawcett, Richard – *The Buildings of Scotland, THE BORDERS* (Yale University Press) 2006
- Dalgleish, Rev William D.D. – *Statistical Account of Scotland Part XII, Number 1. Parish of Peebles*, 1794
- Defoe, Daniel - *A Tour Through the Whole Island of Great Britain 1724-27*

- Devine, T.M. – *The Scottish Clearances. A History of the Dispossed* (Penguin Random House UK) 2018
- Dixon, P.J. and Perry, D.R. - *Bridgegate, Peebles, 1985-87*
- Gunn, Dr Clement – *THE BOOK OF ST ANDREWS CHURCH, PEEBLES – A.D.1195*
- Gunn, Dr Clement – *THE BOOK OF THE CROSS KIRK, PEEBLES. A.D. 1560-1690. PRESBYTERIANISM AND EPISCOPACY - 1912*
- Gunn, Dr Clement – *THE BOOK OF THE CROSS KIRK, PEEBLES. A.D.1690-1784. SETTLED PRESBYTERIANISM* – 1913
- Gunn, Dr Clement –*THE BOOK OF PEEBLES CHURCH – St Andrews Collegiate Parish Church A.D. 1195-1560* – 1908
- Gunn, Dr Clement -*THE CHURCH AND MONASTERY OF THE HOLY CROSS OF PEEBLES – 1261*
- Gunn, Dr Clement -*THE MINISTRY OF THE PRESBYTERY OF PEEBLES A.D. 296 -1910 – 1910*
- Guildry Corporation of Peebles,The – *Members Handbook 2004*
- Haldane, A.R.B.– *THE DROVE ROADS OF SCOTLAND* - (Birlinn Ltd, Edinburgh) 2008
- Jordan, Don & Walsh, Michael – *The King's Revenge. Charles II and the Greatest Manhunt in British History*. (Little, Brown, London) 2012
- Layman, C.H. (editor) *Man of Letters – The early life and love letters of Robert Chamber*s – (Edinburgh University Press) 1990
- Lynch, Michael – *Scotland a New History* (Pimlico, London) 1992
- Mackie, J.D. – *A History of Scotland* (Penguin Books Ltd, Harmsworth) 1964
- Macky, J – *A Journey Through Scotland – in familiar letters from a Gentleman here, to his Friend abroad* – Second Edition (London) 1729.
- Moffat, Alistair – *The Borders* (Birlinn, Edinburgh) 2007
- Pennecuik, Alexander of Newhall – *The Works of, New edition 1815*
- Renwick, Robert – *Peebles Burgh and Parish in Early History* – 1903
- Renwick, Robert – *Peebles During the Reign of Queen Mary* -1903
- Renwick, Robert – *THE BURGH OF PEEBLES : GLEANINGS FROM ITS RECORDS 1604 -52* – (Neidpath Press) 1912

424

- Renwick, Robert (Editor)– *EXTRACTS FROM THE RECORDS OF THE BURGH OF PEEBLES 1652-1714* – (Scottish Burgh Records Society) 1910
- Scott, Sheila (compiler) – *PEEBLES during the NAPOLIONIC WARS* (Sheila Scott, Peebles)1980
- Scott, Sir Walter, *The Black Dwarf* (Introduction) Portrait Edition Vol V (Adam & Charles Black, London) 1913
- Spencer, Charles, *The Killers of the King. The Men Who Dared to Execute Charles I* (Bloomsbury Publishing Plc, London) 2014
- Stewart Family, Earls of Traquair Muniments
- The Register of the Privy Council of Scotland, Edited and abridged by P Hume Brown, M.A., LLD. Second Series, Volume III A.D. 1629 - 1630 (H.M. General Register House, Edinburgh) 1901
- The Royal Commission on the Ancient and Historical Monuments of Scotland – *Peeblesshire Volumes I & II* - 1967
- *The Statistical Account of Peebles-shire by Ministers of the respective Parishes* (Blackwood and Sons, Edinburgh, and 22 Pall Mall, London, MDCCCXLL)
- Thin, James - *James Thin, 1824 – 1915*, from his hand written diary, 1904
- Williamson, Rev Alex – *GLIMPSES OF PEEBLES or FORGOTTEN CHAPTERS IN ITS HISTORY* (George Lewis & Co., Selkirk)1895
- Wordsworth, Dorothy - *Recollections of a Tour Made in Scotland A.D. 1803*

* * * * *

Material has also been drawn from the Stewart Family, Earls of Traquair Muniments.

Index

428

Wycliffe, John 125

Yeomanry Cavalry 354, 370
Yester, Lords of *see* Hay family
Yolande of Dreux (wife of Alexander III)
  58, 61
York, Duke of *see* James VII, King of Scots
  (II of England)